Kal'unek From Karluk

Kal'unek
From Karluk

Kodiak Alutiiq History
and the Archaeology of the
Karluk One Village Site

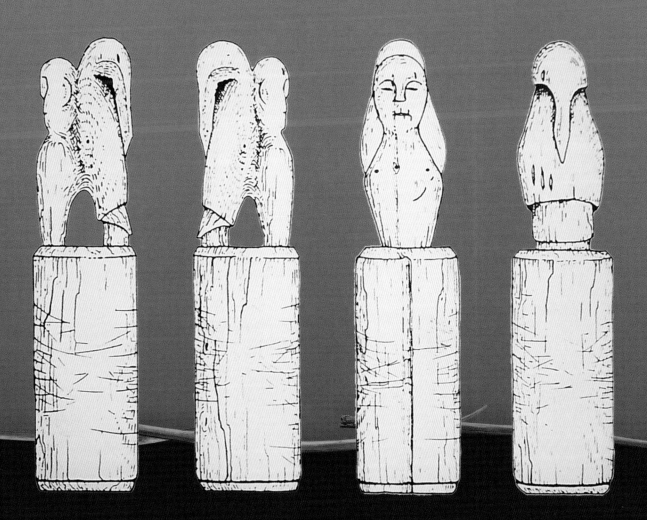

Amy F. Steffian · Marnie A. Leist

Sven D. Haakanson Jr. · Patrick G. Saltonstall

A project of
The Alutiiq Museum and Archaeological Repository, Kodiak, Alaska

University of Alaska Press
P.O. Box 756240
Fairbanks, AK 99775-6240

ISBN 978-1-60223-244-0

Library of Congress Cataloging-in-Publication Data

Kal'unek—from Karluk : Kodiak Alutiiq history and the archaeology of the Karluk One village site / [edited by] Amy F. Steffian, Marnie A. Leist, Sven D. Haakanson Jr., and Patrick G. Saltonstall.

    pages cm

 Includes bibliographical references and index.

  ISBN 978-1-60223-244-0 (hardback : alkaline paper)

1. Pacific Gulf Yupik Eskimos—Alaska—Kodiak Island—Antiquities. 2. Pacific Gulf Yupik Eskimos—Alaska—Kodiak Island—Antiquities—Pictorial works. 3. Paleo-Eskimos—Alaska—Kodiak Island. 4. Excavations (Archaeology)—Alaska—Kodiak Island. 5. Villages—Alaska—Kodiak Island—History. 6. Material culture—Alaska—Kodiak Island—History. 7. Native Village of Karluk—Antiquities. 8. Kodiak Island (Alaska)—Antiquities. I. Steffian, Amy F. II. Leist, Marnie A. III. Haakanson, Sven D. IV. Saltonstall, Patrick G. V. Alutiiq Museum & Archaeological Repository.

 E99.E7K15 2015

  305.897'107984—dc23

            2014023233

Cover and text design by Paula Elmes

Cover illustrations: Objects—wooden snoods and a wooden spool, Karluk One collection, Koniag, Inc., photographs by Sven Haakanson Jr.; upper photograph—Panoramic view of the Karluk One site, 1983. Alutiiq Museum archives, AM193.8-13.P, photograph by Kevin Smith; lower left photograph—Panamaroff Bluff stratigraphy, 1986, courtesy Robert Nelson.

This publication was printed on acid-free paper that meets the minimum requirements for ANSI / NISO Z39.48–1992 (R2002) (Permanence of Paper for Printed Library Materials).

Printed in China

For
Dr. Gordon Pullar, Sr.

and the Kodiak Area Native Association's first culture committee

Nancy Anderson
Thelma Johnson
Julie Knagin
Linda Lester Suydam
Peter Olsen Sr.
Margaret Roberts

whose belief in heritage preservation supported archaeological studies
in Karluk and the journey to create a museum for the Alutiiq people.

Contents

Foreword

Gordon Pullar, University of Alaska Fairbanks

In the late summer of 1983, I learned of a public lecture to be presented at the Kodiak Library by archaeologists Glenn Sheehan and Kevin Smith. They had just returned from a float trip down the Karluk River on which they identified archaeological sites from Karluk Lake all the way down the river to the Sugpiaq village of Karluk, on Karluk Lagoon. Their presentation was on the results of their archaeological survey. I arrived at the lecture room on time and was surprised that it was already full with standing room only. I found a place along the wall and soon became intrigued by what they described. There were *so many sites* representing a very large population of people who had lived on this river of abundance! It was mind boggling. The land at the mouth of the river on Karluk Lagoon had been occupied for thousands of years. That significant numbers of people had lived here was not surprising. This was clearly a desirable place to live because of the rich food resources and relatively mild climate, but this many people for so long? It gave me much to ponder over.

I arrived in Karluk for the first time later in 1983; it was my first visit there as president of the Kodiak Area Native Association (KANA). I was immediately told that I was supposed to pay a visit to Frieda Reft for chai (tea). I quickly understood that this visit was not optional. It was explained to me that Frieda was the matriarch of the village, and being invited to have tea with her was not an insignificant request. I found I was quite nervous as I was being taken across the lagoon in a skiff to the lodge Frieda owned on the other side. At this time, Kodiak Island Natives had been embroiled in some very contentious legal battles with each other over the actions and control of the corporations established under the Alaska Native Claims

Settlement Act of 1971 (ANCSA). It was a divisive time for Kodiak's indigenous people as family and friends were pitted against each other. I feared that I might receive an earful of angry complaints from Frieda, as I had already received from some others.

There was a lot of controversy, and it seemed a majority of the Native population had taken sides in this battle. As the new KANA president, my first directive from the board of directors was to repair the damage that had been done to KANA. The top priority was to save the grants and contracts that funded important programs and services to the Native population. These funds were in jeopardy of being rescinded by their granting agencies because of the instability of the organization brought on by the internal struggles. Next was to look at the long-term future of the organization and find ways to guard against being in this undesirable situation again.

My fears of Frieda's anger were unfounded. She simply wanted to meet me and talk about family and history. Frieda was warm and friendly, and I sat dumbfounded as she recited my Kodiak Island family tree to me with details that I had never heard before. She brought my family history more alive to me, just as the millennia of cultural history would begin to become more visible with the amazing discoveries at the place in Karluk that archaeologists called "Karluk One." Both of these events changed my life. For the first time, I began to see who I really was.

Extensive excavations took place at Karluk One in the following summers, led by Bryn Mawr College archaeologist Dr. Richard (Dick) Jordan. When the well-preserved wood artifacts from Karluk One began revealing themselves to archaeologists, there was surprise, shock, dismay, and pride among the Sugpiat of Kodiak Island. All of these finely crafted items represented periods in the cultural timeline of Kodiak Island that were virtually unknown at a conscious level, yet deeply embedded in the Sugpiaq genetic makeup. It had been precisely two hundred years, 1784 to 1984, since Russian fur traders had militarily conquered the Sugpiat and begun erasing their culture as if it were a pencil mark on a piece of paper. Yet despite the strong efforts of the Russian fur traders, the culture was not totally erased; a small mark remained. This mark, like a tiny spark under a dry haystack, kindled a flame, and the fire of culture began to burn again. Before long, the magnificent items from the Karluk One site inspired people to seek other cultural items stored in museum collections.

Figure 1. Gordon Pullar (L) examines artifacts with Rick Knecht (R) at a gathering sponsored by the Kodiak Area Native Association, Karluk School, 1984. Photograph by Richard Knecht Sr.

In early 1985, Dr. William Fitzhugh of the Smithsonian's National Museum of Natural History visited Kodiak and came by my office. In our discussions, I shared my excitement at seeing the Karluk One cultural items (wood artifacts that had survived for centuries because of wet conditions at the site), and he mentioned rather matter-of-factly that the Smithsonian had many items from Kodiak Island, including wooden masks and intricately woven spruce root hats and baskets. He invited me to visit the Fisher collection when I came to Washington, DC, on a business trip I had planned for later that spring. The Smithsonian artifact collection from Kodiak Island validated the Karluk One discoveries. It seemed there was a lot more information available than we had ever imagined.

I first met Dick Jordan in 1984, after receiving a phone call from him early in my KANA presidency. It was fairly soon after a complete change-over of the board and management at Koniag, Inc., our regional corporation formed under the Alaska Native Claims Settlement Act. Karluk One was on Koniag-owned land, and Dick had gotten permission from Koniag to do excavations there the year before, when Koniag was under the previous administration. The new administration was very absorbed in other things and did not have time to be involved in an archaeology project; so Dick was directed to me to see if KANA would be interested in working with him.

The Karluk archaeology project came at a time when it was most needed. Elders had identified the root of the infighting among the Kodiak Island Sugpiat as a loss of cultural identity and a drifting away from long-held cultural practices. The KANA board and I worked together to seek ways for KANA to address this issue. A beginning was to find funding for cultural programs, especially for the island's youth, and to include a cultural component in each new KANA program. The Karluk archaeological project almost seemed to be a gift from above. It was an opportunity for

young Alaska Natives to work on the project along with archaeologists and learn about their rich history. I proposed this idea to Dick Jordan, and he embraced it wholeheartedly.

The excavations at Karluk One led to many other archaeological excavations around the Kodiak Archipelago. Seeing the cultural items from these projects inspired many people to begin making new items (fig. 1). They carved masks, made traditional clothing, and crafted cultural utensils. Traditional dance groups sprang up around the island, and soon young and old alike were learning the language that was thought to be on its way to extinction. The centerpiece for these activities became the Alutiiq Museum and Archaeological Repository, a Native-owned and run, state-of-the-art museum in Kodiak and home to the Karluk One collection. Karluk One not only produced incredible cultural items that benefited the Kodiak Sugpiat in immeasurable ways but also contributed to science in that many of those who worked on the project at one time or another went on to prominent careers. Rick Knecht, who was Dick Jordan's top graduate student on the project, is now internationally known and respected as an archaeologist. Amy Steffian is the director of research and publication at the Alutiiq Museum, and Patrick Saltonstall is its curator of archaeology. Aron Crowell is the director of the Alaska office of the Smithsonian's Arctic Studies Center. The list goes on as this project continues its impact today as much as ever.

Preface

Karluk One is a large, ancient Alutiiq settlement built at the mouth of the salmon-rich Karluk River. This site is unlike any other archaeological deposit studied in Alaska's Kodiak Archipelago. For six hundred years Alutiiq people built houses here, one atop another, creating a massive mound of cultural debris. Fresh water from a nearby pond seeped through the deposit, preserving many fragile artifacts. Site studies recovered thousands of rare items, many made of wood, bone, ivory, horn, antler, fiber, and even leather, before the meandering river washed away the site. These cultural materials provide a stunning view of ancestral Alutiiq society, revealing everything from the ingenious tools to the spiritual traditions that shaped daily living.

Kal'unek—From Karluk unites the people who excavated the site, cared for its contents, and were inspired by its collection to tell Karluk One's remarkable story. The publication provides a context for understanding the site, an overview of its collection, and a view of the immense impact the site's study has had on the Alutiiq heritage movement.

This volume is not a site report. The Karluk One collection contains roughly twenty-six thousand items collected over more than a decade. We make no attempt to share them all, to provide a comprehensive summary of the site's many features, to follow changes in the assemblage through the layers of the site, or to systematically compare the collection to others from the region. Rather, to make Karluk One's remarkable contents more accessible to the public, we use the collection as a foundation for a prehistoric ethnography. This

work aims to illustrate what life might have been like in Karluk four hundred years ago, looking at the collection as a whole. This is *Kal'unek's* first story. With environmental, archaeological, historic, ethnographic, and linguistic information focused on the Kodiak region, we build a picture of Karluk Village in the centuries before Russian conquest. The result is an imperfect picture, one that relies on both broad historic accounts of Kodiak Alutiiq culture and detailed information from Karluk to understand the site and its contents. As Alutiiq heritage research and investigations of the Karluk One collection advance, the story of Karluk will continue to unfold.

The volume's second story is the far-reaching impacts of the Karluk One project. The foreword, introduction, short essays, and interviews tell this story. Contributors had the choice to be interviewed or to write an essay. For those who preferred to provide an interview, museum staff members recorded and transcribed their thoughts. From these transcripts, volume authors developed written pieces using the interviewed people's own words. Each interviewee reviewed and edited their contribution and approved the final version published here.

With help from Alutiiq speakers, *Kal'unek* presents words in the Kodiak Alutiiq language, also known as Sugt'stun. The book's title is itself in the Alutiiq language. *Kal'unek* (pronounced KAHL - loo - neck) means "from Karluk." There are two styles of Alutiiq spoken in the Kodiak region: a northern and a southern. Since this book is about Karluk people, we list the northern style or accent first in the rare cases where the southern style uses a different term.

This is the way Elders from Karluk speak today, and it is a way of speaking shared in communities found along Kodiak's western and northern coasts. In the instances where southern Kodiak Alutiiq style words are different, terms appear with an (N) or an (S) notation for educational and language-revitalization purposes.

As the volume's glossary explains, many of the artifact names presented here were developed recently with assistance from Elder first-language Alutiiq speakers. This is because many of the items have not been used during the Elder's lives, and the terms once used to describe them are no longer known. Readers may notice that in some Alutiiq words a small capital R appears. This is an orthographic convention that distinguishes the Russian R from an Alutiiq *r*, two unique sounds in the Alutiiq language.

1

The Karluk One Site and Its Role in Community Change on Kodiak

Richard A. Knecht, University of Aberdeen, Scotland

Archaeology isn't really about the past; it is about us. Archaeology lends a very powerful perspective on the nature of time and change, which in turn is essential in gaining an understanding of who we are and how we came to be here, doing what we do every day. All archaeological sites possess at least some of that power over the human imagination, but few sites have changed our collective perception of the cultural heritage of Alaska like the Karluk One site, which from a distance looked like just a few hundred yards of dark-colored earth near the outlet of the Karluk River on Kodiak Island, Alaska (fig. 1.1, 1.2). But it was far more than that, for in the past three decades since our work there first began, the Karluk One collections have become an important catalyst in generating a true Alutiiq cultural renaissance, which has transformed the Kodiak community, Alaska, and the professional world of archaeology in a way that is difficult to overstate (Pullar, Knecht, and Haakanson 2013).

The marvelous artifacts from Karluk One, preserved for centuries by the water-saturated soils, are incredible. But what makes the collections truly special is the reaction of people who encountered the Alutiiq past through them. The initial partnerships between academic archaeologists and the island communities on Kodiak quickly transcended expediency and grew into a collaboration that has set a new, highly visible, and international standard for what community-based archaeological research, preservation programs, and Native-owned museums are capable of. Above all the remarkable transformation of Alutiiq culture from relative obscurity into the highly visible and well-known presence it is today

is the fruit of the love and labor of countless Native and non-Native people. Some of their stories are in this book.

To appreciate how far Alutiiq culture has come, we need only to look back a few decades. It is difficult to imagine now, but when the Karluk One excavations began in 1983, tangible evidence of a living, breathing Alutiiq material culture was nearly invisible beyond a few cherished heirlooms in village attics and a few fragments on display in the local Baranov Museum. Even a mention or photograph of Alutiiq material culture in any book or journal was uncommon, and the professional literature on Kodiak prehistory was either rare or hard to find. Very few owned or had seen

1

FIGURE 1.1

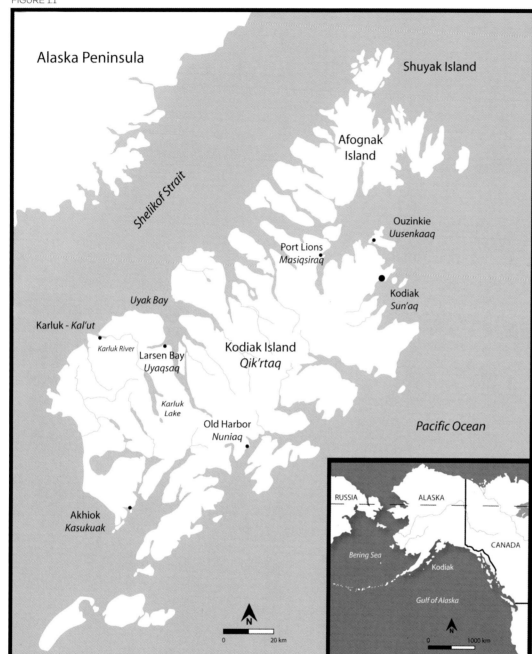

Figure 1.1. Map of the Kodiak Archipelago with contemporary villages. Illustration by Amy Steffian.

Figure 1.2. *Kal'ut*—Karluk. Panoramic view of the Karluk One site, 1983. Alutiiq Museum archives, AM193.8-13.P. Photograph by Kevin Smith.

FIGURE 1.2

Figure 1.3. Teddy Alpiak, Nicky Charliaga Jr., and Shane and Earl Malutin looking at artifacts, 1987. Alutiiq Museum archives, AM628:410. Photograph by Amy Steffian.

a copy of Hrdlička's dated *The Anthropology of Kodiak Island* (1944), and Donald Clark's *Koniag Prehistory* (1974) had been printed by an obscure German publisher and was similarly hard to find. Translations of Russian accounts of Alutiiq life by the Limestone Press and others were just beginning to appear in the early 1980s.

More crucially, many of the Alutiiq people themselves were confused and conflicted about their own cultural identity (Pullar 1992). Many identified themselves as "Aleut," a self-identifier dating from the Russian era use of the word, but were misdirected by literature that used this term to refer to the indigenous people of the Aleutian Islands. Some Alutiiq even called themselves "Russian." Anthropologists were of little help and confused the issue even further by using the term "Pacific Eskimo" (Dumond 1988). And archaeologists referred to the period of late prehistory before the arrival of the Russians as "Koniag," a name some suspected was derived from the name for the regional nonprofit Koniag, Inc., rather than the reverse (it wasn't).

As Gordon Pullar observes in the foreword, the Karluk discoveries came at precisely the right time. There was a long pent-up and openly expressed frustration on the part of the Alutiiq people that while the cultural achievements of other Alaska Natives were celebrated and highly visible, theirs were not. There were no Kodiak dancers at the Alaska Federation of Natives annual gathering, and Kodiak art traditions were largely absent from Alaska galleries, museums, and public spaces, except for the works of modern pioneers like Alvin Amason. Thus, when the Karluk One collection was first displayed in workshops in Karluk and Kodiak, it was a complete revelation because most people had never seen even a single piece of Alutiiq artwork. Suddenly there were thousands of stunning objects to study (fig. 1.3). But in the end, we recovered only a small sample of the site before it was lost to us. We had arrived in the nick of time to get even that.

It Started in Karluk

Allen Panamaroff, Elder

Allen Panamaroff has been a community leader for much of his life. Born in Karluk in 1945 to Alex and Olga Panamaroff, he completed high school at Mt. Edgecumbe and graduated from the University of Alaska before serving in the United States Navy. He returned home to raise a family and worked on the Alaska Native Claims Settlement Act for the Alutiiq people as a Koniag, Inc. board member (fig 1.4). When the Kodiak Area Native Association (KANA) and Bryn Mawr College teamed up to study Karluk One, Allen was the Karluk representative to the KANA Board of Directors. He acted as a liaison between the researchers and the community and helped to share the project across the island. Allen's connection to the site was particularly strong. He grew up at the river's mouth, and his family was the last to leave the settlement. He spoke to Sven Haakanson Jr. about artifacts, archaeologists, and the heritage movement in August 2012.

The Elders didn't like them digging. That was way before my time. They used to try to stop people from digging. They thought it was evil for them to do that. They were really angry at the people who took all that stuff from Larsen Bay, all those skeletons and everything.

We knew even before I was in grade school that there were artifacts in Karluk. There was a teacher who started to find the site where the old school building used to be. He started digging there and found quite a few artifacts. He was a BIA [Bureau of Indian Affairs] teacher in the early fifties. People were telling him not to dig as something would happen. He passed away. I was about four or five years old then. They buried him and they took all the artifacts and buried them too, right in that spit area where all the artifacts were found [fig. 1.4].

I usually took it home to my mom if I found something, or I just left it right there. But mostly I took it home. I found a couple of masks. One was busted, but it had some kind of grass around the eyebrows and something on the nose. I don't know if it was grass; it didn't look like hair. The others were small toys and bidarkies [kayaks]. There was a simple one. It didn't have any design on it. I also found about three or four small kayaks out of bark. One had a little figurine on it and a small paddle. He was holding it up somehow. It just clicked right into the hole in the middle of the kayak. That one was fancy. It didn't have any fancy markings on it, but it had a keel on the back end.

There were a lot of beads, great big bunch of beads in that one area right at the end of that spit before it got washed away—black beads, blue beads, red, yellow. And then there were different sizes; the biggest one I seen was about half an inch thick, and the others were more like one sixteenth of an inch. Frank Carlson, the old man, he came down one day to take look at the area and started fooling around, scraping in one area with one other Native woman. And he just went like this . . . and about five or six hundred black beads came down. No strings or anything, they were just right there. I don't know, they may have just dumped them a long time ago.

It was four or five regular archaeologists and probably eight to ten students. They were from Bryn Mawr College, and they got a permit to come down and do the excavation. Everything the archaeologists found, they let me know specifically, because I was on the Koniag board and also on the KANA board. The people there were using me as a liaison between the archaeologists and their organization and the village and the council. I let them meet all the Elders, so the Elders had something to say about what was happening.

They found a skeleton at Karluk, and right away they came to see me. I said, "Ok, what you guys want to do?" I was going to say no. But they ask me what if they could just go in and take the bones to study. It was a burial site in a barabara [sod house]. When they took it out, they did everything that was requested. They brought them back the next spring, and then they buried them exactly where the people wanted them to, up on the hill. Because there was no way we could bury them in the same spot. That area was being washed out. The archaeologists were really good about that.

One of the first meetings we had on the artifacts, that was in Karluk. It was the end of the year, the digging year, which was during the summertime, August. And I just requested to the archaeologist, "Hey you guys are finding all this stuff, why don't we just get everyone from around the island and bring those people, like the leadership of all the villages, and have a makeshift-type informational meeting. We can have it at the schools, and then we could show not only to our own village but to other villages too." I understood that the artifacts were basically the same all over the island. And so we did, and that was the first information meeting. I did the introductions. We had at least four or five people from each village.

Everyone was invited, if there was room in the planes: people from Old Harbor, Larsen Bay, Ouzinkie, Port Lions, and Akhiok. And that was really interesting. We actually didn't have an agenda or anything. We just let them come here and take a look and have these people talk about what they found. And that's basically what they did. I was on the KANA board of directors, Margaret Roberts was the chairman at the time. We did get the whole board of directors in, mainly because it was a project initiated from KANA at the time— not the digging project but showing the artifacts. It was put together within a week. We had people from all over the place, and that's where that started. Right there.

Figure 1.4. Allen Panamaroff points toward the Karluk Spit, 1970s. Karl Armstrong Collection, Alutiiq Museum archives, AM71:501. Courtesy Kodiak Area Native Association.

Figure 1.5. Crew members excavating, 1987. Alutiiq Museum archives, AM193:344.S.

Sites in southwestern Alaska tend to be large. Resources were abundant; populations were large, and cultural histories are very ancient and complex. Consequently, the scale and richness of the archaeological record here continues to vastly outstrip the resources available to archaeologists to understand it. It wasn't until the mid-1980s that we were able to field a crew large enough to finally excavate a single Alutiiq house. Hundreds of village sites are known on the Kodiak Archipelago, but it will be years yet before archaeologists have excavated even one complete village. The Karluk One site was no exception to this rule. The Bryn Mawr team managed to lead some of the largest field crews ever to dig on Kodiak, with as many as twenty excavators at a time. Nearly all the student excavators were volunteers, working months of

long hours in the wind and rain for no pay. Most students also paid for their own travel and contributed money for food. But even an effort of this scale could hope to recover only a small sample of the site (fig. 1.5). It is unlikely that the current Karluk One collection, impressive as it is, represents even 5 percent of the site contents as we first saw it in 1983. By that time, many meters of the original site had already been lost to the sea, especially after a 1978 storm changed the configuration of the Karluk River mouth to a position where storm surges from the Shelikof Strait could directly impact the site (Rogers 1989). Tragically, the erosion worsened over time until now the Karluk River has entirely erased the village site that it once nurtured. A dedicated few Karluk residents continued to salvage what they could, and some of the finest pieces in the collection were saved through their effort. But in the end, the sum total that we were able to recover, as magnificent as it is, represents only the barest tip of the iceberg. Nevertheless, the Karluk One collection is one of the largest and most important artifact assemblages ever recovered from Alaska. The collection formed the nucleus of what became the Alutiiq Museum, which continues to be the focal point and staging area for the Alutiiq renaissance.

From Little Things, Big Things Grow

Colleen Lazenby, Senior Associate, Jude Monro and Associates

Archaeologists often spend significant amounts of time, money, and energy on research, field surveys, and test excavations before they find important sites. If I told you that the story of rediscovering the vitality and depth of Alutiiq/Sugpiaq prehistory and power—and the extraordinary wealth of information in the sites at Karluk—began with a little wooden transformational figurine in a bar in Kodiak, would you be surprised?

In 1980, archaeologists at Bryn Mawr College in Philadelphia, led by Dr. Richard H. (Dick) Jordan, were just starting to be involved with what is broadly termed Cultural Resource Management (CRM). A wide variety of projects that might have negative impacts on prehistoric-, protohistoric-, and historic-period "cultural resources"—largely represented by above- and below-ground sites—are required by the US National Historic Preservation Act (Section 106) to undertake an assessment for the presence or absence of sites as a first step to protecting important resources. Dick Jordan, born in Alaska in 1947, was already an experienced researcher, university professor, and specialist in hunters and gatherers of the arctic and subarctic regions of the world in 1980. That year Dick was approached by a Pennsylvania-based CRM company to be a principal investigator for assessing the impacts of Kodiak Island's Terror Lake hydroelectric project. Dick, myself, and three staff from the CRM company formed a small crew of investigators and spent several weeks surveying the footprint of the proposed Terror Lake project.

The interior upland areas around Terror Lake and the transmission-line zones showed no evidence of prehistoric use or occupation. But in sections where the impact areas met the shores of Kodiak Island, it was different story. Sites large and small were everywhere. Cultural material and evidence of occupation could be seen in exposed strata next to the beaches. A couple of test pits in an obvious prehistoric site, adjacent to a river, produced remarkable material almost immediately below the surface. One of the less experienced excavators stood up in his test pit one day, announcing that he had found "a pulley!" I saw immediately that it was a black jet labret—breathtakingly beautiful and implying so much about the cultural complexity of people who had lived on Kodiak Island in the distant past. It was clear that there were very important site locations that the hydro project needed to avoid. More than that—even the small sample seen during the test excavations and survey indicated that there was a rich archaeological repository of material about the prehistory of Kodiak that deserved further investigation.

During the period of the project when we worked out of the town of Kodiak, Dick and another crew member met a Karluk resident in a bar one day. Upon hearing that they were archaeologists, the man pulled an object out of his pocket for Dick to examine. He said he had picked it up on the beachfront at

Karluk, near a place where similar objects eroded out of the banks on a regular basis. Dick was stunned. The small wooden figurine was double faced, showing a man on one side and a bird on the other, their backs to each other (fig. 1.6). Both were perched atop a cylinder-shaped base, the whole piece about 10 cm (4 in) high. The preservation of the wood was excellent. And the symbolism of man and animal in one piece was strikingly familiar for an Arctic archaeologist like Dick—such objects are often called transformational figures, and they occur not just in Kodiak prehistory but across the Arctic, in other cultures and sites as well.

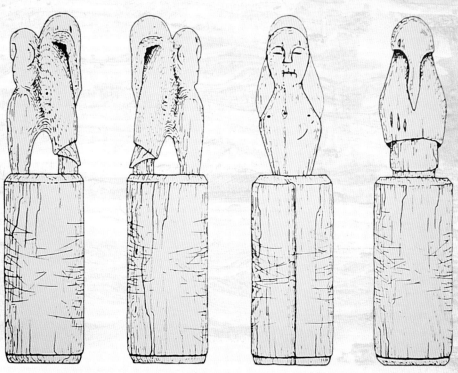

Figure 1.6. Wooden spool featuring carvings of a bird and a man back-to-back. This artifact, found by Ronnie Lind, enticed Richard Jordan to visit Karluk. Courtesy Colleen Lazenby. Illustration by Jill H. H. Lipka, adapted from a drawing by Julie Perlmutter.

The Anthropology Department at Bryn Mawr College was noted for its Arctic program, begun by the famous anthropologist and Alaska researcher, Frederica de Laguna. On Dr. de Laguna's retirement, Dick got the job as her successor. In the late 1970s, he had been co-principal investigator, with William Fitzhugh from the Smithsonian Institution, on the Smithsonian-Bryn Mawr Torngat Archaeology Project in Labrador, Eastern Arctic Canada, for a number of years. The Torngat Project had come to the end of a critical period of fieldwork, and Dick no longer relished the prospect of working with the difficult logistics and climatic conditions of remote Labrador. He was looking for a new research area and had been thinking about Alaska. He may not have initially considered Kodiak, but in that way that the universe unfolds as it should, circumstances conspired to bring Dick to that bar, on that day, and to understand the significance of what he saw in that man's hand.

Dick Jordan was successful in obtaining funding for excavations at Karluk, and a cadre of other researchers, graduate students, and undergraduates worked at the original Karluk One site, other sites around the Karluk Lagoon and adjacent Larsen Bay, and over the years at numerous areas around Kodiak Island. Some of those names are familiar to many of you—Sven Haakanson Jr., Amy Steffian, Rick Knecht, Patrick Saltonstall, and Ben Fitzhugh. Many times, people paid their own costs to be a part of the unraveling of the story and to say that, yes, they too had worked at Karluk.

The cultural material at Karluk is so extraordinary, the sites are so deep and well preserved (in some places between 10 and 12 feet of accumulated material), and the emerging information on the settlement pattern and projected population densities so extraordinary. Taken together, the story they tell about the complexities of the past on Kodiak is as compelling as any you will ever hear. Dick Jordan and Gordon Pullar, then president and CEO of the Kodiak Area Native Association (KANA), enthralled twelve visiting US senators one night at the Karluk fishing lodge with a talk about thousands of years of history represented by the sites around them.[1] Supported by KANA, Dick testified before a US congressional

Figure 1.7. Karluk residents Zoya Shugak (middle) and her daughter Marie talk to Richard Jordan about a figurine found in the excavation, 1987. Courtesy Colleen Lazenby.

committee about the critical relationship between an understanding of and appreciation for the antecedents of their cultures for Alaska's Native people and their present-day health and well-being. And it surprised no one knowledgeable about Kodiak's prehistory when *National Geographic* writer Gene Stuart contacted Dick and asked to visit the archaeology sites and review the material. Stuart included the results of this expedition in her book on ancient cities of the Americas (Stuart 1988), alongside chapters about pre-Columbian cities such as the Anasazi cliff dwellings at Mesa Verde, Colorado; the Makah occupations at Neah Bay, Washington; and the Olmec cities of Mesoamerica.

The people of Karluk Village itself had critical parts to play as excavators, supporters of the project, and friends to the researchers and crewmembers (fig. 1.7). Just as important to this story is the meeting of the minds that took place when Dick Jordan and Gordon Pullar, representing KANA, came to know each other in 1983, marking the beginning of a strong friendship that ended with Dick's untimely death in 1991. Under Gordon's leadership, KANA supported the investigations and many years of the Karluk archaeology project. KANA provided small amounts of funding, project logistics and administrative support, an authoritative voice for the Alutiiq people on how the project should be delivered, and a source of information about annual results and outcomes. James Clifford notes that "Gordon Pullar has been a leader in Alutiiq heritage projects since the early 1980s." Clifford also recognizes that "The Karluk project, with its Native participation and local dissemination of results, would become a model for subsequent excavations in Alutiiq communities" (Knecht 1994).

So much of what we now know and appreciate—and so much of the struggle and the successes—began in partnership with KANA and people in Karluk, and with enthusiastic receptions in the academic community and the public. Among the most noteworthy outcomes was the repatriation of the Larsen Bay skeletal and cultural material, "a landmark in the wider renegotiation of relations between United States Indian communities and scientific institutions that resulted in the Native American Graves Protection and Repatriation Act (NAGPRA) of 1990, and it was a rallying point for the dispersed Native peoples on and around Kodiak Island who were coming to see themselves as custodians of a distinctive "Alutiiq" history and culture" (Clifford 2004:10). As Paul Kelly and Kevin Carmody (1991) wrote in their song about the successful Aboriginal land claims settlement of the Gurindji people of Australia,[2] "from little things, big things grow." Take one small wooden figurine, put it in the hands of the right man . . . and see what happens. Vale Richard Heath Jordan 1947–1991.

The Karluk Archaeological Project began in a conventional enough way but continues to evolve into something very far beyond what anyone involved imagined. Our team at Bryn Mawr was led by Dick Jordan, an Alaska-born, cigar-chomping archaeologist, gruff and driven beyond his years. He had spent most of his career in the eastern Arctic sites of Canada and Greenland and was determined to "skunk out" Arctic prehistory and wondered "what Eskimo culture would be like if people had all the food and wood they wanted" (Jordan, pers. comm. 1983; Knecht 1995:21). Earlier archaeologists on Kodiak had remarked about the archaeological potential of the famously salmon-rich rivers there (Hrdlička 1944). The beaches in the Karluk area were lined with piles of driftwood often several meters deep; this was clearly the right place to learn about the achievements of precontact Alutiiq society.

Tidelines: Re/Visiting Karluk

Katharine Woodhouse-Beyer, Lecturer, Rutgers University

For twenty-five years I have kept a small photograph over my desk: a panoramic view of the Karluk River coursing to its junction with Shelikhof Strait. The village of Karluk is a small speck within this serene but powerful landscape, and Cape Karluk looms in the distance, a vigilant sentry over the mouth of the river and the expansive vista. The photograph reminds me of the power of the natural environment, the long history of Alutiiq settlement in Kodiak, and my own journeys to this unique location, first in 1987, and again in 1994.

My first visit to Karluk was in 1987 as one of the Bryn Mawr College students picked by Dr. Richard Jordan to assist in the excavation of the Karluk One site. Dr. Jordan explained to us that the site was in peril due to the powerful forces of the weather, especially winter storms. We were to live in the village of Karluk for three months and to combine our excavation and research efforts with that of the Kodiak Area Native Association and Karluk villagers. He recommended that we prepare for our journey by reading texts on Alaskan archaeology—and loading up on flannel shirts and rain gear.

For the next three months, we excavated two semi-subterranean sod houses with central hearths and adjoining side rooms (fig. 1.8). Digging energetically with shovels, trowels, and, at times, bare hands, we recovered a multitude of extremely well-preserved artifacts made out of wood, bone, coal, slate, and ivory. We marveled at how the anaerobic site conditions preserved wood, basketry, and even blades of grass from centuries before. Dr. Jordan would often hop into the unit we were working in and instruct us to find the house floor. As we approached a house floor level, we would see the soils become darker. The soils would start to smell like seal oil, and the compacted grass thatch we encountered would reveal artifacts and animal remains.

Every day started with the long walk to the site through the modern village, up the hill past the airstrip, and down to the dig. The days passed quickly with our tasks of excavating, hauling heavy buckets, and recording finds. Nearly every fifteen minutes someone would excitedly report the find of a new architectural feature or an object in remarkable preservation. We excavated rain or shine—and, as I remember, mostly through rain. Our daily uniform usually consisted of colorful orange or yellow Grundens rainwear

Figure 1.8. Excavations at Karluk One, August 1987. From left: Richard Jordan, Colleen Lazenby, Chris Donta, Beth Workmaster, Richard Jordan III, Brandt Feuerstein, Pam Innes, and Philomena Hausler. Courtesy Katharine Woodhouse-Beyer.

layered over jeans, flannel shirts, and Xtra Tufs or hip waders. Our excavation notes were housed in aluminum folders or large plastic Ziplock bags. At the fresh salmon dinner, we enjoyed after the long workday, the "Alaska Plate," a well-worn, tourist plate salvaged in an earlier season, was awarded to the person who had found the most interesting object or feature that day. On many evenings, some of us would carefully copy the information on the wet, smudged recording sheets used that day onto fresh grid-lined pages (fig. 1.8).

Aside from the excavation, there were many interesting experiences that summer: learning how to cook for a twenty-plus-person crew, becoming friends with Karluk residents, kayaking up and down the Karluk River, learning how to fish salmon with the instruction of local fishermen, and, on Sundays, our only day off, hiking and backpacking. A photo taken on one of those early hikes is now the one above my desk. I went back to Bryn Mawr College that fall and volunteered to help with the conservation and processing of the artifacts—my job was to draw pictures or take photographs of the artifacts, place the wooden artifacts in tubs of water or polyethylene glycol, and then monitor the conservation process. Some of those artifacts were later featured in the Crossroads of Continents Smithsonian exhibit and catalog, and now the objects are central pieces in displays at the Alutiiq Museum, the Kodiak Alutiiq community's national museum.

In 1994, and as a professional archaeologist, I returned to Karluk on the invitation of Dr. Richard Knecht, Director of the Kodiak Area Native Association's Alutiiq Culture Center. The Karluk One site was severely eroding. Each tide and storm threatened to wholly annihilate the site. Knecht was assembling as many excavators as he could to help with the rescue and salvage excavation of the site. Over a month, and a mix of new and former crew members, we excavated as quickly as we could, again with attention to context and provenience. We again marveled at the architecture of the semi-subterranean structures, the well-preserved and diverse artifacts, and the way in which the site continued to reveal more information about the Alutiiq past. But with each tide, we saw the waters creeping closer. Depending on the tide levels in the morning or afternoon, we would sometimes wade to or from the site by way of the river shore, searching to save wooden artifacts that had been washed out of the site. The emphasis that summer wasn't only on what we found but on what we found out: the site was in such peril that our salvage efforts might very well be our last opportunity to investigate.

As the decades have passed, I have often thought of our archaeological work at the Karluk One site. The site was where I received my first fieldwork training, as well as my first experience of professional archaeologists and local communities working together from initial project research design through to excavation, conservation and analysis, and public presentation. At the end of the 1987 field season, I decided that archaeology would be my career path. I continue as an archaeologist today with one foot in the university teaching world, and the other foot in the world of cultural-resource management; excavations at Karluk One have been an integral, and influential, part of my journey. As an archaeological consultant, I work with diverse individuals and groups to identify, evaluate, and mitigate sites and other cultural resources in the face of development; there have been times when I've had to defend the integrity of a site, champion the importance of the past to the present, and speak to the importance of community values and cultural heritage. As a university lecturer working in the fields of anthropology, art history, and cultural heritage, I find ample opportunity to speak about the Karluk One site, the many benefits of collaborative archaeological work, and the way in which archaeological findings and the Alutiiq Museum and Archaeological Repository have contributed to Alutiiq community pride, persistence, and strength. I am deeply grateful for my Karluk experiences and being invited to work and visit with the Alutiiq community at this most remarkable and important site—*Quyanaa*.

Our crew first arrived at Karluk Lagoon in May of 1983. I was completely new to Alaska, and along with fellow crew members Alexander Dolitsky and Marianne Smith, I had been sent out as an advance team to finalize arrangements and ready our quarters. As our little plane circled Karluk Lagoon, I strained to make out the lines of old house pits dotting the shoreline. My rubber boots and raingear were spanking new and I clutched my barf bag with both hands as we bounced in the gale winds tearing across Shelikof Strait. Karluk Mayor Larry Shugak met us on the gravel airstrip and was nice enough not to laugh at a group of adults who were as ignorant as toddlers about their surroundings. Jerry Sheehan got us settled in a recently abandoned but still comfortable house that overlooked "New Karluk" on the south shore of the lagoon (fig. 1.9).

Dick Jordan arrived a few days later, and we began to work, testing and surveying new sites as

Figure 1.9. Looking east toward Karluk One across Karluk Lagoon, 1983. Bryn Mawr College Archaeological project, Alutiiq Museum archives, AM278:478.

we went. He was inexhaustible, and we worked for the next three weeks nearly without a break. Jordan's enthusiasm was contagious, and it was easy to share his absolute certainty that Arctic archaeology was the most important research that one could hope to do. Soon the kitchen table was covered with dirty field maps of sites, and Jordan exulted over them far into the night by the light of a hissing Coleman lantern. However, while the importance of the Karluk region in Kodiak prehistory was quickly apparent to us all, the value of the Karluk One site was not. It was an impressive site to be sure, with artifact-rich soils nearly 4 m thick. On sunny afternoons, women from the village dug through the top layers with teaspoons and filled small jars with brightly colored glass trade beads. Recently abandoned houses still stood on the site, many constructed of recycled parts of

nineteenth- and early twentieth-century cannery buildings that once stood on the spit (fig. 1.10). The preservation was impressive; carved wooden fragments and floorboards jutted everywhere from the soft, dark soil. The preservation added to our impression that it was a late site, and, frankly, we preferred something a bit older that would tell us more (or so we supposed) about Kodiak's prehistory. So Jordan turned his attention more toward the deposits on the north shore of the lagoon (KAR-031) near the Karluk Lodge, which were even deeper and seemed to have better stratigraphy. Kevin Smith, however, had worked on late prehistoric sites in the Barrow area that looked very much like Karluk One; he recognized the potential of the site and did some small excavations and profiled the site that first summer. In the end, both of these sites were excavated, and while both

Figure 1.10. Empty houses rest on top of Karluk One, 1983. Alutiiq Museum archives, AM193:8.S.

contributed mightily to what we learned about the prehistoric cultural sequence, it was the Karluk One site that left us all dumbfounded, archaeologist and Karluk resident alike.

When the Karluk One collection was first displayed in public workshops in Karluk and Kodiak, it was a complete revelation. Suddenly in front of us all were hundreds, then thousands, of magnificently made wooden weapons, tools, bentwood bowls, figurines, dolls, masks, and much more. It was tremendously exciting for everyone, and it was that shared sense of wonder and discovery that first brought together scientists and the Alutiiq community and then the entire island. Indeed, I think you will find that this sense of wonder still infuses this book.

The scientific view of Alutiiq culture was similarly changed by the Karluk project and all those that followed. The Alutiiq had been viewed for many years as a kind of anomaly because here on the North Pacific were people with clear linguistic and cultural links to the Yup'ik and Inupiat Eskimo peoples to the north and beyond. The Western stereotype of an Eskimo/Inuit had been formed by early encounters between Europeans and Inuit living on the icy shorelines of the eastern Arctic. Surely any speakers of an Eskimo language on the ice-free coasts of the Gulf of Alaska must represent some late intrusion from the north.

But the Karluk research told a different story, one of long-term continuity. There was input from neighboring groups on all sides; the collections showed influences or even imported objects from the Unangan, Yup'ik, and Tlingit, among others. But there was no sign of any sudden in-migration of outsiders from the north, just a fruitful and steady exchange (Jordan and Knecht 1988). And this cultural continuity seemed to extend back to the very first known occupation of the Kodiak Archipelago some seven thousand years before. In fact, it seems increasingly likely that many features of what we now know as Eskimo/Inuit culture may have had their origins in south Alaska. The range and complexity of the material culture from Karluk One also opened many eyes in the archaeological community. Here was dramatic evidence for a level of cultural complexity that was far beyond what most nonagricultural peoples could hope to achieve. In 1988, KANA hosted the Kodiak Island Cultural Heritage Conference, and for three days more than forty scientists and scholars from all over the world discussed this new perspective on Alutiiq culture. Conference attendees and the island community came away with a new sense of respect for heritage and ultimately themselves.

The cultural landscape of Alaska and indeed of the northern world has been forever changed by the rise of the vibrant arts and culture of the Alutiiq people in recent decades. Today, visible reminders of this cultural renaissance exist in museums, bookstores, schools, and art galleries around the world. This volume is just the latest expression and evidence of this movement, and Karluk One was where it began.

Rescue Archaeology Invites Fresh Perspective in School Lessons

Cheryl Heitman Meunier, Educator and Alutiiq Descendant

My participation in Karluk archaeology followed the Exxon Valdez oil spill and the beginning years of my career as a teacher. At that time, rescue archeology was the focus. The Karluk River was changing its course. Researchers sought to learn as much as possible before structures, artifacts, and information about a rich and flourishing culture washed completely out to sea. Due to my previous field experience and interest in my own culture, I was invited to help. The ability to reach down into the earth, thick with mud from days of rain, to "rescue" fully intact artifacts—one after another, after another—was a privilege. This was not the typical experience of an amateur archaeologist.

In spite of my minimal experience, what I discovered working in the field and beside archaeologists spilled into my classroom. It inspired lessons that required students to learn about Kodiak and its people. My students believed that all of Kodiak's indigenous people and their way of life died with Russian contact. I understood their perspective. I never really identified myself as Native until I participated in archaeology and began to have an understanding of what it meant to be a descendant. I do not recall ever being taught Native history in school.

These perspectives were reinforced by student participation in a play highlighting the massacre of Alutiiq people at Sitkalidak Island. We taught a curriculum about the history of Kodiak whose lessons stemmed from documentation of the brutal period of Western colonialism. What we knew about Alutiiq life was Russian conquest. However, there was very little about how Alutiiqs lived before exposure to an outside culture. Colonial exploitation of the indigenous people occurred in large part because Kodiak's Native people were masters of living in their environment. Europeans needed their expertise to expand trade. So how did the indigenous people live?

Comparing and contrasting life in today's modern society to life during a time period so far removed from my elementary-aged students was equivalent to expecting a five-year-old to write a paragraph! They did not have enough background experience transitioning between the abstract and concrete to develop a global perspective. However, guest speakers fresh from ancient sites provided immediate access to unearthed artifacts and photographs. Students became part of a forum where discussion was possible, not canned responses. As a result, their interest in exploring questions like, "What was the purpose of miniature kayaks?" was ignited with possibility, and with an artifact in view.

Figure 1.11. Painted toy war club and slat armor. Sheehan avocational collection, AM38:358, Panamaroff avocational collection, AM15:418, UA85.193:5841, UA84.193:1408.

In my classroom, discussion revolved around the uses of natural resources and how technology advanced daily living. This prompted essential questions about what life was like on Kodiak Island thousands of years ago. What tools helped hunters succeed on land and at sea? What kind of bone was found in a midden? Why was wooden armor needed? Who was fighting and why? It can be intimidating for a teacher to not have an answer when a question is asked. Yet, I did not always have the answer (fig. 1.11).

With subsequent archaeological digs, and the opening of the Alutiiq Museum in 1995, teachers and students now have the opportunity to be directly immersed in the history found right in our own backyard. At the end of each field season, we can now change and adapt our lessons as new or supporting evidence expands knowledge of our deep heritage.

Shortly after the museum opened, I was consulted as to whether or not educational kits assembled by the Alutiiq Museum would be used in the classroom. Yes! The kits consisted of artifacts from local sites and accompanying information that could be used in hands-on lessons to teach about Alutiiq history. There is no better concrete experience than holding a six-hundred-year-old artifact from Karluk—an object that can be touched and studied—to prompt questions that connect students to the study of people and their environment!

The Karluk One site provides information and acknowledgement of a culture that predates Russian contact. What we are learning from this site is a story with many fascinating elements that took place before the influence of invaders. It's a story we can be proud of it. It's a story we can teach joyfully. It's our story.

Chapter One Notes

1. In 2013, Gordon Pullar told the author that he and Dick were milling around the main room after dinner in the Karluk Lodge, wondering what next, when Senator Barbara Mikulski came up to Dick and said, "Professor Jordan, time to get things underway, I think. Maybe you should call us all together." And Dick said, "Um, Senator I wouldn't know how to call a bunch of United States senators together." Senator Mikulsky turned around and instructed her fellow senators in her inimitable style: "Alright, gentlemen, gather round, and let's get this show on the road!"

2. The song tells the story of the Gurindji people and their champion Vincent Lingiari, and a protest that sparked the indigenous land rights movement in Australia, leading directly to the *Commonwealth Aboriginal Land Rights (Northern Territory) Act* in 1976. The act gave indigenous people freehold title to traditional lands in the Northern Territory and the power of veto over mining and development on those lands. In 1975, on an occasion marked with huge symbolism and celebration, 3,236 km² of land was handed back to the Gurindji people by the commonwealth government.

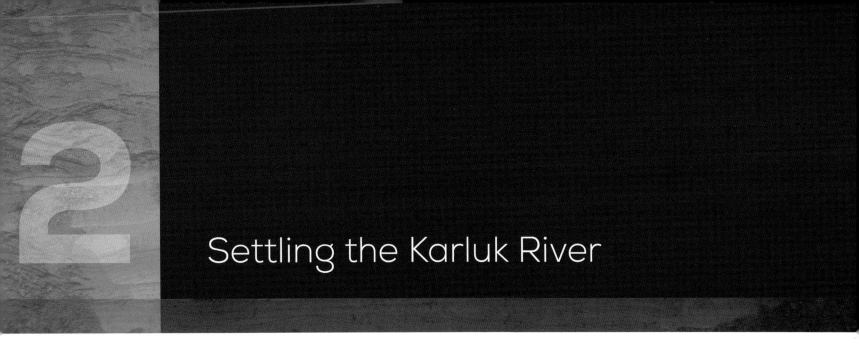

Settling the Karluk River

By Alaskan standards, the Karluk River is small. From its headwaters at Karluk Lake, this narrow freshwater stream travels just 35 km (22 mi). Draining mitten-shaped Karluk Lake, it weaves through the low, brushy, mountains of southern Kodiak Island emptying into Shelikof Strait and the North Pacific Ocean (fig. 2.1). Despite its modest size, however, the Karluk River is one of Alaska's most productive salmon streams. Five species of Pacific salmon spawn here, returning annually in spectacular quantities. From May through December, salmon are an abundant, predictable resource in the Karluk and a staple food for both people and animals.

Drawn to this bounty, Alutiiq people have lived on the banks of the Karluk for at least six thousand years. The remains of over a hundred settlements record their activities and the development of fishing and food storage practices. Villages, camps, fish-processing sites, cairns, and trails are all part of the river's history and illustrate how Alutiiq people harvested fish with increasing efficiency to feed growing communities. The Karluk River region holds both profoundly important natural resources and some of Kodiak's richest cultural deposits. This chapter explores the natural and social environments of the Karluk River to illustrate Karluk One's place in local history. When occupied, Karluk One was once one of seven major prehistoric villages in the Karluk drainage and part of one of the most densely populated regions of the Kodiak Archipelago.

Karluk Lake and River

Glaciers formed the low rolling mountains of southern Kodiak and the small valley that holds Karluk Lake and Karluk River. For tens of thousands of years, massive streams of ice flowed out of the Kodiak Mountains. Geologists believe that this process began about one hundred twenty thousand years ago, during the Pleistocene, with three major periods of ice advance followed by melting and retreat (Karlstrom 1969:29).

Across the archipelago, intense glaciation carved steep-sided mountains and deep fjords out of bedrock. Kodiak's rugged mountains and protected bays reflect the removal of rock from the land. Streams of ice cut and carried this material out to sea, creating valleys that filled with ocean water when the ice eventually melted

(Capps 1937). Along the island's western coast, glaciers flowing out of Cook Inlet aided this process (Heusser 1960:14; Karlstrom 1969:33). This ice cut the vertical cliffs flanking the entrance to Karluk Lagoon (fig. 2.2), as well as the deep trench that holds Shelikof Strait.

During the first major glacial advance, ice covered the entire archipelago. Only the highest mountain peaks rose above the glaciers. During the next two periods of glaciation, however, parts of southwest Kodiak Island were ice free. At sixty-five thousand years ago, and again at about twenty thousand years ago (Karlstrom 1969:41), large lakes formed in front of Kodiak's mountain glaciers in the area between present-day Uyak Bay and Olga Bay. This included much of the future Karluk River basin. Trapped between Kodiak's glaciers and the ice filling Shelikof Strait, these large lakes deposited sediment that helped to create the region's distinct topography. Today, southern Kodiak lacks the steep mountains and fjords found elsewhere in the archipelago. Lakes and rivers rest in valleys cut by glaciers and then filled with lake sediment. Mountains are older and more weathered, rounder than their northern cousins. In short, while glaciers carved fjords to the north, they built and softened landscapes in the Karluk valley.

Geological data from the neighboring Alaska Peninsula suggest that deglaciation of the region began about seventeen thousand years ago (Misarti et al. 2012), with rapid melting (fig. 2.3). Geological data from Kodiak suggest that western areas of the archipelago were ice free by fourteen thousand years ago (Peteet and Mann 1994), although mountain glaciers both grew and shrank over the long period of melting. As the ice retreated, freshwater filled valleys in interior, southwest Kodiak, forming the large lakes present

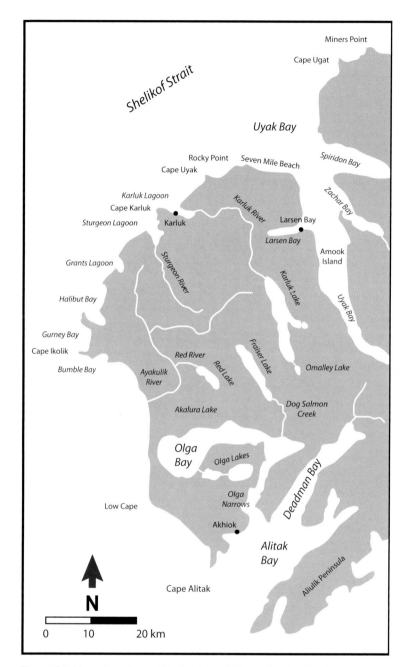

Figure 2.1. Map of southwest Kodiak Island. Illustration by Amy Steffian.

today—Karluk, Red, Fraser, Akalura, Olga—and the rivers and streams that drain them.

Biologists believe that plants and then mammals colonized the ice-free landscape relatively quickly. Chapter 5 considers the natural resources

Figure 2.2. Cliffs south of Karluk Lagoon, 2008. Alutiiq Museum archives. Photograph by Jill H. H. Lipka.

Figure 2.3. The Koniag Glacier—a remnant of the glaciers that once covered the archipelago, view east toward Sitkalidak Island. Photograph by Patrick Saltonstall.

of the Karluk region in detail. However, pollen studies suggest that a variety of herbaceous plants were the first plants to arrive, followed by ferns (Peteet and Mann 1994). At least seven thousand years ago alder and birch colonized the region, followed by a succession of modern plants (Heusser 1960:183). Biologists hypothesize that mammals, particularly bear, fox, river otter, and ermine, reached the archipelago by swimming or traveling over winter sea ice (Rausch 1969:230). For other species, like moose and caribou, water and ice were barriers to colonization. People were the island's final settlers. They arrived at least seven thousand five hundred years ago, thousands of years after the island's other mammals.

Pollen Studies in the Karluk River Region, Alaska

Robert E. Nelson, Professor, Colby College

I came to Karluk in 1986, as a relatively new PhD in Quaternary Paleoecology, amazed at how lush and green Kodiak was compared to the Seward Peninsula and North Slope where I'd worked previously. Though my previous studies had been on materials much older than the first known human presence in the New World, it was exciting to think that I was going to be working in association with a major archaeological undertaking and helping to interpret the environments in which the Alutiiq people had lived here for thousands of years.

The broad U-shaped valley of the lower Karluk River was clear evidence that, prior to human arrival, the region had been glaciated. Previous geological studies indicated that, contrary to what might be expected, the ice here moved inland from Shelikof Strait. Ice derived from the Alaska Peninsula, and even the distant Alaska Range, flowed down through what is now Cook Inlet and continued on down the strait and up onto the island. A broad ridge of material deposited by this ice is, in fact, responsible for why the Karluk River, flowing north from Karluk Lake, turns abruptly to the west to follow its current course. The glacial river flowing down this new course eroded much material, depositing it in the layers of gravel exposed in some of the bluffs around Karluk Lagoon. It was also ice from Shelikof Strait that pushed up the mud from the sea floor into layers that can be seen in the cliffs on either side of the Karluk River mouth, mud that was used by ancient Alutiiq people to line some of the fire pits in their homes.

To reconstruct the vegetation history of an area, we use pollen preserved in sediments. But the pollen in glacial sediments will be mixed, as the glaciers have bulldozed the landscape and carried everything forward. So, we look for small ponds or bogs, in which the sediment that has accumulated has come from a very local area. Since there were none that looked particularly promising in the Karluk area, we crossed over the pass into the Sturgeon River drainage. There, Patrick Saltonstall and I dug a pit in a broad depression atop the glacial deposits, down to the glacial deposits themselves. This gave us easy access to sediments that had washed into this basin from the immediate area, capturing the pollen that was coming from the surrounding plants, and depositing it in layers, year upon year, and capturing as well the periodic volcanic ash falls (fig. 2.4).

As elsewhere on western Kodiak, radiocarbon dating indicated that our area only became stable and began accumulating nonglacial sediments around five to six thousand years ago. The radiocarbon date

on the organic materials at the very base of our excavation indicated that it was in fact only about 4,800 calendar years old, which was comparable to two previously published radiocarbon dates from the Karluk area. The pollen from this section indicated that alders and ferns quickly covered the landscape but soon diminished dramatically; by three thousand years ago, the landscape became covered with the grass-sedge vegetation and miscellaneous wildflowers that we see today. There was no indication that the area was ever forested; even birch, poplar, and spruce were rare. So, other than the periodic volcanic ash falls—one of which left at least an inch-thick blanket on the landscape around the year AD 400—the ancient people here lived in an environment that, at least as far as the vegetation indicates, was relatively stable and much as it is today.

Wondering if maybe I could find something that would give us a vegetation record extending farther back in time, I sampled the deposits exposed in the bluff that faced the ocean from inside the lagoon: a land formation parallel to the modern beach but between the river mouth and the modern village site. In my notes, I named the site Panamaroff Bluff, since it lay in front of a summer cabin that belonged to Lawrence Panamaroff. These deposits seemed quite interesting, showing ripples in the bedding that indicated alternating stream-current directions, so they had likely been deposited in a lagoon that was subject to significant tidal action. The volcanic ash beds in the deposits were also completely weathered to blue clay and as stiff and waxy as a bar of soap (fig. 2.5).

The pollen from these deposits was completely different from that in the excavation in the Sturgeon River valley and different from anywhere

Figure 2.4 (above). Layers of sediment in the Sturgeon River basin, 1986. Courtesy Robert Nelson.

Figure 2.5 (below). Panamaroff Bluff stratigraphy, 1986. Courtesy Robert Nelson.

on modern Kodiak. There was very little pollen of grasses, sedges, or anything other than trees here, along with spores of ferns. But the pollen was dominated by tree-type alders, with a good deal of tree birch. The exotic trees that were represented, however, were mind-boggling though no one type was abundant, there was pollen of spruce as well as of hardwoods such as oaks, hickories, walnuts, elms, holly, and even wingnut—a tree today found only in China and adjacent Asia, though it has relatives in the southeastern US mainland. Comparison with mainland Alaska pollen floras indicate that these deposits are probably in the age range of fifteen to eighteen million years old.

Apparently, the ice that came onshore from Shelikof Strait was finished with its eroding work by the time it stretched this far inland and was only depositing its sediment load. The older Panamaroff Bluff deposits were merely overridden by that ice and its debris as it pushed upvalley. That would explain the incredible age of the deposits and why the volcanic ash was so stiff, like a waxy clay.

I have for many years thought that it would be marvelous to return to resample this bluff, to try to recover enough material to gain an accurate age determination on these wonderfully old materials. It would definitely be a major reference for further studies of the vegetation history of Alaska and of the tundra development.

The Karluk River valley of today looks much like the region the Alutiiq people settled. Karluk Lake fills a deeply cut glacial trench, and the river descends to the ocean in a valley partially confined by mountains. Although abandoned channels, stream-cut terraces, eroding banks, and migration of the river mouth indicate that the river has meandered along the valley bottom (Rogers 1989), surrounding mountains and shallow water have kept the waterway from dramatically altering its course. Both the lake and river have been present in a similar position for a very long time, providing habitat for wildlife and a home for the Alutiiq.

Alutiiq people settled the entire length of the Karluk system—from the very head of Karluk Lake to the mouth of Karluk River. Understanding the watercourse and its features is important to understanding the ways people used the region. Karluk Lake is the largest body of freshwater in the Kodiak Archipelago (fig. 2.6). Twenty-two

Figure 2.6. Panoramic view of the southern end of Karluk Lake, 2009. Alutiiq Museum archives, AM620. Photograph by Patrick Saltonstall.

kilometers long and up to 3 km wide, the lake rests about 122 m (400 ft) above sea level. This long oval feature has three small islands near its center and a small bay on its eastern shore known as East Arm or the Thumb. At the end of both Karluk Lake and East Arm lie two smaller lakes—O'Malley Lake and Thumb Lake, respectively. Each small lake drains into Karluk Lake through a very short stream less than 2 km long.

The shores of Karluk Lake are generally steep and brushy. Surrounding mountains rise from the water creating little room for settlement. In places, however, streams running down the mountains have formed small deltas at their mouths, with pockets of flat land suitable for building. Moreover, sockeye salmon spawn in the lake's tributary streams and along its pebbly shores, making settlement of the lakeshore desirable. The head of

Karluk Lake, the head of East Arm, and the banks of the small streams emptying into each also have large areas of level ground and excellent access to spawning sockeye, coho, and pink salmon.

Karluk Lake empties into Karluk River at its northern end. The lake outlet is open, surrounded by a low-lying, marshy area known as the flats. From the outlet, the river's clear, shallow waters flow north through a single channel. Low, flat terraces border the river for about 3.5 km below the outlet, before the surrounding area becomes low and marshy. These higher, drier landforms provide ample space for settlement. Archaeological data indicate that people built communities on these terraces.

The upper Karluk River meanders through the flats, over hummocky, muskeg-covered terrain dotted with small ponds (fig. 2.7). Here the

Figure 2.7. The upper Karluk River, 2011. Alutiiq Museum archives, AM620. Photograph by Patrick Saltonstall.

waterway is wide and shallow (Heusser 1960:55) with a commanding view of the surrounding valley. River waters are typically less than half a meter deep and can be very low in summer. This can make it difficult to boat along this section of the river, and people are known to walk in the channel and even drag their vessels through the stream (Bean 1890:10, 15; Dodge 2004:128). The shallow waters, however, make this one of the best places to capture fish. Sockeye, coho, pink, and often chinook salmon either spawn in the upper river or pass through on their way to Karluk Lake. Fisheries biologist Tarleton Bean, who studied the river in 1889, photographed lines of boulders used to build salmon traps in this location (Bean 1890:Plate XXIV). Recent archaeological surveys confirm the presence of V-shaped alignments of stones in the river, the remains of fish traps.

About 13 km below the lake, the river begins a gradual swing to the northwest, entering an area more closely rimmed by mountains. At the northern end of the flats lies the Larsen Bay portage. This long-used, easily hiked trail crosses the flats and descends to the head of Larsen Bay, a marine waterway and arm of larger Uyak Bay (Bean 1890:15; Dodge 2004:185; Mulcahy 1986:64). Like Karluk River, this trail is one of the region's major avenues of travel. It connects the riverine environment of the Karluk with the protected marine waters of neighboring Uyak Bay about 4.5 km to the east. Near the portage, river waters are deeper. Chinook salmon spawn here and steelhead overwinter in pools of quiet water (fig. 2.8).

From the portage, the river channel narrows gradually and the current intensifies as the waterway turns west and snakes through mountainous terrain. Small tributary streams empty into the river and the channel braids, forming a few small islands (fig. 2.9). Terraces continue to line the riverbanks, although with a more limited view.

Figure 2.8. Steelhead fishing at the Karluk River Portage, ca. 1960. Nekeferoff Collection, Alutiiq Museum archives, AM580:415.

About 21 km below the lake, the river enters a canyon, confined on either side by steep mountains. Here, river waters run swiftly over the rocky bottom, creating small areas of rapids. The steeper topography and the faster running water make this area less desirable for settlement and fishing, although sites are recorded here.

About 5 km from the ocean, the river widens, forming a broad lagoon. The upper part of this feature, known as the inner lagoon, is an oval basin (Rogers 1989). Two prominent points of

Figure 2.9. Lower Karluk River, 2012. Alutiiq Museum archives, AM620. Photograph by Patrick Saltonstall.

land separate the basin from the lower lagoon, a broad triangular waterway up to .8 km across. The lagoon, with its expansive terraces and access to both riverine and marine resources, is an excellent place for settlement. All salmon entering the Karluk system pass through the lagoon. This includes chum salmon only found in the river's lowest course.

Marine waters flood the lagoon twice daily, mixing ocean water with fresh and raising the water level as much as five feet. A heavy barrier beach formed by cobbles eroded from glacial deposits separates the ocean from the lagoon. At present,

the mouth of the river cuts through this beach on the southern corner of the lagoon. However, geologists note that the mouth of the river has shifted numerous times in its history (Rogers 1989). Storms, shoreline erosion, and tidal forces periodically redirect river waters, breaking through the cobble spit and creating a new entrance. In January of 1978 (Mason et al. 1997:89), these forces damaged Karluk homes and a bridge across the river, leading to the relocation of the village (Lind essay Chapter 2) and the eventual destruction of the Karluk One site.

The Storm that Changed Everything

Ronnie Lind, Karluk Elder

Ronnie Lind, the son of Andrew and Nancy Lind, was born in Perryville, an Alutiiq village on the southern Alaska Peninsula. Raised by his grandmother, Barbara Shangin, he attended school in Kodiak in the 1970s. Here, he met Betty Pavaloff, a girl from Karluk. They married and moved to her village, where they have lived since. Betty is the Karluk postmaster and a community health aid. Ronnie is a subsistence harvester and a carver and runs a lodge for visiting fishermen. He has a deep interest in Alutiiq objects. He shared his thoughts about Karluk history and archaeology in an interview with Sven Haakanson Jr. in March, 2012.

The bridge caught my eye when I first came to Karluk. People had stories about living in barabaries [sod houses] behind the bridge (fig. 2.10). They talked about how they used to go back and forth to the other side. It always fascinated me how they kept the site quiet for so many years.

When the storm took out the bridge, it created chaos. Then the village split into two different worlds. They lost access to the school and theater when the spit broke. They lost all the fuel during that storm, and we could get no assistance to help. OEDP [Overall Economic Development Plan] was asking for repayment of the fuel lost in the storm. We had to get a loan to get the oil, so we had to get another loan to pay for the loss. This was a great disaster, and out of this, a new village site was selected in a new area.

The other things that happened was the artifacts started washing out. I found some, and then others started seeing them. The next ten to fifteen years artifacts by the thousands were washed out with the storms. The Elders knew about the artifacts. Before, they would find little things: beads, fishhooks, spears. After the storm, they would find large amounts of artifacts. Not one or two pieces but thirty to forty pieces a day: kayak parts, spears, and so on. The site changed. So people would spend their time looking for artifacts. There were thousands of pieces found, and many still have them. There were beads, wood, crosses, all sorts of designs, but there were a lot of them.

The people moved to the new site a mile up the river. No one really agreed on this, but no one had a choice. For the first year [after the move], there was no running water or sewer. Also, you could hear everyone next door, and this was uncomfortable. While this was happening, the site was eroding and no one paid attention. The site was being destroyed, washed out. Then the archaeologists came, two or three years after the storm. The artifacts were not paid attention to. The Elders did not mind them being lost. But the archaeologist Dick Jordon asked permission to dig and got it.

When they were digging, the archaeologists would have a display every week. They had cookouts and parties, but they worked very hard. [But even their work] was still not enough. When they left, after storms the artifacts would wash out. You would find coins, beads, flintlock-gun parts from the American to the Russian period.

The archaeology project was a beautiful thing at the beginning. It was seeing what others did not, our ancestry. The archaeologists came in taking, doing assessments, and showing all the amazing things that were from the past. There were things from all over the world right here—Chinese, American, Russian, Aleut. All the artifacts that came out of the site were amazing.

Figure 2.10. New Karluk, 1962. William Laughlin Collection, Alutiiq Museum archives, AM50:7.

It was so neat to see the different stages of how the houses were built, to see how they lived in the past. Even today, this is the beauty of what was here. I can picture the past, sitting on the beach imagining what it was like. Our ancestors were living, kayaking, hunting, fishing, carving, and surviving with so little but so much to them.

They would tell stories of them coming over to dance. It is hard to imagine how in the past this village was a central place for people. It is going extinct now. Mother Nature is taking over now. The change is sad. Karluk was Kodiak in the day. It was where everyone met, worked, and made money in the past. It took awhile for me to understand how important a role this place had. It is interesting how so many people came here from around the world. It was a central point, yes, for work, but they came here. So many cultures came here at one time.

In my time, I would find a lot of objects. I was being driven to pick up the artifacts. The shaman dolls—I would leave them to be taken out to sea. The artifacts were not for my keepsake but for my grandchildren. When I was collecting them, I had to have this stuff. It was so phenomenal. I want to share with my kids what I found. When we showed them to visitors, Betty would tell everyone this was what my ancestors made. One thing you can say for the objects I found, they are from Karluk only. Now they are at the museum.

Dick Jordon was chasing me around for a couple of years there. I had this little bird-and-man figure. You have that in the museum now. I found that figure, and it got them interested in Karluk. I preserved that doll. I put it in a mayonnaise jar and filled it with vodka. It stayed like that until I met Rick, and they got a hold of it. This was the first artifact. Then there was a lopsided face [mask] and a drum handle. The lopsided mask was the ugliest artifact I have ever seen. I would not allow it into my house. I've never seen collections like that from other sites. There is no other site like Karluk.

Karluk should be given credit for the starting of the museum. Most of the stuff from Karluk is in the museum. Karluk made that museum. That should be recognized. This was the first site that helped establish this museum and the changes that have happened since. Yes, now you are collecting things from around the world, but the site is important.

The Elders pointed out that Karluk was the most unique place in the world. They knew Karluk would fade out. Life is change. They were right. The future remains like the artifacts. We need to heal to change the future. We should have listened because our future was set. The Elders knew the storm would change everything. We are going through a cycle.

The climate of Karluk mirrors that of Kodiak. Cloudy, cool, wet, maritime conditions prevail, with fog and drizzle in the summer and wind, rain, and snow in winter. In the coldest winter weather, Karluk Lake and River freeze, creating a route through the valley. People take advantage of easy walking at this time of year to access inland areas (Bean 1890:20).

Despite its maritime climate, the Karluk region receives significantly less rain than eastern Kodiak Island. On average, a storm crosses the Gulf of Alaska once every four to five days in the winter, stalling against Alaska's high coastal mountains and dropping an abundance of rain (Wilson and Overland 1986:32). On Kodiak, the mountainous, northeast trending spine of the island forms a rain shadow, reducing the amount of rain that reaches the island's western shores. Eastern Kodiak Island can receive as much as 284 cm of precipitation a year, as compared to less than 122 cm in the Karluk drainage (Karlstrom 1969:24). This is another appealing characteristic of Karluk and an important consideration for

people who rely on drying fish for winter food. Although fish can be harvested in vast amounts around Kodiak, Russian observers noted that thousands of drying filets spoiled in the persistent rain (Wiswell 1979:115). Not only is the Karluk River the most productive salmon stream in the Kodiak Archipelago, it has some of the best local conditions for transforming fish into storable food.

Archaeological Studies Along the Karluk

Today, Karluk is home to about forty-one people (Alaska Department of Commerce 2013). The modern Alutiiq community lies on the western shore of Karluk Lagoon, about 1.6 km from the river's mouth. In 1980, villagers moved to this location from homes surrounding the river's mouth (Rogers 1989:24). Wood-framed houses, a school, a chapel, a tribal office, a clinic, a post office, a handful of private lodges, gravel roads, a landfill, and an airstrip represent the community's central facilities (fig. 2.11), serving the region's smallest population in several thousand years.

How do we know? The Karluk River, with its broad banks and relatively stable course, holds over a hundred archaeological sites documenting the history of Alutiiq settlement. Archaeologists walking the riverbanks have recorded depressions formed by collapsed houses, grassy mounds that cover ancient garbage, eroding layers of charcoal from past campfires, and patches of luxuriant plant growth. Elderberry, salmonberry, nettles, and cow parsnip thrive in the nutrient-rich soils of abandoned village sites.

Although erosion has damaged settlement sites along the watercourse, many are still present and in good condition. Along the Kodiak coast, Alutiiq people commonly built their homes one on top of the next. Limited space and competition for access to harvesting areas encouraged people to stay in one place. As houses aged, residents undertook the major task of rebuilding them—salvaging materials, establishing a clean, dry foundation, and building a new structure. This process created large piles of debris along the coast. Deep deposits of house remains and garbage accumulated over hundreds of years. This is not the case along the inland shores of Karluk Lake and River, where there is ample building space. Here, people settled along terraces overlooking the river, moving their communities as needed. Adjacent occupations overlap little, and many archaeological sites have neighborhoods, spatially distinct clusters of houses that reflect different episodes of settlement.

The exception to this pattern is in prime fishing locales—the mouth of Karluk Lagoon, Karluk Lake outlet, and the stream mouths at the head of Karluk Lake and East Arm. Here, settlements overlap significantly. At Karluk One, for example, as many as ten superimposed house floors illustrate that people rebuilt at the river mouth over

Figure 2.11. Karluk village, 2008. Alutiiq Museum archives. Photograph by Jill H. H. Lipka.

centuries, often directly on top of a previous house. In a few key fishing spots, moving to the next suitable terrace was not the preferred option. Presumably building in desirable spots helped people maintain control over these locations and the resources they held.

Archaeologists did not always recognize the potential for settlement along the Karluk River or in other areas of Kodiak's interior. Historic accounts of marine hunting and fishing, the presence of numerous large villages in coastal settings, and a lack of riverine settlement in the historic era (Black 1977:82) led many to believe that Native people used Kodiak's interior very little (Huggins 1981:3; Wrangell 1980:59). Recent research indicates this view is incorrect.

We now know that as part of their broad use of maritime resources, Kodiak's Alutiiq people harvested extensively from salmon streams and that the type of stream influenced the type of use. Larger and more productive streams experienced more intense use. Rivers without lakes and spawning habitat for one or two salmon species tend to have settlements only around their mouths. This includes the sizable, unnamed streams found in the heads of bays throughout the archipelago. Small lake-headed systems, like the Buskin River or the Uganik River, tend to have settlements around the river mouth and at the outlet to the lake. Here, people built beside the best areas for catching fish and passed by the spaces in between. In contrast, mega systems—the Karluk, the Red/Ayakulik, the Olga—long, lake-headed rivers that support four or five salmon species, have settlements along much of their courses. In addition to building in prime fishing locations, the sheer abundance of fish allowed people to live successfully in many additional streamside settings. Importantly, these major salmon systems all occur on southwestern Kodiak Island, promoting a

distinct regional pattern of settlement and subsistence. Northern archipelago fishermen fished at the mouths of salmon streams, likely combining late summer and fall fishing with activities like seal hunting, duck hunting, and plant and shellfish collecting in shoreline environments. In contrast, fishermen living in southwestern Kodiak focused on fishing in interior environments, combining their efforts with duck hunting, trapping, and plant collecting in the surrounding marshes and hillsides. Information gathered by archaeologists illustrates this pattern in the Karluk drainage.

Historic accounts of Karluk indicate that the lagoon had from two to five areas of settlement in the late 1700s. People lived in the location of Karluk One, immediately across the lagoon at Old Karluk, and possibly in several other locations on the lagoon shore and beachfront (Black et al. ca. 2003). In 1889, fisheries biologist Tarleton Bean confirmed the presence of settlements on either side of the lagoon mouth and noted a sod house called "Nicolai's" at the juncture of the river and the Larsen Bay portage trail (Bean 1890:15). Other accounts of settlement along the river come from Smithsonian Institution physical anthropologist Aleš Hrdlička. Hrdlička visited Karluk in 1932, while traveling around the island in search of archaeological sites. He journeyed upriver as far as the head of the inner lagoon (Hrdlička 1944:102), encountering at least nine areas with sod houses. He also learned of old barabaras [sod houses] on the lower river, and at two places on Karluk Lake (Hrdlička 1944:104). Hrdlička did not visit Karluk Lake. Villagers probably told him of these settlements, as they did later archaeologists (Sheehan 1983:51–52).

In 1949, archaeologist Frederick Milan visited the Karluk region and observed a number of sites in both Karluk Lagoon and along Karluk Lake, supporting Hrdlička's report of far inland villages

(Milan 1974:85). Although he did not study any of these deposits, Milan returned in 1952 to explore sites in the lagoon and test Karluk One (see Chapter 4).

Research on Karluk area settlement picked up again in the later decades of the twentieth century. In 1976, archaeologist Linda Yarborough investigated Karluk Lake for Koniag, Inc. (Yarborough 1976). While helping the corporation to select lands for ownership under section 14h(1) of the Alaska Native Claims Settlement Act, she identified, mapped, and tested three ancient settlements overlooking the southern end of the lake. Her work confirmed the presence of lakeside settlements and provided the first detailed description of these deposits.

A more comprehensive effort to locate sites in the valley began in the 1980s, when Bryn Mawr College crews surveyed large portions of the Karluk system through a multiyear project directed by Richard Jordan (Jordan 1983). In 1983, graduate students Kevin Smith and Glenn Sheehan spent two weeks in the region, traveling by raft from O'Malley Lake to Karluk Lagoon (Sheehan 1983, Smith 1983, Smith essay Chapter 2).

Their work focused on Karluk Lake but included portions of the upper river. Across this area, they found seventeen additional sites, including several very large sod-house settlements. A test in one of these sites revealed substantial quantities of marine fauna—clams, mussels, and cockles. Shellfish available only on the distant coast were a common component of the site's garbage deposits. The large number of sites, some of them extensive and filled with unexpected evidence of coastal resources, suggested a much more intensive use of the interior than previously imagined.

Intrigued by mounting evidence of extensive interior settlement, Jordan and his students returned to the lake and river numerous times, locating additional sites and mapping hundreds of house depressions (Jordan and Knecht 1988). Their research illustrated the presence of sites spanning Kodiak's history and the use of key fishing locales—the heads of East Arm and Karluk Lake, the river outlet, and the lagoon. As crews excavated the remarkable deposits at Karluk One, it became evident that this large site was part of a major settlement system spanning the entire Karluk River.

First Survey, First Steps: The Beginning of the Karluk Archaeological Project

Kevin P. Smith, Deputy Director/Chief Curator, Haffenreffer Museum, Brown University

The Karluk Archaeological Project began in the winter of 1981, in conversations between Glenn Sheehan and myself. Anthropology was just starting to recognize complex hunter-gatherers, ridding itself of a lock-tight vision of highly mobile "bands" as the norm for hunting and gathering communities (Lee and DeVore 1979; Service 1962) and seeking good examples in the archaeological record. Glenn and I had been working in Barrow, Alaska, on SUNY Binghamton's Utkiagvik Archaeological Project, and I was looking for a place to do dissertation fieldwork in Alaska. Lydia Black's then-recent (1977) translation of Bolotov's and Gideon's descriptions of Koniag society suggested that Kodiak might be an area of unrecognized potential. The pioneering work of Hrdlička (1944), Heizer (1956), Don Clark (1966a,b, 1970a,b, 1974, 1979), Workman (1966), Dumond (1971, 1981), Gerald Clark (1977), and Henn (1978) had established a cultural-historical framework for the region. Yet with the exception of a brief mention by Hrdlička of sites near the lagoon, no one had identified Karluk as a place of archaeological interest. The historic scale of its salmon fisheries, coupled with early Russian statements about the importance of salmon fishing in Alutiiq culture, suggested to us that the Karluk River drainage was an important a place to investigate.

In the summer of 1982, Glenn and I flew to Karluk, met the community, and got a sense of the region's archaeological potential. In just one day, the richness of the sites at the mouth of the river became apparent, and we identified at least four new settlements spanning Kodiak's cultural history. That fall, we wrote a grant proposal to the National Endowment for the Humanities and asked Dick Jordan, a Bryn Mawr College professor working in Greenland but with previous survey experience on Kodiak, to submit it on our behalf, as we were both graduate students. The proposal laid out a fairly simple model and research plan coupling surveys along two adjacent rivers—the Karluk and the Sturgeon—and their lagoons with excavations to clear eroding bluff faces at the two most deeply stratified sites in Karluk Lagoon. These would help us interpret survey results and determine these sites' potential for future research.

In 1982, little was known archaeologically about the interior of Kodiak Island. Although Linda Yarborough (1976) had documented three sites near the south end of Karluk Lake, most archaeologists assumed that the Alutiiq people occupied the coastal fringes, pursuing a dominantly marine diet. We suggested, instead, that many of Kodiak's prehistoric communities relied on the salmon fishery; that stored, smoked, and dried fish fueled Kodiak's prehistoric chiefdoms; and that the rise of cultural complexity on Kodiak could be tied to changes in the utilization and accessibility of the island's fisheries. We suggested that the Karluk River's multiple runs of salmon, as well as its year-round char, steelhead, bears, birds, and

Figure 2.12. Kevin Smith and Glenn Sheehan returning from the Karluk Lake and River survey, 1983. Bryn Mawr College Archaeological project, Alutiiq Museum archives, AM278:406.S.

wild plants would have made it a magnet for human settlement, while the smaller, adjacent Sturgeon River might have been settled later or less extensively. We argued that evidence for Alutiiq communities' earliest focus on salmon as a staple resource would be documented by the initial colonization of sites along the river best suited for intercepting seasonal salmon runs. We thought that information on changes in the importance of salmon to the Alutiiq diet and economy would be seen in the expansion and contraction of fishing sites throughout the river and lake systems. Finally, we proposed that changes through time in the ways prime fishing locations were shared or monopolized would help us to understand whether prehistoric communities were organized along egalitarian or hierarchical principles and how this changed through time.

The grant was funded, and in the summer of 1983, our small team flew to Kodiak to begin the project. Jordan agreed to come along for two weeks to help set up a field base in Karluk while Glenn and I did a ten-day survey by boat along the Karluk River (fig. 2.12). Everyone, even people in Kodiak, assured us that the survey would be a waste of time. The consensus was that we might locate a few small fishing camps where Alutiiq people labored for the Russian artels, but that the ten days we'd planned would be eight too many. On the other hand, people suggested that the work around the lagoon might be more promising.

Within 2 hours of arriving by float plane at the southern end of Karluk Lake, Glenn and I had identified 1 historic and 2 prehistoric sites, the largest clearly a major village with sod houses lined up along the shoreline adjacent to the O'Malley River's outlet into Karluk Lake. Less distinct depressions behind this front line suggested either storage facilities or earlier occupations. Two test pits revealed deep stratigraphy; abundant fish, bird, and eagle bones; late-prehistoric artifacts; but no evidence of Russian- or American-period activity. Over the next 10 days, working nearly around the clock and traveling in a 6-foot-long inflatable raft with a 1.5 horsepower motor, we documented 33 previously unknown prehistoric sites around Karluk Lake and along the upper and middle sections of the Karluk River. One memorable plunge of my hand into the frigid waters of the Thumb River brought up the midsection of an Ocean Bay 2-style ground-slate bayonet, in an instant extending the known prehistory of Kodiak's interior by 4,000 years. A later return to that location resulted in finding the site from which the bayonet had eroded, although the visit was interrupted by an equally memorable close encounter with a large bear! Other sites were clearly Kachemak or Koniag, with both small settlements and deep, spatially extensive deposits representing villages. We quickly abandoned test pitting as the sheer scale of the regional archaeological record became apparent and instead used careful scrutiny of erosion faces and bear trails, vegetation-community changes, and the layout of surface features to make preliminary assessments of most sites' ages. By the end of ten days, having run out of food, we were forced to shoot the lower course of the Karluk River without further survey, although we observed large and small sites along the banks as we dodged bears and eagles.

The 1983 survey extended the known prehistory of interior occupation into the mid-Holocene, documented unexpected and extensive settlement throughout late prehistory, and suggested rapid and nearly complete abandonment of the river during the Russian and American periods. Rather than small fish camps, we mapped several villages of sod houses extending more than a kilometer along the river's banks and the lake's shorelines, networks of fishing weirs, and smaller settlements at the mouths of small tributaries and landing beaches. Together, these sites suggested a hierarchy of settlements linked to the scale of fisheries around the drainage and that the earliest and the largest later sites would be found at the most productive locations, as our model had predicted. In the long run, ten days of survey proved to be at least twenty days too few. More than a month of intensive survey by the Alutiiq Museum has recently confirmed our finds and located more sites in this resource-rich interior region of Kodiak Island.

Investigations of fishing practices, food storage, and settlement led Alutiiq Museum archaeologists back to Karluk. Patrick Saltonstall, a veteran of Jordan's field crews and a leader of efforts to document sites along other Kodiak salmon streams, recognized that the Karluk settlement data was impressive but incomplete. Working in collaboration with Koniag, Inc. and the US Fish and Wildlife Service, he set out to review the entire system, returning to known sites and examining areas not yet intensively investigated (VanDaele essay Chapter 2). Between 2008 and 2012, he visited the region four times, inspecting lakeshores and river terraces. In particular, he focused on the middle course of the Karluk River, locating sites in the little-studied region between the portage and the inner lagoon. The results were astonishing. Saltonstall's survey doubled the number of known sites, revealing an even more intense use of the river than imagined. To date, archaeologists have located 127 sites in the Karluk lake and river region, and mapped more than 1,100 house depressions. These sites document at least 207 distinct occupations—unique periods of settlement. Evidence of settlement now spans Kodiak's human history, from the camps of early Alutiiq fishermen to the massive prehistoric villages of the recent past.

Archaeological Conservation in the Twenty-First Century

Matthew VanDaele, Environmental Scientist, Koniag, Inc.

The passage of the Alaska Native Claims Settlement Act (ANCSA, 43 USC 1601–1624) in 1971 dramatically changed land management in Alaska. ANCSA attempted to resolve the disparity in land stewardship issues, specifically the friction caused when the US government, and later the State of Alaska, took ownership of Alaskan Native's lands with minimal acknowledgement of their traditional uses or cultural importance.

ANCSA conveyed a total of 148.5 million acres of land to the twelve newly established Alaska Regional Native Corporations and 208 Village Corporations. After several centuries, approximately 10 percent of Alaska's land was about to be managed again by its original stewards.

Koniag is one of the twelve Alaskan Regional Native Corporations formed through ANCSA. As the Regional Native Corporation for the Kodiak Alutiiq people, Koniag is entrusted with making land-management decisions that benefit both present and future shareholders and with ensuring that these management strategies result in land conservation through a balance of development, stewardship, and protection.

Growing up in Kodiak, I learned that any effective environmental-conservation plan must have archaeological stewardship as a core consideration. Throughout high school, I participated in the Alutiiq Museum's annual community-archaeology program and learned about Kodiak's unique and rich heritage. I also gained a greater appreciation for the distinct history all regions gain through generations of interaction with the land.

Much can be learned through the study of archaeology, but unfortunately archaeological sites are nonrenewable resources. Archaeological resources can be lost forever, particularly in areas disturbed by unregulated public access and threatened by natural forces, such as bank erosion and changes in sea levels. If proper conservatory steps are not taken in time, the cultural heritage these sites preserve can be lost forever.

Conservatory steps

When I joined Koniag's Department of Land and Natural Resources team, it was common knowledge that the Karluk Basin has a rich archaeological heritage. This area is the ecological cornerstone of southwest Kodiak and throughout history drew numerous human inhabitants to its natural bounty. In the Kodiak Archipelago, it has an unparalleled history and tradition of Alutiiq habitation, which has also drawn interest from past archaeologists.

Detailed, accurate information about the location, characteristics, and disposition of sites are essential for land managers to determine appropriate management strategies. Reviewing the management of Koniag's lands in the Karluk Basin made it apparent that there were critical gaps in our knowledge. Broad tracts of Karluk Lake and River had either never been thoroughly investigated or, in some cases, even visited by archaeologists. Before we could develop an effective management plan, we needed to know what we were working with.

Figure 2.13. Matthew VanDaele uncovers a clamshell in a test pit on the Karluk River, 2013. Alutiiq Museum archives, AM620. Photograph by Patrick Saltonstall.

In 2008, in partnership with the Alutiiq Museum and funded through federal grants, Koniag initiated the Karluk Basin Survey. Over the next four years, Alutiiq Museum archaeologists and Koniag staff surveyed the extent of Koniag's land along Karluk Lake and River, and this effort enabled development of a complete picture of the basin's archaeological resources—both total numbers and ages of sites and, just as importantly, estimates of the stability of these sites (fig. 2.13). As I attempted to keep up with Alutiiq Museum archaeologist Patrick Saltonstall hiking through the brush and read the Museum's previous reports, a clearer picture began to form about the importance and extent of necessary site stewardship.

Accurate information enables better management . . .

By building on the work started in Karluk many years ago (Jordan and Knecht 1988), with the completion of the Karluk Basin Survey, Koniag finally has a strong understanding of the location and disposition of archaeological sites along the Karluk—and this information was timely. In December 2013, a decade-old conservation easement between Koniag, the Kodiak National Wildlife Refuge, and the Alaska Department of Fish and Game expired, and management rights and responsibilities for more than fifty-six thousand acres of Koniag's land in southwest Kodiak returned to Koniag.

As it was with the passage of ANCSA over forty years ago, Koniag was again thrust into a prominent role managing its lands—the difference now being excellent information gained through the Alutiiq Museum's comprehensive efforts to evaluate and catalog every site in this area.

This complete picture was instrumental in allowing Koniag to determine areas that could be compatible with continuing permitted public access and camping and other more sensitive sections that needed to be set aside for other uses.

. . . but it takes a community to make it work!

For management to be fully successful it needs buy-in from a wide range of stakeholder groups, especially in an area such as the Karluk Basin. One of the many things that defines Kodiak and makes it great is the diverse ways our community comes together for mutual support and the important role non-shareholders play in preserving the archipelago's archaeological heritage.

Koniag is now working with the Alutiiq Museum to compile information on the sites in its care through archaeological surveys of the rest of Koniag's land. With funding from a National Park Service grant, we are completing this effort and sharing what we are learning about integrating site stewardship and management programs with the Kodiak Archipelago's other Native corporations.

Trusted volunteers from the Alutiiq Museum's Site Stewardship program are also an excellent example of the community's joint effort to protect archaeological sites; it is very beneficial for landowners to have trusted eyes and ears in the field to assist with protection of our resources. The museum's network of guides, set netters, and air-taxi-pilot site stewards are a tremendous asset to our land-management team, and continue Kodiak's rich tradition of the community coming together for the greater good.

Alutiiq Settlers

The combined results of settlement studies and excavations now provide a detailed picture of Alutiiq history in the Karluk region and patterns of subsistence and settlement along Kodiak's interior waterways. Broadly speaking these studies show that Alutiiq people settled the full length of the valley, from remote regions on O'Malley Lake to the narrow Karluk River canyon and the shores of the entire lagoon. Although preference for specific locations varies through time, all settlement focused on areas immediately adjacent to the waterway. People avoided low wet spots and sloping terrain, picking dry, flat terraces on which to build. Areas by shallow water, the mouths of tributary streams, and the pea gravel beaches flanking the lakeshore were particularly popular spots because salmon spawn in these locations. This includes the outlet to the lake and locations flanking the streams that drain O'Malley Lake and Thumb Lake. Similarly, the lagoon with its access to both marine and riverine species has been a settlement hub throughout Alutiiq history. These settlement preferences are remarkably similar to those observed along the Ayakulik/Red River system and the Olga Lakes system (Saltonstall and Steffian 2007; Steffian and Saltonstall 2004),

Kodiak Island's other major salmon streams. Alutiiq people purposefully and systematically built villages along these streams for more than six thousand years, living beside the areas where salmon spawn in large and predictable numbers.

Adversity in Archaeology

Mark A. Rusk, Alutiiq Archaeologist

Early in my career as an archaeologist, it became apparent that working at remote archaeological sites required great sacrifice, both physical and emotional. While excavating at the Karluk One site during the summer of 1994, Dr. Richard Knecht, Patrick Saltonstall, and I built a sandbag-and-beach-boulder retaining wall in an attempt to protect the site from further erosion. As a group, we filled, carried, and placed sandbags and added nearby, smallish boulders; we constructed what appeared a sufficient line of defense against a changing river course and winter-storm wave action. This effort proved insufficient. Months later, I learned the very first winter storm packing waves over fifteen-feet tall erased within hours what took days to complete. Despite a bitter end to a great effort, many artifacts and associated information from Karluk One rest at the Alutiiq Museum waiting for researchers to study questions in Alutiiq history.

Through completing the sandbag wall, I learned that participating in remote archaeological projects requires facing challenges and responding with sacrifices. Difficult situations have to be addressed, and they often require a major effort to overcome. At the Karluk One site, we were faced with preserving this important place. How were we going to ensure that the unexcavated portions of Karluk One would survive another winter? The answer was to build a retaining wall. However, this construction effort required sacrificing our bodies. As a group, we offered our labor, resulting in sore backs from carrying the sandbags. Also, our hands were bloodied from filling and handling the plastic sandbags. By the time the wall was completed, our backs ached and our hands looked and felt like we had been handling a crab pot line for months.

This theme of facing adversity and making sacrifices recurs throughout my archaeological career. During recent surveys of the Karluk drainage, Patrick Saltonstall and I would locate a site and begin the process of mapping it. While the site was being mapped, I would check the opposite bank for cultural deposits. I would hike down one bank of Karluk River, ford the river, and hike back upstream looking for sites, then return and ford the river again to rejoin those mapping. During the Karluk Lake survey, Patrick and I paddled the west shore at the head of the lake, traveling two miles in a small inflatable canoe. Due to the lateness of the day, we needed to return, but instead of returning the way we came, we decided to make the most of our survey time and paddled across the lake to survey its eastern shore (fig. 2.14). These examples illustrate the challenges faced daily while conducting remote archaeological research. In each case, the sacrifices made included a willingness to become fatigued and a willingness to overcome the difficult situation through any method.

To me, this is the legacy of Karluk One and the Karluk Project, and one that directs my approach to the practice of archaeology. The sacrifices made while conducting remote research are justified. They pay dividends not only to those who participate in the research effort but also to local people. In the case of the Karluk Project, the residents of Karluk as well as the entire Kodiak Alutiiq community learned about their past; some as participants, others through hearing or reading results. The Karluk Project, while focused upon archaeology, sought to facilitate positive social change within the Alutiiq community. With this basic tenant, I approach archaeology. The sacrifices made and the adversities faced become negligible when field findings can inform communities about their past, a past which can be built upon as a foundation for a positive future.

Figure 2.14. Mark Rusk paddling on Karluk Lake, 2008. Alutiiq Museum archives, AM620. Photograph by Patrick Saltonstall.

Despite these broad patterns of settlement, use of the river changed over time as salmon runs grew in size and stability and climate changes influenced the availability of many resources (Foster 2009; Knecht 1995). Archaeologists divide the ancient history of Kodiak into three related traditions—Ocean Bay, Kachemak, and Koniag—each reflecting a distinct way of life (table 2.1).[1] Artifact types, housing styles, and patterns of land use indicate continuity between these traditions. On Kodiak, cultural changes reflect the evolution of one cultural group over thousands of years (Clark 1997; Fitzhugh 2003; Jordan and Knecht 1988). Over time, Kodiak's hunting, fishing, and gathering societies grew, adopted new technologies, and harvested resources with increasing intensity and efficiency. Ultimately, this process resulted in the development of late prehistoric Alutiiq culture, with its large communities, sophisticated technologies, and complex social, spiritual, and artistic traditions. Karluk One reflects this process. It is a late prehistoric Koniag tradition village. Due to its remarkable preservation, it provides some of the most detailed technological information on Alutiiq culture in the centuries before Russian conquest and is part of a broader pattern of cultural change recorded in the ancient sites of the Karluk River valley.

Early Hunters—The Ocean Bay Tradition

Kodiak's first settlers paddled to the archipelago from the mainland, arriving in seaworthy boats with the technologies needed to harvest food from the ocean. Where did the island's first colonists come from? An Alutiiq legend suggests that people arrived from the west, settling Kodiak from the Alaska Peninsula (Lisianski 1814). Ancient sites on the Pacific coast of the peninsula confirm a cultural connection with Kodiak. Early artifacts and technologies from both shores of Shelikof Strait share many similarities, suggesting that the region was part of one broad cultural area. Moreover, some of the Kodiak's oldest artifact collections contain raw materials whose sources are likely from the Alaska Peninsula (Fitzhugh 2004:29).

Archaeologists named the culture of Kodiak's earliest settlers the Ocean Bay tradition (table 2.1), after the bay on Sitkalidak Island where this cultural era was first identified (Clark 1966b; 1979). Ocean Bay sites date from about seven thousand five hundred to four thousand years ago and are widely present along the archipelago's coast (Fitzhugh 2003). Excavations on northeastern Kodiak Island have revealed a variety of small Ocean Bay settlements and task-specific sites like hunting camps. People lived in both sod-walled structures and tents identified by circular piles of slate slabs used as a foundation for hide coverings (Steffian et al. 1998; Steffian and Saltonstall 2014). Over time, residents began to build single-roomed houses in foundations dug into the ground. One hallmark of this early culture is the development of slate tools (Clark 1982). By at least six thousand years ago, craftsmen shaped Kodiak's hard black slate into long, slender killing lances. Like their descendants, people also used barbed harpoons to hunt for sea mammals and delicate bone hooks to catch marine fish.

These early settlers were relatively mobile, moving their settlements at least seasonally between harvesting areas and occasionally trading with or visiting neighbors on the Alaska mainland.

Evidence of Kodiak's earliest settlers is rare in the Karluk River region. There are just eleven deposits with occupations dating to the thirty-five hundred years the tradition covers, and only two from Ocean Bay I, the first half of the tradition (table 2.1). Both of these sites lie on the shore of the outer lagoon, indicating that early residents inhabited the protected, productive mouth of the waterway. One site, excavated by archaeologists, contains the remains of a small structure radiocarbon dated between five thousand nine hundred and five thousand three hundred years old. Postholes surround a floor filled with red ochre, chipped-stone tools, and a substantial stone-lined hearth in the center (Jordan and Knecht 1988:239).

Cultural materials from the first fifteen hundred years of Kodiak's human history have not been found along the Karluk drainage. Such deposits may be located in the future, and the absence of sites does not necessarily indicate the absence of people.[2] However, it is interesting that the region's single dated Ocean Bay I site likely postdates the development of large salmon runs. Based on nitrogen levels in Karluk Lake sediments, Finney (pers. comm. 2013; Finney et al. 2000, 2002) believes salmon were present in the Karluk system before this time but in low numbers. In adjacent regions of Alaska, scientists believe salmon runs were in place about six thousand years ago (Misarti 2007). Fish runs would not have been as large or predictable as those recorded historically, but they were present and probably most easily intercepted at the mouth of the river. Thus, like later residents, the Karluk's first settlers may have been drawn to the river by its salmon. Elsewhere in the archipelago, Ocean Bay I sites are known from the mouth of the Afognak River (Clark 1979) and the shore of Olga Lake (Saltonstall and Steffian 2007).

Sites from the later centuries of the Ocean Bay tradition are more common along the Karluk River and appear in a variety of locations. These include the head of the lake, tributary streams, the upper river, and the lagoon (table 2.2). Thus, by at least four thousand years ago, Kodiak fishermen were making use of locales throughout the river valley, with prime spawning areas the focus of their activity. Their fishing gear included lances, long narrow projectiles ground from slate. Found throughout the archipelago in streamside camps of this age, these lances suggest people speared individual fish in shallow river waters.

Fishing Villages—The Kachemak Tradition

By about four thousand years ago, the first streamside villages appear along the Karluk River, marking a change in fishing practices and a new cultural tradition. Clusters of small, circular, grass-covered depressions represent the remains of single-family houses of the Early Kachemak tradition. Early Kachemak sites are hard to recognize, as they often look like later deposits (Steffian et al. 2006:95). There are just six recorded for the Karluk River, and this is likely an underestimate. In contrast, there are forty-eight sites attributed more generally to the Kachemak tradition. This group probably includes a number of deposits from the early phase. As such, we consider all fifty-four of the Karluk River's Kachemak settlements as a group (table 2.1).

During the Kachemak tradition (four thousand to six hundred fifty years ago; table 2.1), Kodiak residents developed new harvesting, butchering, and preservation technologies and began to fish more intensively. These cultural changes reflect a shift from fishing for immediate use to fishing for storage—a focus that became the foundation for later cultures. To harvest more fish, people of the Kachemak tradition used nets. Notched pebbles occur in large numbers in Kachemak sites. These smooth, oval, slate and greywacke cobbles with notches chipped into both ends occur in large numbers throughout deposits, particularly in sites adjacent to salmon streams. They are net sinkers, stones used to weight the base of nets and keep them open in the water. Along the Karluk River, Kachemak sites occur in all potential settings, including the lakeshore and the course of the lower river. Assuming the modern geography of the lake and river are similar to that of the past, use of these areas supports the idea that people were net fishing. A cluster of Kachemak sites along the lower river lies adjacent to deeper river waters, a better place for net fishing than spear fishing. This is also a place where chinook salmon spawn. Similarly, sockeye salmon spawning along the gravel shores of the lake are not easily intercepted but could be captured with nets in shallow, near shore, lake waters.

Indications of fish processing are also common in Kachemak sites. People made hundreds of simple knives from beach cobbles by knocking off a sharp-edged piece of stone. They also used a new type of knife, the ulu, to split and clean fish. Ground from slate, these knives had a long edge well designed for butchering, and they could be easily resharpened. Pits and small structures filled with wood charcoal and fire-cracked rock are also present throughout Kachemak sites, suggesting that people dried their catches in covered areas with the help of slow burning fires. Excavations at Karluk Lagoon uncovered such a structure. Multiple pits in its floor are filled with wood charcoal and fire-cracked rock. Outside the structure were dumps of fish bones, wood charcoal, wood

Table 2.1 Cultural traditions of the Kodiak Archipelago

TRADITION	PHASE	YEARS BEFORE PRESENT	CALENDAR YEARS
Ocean Bay	Ocean Bay I	7500 to 5000 BP	5500 to 3000 BC
	Ocean Bay II	5000 to 4000 BP	3000 to 2000 BC
Kachemak	Early Kachemak	4000 to 2700 BP	2000 to 700 BC
	Late Kachemak	2700 to 1000 BP	700 BC to AD 950
	Transitional Kachemak	1000 to 650 BP	AD 950 to AD 1300
Koniag	Early Koniag	650 to 550 BP	AD 1300 to 1400
	Developed Koniag	550 to 200 BP	AD 1400 to 1763
Alutiiq	Russian	200 BP to 100 BP	AD 1763 to 1867
	American	100 BP to present	AD 1867 to present

NOTE: Years before the present = before 1950, the beginning of the atomic age.

ash, and gravel—the refuse created by cleaning and drying fish (Jordan and Knecht 1988:239).

Why did people begin harvesting larger quantities of fish? Changes in Kodiak's weather may have played a part. The final centuries of the Ocean Bay tradition coincide with the onset of the Neoglacial, a period of cool, stormy weather (Nunn 2007:3). Stormy weather makes it harder for people to harvest fresh foods and increases the risk of seasonal food shortages. Storing foods helps communities bridge both predictable and unpredictable periods of scarcity. Archaeologists also suspect that, by this time, human harvesting had reduced the availability of seals and sea otters (Kopperl 2003). Faced with an increasingly seasonal environment and fewer sea mammals, Kodiak residents appear to have developed new ways to harness the abundance of the archipelago's most predictable resource—salmon. People turned their attention to fishing, settling salmon-rich areas like Karluk and harvesting and storing fish in large quantities (Steffian et al. 2006).

Table 2.2 Distribution of Karluk area settlements by cultural tradition and area

TRADITION	THUMB/ O'MALLEY	LAKE SHORE	UPPER RIVER	LOWER RIVER	LAGOON	TOTALS
Ocean Bay I	0	0	0	0	2	2
Ocean Bay II	2	0	4	1	4	11
Kachemak	5	7	12	18	12	54
Transitional Kachemak	3	4	5	9	4	25
Koniag	6	11	21	24	22	84
TOTALS	16	22	42	52	44	176

Importantly, the cooler wetter weather that creates difficulties for mariners promotes strong salmon runs (Finney et al. 2002).

During the Kachemak tradition, net-fishing practices and food storage led people to spend more time in their settlements. Communities grew as people moved less and used larger, more permanent villages and camps. Kachemak sites in the Karluk River have from one to twenty-three houses, with an average of five structures (table 2.3; fig. 2.15). However, there are two large settlements with twenty or more structures. While we do not know how many of these structures were occupied at the same time, the largest sites occur in prime fishing locations where people probably returned for centuries, building houses as needed. Whatever the answer, streamside houses of the Kachemak tradition were designed for use over decades.

Excavations of one such house on the shore of Kodiak's Buskin Lake illustrate that homes were well built and well equipped. An insulating sod roof, earthen benches for sitting and sleeping, and a central hearth surrounded by clay-lined pits for cooking, are among their common features and match those seen in sites on the coast (Steffian 1992b). Despite similarities between the houses found in coastal and interior settings, the tools from these sites differ. Coastal villages yeild very diverse sets of tools. Artifacts represent a broad range of harvesting and manufacturing activities (Steffian 1992b). In contrast, streamside sites hold a limited set of tools with large numbers of items related to fishing—net sinkers, slate ulu knives, and whetstones for sharpening ulus. Together, the houses and tools indicate that people moved seasonally from the coast to long-established interior camps. The presence of well-built homes along the Karluk River also likely acted as territorial markers. They signaled their owners' intended to return to a particular fishing spot.

During the course of the Kachemak tradition, trade with neighboring areas increased dramatically. People began importing quantities of ivory, coal, antler, and glassy volcanic stone from the Alaskan mainland (Steffian 1992a). On Kodiak, craftsmen fashioned these materials into a great variety of objects, including items of personal adornment. Labrets, beads, pendants, and nose rings became popular, as did an array of small carvings (Steffian and Saltonstall 2001). Signs of territoriality and warfare appeared in the later

Table 2.3 Characteristics of sod house settlements in the Karluk River valley

TRADITION (YEARS BEFORE PRESENT)	OCCUPATIONS	HOUSES PER OCCUPATION	AVERAGE NUMBER OF HOUSES PER OCCUPATION	AVERAGE MAIN ROOM AREA M²
Ocean Bay I (7500–5000)	2	—	—	—
Ocean Bay II (5000–4000)	11	—	—	—
Kachemak (4000–1000)	54	1 to 23	5	10.8
Transitional Kachemak (1000–650)	25	1 to 39	12	9.1
Koniag (650–200)	84	1 to 69	9	17.8
TOTALS	176			

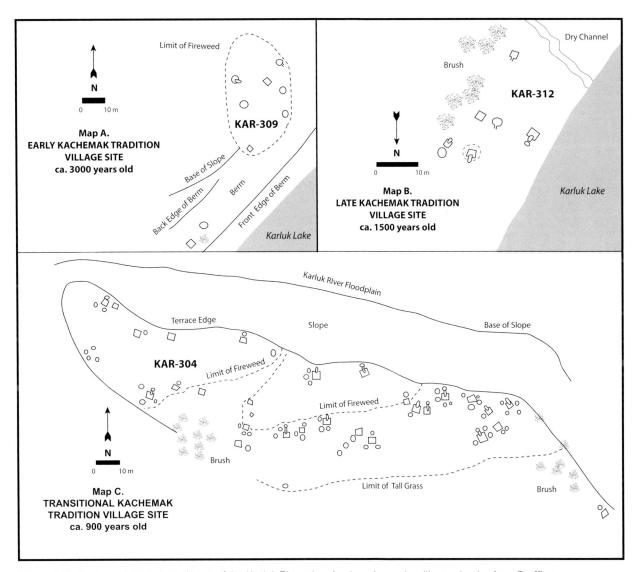

Figure 2.15. Kachemak tradition villages of the Karluk River showing housing styles. Illustration by Amy Steffian.

centuries of the tradition, perhaps in response to increased competition for resources among members of a growing population.

Through time Kachemak settlements grew larger, culminating in a distinctive set of sites and house styles. Sites from the three hundred years at the close of the Kachemak tradition (the Transitional Kachemak phase 1,000–650 years ago[3]; table 2.1) feature artifacts similar to those used in preceding centuries. This includes the use of nets for fishing. However, people built a new style of house—small multi-roomed structures with numerous surrounding pits (see fig. 2.15). Archaeologists believe that these early multi-roomed houses reflect efforts to control the food supply, as activities associated with processing and storing food move from external structures into family homes (Saltonstall and Steffian 2007:112). This change in location may have helped families better protect their winter food supply. Excavation of a Transitional Kachemak house at the Flies and Grass site on the Olga River

(Saltonstall and Steffian 2007:79–80), suggests that individual families lived in these houses, drying fish inside the central, main room and using tiny side rooms for sleeping and steam bathing. Like earlier streamside sites, Flies and Grass produced a limited set of tools. The artifacts include an array of cutting and sharpening implements but little else. In short, household activities, tools, and the site's setting also suggest a focus on harvesting and preserving fish by people who visited the settlement seasonally.

Transitional Kachemak sites occur in a variety of settings, but they are best known from the shores of lake outlets, where people gathered in impressive numbers to harvest fish. At the outlet to Kodiak's major salmon-producing lakes, there are huge numbers of early multi-roomed houses indicating a heightened focus on late-summer and fall fishing. In the Karluk River drainage, there are twenty-five settlements from this time with an average of twelve houses. This is double the average number of houses from the preceding Late Kachemak phase. Moreover, there are four settlements with more than thirty houses (see fig. 2.15).

Increases in the size of settlements and the number of houses they contain suggest that the local population rose. To better understand these changes, table 2.4 shows the number of settlements divided by the number of centuries in each tradition.[4] The resulting values indicate that settlement of the region increased gradually until about one thousand years ago—at the onset of the Transitional Kachemak.[5] At this time, there was a dramatic rise in settlement in the Karluk region, suggesting an influx of people.

Who were these people, and why did they move to the Karluk area? It is possible that residents of neighboring areas came to the archipelago. The early centuries of the second millennium AD are a time of shifting settlement and social reorganization across the Gulf of Alaska (Maschner et al. 2009). Some archaeologists argue that colonists from the west settled Kodiak, people from the Bering Sea who brought a new language and new technologies (Dumond 1988; Maschner et al. 2009:38). Based on finds from Karluk One and a variety of other settlements, others believe that Alutiiq societies evolved from Kodiak's older

Table 2.4 Occupations and houses per century in the Karluk River valley

TRADITION (YEARS BEFORE PRESENT)	OCCUPATIONS	CENTURIES	OCCUPATIONS PER CENTURY	TOTAL HOUSE DEPRESSIONS	HOUSES PER CENTURY
Ocean Bay I (7500–5000)	2	25	0.08	0	0
Ocean Bay II (5000–4000)	11	10	1.10	0	0
Kachemak (4000–1000)	54	30.5	1.77	206	6.7
Transitional Kachemak (1000–650)	25	3.5	7.14	278	79.4
Koniag (650–200)	84	4.5	18.67	599	133.1
TOTALS	176	73.5			

NOTE: This table does not include occupations or structure depressions associated with the historic era.

cultures in response to changing environmental and social circumstances (Clark 1997, 1998, 2008; Fitzhugh 2003; Jordan and Knecht 1988; Kopperl 2003; Partlow 2000; Steffian and Saltonstall 2005; Yarborough and Yarborough 1998).

Possible explanations for Karluk's increasing population include an influx of people from adjacent regions to Kodiak. During the Transitional Kachemak, some areas of the Alutiiq world, like Kachemak Bay, experienced population declines. The growth in Karluk's population could also reflect changes in subsistence practices that reshuffled the archipelago's existing population around key resources. Transitional sites with large numbers of houses occur beside the region's most productive harvesting areas: Cape Alitak where whales pass near the shore, the entrance to Uganik Bay adjacent to a cod nursery, and the outlets to major salmon streams (Haakanson et al. 2012; Saltonstall and Steffian 2006). A similar pattern occurs on the western Alaska Peninsula about seven hundred fifty years ago. Here, coastal sites are present, but they are small in comparison to extensive settlements established on salmon streams (Maschner et al. 2009:48). Interestingly, Kodiak's Alutiiq culture spread into the major salmon rivers of the northwestern Alaska Peninsula about six hundred fifty years ago, bringing artifact and house styles closely mirroring those of the Early Koniag found on Kodiak (Dumond 2005:41–42; Saltonstall et al. 2012:37). In short, the economic focus on Kodiak's major salmon streams may have included settlement of similar streams on the adjacent Alaskan mainland.

Importantly, the Transitional Kachemak coincides with a period of rapid climatic cooling that led to the Little Ice Age (Nunn 2007:13–14). This was a time of highly variable resource productivity in the Gulf of Alaska (Maschner et al. 2009:46), but one when salmon populations were consistently more abundant (Finney at al. 2002). As with the end of the Ocean Bay tradition, the cooling climate likely brought stormier weather, less predictable open-water hunting and fishing, and pressure to store quantities of food. In this situation, harvesting even more of the Karluk River's abundant, predictable salmon resources would have been a logical choice. Whatever the cause, the Karluk River continued to increase in economic importance, supporting more people in larger aggregations. This pattern intensified in the final centuries of the prehistoric era in the Koniag tradition.

Chiefly Societies—The Koniag Tradition

The most intensive settlement of the Karluk River occurred after 650 years ago. The culture of this time is characterized by heightened ritual practice and the development of ranked societies (Fitzhugh 2003; Jordan 1994). During the Koniag tradition, extended families began working together to harvest, process, and store resources in massive quantities. Leaders emerged to manage labor and stores, and held elaborate winter festivals to demonstrate their wealth and power. Archaeologically these changes are recognized through increases in the size, number, and variety of sites. People began to build very large villages filled with multi-roomed houses, designed to shelter large, extended families (fig. 2.16). Historic sources report that groups of related women lived in these houses with their families (Black 1977:85), suggesting an increased emphasis on family ties and perhaps the development of lineage-based clans (Jordan 1994:166). Very large Koniag settlements occur along the banks of Kodiak's largest salmon streams (Saltonstall and Steffian 2007; Steffian and Saltonstall 2004), as well as numerous coastal locations. Karluk One is such a village.

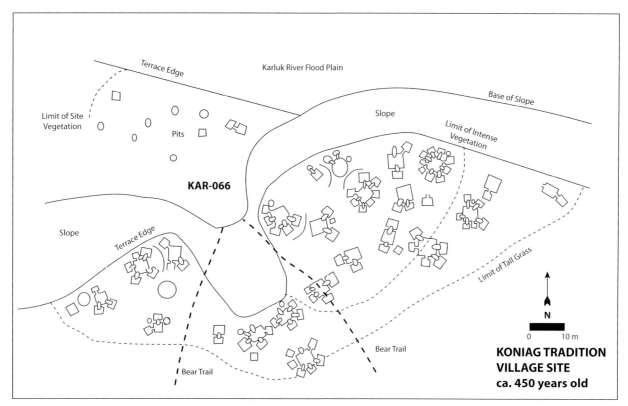

Figure 2.16. Koniag tradition village of the Karluk River showing housing styles. Illustration by Amy Steffian.

In the Karluk River drainage, Koniag settlements contain from one to sixty-eight houses, with an average of nine structures. Although houses are larger than in the preceding era, with more residents, this is a lower average number of structures. It reflects the presence of many small sites. While the size of the largest occupations increases dramatically, those with five or fewer structures make up more than half of the sample. What were these smaller sites used for?

Historic reports of Alutiiq settlements suggest the presence of both villages and seasonal camps. Bolotov noted that families moved seasonally between the coast and salmon streams and reported that "Almost every family has its own dwelling, and many have more than one dwelling in various places" (Black 1977:85). Billings adds that "In the month of April, they move from winter

to summer dwellings, which are in places rich in fish and whales" (Billings in Merck 1980:206). He also notes that people moved back to winter settlements in October, taking stores of summer foods with them. Moreover, historians (Pierce in Gideon 1989:165, 171) note a distinction between the Russian terms used to describe Alutiiq houses. Barabara referred to a "small summer dwelling or camp," whereas yurt specified a "large semi-subterranean" house.[6] This matches Glotov's account of summer huts (Coxe 1780:110).

Along the Karluk River, differences in house construction between small and large settlements support the idea that smaller settlements functioned as fishing, trapping, or hunting camps. Here, small-sized settlements (≤ 7 houses) have smaller average house areas than medium (eight to eighteen houses) and large settlements (nineteen or more houses), as well as fewer side rooms. While they contain permanent structures and were home to more people than structures from proceeding eras, these houses were not constructed to hold large numbers of people or quantities of stores.

Archaeologists have yet to excavate a small Koniag settlement in the Karluk River region. However, studies of the Outlet site on the bank of Buskin Lake support the idea that they were used for specific tasks. Here, the Koniag occupation contained just a single, small, lightly built Koniag house. This house lacked thick sod walls, features dug into the floor, and sunken entrances to its two small side rooms. The small central room (ca. 9 m²) had a large central hearth surrounded by a mound of fire-cracked rock and charcoal as well as artifacts dedicated to fish processing (Saltonstall and Steffian 2006:94). This contrasts with the houses studied at Karluk One, which were larger and built with massive wooden frames, sunken entrance tunnels, and numerous in-floor features. Inside, they were filled with multiple types of artifacts indicating a variety of activities, such as food preservation, cooking, food and gear storage, manufacturing, and recreation. These differences in construction suggest the presence of short-term and long-term houses. The Outlet site house appears to have been used for brief periods by a few people. In contrast, the large, heavily built houses at Karluk One appear to have been occupied for a large portion of the year by an extended family.

Koniag houses resemble those of the Transitional Kachemak, only bigger. The size of the main room expands creating a much larger interior space. In the Karluk River drainage, Transitional Kachemak houses had an average main room area of about 9 m², as compared to about 17 m² for Koniag houses (table 2.3). Similarly, Koniag houses also had larger, more formal side rooms

than earlier houses, with as many as eight side rooms. These rooms range from about 2 to 25 m², making the average interior space more than 32 m². Some exceptionally large houses had more than 100 m². These large houses required a new type of roof. While heavy blocks of sod were used to build walls and cover side rooms, they were not used to cover roofs. Historic accounts suggest that people thatched their homes, using grass and even fireweed stems to cover the large wooden framework (Gideon 1989:40; Matfay 1990), and archaeologists testing sites along Karluk River and throughout the archipelago confirm that Koniag-aged structures generally lack roof deposits over their central rooms (see Chapter 6).

Large villages also contain a number of features not present at smaller sites. Here, archaeologists have found substantial piles of garbage: small, single-roomed structures that may be storage sheds; huts used to isolate the dying or for secluding women in labor or menstruating (Gideon 1989:51; Lisianski 1814:184, 200–201); and extremely large structures that may be examples of historically recorded community houses. Such structures were gathering places where men prepared weapons, planned trips, discussed politics, and hosted winter festivals (Gideon 1989:40). Their presence in large interior villages suggests that these sites were lived in for a large part of the cold season, perhaps from the fall salmon-fishing season until early spring.

The Late Prehistoric Population

How many people lived in the Karluk River drainage during the Koniag tradition? Estimating past populations from archaeological data can be very difficult. While house styles, artifact types, and even radiocarbon dates can help to determine a site's age, they provide only estimates. They cannot give an exact date of occupation, determine the length of time a site was used, or indicate with precision which sites or houses were occupied at the same time. Despite these difficulties, the well-preserved deposits from the Karluk River's Koniag sites provide some clues to regional population.

First, based on variation in the size and character of sites, we believe that there were both long-term settlements and camps along the river. If we exclude camps (temporary sites presumably used by the residents of large settlements), there were seven villages in the drainage with between fifty-one and sixty-eight occupations (distinct periods of use based on the character and spatial distribution of houses). Second, we know that as a set, these sites were occupied for about four hundred years. Third, carbon dates from the stack of house floors at Karluk One suggest that a sod house lasted about fifty years before it required complete rebuilding. This rate could be unique to Karluk, where wet conditions may have encouraged more frequent rebuilding than elsewhere. However, this rate provides a way to estimate the length of a site occupation. Finally, a historic account tells us that about eighteen people lived in an Alutiiq house (Lisianski 1814:193).[7] As late prehistoric houses vary dramatically in size, and this is just one account, it must be considered an estimate. However, it provides a starting place for estimating the number of people living in the houses associated with each site occupation.

Combining these four assumptions with a careful review of house data from the occupations at each major site, we conservatively calculate that there were between nine hundred and twelve hundred people in the Karluk drainage at any one point during the Koniag tradition. We also suspect that the population of the region rose over the course of the Koniag tradition, but additional research is needed to better define and

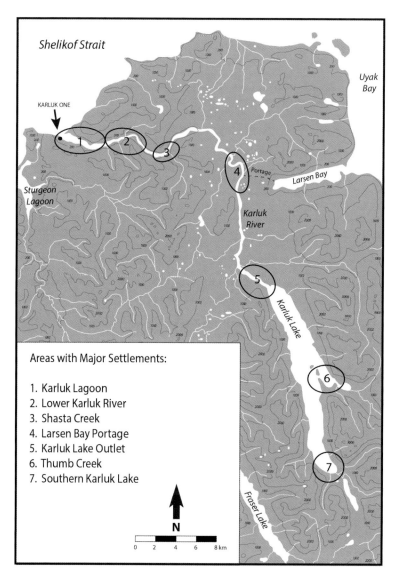

Figure 2.17. Major areas of settlement along the Karluk River in the Koniag tradition. Illustration by Amy Steffian.

date individual settlements. While our assumptions may prove wrong, and there are many ways the settlement data could be interpreted, this preliminary estimate illustrates the magnitude of settlement. The Karluk River was a population hub during the Koniag tradition, with hundreds of people present.

The number of large settlements and the region's high population has implications for life at Karluk One. The village was inhabited throughout the Koniag tradition, from about six hundred years ago into the historic era (West essay Chapter 3). During this time, the river valley was filled with groups of people harvesting a similar set of local resources—salmon, plant foods, land mammals, and waterfowl (fig. 2.17). Like bad weather or high mountains, other people can create barriers to subsistence harvesting. Population increases can cause competition

Figure 2.18. "People would go all over these mountains and they'd work their hills." Sven Haakanson Sr. (Haakanson 1987). Barbara Cellarius beside a stone cairn, possibly a territorial marker, on the mountain ridge overlooking the northeast side of Karluk Lagoon, 1984. Alutiiq Museum archives, AM278:279.

between adjacent communities seeking to harvest similar plants and animals or even deplete a region's resources. We do not know if either of these situations occurred in the Karluk River valley. However, it seems likely that the presence of large villages, spread through the drainage and occupied for extended portions of the year restricted Karluk One's access to some interior resources and harvesting locales. In short, every community likely had harvesting areas used by its members and respected by others. Elders report that the stone cairns on the mountain ridges overlooking Karluk and other villages are boundary markers, left by harvesters to note the limits of their traditionally used land (Haakanson 1987) (fig. 2.18). Similar practices remain in place today around Kodiak. For example, ladies pick berries from patches used by their families for generations and from which others will not harvest. Thus, as the social landscape of the Karluk River became increasingly populated, harvesters faced new challenges. They also found new opportunities.

The presence of seven long-term villages in the drainage also suggests the possibility of collaboration and trade. While Karluk One residents may not have harvested from the banks of the upper river or Karluk Lake, their community at the river's mouth had access to valuable marine resources and coastal neighbors carrying trade goods. Access to marine resources must have remained critical even to the most successful inland fishermen. Sea mammals are the central sources of both fat and large hides in the Kodiak region. The presence of both seal bones and marine shells in ancient Karluk River villages (Morrison 2009) indicates interior communities were tied to coastal areas and their resources. We don't know how the late prehistoric villages of the Karluk River were related. However, we speculate that sets of villages functioned as social communities based on the need for marine resources and their proximity to ocean areas.

There are three major gateways to the ocean from the Karluk River region—Karluk Lagoon, the Larsen Bay portage, and the valley at the southern head of O'Malley Lake. This low area leads to the Dog Salmon River and Olga Bay over a distance of just 18.5 km. It provides one of the few easily traversed passes through the mountainous spine of Kodiak Island. The spatial distribution of major Koniag villages in relation to these access areas suggests that certain communities were connected to certain ocean areas. The three major settlements of the lower Karluk are adjacent to Karluk Lagoon and Shelikof Strait. Similarly, villages associated with the portage and the upper river lie near the short trail to Larsen Bay. The major sites near Thumb River and O'Malley Creek may have been linked to the Olga Bay area. It is perhaps no coincidence that an extremely large Koniag tradition village, with more than one hundred house depressions, lies in the Dog Salmon River flats, a sentinel at the overland entrance to Karluk Lake.

Whatever the relationships between the river's major villages, Karluk One residents were likely middlemen in an extensive social network that moved goods between the coast and the river valley. Throughout the region's history, people settled the banks of Karluk Lagoon, illustrating both the economic and environmental importance of this location at the juncture between riverine and marine environments, as well as its strategic geographic placement. It is not insignificant that villagers built their houses on the bluff and beach directly beside the river mouth. Anyone entering the narrow river mouth would have had to pass by Karluk One. Moreover, as disease, enslavement,

economic pressures, and social change ravaged the Alutiiq community, settlement contracted to the lagoon. This was the primary locus of settlement in the historic era (Bean 1890; Gideon 1989; Lisianski 1814), and it is the only part of the river inhabited today.

Southwestern Kodiak with its sizable river valleys and extraordinary abundance of salmon offered a unique set of settlement and subsistence opportunities. For at least six thousand years, residents took advantage of the region's numerous dry flat terraces to settle the far inland course of salmon streams. Settlement occurred primarily along areas of shallow water where salmon spawn, and from these streamside locations, people harvested, cleaned, and dried fish to feed their families. Over time, both settlement and fishing practices changed.

Archaeological data illustrates that the use of inland environments expanded. As the river's human population grew, settlements became larger and more permanent, and people harvested fish with increasing intensity. These changes occurred despite fluctuations in the productivity of salmon. Karluk's salmon runs are so great that even periods of lower abundance (cf. Finney et al. 2002) did not deter ancient fishermen from harvesting large quantities of fish.

The first occupations of the region seem to have occurred after the establishment of salmon runs. Along the river, early fishermen speared individual fish from small, short-term camps located at prime interception areas. The first settlements were in the lagoon, where people built small earthen homes, and eventually spread into the river valley. Starting about four thousand years ago, fishermen built small sod-house camps beside streams, returning repeatedly to the river to fish with nets and dry their catch over smoky, slow-burning fires. Over the span of this era, the population increased and fishing intensified once more. Fishermen began building bigger houses and processing, drying, and storing fish inside.

By the late prehistoric period, harvesting shifted to areas of shallow water where fish trapped behind weirs were taken with specially designed fishing harpoons. At this time, there were hundreds of people living in the valley in a series of large villages surrounded by smaller camps.

Karluk One was one of seven major settlements likely occupied for a large portion of the year. Housing styles, midden mounds, and special structures suggest that these were cold-season villages, places where people fished for salmon in late summer and fall, processed and stored their catch, and settled in for winter. The remarkably preserved objects from Karluk One illustrate the activities that took place in such villages as well as the ingenuity of their residents.

Chapter Two Notes

1. To enhance public understanding of these terms and the historical trends they represent, the Alutiiq Museum uses the following descriptive terms in place of the archaeological-tradition names Early Hunters (Ocean Bay), Village Fishermen (Kachemak), and Chiefs and Slaves (Koniag).

2. The small number of sites from the Ocean Bay tradition is not surprising, given the limited number of carbon dates and the difficulty archaeologists have identifying older, more deeply buried deposits. Older sites often lack surface features and are only found through subsurface testing or if they are eroding. Moreover, many early sites may have been lost to millennia of shoreline erosion.

3. Archaeologists have begun referring to the period between about 950 and 650 calibrated years before present, as the transitional era (cf. Jordan and Knecht 1988), or as we propose, the Transitional Kachemak phase (Steffian et al. in press)..

4. Variations in the number of sites associated with each cultural tradition can be deceptive as the cultural eras they represent arc of different duration. The Kachemak tradition, for example, spans 30.5 centuries, whereas the Koniag tradition lasts just 4.5. To control for this bias, we divided the number of sites associated with each tradition by the number of centuries in that tradition. This produces site frequency values that can be better compared.

5. In part, this rise in occupation reflects our methods of calculation and the ease with which we can identify Transitional Kachemak sites. When more Kachemak sites are dated, and we are able to separate early and late occupations, we believe the frequency of Late Kachemak occupations will increase and the difference between the frequency of Late and Transition Kachemak occupations decrease. However, even if all 54 of the occupations assigned generally to the Kachemak tradition were from its late phase (2,700 to 950 years ago), the relative Late Kachemak occupation frequency would only be 3.1 (fifty-four occupations / 17.5 centuries).

6. Karluk hunters and travelers report constructing temporary shelters, small tents made from flexible branches tied at the top (Russell 1991:58). Two archaeological sites representing these types of simple overnight camps have been found, one each on O'Malley Lake and Red Lake.

7. See Appendix I for a summary of eighteenth- and nineteenth-century ethnographic sources on the Kodiak Alutiiq people.

3

Kal'ut—Karluk Village

Alutiiq speakers refer to Karluk as Kal'ut, or "sun sets." This is a fitting name. The community rests on one of the most westerly points of Kodiak Island (fig. 3.1). Here, the sun makes its final descent over the archipelago, sinking behind the horizon and the volcanoes of the Alaska Peninsula beyond. Kal'ut is an ancient name, given to the area and the community by Alutiiq people. The first European visitors to southwestern Kodiak Island recorded the name as Karluk (Black 1977:90), as well as Carlook, Karlooch, Karlouski, and Karluta (Campbell 1816:86; Lisianski 1814:169, 186; Orth 1971:496), versions of the Alutiiq term still used by Elders.

Figure 3.1. Evening at New Karluk, view west toward the Ascension of Our Lord Russian Orthodox chapel and Cape Karluk and across the Shelikof Strait toward the Alaska Peninsula, 1983. Bryn Mawr College Archaeological project, Alutiiq Museum archives, AM278:65.S.

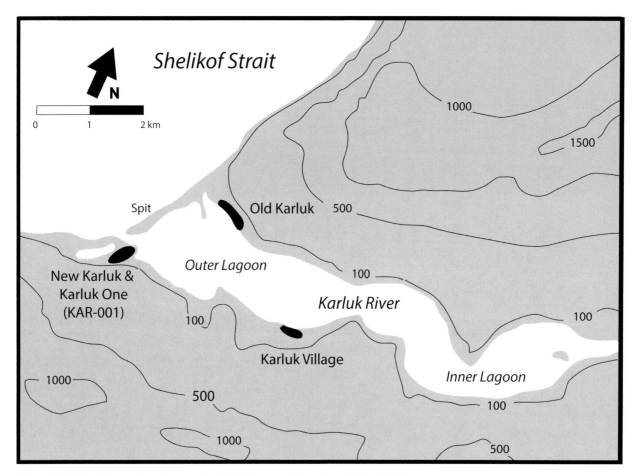

Figure 3.2. Map of recent settlements in Karluk Lagoon. Illustration by Amy Steffian.

This chapter examines the history of Kal'ut, from its origins more than six hundred years ago to its destruction by the meandering Karluk River less than twenty years ago. The discussion focuses specifically on the settlement, its location, preservation, history, and study.

As people lived at Karluk One for over six centuries, and as the village was both an archaeological site and one of several actively used parts of the twentieth-century Karluk community, it is important to consider the terms used to describe it. Throughout this chapter, Karluk One refers to the archaeological remains of the prehistoric village on the southwestern shore of the Karluk River mouth (fig. 3.2). This name comes from a number

assigned to the site by the Alaska Office of History and Archaeology. Karluk One (KAR-00001) is the first site recorded in the US Geological Survey (USGS) Karluk Quadrangle, the topographic map of the area. As such, Karluk One is an American term, established to link the site to a statewide database. In contrast, New Karluk, or the Spit, refers to the historic and modern community that rested on top of the Karluk One site. This is a term used by residents, created to distinguish the settlement from another located on the northeast side of Karluk Lagoon. This second settlement, known as Old Karluk, lies opposite New Karluk on the north shore of the lagoon (fig. 3.3). Old Karluk also contains modern, historic, and prehistoric deposits (KAR-00031; Jordan and Knecht 1988). Finally, Karluk Village refers to the modern community of Karluk, established in 1980 about 3.5 km from the river mouth on the southwestern shore of the lagoon.

Location

Native people have lived at the mouth of the Karluk River for at least six thousand years. Sites reflecting their activities lie on both shores of the lagoon especially beside the river's mouth. Here, people settled over and over, drawn by the commanding view and excellent access to both ocean and river resources. Despite these features, the river's mouth is geologically active and unstable.

Winter storms periodically rework the cobble spit separating the lagoon from the ocean waters of Shelikof Strait, filling the river mouth and forcing the river to cut a new exit. Periodically, the river breaks through the spit, dramatically reworking the entrance to Karluk Lagoon. In recent centuries, the mouth of the Karluk River has emptied into the Shelikof from either end of the spit. Eighteenth-century maps and nineteenth-century photographs show the river turning south at the head of Karluk Lagoon and flowing along the outer shore before meeting Shelikof Strait at the far southern end of Karluk Anchorage. On January 8, 1978, 24 hours of intense northern winds and a monthly high tide combined to create heavy surf and flooding in Karluk (Mason et al. 1997:89),

Figure 3.3. School (center) at Old Karluk, view northeast, ca. 1960. Clyda Christiansen collection, Alutiiq Museum archives, AM680:206.

and the river breached the spit directly opposite New Karluk (Rogers 1989) (see fig. 3.2).

A period of intense shoreline erosion accompanies each reworking of the river mouth, as the river cuts a new channel and gradually assumes a new position. For example, in the twenty years following the 1978 storm, the river completely eroded New Karluk and Karluk One as it cut a new course. Reorientation of the river mouth is an ancient, recurring process. New Karluk is probably not the first community to be destroyed at the river's mouth. Much older sites are known from the opposite shore of the lagoon (Jordan and Knecht 1988), illustrating that people settled the mouth of the river for thousands of years. Moreover, remnants of older settlements are known from the hillsides behind Karluk One.

As the river erodes the shoreline, it creates new beaches and excellent places to settle. Gravel spits and bars were once favorite spots for house building, as they drain water and help to keep houses dry. About six hundred years ago, perhaps after an event that reworked the river mouth, people began to build houses on the beach at Karluk One.

The prime location on a dry gravel bar at the outlet to the lagoon gave residents exceptional access to the millions of fish that ascend the river each summer. It also allowed them to pursue the birds, fish, and sea mammals common along the coast of southwest Kodiak Island and to watch for visitors. In short, the mouth of the river was well situated for harvesting, trade, and travel (fig. 3.4).

The availability of fresh water also likely drew residents to this spot. A small stream draining the

Figure 3.4. Unidentified man and Arthur Panamaroff beach seining for red salmon at the mouth of the Karluk River, 1995. Alutiiq Museum archives, AM193:1200.S. Photograph by Patrick Saltonstall.

Figure 3.5. Grass matting covering boards on house floor 5 at Karluk One, 1987. Alutiiq Museum archives, AM193:397.S.

the organic materials were buried in the cool wet village deposits, they did not decompose. When archaeologists first visited, there was a 4 m mound of sod, wood, grass, rock, and animal remains resting on the gravel beach.

The organic preservation at Karluk One was exceptional. Without such preservation, it can be difficult to interpret the remains of a house. All that is left are floor deposits, remnants of sod walls, and holes where posts once stood. At Karluk One, however, the actual boards, beams, and posts used to build houses were common finds. Lengths of wood cut and hewn for use in construction occurred throughout the site, often in layers that required a hatchet to remove. Floorboards used to cover ancient drainage ditches were in such great shape that they could support the weight of archaeologists.

In addition to sturdy pieces of house lumber, archaeologists uncovered many delicate items—twigs, fur, bundles of human hair, grass, leaves, bug carcasses, and even a few scraps of leather. Grass was a particularly common find, indicating that residents repeatedly covered the floors of their houses with layers of clean dry grass (fig. 3.5). Rolls of grass also occurred along the edges of houses. Some of this grass was still green when unearthed, fading quickly to brown when exposed to the light and air. Even some of the unpleasant residues of village life were preserved. The deposit smelled faintly of fish and rotten oil, the results of centuries of storing seafoods and rendering oil from sea mammal blubber. Turn over a board and you might find maggot casings or feces filled with berry seeds.

History of the Settlement

Settlement around the mouth of Karluk River is ancient. People have long been drawn to this

low rolling mountains behind the site provided immediate access to water for drinking, cooking, sweat bathing, and other household activities. The stream emptied into a small pond behind the settlement. This pond was probably a remnant of an older river channel, cut and abandoned before the creation of Karluk One.

To build on the beach, residents collected logs washed onto the spit and harvested sod, dirt, and grass from the hillsides nearby. These bulky materials quickly covered the beach, and with food scraps, manufacturing debris, and the rock rubble from cooking and steam bathing, village deposits built up rapidly. Based on the age and thickness of the deposits, it appears that people rebuilt their houses about every fifty years (West essay Chapter 3), creating new structures on top of older ones.

The settlement grew so quickly that house remains and discarded objects were buried rapidly. Moreover, water from the pond seeped into the site saturating everything. This is the reason that Karluk One had excellent organic preservation. Wet conditions prevailed for centuries. Once productive spot where river and ocean meet. While erosion from the meandering river mouth and fierce winter storms have combined to alter the landscape, evidence of human activity remains plentiful.

The bluffs behind Karluk One were first settled at least five thousand years ago. Here, archaeologists have found distinctive ground-slate bayonets, spears likely used for both fishing and hunting by people of the Ocean Bay tradition. Net sinkers, small notched stones used to weight the bottom edge of fishing nets, are also present. These tools were only common on Kodiak after four thousand years ago, suggesting that later peoples settled the bluff overlooking the river. Despite these finds, most of the deposits on the southwest side of the lagoon have been destroyed. Evidence of early prehistoric people is better preserved on the opposite shore at Old Karluk. Here, people built sturdy houses as early as six thousand years ago and continued to live along the riverbank till the present day (Jordan and Knecht 1988). The tantalizing evidence of earlier technologies suggests that the same is almost certainly true for New Karluk, although the river had reclaimed most of the evidence in the distant past.

The story of Karluk One begins about six hundred years ago, near or just before the onset of the Little Ice Age. This was a period of cold temperatures and stormy weather in the North Pacific (Foster 2009; West et al. 2011). The description of ancient village life presented in this book reveals the character of the community in its first four hundred years, till the time of Russian conquest.

The origins of Karluk One coincide with the early centuries of the Koniag tradition (see Chapter 2). At this time powerful chiefs led villages, people harvested huge quantities of foods to feed growing communities, men traveled long distances to trade and wage war, and powerful leading families invested the resources harvested in summer in lavish winter festivals designed to thank the spirit world, honor ancestors, and display their wealth.

The bottom of Karluk One features examples of multi-roomed houses and objects such as hollow ground points and incised pebbles typical of the fifteenth century on Kodiak. In 1995, archaeologists observed the wooden superstructure of one of the settlement's earliest houses, uncovered by tides that had washed away overlying deposits. Upright planks and posts associated with the structure's entrance tunnel and with shorter tunnels leading to side rooms were all visibly exposed on the beach. This house resembled a late prehistoric multi-roomed house much like those excavated in more recent layers of the site (see Chapter 6) and in settlements elsewhere around the Kodiak Archipelago (Saltonstall 1997). This style of house matches recent radiocarbon dates of ca. AD 1450 from the bottom of the site (West 2011). Thus, when people began building Karluk One, family groups were living together, sharing labor and resources in ways very similar to those described in historic accounts. This way of life, chronicled in this book, persisted for nearly four hundred years, until the late eighteenth century and the arrival of Russian traders.

How Old Is Karluk One?

Catherine F. West, Research Assistant Professor, Boston University

As archaeologists peeled back the layers at Karluk One, they found the remarkably preserved houses of Alutiiq people. Layers of collapsed structures indicated that people lived on this scenic spot at the river mouth for many generations, building one house on top of the next. But when were they here, and how long was each house used? To better understand the history of events represented by the site, I worked to date its layers.

The first method for estimating how long people lived at Karluk One was *relative dating*. By looking at the superposition of the pancake stack of houses, archaeologists knew that the layers at the bottom of the site should be the oldest, and the layers at the top of the site should be the most recent (fig. 3.6). We knew the site was occupied until about forty years ago. The remains of wood-framed houses, Russian- and American-period artifacts, and historic photos told us that people lived on top of the archaeological deposit until a winter storm badly damaged the community in 1979. Beneath the modern buildings, which dated to after about 1900, excavators encountered the remains of ten sod houses, built on top of each other. If we estimate that each house was occupied for about fifty years, we could say that ten layers of houses represent about five hundred years of occupation. Subtract this from 1900 and site deposits may be up to six hundred years old.

To get more accurate dates for the occupation, archaeologists used *absolute dating*. This set of measures helped to determine a specific calendar date for the layers in the site, using radiometric—or chemical—methods. The most common of these methods is radiocarbon dating. Radiocarbon dating is based on the idea that all living things contain carbon 14, or unstable, radioactive carbon. When an organism dies, its carbon 14 begins to decay at a constant rate, which can be used as a measuring stick. For instance, a tree may have been used to build a house on Kodiak. When this tree died, its radioactive carbon 14 began to decay, and the remaining amount of carbon 14 can be measured to date when the house was built.

When Karluk One was first excavated in the 1980s, the archaeologists working at the site collected pieces of wood, charcoal, and other organic material so they could radiocarbon date the site to get an accurate picture of when it was occupied. Because large pieces of wood were well preserved throughout the site and provided

Figure 3.6. Layers of boards in the west wall of the 1984 excavation represent a series of house floors. Alutiiq Museum archives, AM193:163.S.

excellent samples, the scientists chose to date a selection of large logs. Based on these radiocarbon dates, they found that the site's buried houses represent occupations from about eight hundred years ago until Russians settled at Karluk in the nineteenth century (Jordan and Knecht 1988; Knecht 1995).

However, when I was working with the Karluk One collections, I found that dating logs posed a problem. The best source of large logs on Kodiak is driftwood. People living at Karluk probably collected wood to build their houses from the beach after the logs had floated to Kodiak (Shaw 2008). So, how do we know when those trees died? Because the trees may have died long before they floated to Kodiak and were used by Alutiiq people to build houses, it is difficult to know whether radiocarbon dates from their remains actually represent the age of Karluk One houses! Dating this "old wood" presents a chronological problem (Shaw 2008).

To address this problem, I decided to redate the site (West 2011). Because the excavators collected a huge variety of organic material, including animal bone, hair, twigs, logs, seeds, shells, and bark, I was able to select the best specimens to represent all the houses through time. To avoid dating old wood, I decided to use shorter-lived twigs and berry seeds. Because these materials don't have a long life, they were likely collected and used by Karluk people right away, so they had the potential to provide a more accurate occupation date.

I sent twenty-one samples to the National Ocean Sciences Accelerator Mass Spectrometry laboratory in Woods Hole, Massachusetts, where they were radiocarbon dated. When the results came back from the lab, I was surprised to learn that the site was almost three hundred years younger than previously thought! The oldest house at Karluk One dated to AD 1400–1450, or just over five hundred years ago. The other dates indicated that the houses were rebuilt approximately every fifty years and that the most recent sod house was probably built in the nineteenth century (West 2011).

The new dates place the Karluk One site firmly in the late-prehistoric Koniag tradition and help archaeologists to understand the history preserved in this remarkable collection.

With Russian colonization, people moved out of inland regions of Kodiak's major river systems. Historic artifacts, common to this time, are absent from sites found along interior stretches of the Karluk, the Ayakulik, and the Olga rivers. Archaeologists have never found the beads, metal axe heads, or European ceramics that indicate the presence of an early historic village. The only early Russian-era artifact from an interior setting is a gunflint recovered near the outlet to Karluk Lake (Alutiiq Museum collection AM176:71). Moreover, Russian accounts report that Alutiiq people lived on the coast and not inland (Black 1977:82). We do not know why the

Alutiiq stopped settling the interior. Perhaps the diseases that accompanied European traders in Alaska traveled through the Native population and altered settlement before traders actually set foot on Kodiak Island. Or perhaps Russian traders forbade inland settlement. Whatever the answer, the settlement history of Karluk since this time is relatively well known.

Russian colonists came to Karluk shortly after entrepreneur Grigorii Shelikhov built the first formal outpost at Three Saints Bay in 1784 (Crowell 1997; see Appendix I). The first known written description of Karluk dates to 1787. At this date, a large party of Russian and Alutiiq men led by Delarov wintered in the village, after returning from explorations in Cook Inlet. During their stay, Delarov and his party established an artel on the riverbank (Black 2004a:108; Tikhmenev 1978:16), a workstation designed to process the abundance of Karluk salmon for distribution to other Russian posts. This was the first Russian post on the western coast of Kodiak (Luehrmann 2008:74). A map of the Kodiak Archipelago drawn in 1784 by Izmailov and Bocharov shows two settlements on interior shores of the lagoon and a third near the river mouth at the location of Karluk One. An 1805 map of Kodiak published by Urey Lisianski places the artel and historic village behind the Karluk One site (Lisianski 1814:168), as does Teben'kov's 1849 map and narrative (Pierce 1981:50).

Hiermonk Gideon (Black 1977:90) described the Russian settlement sometime between 1804 and 1807 as follows:

On the hill near the river Karluk is a fort, surrounded by a small earthen wall: on the seaside, about 27 sazhen' in length, on other sides about 50 sazhen'.[1] Inside this fort are the following structures: a rather clean and light barracks, constructed of boards covered with sod, 7 sazhen' in length and 4 in width, with 11 urun (see glossary[2]) for Russian hunters and quarters for the baidarshahik.[3] Further up there are two summer rooms, a foreroom, and a kitchen. There is also a balagan[4] of 8 by 4 sazhen'. Hereabouts, in the course of a good summer, they put up to 300,000 yukolas.[5] There are two barabaras[6]: one for the foodstuffs, in which 200 ishkat (see glossary[7]) of sarana,[8] 20 casks of shiksha[9] (each cask holding 25 buckets), three vats of whale oil, and two casks of moroshka (see glossary[10]) are

stored; the second barabara is used for storage of various items; there is also a root cellar for preservation of potatoes and turnips, a summer kitchen, a sweat bath, a gear storage shed or barn, a sentry post and a watch room. Beyond the fort, not too far from the gate, are the cattle yard, hay barn, piggery and a kazhim[11] and a yurt about 3 sazhen' in length by 4 sazhen' in width for the kayurs.[12] There are at this artel' present and accounted for 20 kayur men and 18 kayur women. In addition, for preparation of the fish they employ here 25 women from various settlements. At the foot of the hill there is the shed for the baidaras and baidarkas.[13]

In 1984, archaeologists mapped some large foundations on the bluff behind Karluk One. These sit in an area surrounding the village's modern Russian Orthodox chapel, directly overlooking the Alutiiq village on the beach below. They may in part represent the remains of the artel. In addition, the top layer of the Karluk One excavation contains a number of early Russian-era artifacts. Pieces of porcelain and large blue and yellow beads from China indicate there was a settlement at the location before the Russian American Company established its contract with the Hudson Bay Company in 1839. After that date, the trade goods found in Alaska changed dramatically (Jackson 1991; Knecht and Jordan 1985:24).

The influx of roughly 170 people from Delarov's party and the construction of a workstation must have had significant economic and social impacts on Karluk residents. The Russians positioned themselves to watch over activities in the Alutiiq community and ultimately asserted a powerful influence over the daily lives of villagers (Solovjova and Vovnyanko 2009:34). From places like Karluk, Russian colonists also fueled antagonisms between Alutiiq communities on the eastern and western coasts of Kodiak, creating divisions in the Native community that helped to prevent a coordinated uprising (Black 2003:109). After the Russians arrived, Karluk's population dropped dramatically from 344 in the Baranov Census of 1795 to 57 in 1841 according to church records (fig. 3.7).

By the tenth US Census in 1881 (Petrof 1884), the village population was back up to 302 people. Shortly after this, with the arrival of the commercial canneries and seasonal workers, it exploded to 1,123, with between 181 and 187 permanent, mostly Alutiiq residents. In the early twentieth century, the Alutiiq population of Karluk steadily declined, dropping to just 75 in 1914.

The primary company activities at Karluk were fishing, trapping, berry and root picking, and bird harvesting (Black 1990; Gideon 1989; Khlebnikov 1994). A 1833 report by V. I. Kashevarof notes that Russians brought Alutiiq women to Karluk to help process the fish and presumably collect berries and roots (Black 1990:29). The need for imported labor reflects either the wealth of local resources or the fact that the Russians employed village men elsewhere to hunt birds and sea otters. In summer, men from the village travelled by *angyaq*—open skin boat—to the Alaska Peninsula to harvest birds for their skins. Back on Kodiak, these skins were distributed to Alutiiq seamstresses to sew into parkas, which were in turn used as payment for the work of Native laborers (Khlebnikov 1994:27). In the fall and winter, men traveled up the frozen river, using Russian-supplied traps to catch fox and river otters. Sometime in the 1820s the Karluk artel was downgraded to an odinochka—a post manned by a single Russian overseer (Black et al. ca. 2003). Still, Russian American Company officials continued to take the resources harvested by Alutiiq people, often

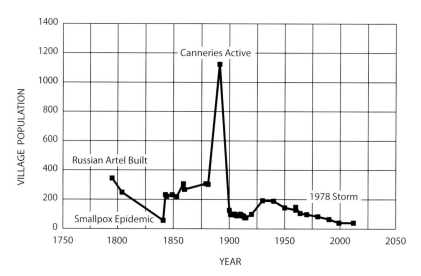

Figure 3.7. The population of Karluk, 1795–2012, from statistics compiled and provided by Donald W. Clark. Illustration by Amy Steffian.

in return for inexpensive trade goods like beads and copper rings. Moreover, forced indenture to the company left little time for traditional subsistence activities and led to deprivation in the community (Huggins 1981:3; Gideon 1989:69–71; Langsdorff 1993:29–31). For the first time in perhaps millennia, Karluk villagers may not have had enough food.

Karluk was not as hard hit by the 1837 smallpox epidemic as some Kodiak Alutiiq communities. Word of the spreading disease reached the odinochka's overseer, who preemptively vaccinated villagers. The overseer was later honored for his actions (Black 2004a:206, 279; Black et al. ca. 2003). After the epidemic, Russian authorities consolidated the island's much reduced Alutiiq population into seven villages—one of which was Karluk (Knecht and Jordan 1985; Luehrmann 2008:39; Tikhmenev 1978:200). The population of Karluk grew at this point, as the surviving residents of villages in Uyak and Uganik Bays moved to a newly founded settlement named Nunakakhnak. This village was located about two km inside the lagoon, just north of present-day

Karluk Village (Knecht and Jordan 1985). The re-settlement village appears both on an 1849 map drawn by Teben'kov and in his description of the area (Pierce 1981:Chart XXII). It is shown more clearly on an 1849 Russian American Company map created by Illarion Archimandritov (Baranov Museum Accession 76–51–2),[14] where the village name is recorded. On both maps, the odinochka rests on the bluff at the mouth of the river, above Karluk One.

An archaeological map of Nunakakhnak shows multi-roomed houses lining a low terrace adjacent to the lagoon (Knecht and Jordan 1985:22). Teben'kov's Russian American Company map of the settlement also shows house depressions and includes a large building behind the village

that historians interpret as the Russian Orthodox chapel (Black et al. ca. 2003). Historic records indicate that the company built a chapel in 1843 in an attempt to promote community unity (Arndt 2002), although its precise location remains uncertain. However, this chapel may be represented by a raised, 7 m² foundation on the archaeological map (Knecht and Jordan 1985:22).

Nunakakhnak was the focus of investigations in 1984, when archaeologist Rick Knecht excavated a complete sod house (fig. 3.8) and collected artifacts from the site's extensive, eroding banks. This study revealed fragments of British china—teacups, saucers, and plates—as well as metal tools and glass beads. The site also produced a slate tablet with Cyrillic writing, bullet molds, and even

Figure 3.8. House 1 at Nunakakhnak (KAR-037), as exposed by excavations in 1984. Alutiiq Museum archives, AM257:128.S. Photograph by Rick Knecht.

a Russian coin. All of these materials are characteristic of the late Russian era. Researchers also recovered tools of Alutiiq manufacture including slate ulu knives, slate whaling lances, stone anvils, a greenstone adze, hammerstones, pumice abraders, whetstones, and stone gaming pieces (Knecht and Jordan 1985:27–29). Together the house and its contents illustrate Alutiiq people living largely in the manner of their ancestors with the adoption of a variety of European tools.

It is not clear whether Alutiiq people continued to live at Karluk One during the occupation of Nunakakhnak. According to the 1849 Archimandritov map (Baranov Museum Accession 76–51–2), it was still the location of the Russian odinochka. However, available records do not address this point, and disturbance of Karluk One's upper layers makes it difficult to determine from archaeological data. Whatever the answer, Nunakakhnak was probably abandoned within a few decades, perhaps by 1867 when the United States purchased Alaska. Under American rule, and after the removal of Russian American Company control, many Alutiiq people moved back to their ancestral villages (Black et al. ca. 2003). When fisheries biologist Tarleton Bean mapped and photographed Karluk Lagoon in 1889, he documented Alutiiq settlements at Old Karluk and New Karluk but not at Nunakakhnak. Historic records also indicate that villagers built a Russian Orthodox chapel on the bluff overlooking Karluk One in 1876 (Arndt 2002; National Register of Historic Places 1980) and that community members paid for the construction. Together the location of the chapel and community investment in its construction suggest that people were once again living at New Karluk by at least the late 1870s.

The American era at New Karluk began with the development of the commercial fishing industry,

bringing more social and economic changes. By the mid-nineteenth century, the Kodiak fur trade had ceased to be productive, and entrepreneurs were searching for new ways to turn the island's resources into cash. Harvesting and selling the wealth of salmon became their focus. Early commercial efforts focused on salting fish and shipping it south in barrels. However, canning proved to be a more efficient and reliable way to preserve fish. The first cannery on Karluk spit was built in 1882 (Roppel 1985:6).

Rapidly, newcomers swamped Karluk. In 1890, the eleventh US Census recorded 1,123 people at Karluk (Porter 1895:6). Most of these people were seasonal workers traveling to Karluk to work in the canneries. There were just 180 Alutiiq living in the village (Porter 1895:4,79). By 1889, there were five canneries lining the spit opposite the village (Porter 1895:79; Roppel 1985:20) (fig. 3.9, 3.10). Porter (1895:79) described the Karluk canneries and their facilities in 1891:

> Each firm has its superintendent's residence, mess house, bunk house, blacksmith and carpenter shop, Chinese quarters, cannery proper, warehouse, cooper and box-maker shop, and many also a trading store, while both bay and beach are fairly covered with steam launches, fishing dories, lighters, and boats of all kinds. Farther offshore moorings are laid down for the larger craft, the ships, barks, and steamers which carry the pack to San Francisco, and lastly quite a fleet of steam tenders for local traffic.

As the commercial fishing business boomed, wood-framed structures began to appear at New Karluk, built atop the ancient deposits and amid the comfortable, well-furnished sod houses of Alutiiq families (Porter 1895:79). These buildings included a store, a post office (Orth

Figure 3.9. Canneries lining Karluk Spit, 1889. Albatross Collection, National Archives, Washington, DC, 22-FFA-2093. Note the location of the river mouth at the far southern end of Karluk Anchorage (foreground).

Figure 3.10. View of Karluk Spit from New Karluk, Sept. 27, 1900. William J. Aspe Collection, Anchorage Museum, gift of Mary Rolston, B1990.013.5.

1971:3500), a schoolhouse and teacher's residence (Porter 1895:79), and a renovated Chapel of the Ascension of Our Lord, Karluk's iconic Russian Orthodox chapel. The Alaska Packers Company provided the materials for the renovation, which was designed and built by Charles Smith Hursh in 1888 (National Register of Historic Places 1980). In 1896, the company also built a salmon hatchery in the inner lagoon, about 3 km upriver from the village (Moser 1899:155–156), which was partially supplied with fish harvested by Native people (Moser 1902:246). By the mid-1920s, most Alutiiq families lived in American style, wood-framed homes. Lucille Davis (1997b), born in Karluk in 1924, remembered playing in the old sod houses, but that no one lived in them anymore. In contrast, Lucille's mother, Fedosia Malutin Achuguk, born in 1900, lived in a sod house as a child.

At the turn of the twentieth century, Karluk seems to have been a boomtown, a place where thousands sought to make money and where regulations were not in place to guide their actions. The canneries were segregated communities with Caucasian union laborers beach seining—those of Scandinavian ancestry fished along the Karluk beachfront, those of Italian ancestry along the beach at adjacent Tanglefoot Bay (Moser 1902:236). Alutiiq fishermen harvested in the lagoon, and Alutiiq and Chinese laborers processed the catch (Goode 1887:94; Moser 1902:246; Porter 1895:79). Cannery manager Mont Hawthorn (McKeown 1948; Moser 1899:151) tells colorful tales of the conflicts between ethnic groups, and describes how the different canneries established their own laws to ensure that some salmon had a chance to escape upriver to spawn. Maintaining salmon runs by allowing enough fish to escape and spawn was a central concern for both canneries and the

United States government (Moser 1902; Bean 1890). With the canneries and beach seiners at full operation it was difficult for Karluk's Alutiiq residents to catch fish for subsistence purposes. The canneries and union beach gangs dominated the outside beach (fig. 3.11), while the Alutiiq fished the lagoon and river (Moser 1899:149). In 1895, the Russian priest of the Kodiak parish, Father Tikhon reported:

> From the strait, one does not notice the Aleut barabaras at all—only the beautiful houses of the company, canneries, store houses. Many million cans of fish are produced at the canneries here; they have already made many tens of millions of dollars out of the Karluk River. Only the Aleuts are poorer here than at other places, only they, the rightful owners of the river and the wealth of fish, are made homeless by robbery and the already too insatiable exploiting instinct of the factory owners, as well as by the destructive influence of the transient cannery workforce, more than 300 strong, without home or family, of mixed origin and tribes. (Luehrmann 2008:109)

There were also social tensions. Transient, seasonal fishermen brought alcohol, violence, and disease to the community and exploited villagers (Shalamov 1898 in Davis 1979:108). Some men working in the community wooed and married Native women. Many of the Scandinavian names found in Alutiiq communities date to this era (Mishler and Mason 1996). Sometimes, these relationships were successful, other times, they were not. Men who tired of life in Alaska reportedly packed up and moved south, abandoning their wives (McKeown 1948:56). The cannery stores were also abusive. They introduced a great variety of American goods, bringing Alutiiq people further into the cash economy. Alutiiq cannery workers applied their wages toward purchases of food, cloth, tools, and other items. High prices and the practice of extending credit ensured that workers became indebted to the canneries and had to work the following season to pay their debts (Luehrmann 2008:101).

Commercial fishing in Karluk came with other challenges as well. One was the lack of a harbor to shelter the large ships that brought goods to the canneries and transported canned fish to markets on the west coast. By 1911, the canneries on Karluk Spit ceased operations and moved to nearby Uyak Bay (Grantham 2011; Roppel 1985:152). Salmon were still caught around the mouth of Karluk River, but they were transported to Uyak Bay for processing.

In 1918, in an effort to conserve overfished and dwindling salmon stocks, the US Bureau of Fisheries made it illegal to seine for fish inside the mouth of the river (Grantham 2011). This law effectively denied the Alutiiq easy access to salmon. The unionized laborers working the beach seines claimed exclusive access to certain portions of the outside beach because their members had cleared the intertidal zone of large rocks that fouled the nets. Alutiiq fishermen were forced to seine at the extreme ends of the beach where fishing was the least productive. In these early decades of the twentieth century, Karluk men worked in four beach seining gangs, each led by a village man appointed by a cannery to run a crew (Taylor 1965:31).

Figure 3.11. Beach seiners on Karluk Spit, ca. 1890. Albatross Collection, National Archives, Washington, DC, 22-FFA-1144.

In 1938, the union beach seiners stopped working the beaches and Alutiiq people regained control. However, by this time, the canneries had adopted more efficient motorized purse seiners. The Alutiiq were fishing for the canneries from the beach but using obsolete gear (Grantham 2011). The Bureau of Indian Affairs attempted to rectify this situation by creating a fisheries reservation that provided villagers with exclusive access to the mouth of the Karluk River. In 1943, Secretary of the Interior Harold Ickes set aside thirty-five thousand acres, including three thousand feet off shore, as the Karluk Fishing Reservation. However, cannery owners objected and took the matter to court. In 1948, in *Hynes vs. Grimes Packing Company*, the Supreme Court decided that the reservation could not limit access to the resources (Case 2012:102–106).

As the intense turn-of-the-century commercial fishing activities came to a close, life in Karluk returned to a quieter rhythm. Elders recall the middle of the twentieth century as a time of cohesion and self-reliance. Herman Von Sheele and his sons, Afognak entrepreneurs, maintained a small store in Karluk and carried supplies to the village roughly twice a month via mail boat (Harvey 1991:198, 222; Tiffany 1995). Floatplanes landed in the lagoon occasionally, but the airstrip—a reliable connection to the outside—was not built until 1964. Tim Smith (2005), who traveled by boat to Alutiiq villages with his missionary parents, noted that Karluk in the 1950s was isolated. It took an effort to reach the village, and Karluk residents rarely visited the City of Kodiak. There was little law enforcement in the community. The deputy US marshal in Kodiak could be called in emergencies but seldom visited. He handled complaints by mail (Dizney 1952).

Most people had kitchen gardens, and one family raised cattle that roamed the beaches in summertime (Rostad 1980:8). Everyone participated daily in activities surrounding the harvest of wild foods (Taylor 1966:214–215). Photographic collections at the Alutiiq Museum show American-style wood-framed houses replacing sod houses. They also record the social and spiritual aspects of village life that Elders reminisce about today—hanging laundry, picnicking, berry picking, ice fishing, skating on the frozen lagoon, children playing, birthday parties, worship in the Karluk chapel, and holiday caroling and masking traditions.

The chapel and the school were community focal points. All members of the community belonged to the Russian Orthodox Church (Taylor 1965:11, 35), and a priest from the Kodiak parish visited the Ascension of Our Lord chapel in Karluk periodically to lead services and perform baptisms and marriages (McKeown 1948:40; Taylor 1965:11). In the 1960s, villagers typically requested a visit from the priest in fall, following the fishing season. Between visits, a committee of community leaders cared for the chapel building and oversaw both weekly and holy day services (Porter 1895:182; Taylor 1965:35). The Karluk church committee included two lay readers, a caretaker, the community's most experienced midwife, two experts on Russian Orthodox marriage rules, and the village chief (Taylor 1965:35). Olga Panamaroff, a resident of New Karluk, was one of the lay readers and one of only a handful of women to serve the Orthodox Church in Alaska in this important way (Oleksa 1992:156).

Karluk students attended a government school run by the Alaska Native Service until the early 1950s and then by the department of education associated with Alaska's territorial government (Territory of Alaska Department of Education 1952). The first schoolhouse was built in New Karluk in 1890 (Porter 1895:190) and was one of

Figure 3.12. Children traveling to school from New Karluk to Old Karluk in a dory. Alutiiq Museum library. Courtesy Marie Jones.

Figure 3.13. Bobbing for apples at Karluk School, ca. 1955. Alutiiq Museum library. Courtesy Marie Jones.

the first schools in the entire Kodiak Archipelago (Davis 1979:106). Subsequent schoolhouses were built both in Old Karluk and New Karluk (Shugak 1978b).[15] Patty Mahoney, who grew up in Karluk in the 1950s, remembers watching a dory carrying students from New Karluk to school at Old Karluk prior to the construction of the suspension bridge that connected the two sides of the village (fig. 3.12) (Mahoney pers. comm. 2013). Warren Tiffany (1995), who taught in Karluk from 1944 to 1946, described the community as caring and supportive, the students helpful and eager to learn, but the school building decrepit. Nevertheless, the poorly heated school was a community gathering place (fig. 3.13). Tiffany (1995) reports:

Since the school was the setting for all community activities outside of church services we met, socialized and worked with village adults on a regular basis. We did not have a motion picture projector so entertainment was really homemade. Weekend dances were very popular with the music also homemade, including guitars and accordion. The religious plays were also a big event.

During the mid-twentieth century, the Alutiiq population of Karluk slowly declined. Now tied to Kodiak's cash economy, Alutiiq families sought income. Some solved this problem by participating in seasonal work for canneries located in other communities. As a teenager, Lucille Davis was employed seasonally in the cannery in Carmel, working the patch table, the slime line, and the can lock beside her mother and aunties (Davis 1997b). Julie Knagin traveled to the Alaska Peninsula to work in the Kukak clam cannery (Johnson 2002:10). Many Karluk men worked on small boat crews under the direction of a local crew leader appointed by an area cannery. In the early 1960s, all but one Karluk family had members employed in this way, for a total of forty-four fishermen on eleven different crews (Taylor 1965:11, 26). "In 1963 there were seven Karluk men fishing as skippers on purse-seining boats, of four man crews, and one man who was "boss" of the twelve-man beach-seining crew. Five village men fished as crew on boats from other villages" (Taylor 1965:26). Still, a number of residents moved permanently to villages with better employment opportunities. Larsen Bay, with its active canneries, was a favored destination. Many Karluk families also chose to settle in Afognak village.

For the most part, Karluk was spared the major calamites of the twentieth century that deeply impacted other Kodiak area communities. On June 6, 1912, when Mt. Novarupta exploded on the Alaska Peninsula sending 30 km of volcanic ash into the air, the wind was blowing out of the southwest. According to Karluk resident Lakop Laktonen, who witnessed the eruption, this strong southwesterly wind directed ash away from the village (Milan 1974:82). Karluk and the southern part of the Kodiak Archipelago saw only a dusting of ash from the largest recorded volcanic eruption in North America, while northern areas of the archipelago were buried in debris (Griggs 1921). Although little ash fell in Karluk, area beaches were clogged with pumice, including some pieces as large as a garbage can (Naumoff 1978:63). Karluk residents collected pumice along area shores for decades following the eruption (Smith 2005). Similarly, according to US Census figures, the 1918 flu epidemic did not devastate the village. This epidemic wiped out entire Native villages in other areas of Alaska, but Karluk's population shows little decline. And finally, the Great Alaskan Earthquake of 1964, while felt strongly in Karluk for about four minutes, did not cause substantial damage (Kachadoorian and Plafker 1967:F40). Olive Norrel recalled that people from Old Karluk evacuated to the chapel and that those from New Karluk climbed the hill behind the village (Shugak 1978b). Along the eastern coast of Kodiak, tidal waves and massive subsidence killed people, swept villages away, destroyed natural resources, and forced entire communities to relocate (Davis 1971). In contrast, while Karluk residents noted rising ocean waters, this water did not flood the shoreline. Moreover, lands around Karluk subsided just 45 cm (Kachadoorian and Plafker 1967:F40).

Winter storms are another story, however. Throughout the twentieth century, severe weather battered the Karluk Spit. The consequences

Figure 3.14. Drift logs washed against cannery buildings on Karluk Spit, 1950s. Alutiiq Museum library. Courtesy Marie Jones.

of these storms are a common theme in family photographs from Karluk. Pictures show piles of driftwood carried in by waves and dramatic beach erosion (fig. 3.14). Patty Mahoney who lived in one of the old cannery buildings on the spit remembers during one such storm that a storm surge hurled a driftwood log through a window of their house (Patty Mahoney pers. comm. 2013).

In 1978, a major storm washed ocean water over the spit creating a 244 m breach in the spit and a new river channel directly opposite New Karluk (Kodiak Island Borough 1978). The suspension bridge connecting the two sides of the village and their important amenities—the school and the chapel—was destroyed. Following the destruction, the Karluk Tribal Council voted

to relocate the village. In 1980, with help from the US Department of Housing and Urban Development, community members moved into new houses constructed on the south side of the lagoon (Lind essay Chapter 2). This present village lies adjacent to the location of the site of the 1841 resettlement community of Nunakakhnak.

The breach in the spit exposed the Karluk One site to the fury of Shelikof Strait weather and initiated massive shoreline erosion around the lagoon (Rogers 1989). As erosion at Karluk One began to escalate, archaeologists learned of Karluk and discovered what village residents had long known. Under the debris of recent decades lay a treasure chest of community history.

Give and Take

Gerald Sheehan, Educator, Kodiak Island Borough School District

Jerry Sheehan lived in Karluk for twenty years and participated in the Karluk One excavations as both a community member and an educator. Raised in Salem, Oregon, he became a VISTA volunteer in 1978 and moved to Kodiak Island to assist communities with grant writing. In 1979, he met and married his wife Jessie, and they moved to her hometown, Karluk. A massive winter storm had inflicted severe damage on the village around the archaeological site, and plans were underway to create a new town site inside the lagoon. Jerry spent two summers working on the Karluk Archeological project, one as a volunteer, the other for college credit. When the Karluk River changed its course again in 1994, colliding with the site, Jerry and his students collected artifacts from the beach and sent them to the Alutiiq Museum for safekeeping. Jerry shared his memories of Karluk archaeology in an interview with Danielle Ringer of the Alutiiq Museum in September, 2012.

Before there was even an archaeological dig, I remember walking down to the Karluk One site. I moved to Karluk right after the disaster, and water was still flowing through the old river month. The midden on the bank was high, fifteen feet high or perhaps higher, and there were a lot of people in the community that would go down to look for beads after high tide.

The Elders had known for generations that there were people buried in the midden. They believed that you used the land but that you didn't take things from it, out of respect. They had a kind of a cemetery respect for people and their property in the ground. Some of the Elders were very disturbed by the [archaeological] project. I think they were torn, but they were still disturbed.

I was a history major in college. I've always had an interest in history, so the dig was a natural fit. I enjoyed Rick and Dick's friendship, and they encouraged me to join the dig. I enjoyed it. There were a lot of memorable moments. I guess I can joke about how I always seemed to find a lot of the incised pebbles in the roof sods, most of which people couldn't see (fig. 3.15). I guess I had an eye for it. The best part of the dig was the recovery of the artifacts—being the first human to touch an artifact in at least two hundred years, or longer. Now I see those same artifacts locked up where no one can touch them. That is a neat thing. The project revalidated a lot of my feelings about local culture, local history. It made me question a lot of history.

I also have fond memories of mapping the Karluk Lagoon area one summer. We spent days mapping [sod house] sites. I was amazed by the number of homes that were in the area. It is sobering to realize just how populated the area was at one time.

Working with the youth was also valuable experience. They began to appreciate culture. They began to see the value of the art and the importance that people gave it. Prior to the project, wooden artifacts and

Figure 3.15. Incised slate pebble, UA84.193:2610. This etching of a figure is on a small repurposed ulu that is 8.5 cm high and 4 cm wide. Incised pebbles are difficult to recognize, and Jerry found many.

basketry would be destroyed by exposure to the air. Stone artifacts would be collected for personal collections or trade. Now everything is in a repository for future generations to appreciate.

I believe that erosion did far worse damage than anything that was removed. In retrospect, I'm sorry that the Elders weren't listened to. At the same time, if we hadn't recovered the artifacts from the K1 site, they'd be gone, and the ocean would have claimed them. So, there is give and take on that.

I salvaged artifacts from the beach because I felt they were important to save. I am glad to reflect that my children and grandchildren can now view items in the Alutiiq Museum that may have been lost forever. I can only imagine that the items we found were a small percentage of the things that were washed out. I still remember finding one mask in the dirt, with the ocean kind of coming up around my feet. I went and got Ronnie, and we got it out of the frozen ground. The whole area we got it out of was gone the next day. So, it was important. Those things would never have been seen.

The prejudices that existed before the wet sites were excavated—that Alutiiq people had a crude society with just stone tools—that's way gone. The woodwork and the basketry were exquisite. It's ironic that artifacts collected in the 1800s have been in museums around the world. Those too have been re-found.

There are mixed feelings from people in Karluk that the artifacts are in Kodiak and not in Karluk, and that perhaps Karluk has no ownership, that they are owned by Koniag. The community of Karluk always wanted their own repository. I believe they appreciate the Alutiiq Museum, but the community had a strong desire to have their own Alutiiq Museum, to let the artifacts be returned. So in some ways the project's been a barrier, and in others, it is knocking down barriers.

Earlier, I saw more competition between our communities. Today, I see more cooperation within our villages. I see this with our youth in the schools now. We're becoming one large Alutiiq community, with a greater willingness to communicate and share with each other; the project had something to do with that, allowing a shared sense of culture and history.

I'm proud that I was here at this particular time when there was something of a renaissance in the local culture. I see it still flowering and blooming.

Excavations At Karluk One

When archaeologists from Bryn Mawr College arrived in Karluk in the early 1980s, most people were living in Karluk Village, the recently built community. Just two families remained at New Karluk. Alex and Olga Panamaroff lived in a small, two-story, wood-framed house overlooking the pond. Their son Alan Panamaroff, his wife Barbara, and their sons lived next door in a modern ranch-style home. At this time, the prehistoric village site provided a formidable barrier between the Panamaroffs' homes and the river. The deposit was 4.2 m high and formed a peninsula up to

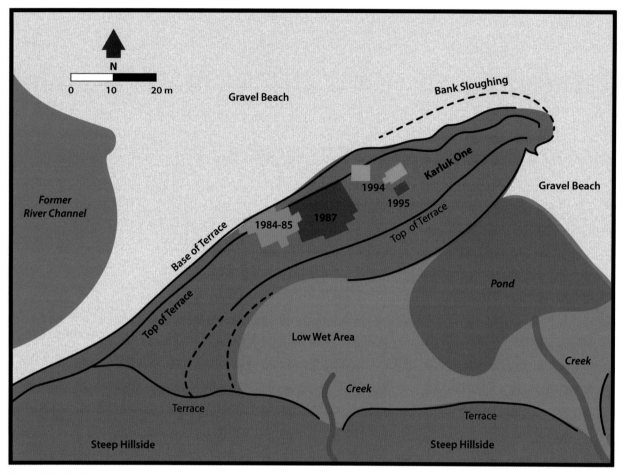

Figure 3.16. Karluk One plan view, based on a site map created in 1983 and updated in 1985. Illustration by Patrick Saltonstall and Amy Steffian. Original map on file in Alutiiq Museum archives, AM193.

30 m wide and 125 m long (Jordan 1994:154), stretching northward from the base of a bluff out onto a wide, flat gravel beach (fig. 3.16). Resting on top of the prehistoric layers was a collection of battered buildings and equipment, which was the remains of the village occupied just a few years earlier. Homes, boardwalks, stairs, a fishing cooperative building, fish boxes, a wooden dory, generator sheds, fuel barrels, and even a bulldozer capped the site and represented its most recent uses. However, while people continued to salvage materials from their former homes, the wind, rain, and lush vegetation of southwestern Kodiak were beginning to reclaim the settlement.

The archaeological site was eroding. Chunks of turf fallen from the ground above lay along the front of the sloughing, sloped bank; ancient boards stuck out of the soil; and fire-cracked rock, animals bones, and artifacts tumbled down the bank (fig. 3.17). The exposed cultural deposits helped archaeologist learn of the site, study its character, and place their excavations. Preservation was best near the center of the deposit, diminishing away from the pond toward the bluff to the southwest. Similarly, this central part of the site was the broadest, a place where horizontal excavations could uncover large portions of the houses preserved deep in the midden. Koniag, Inc. the landowner, provided permission for the study, as did the residents of Karluk (Panamaroff essay Chapter 1), and excavations began near the center of the peninsula. Archaeologists chose an area to dig on the site's ocean-facing side, just in front of the old fishing cooperative building. Working on this face of the deposit allowed the researchers to salvage objects and information from an area that was eroding. It had the added benefit of providing some privacy for the Panamaroffs, as the crew was essentially working in their front yard.

Between 1984 and 1987, the field crew, under the leadership of Richard Jordan, excavated a 56 m² area, eventually removing the concrete foundation of the derelict cooperative building to reach the prehistoric deposits below.[16] The first season of investigation focused on learning about the structure of the site. In 1984, a small excavation, 4 x 6 m, uncovered portions of six successive house floors and illustrated the remarkable information preserved at Karluk One. In 1985, crews expanded the excavation around the 1984 hole, capturing more of the house floors glimpsed in the previous year. They also excavated deep into the site, gaining a sample of materials from a broader span of its occupation. This work revealed a series of ten successive house floors and two midden deposits. In 1987, the research team reached the bottom of the site in a 6 x 4 m area, and expanded to the north, capturing an adjacent series of sod houses. This revealed an additional six house floors.

Over three summers, excavators spent twenty-eight weeks studying the site, with the assistance of 64 crew members (Appendix II). This

Figure 3.17. Archaeologists examine the eroding bank at Karluk One, 1983. On bank, graduate students Glenn Sheehan and Kevin Smith; on beach, Dr. Richard Jordan and US Fish and Wildlife Service archaeologist Chuck Dieters. Courtesy Colleen Lazenby.

included Karluk School teacher Jerry Sheehan, who participated in the project for college credit, as well as eight of his middle- and high-school students. Youth from the village worked as paid project interns through a summer program organized and supported by KANA. Many of the Karluk interns were members of the archaeological crew in multiple years, both in Karluk and in subsequent research projects in Larsen Bay and near the City of Kodiak. Local youth worked side by side with student archaeologists from Bryn Mawr College, Haverford College, Harvard University, the University of Michigan, the University of Arkansas, the University of New Mexico, and the Smithsonian Institution. Most of these students paid their own way to Karluk and contributed to the cost of groceries for the privilege of participating.

Community leaders and visiting researchers were other common additions to the crew. Gordon Pullar, then president of KANA, visited regularly to provide support and follow the finds (Pullar 1992). Physical anthropologist Charlie Utermohle assisted with the study of burials (Utermohle 1988), uncannily arriving just as researchers uncovered human remains in the 1985 excavation area. Geologist Bob Nelson spent several weeks reviewing local landforms and collecting pollen samples to examine past environments (Nelson 1999; Nelson essay Chapter 2; Nelson and Jordan 1988). Zooarchaeologist Tom Amorosi (1986, 1987) participated in survey work along the Karluk Lake and River, collecting samples of animal remains to study past subsistence practices.

Seven Years as an Archaeologist

Philip McCormick, Student, University of Alaska Fairbanks

Philip McCormick was fifteen years old when the Karluk Archaeological Project began. He remembers the archaeologists coming to his village. They worked in his front yard. At the time, Philip and his extended family were living in two small houses behind the site and the pond that had preserved its ancient objects. They were the last residents of Karluk One. In 1979, a brutal winter storm battered the small community built on and around the site. By 1983, most residents had moved about a mile upriver to new housing in a new village site. In a 2012 interview with Amy Steffian, Philip remembered his years working with archaeologists.

Kevin and the others were digging in the dirt out front. I started getting curious, wanted to know what they were doing. I started asking questions and getting interested. *That is a rock, but it's shaped funny.* I wanted to know what those rocks were. I was very intrigued with what was going on. I hated history, but this was hands-on learning that I was very interested in. This was a part of history I wanted to learn.

I started working in 1985. No one else my age was that curious. I worked for seven years with you guys. My interest was there, I don't remember getting paid the first year. It didn't matter either way to me 'cause I was learning something I didn't know. I got paid every year after that.

I enjoyed it. I enjoyed the people I was working with. I had more friends out of the State of Alaska than I did out of the village. I got to teach the college kids some of my ways, and we got to go camping.

I was also learning to identify different artifacts and different layers of the site. The concept of meters versus feet still boggles me, although I do remember working in 2 m squares. I really enjoyed it. Learning what was going on, that was my favorite part, learning the history of my ancestors, how the people lived back then. My favorite find was an ulu I picked up on the beach with a sailing ship sketched on it (fig. 3.18). I found it sticking out of the mud. I really liked it. It's in the museum now.

The worst part was having to get up and play in the mud when it rained. I remember one year, in '85, we had like two or three days of sunshine and the rest of that summer was all rain. None of the dirt would come out of the buckets. There were a lot of fun times too, throwing dirt balls at each other. And if I didn't get interested, I would never know now what I do about my history and my ancestors' history. It opened my eyes. I've learned that's where my roots come from.

All of the men in my family were fishermen, and at the age of eight, my grandfather would have started me fishing if he'd been alive. Working with archaeologists when I was young gave me another option, something other than the family tradition of fishing. It opened a different door. It gave me another choice. People asked me why I didn't go fishing to earn more money. I say "learning about my ancestors' history I don't get to do every day." One year I didn't work [at the site]—1990—I was offered a fishing job. I regret that moment.

It has changed my life in a way. Once I graduated high school in 1987 I was never going to go back to school. Dick Jordan and his wife Colleen influenced me to go back. So I ordered the course information on the vocational school in Seward. . . . I didn't regret it. It did change my life. It's been twenty-five years since I went to that school, and now I'm back in school. If I hadn't done archaeology, I probably never would have gone [back after high school]. Having the care of people who wanted to help me sent me in a different direction than the one I was going in. If I didn't get interested in archaeology, who knows which way I would've gone.

I still have my trowel, the very same one with the lightening bolt on it.

Figure 3.18. The etching on this ulu blade depicts an American whaling ship and a sod house. The trywork, a big iron kettle in which whale blubber was boiled into oil, is visible on the deck of the ship. The rendering of the ship's rigging reflects American-era whaling vessels. Depicted on the reverse is a gaff-rigged sloop with a flag on top of the mast, writing in Cyrillic, and fish. McCormick avocational collection, AM13:2.

Going to School at Karluk One

Ben Fitzhugh, Associate Professor, University of Washington

July 9, 1987—I finally went out to the site today. They finished breaking the [twentieth-century founda-tion] cement yesterday and the exposed excavation was now continuous . . . It was incredibly interest-ing to actually be able to figure out floors from other layers over several squares (fig. 3.19). I started to see the overall picture of archaeology; how things fit together and, even more importantly, why I want to be an archaeologist. I sort of took it on faith for several years, but watching House Floor 2 unfold under my trowel and looking out over the Shelikof, I really began to put it all together . . . how ethnography contrib-utes to archaeological interpretation and how knowledge of collections in general applies. I started to feel confident of what I was doing. I also saw the Alaskan [sub]arctic as a much more realistic research area.

This diary entry was penned midway through the three-month field season at "Karluk One." I was twenty and had participated in my archaeologist-father's field projects since I was barely old enough to walk. I came to Karluk as one of the experienced "trowels" on the project, [a student] with two years of col-lege archaeology and anthropology coursework and an active archaeological crew member for at least three previous seasons in the eastern Canadian Arctic. I thought I knew something about archaeology. But Karluk One brought home something that had previously eluded me. It gave me the opportunity to see more clearly than in previous experiences relationships and connections . . . in the spatial arrangements of artifacts and features across a floor . . . in the relationship between floors as they connected people and activities through time . . . in the relationship between a site and its surrounding landscape . . . and in the connection between the past and the present.

This sense of awakening was facilitated by the incredible preservation of the site. On any given day, we would expose numerous gambling pieces, spoons, bowls, dolls, and similar artifacts. Notable dis-coveries I made or witnessed included that of a bentwood bowl full of sea-urchin shells, a puffin-beak rattle hoop, a storage box full of ceremonial dance paraphernalia, and the so-called Karluk Madonna—a wooden doll with human hair implants depicting a woman in the throes of labor. So many objects would be discovered in any given day of excavation that someone was almost always mapping in something with the surveyors transit. The richness of finds was unparalleled in my experience.

The objects and artistry those finds reveal have been of great importance for understanding past activities and as a stimulus in the cultural-heritage movement on Kodiak. But at the time, I was most influ-enced by the layout of floors and floor plans with hearths, plank-covered drainage trenches, the bases of posts left in their postholes, five-hundred-year-old grass flooring—green as the day it was cut—turning brown before our eyes with exposure to air, and clippings of hair from dozens of trims hundreds of years in the past. The floors were so well preserved and so undisturbed that it took little effort to imagine how they were lived in and used. The preservation of floors and the ease with which we could distinguish them was aided by the unusual stratigraphic separation between them. Some combination of collapsed old roof sods and the addition of new sod blocks to even out and lift the new floor above the poorly drained layers below ensured that older floors were insulated from subsequent activities. As a textbook case of archaeological stratigraphy and spatial organization, few sites match Karluk One. Complete with the re-markably preserved organic artifacts, often found in context on floors or in the drainage trenches, it was relatively easy to envision people engaged in their everyday lives at Karluk several hundred years ago (fig. 3.19). This puts Karluk One on a par with such famous sites as Ozette on the Olympic Peninsula in Washington State and Pompeii in Italy.

Figure 3.19. Portion of the 1987 excavation of house floor 1 found intact and beneath the concrete pad of the former fishing cooperative building. It took many days of hard labor for the crew to remove the pad with sledgehammers. Courtesy Ben Fitzhugh.

My awakening at Karluk was not purely methodological or interpretive. It was also intimately tied to the role that the site and our work there was playing in the unfolding heritage movement on Kodiak. Visits to the site from leaders of the Kodiak Area Native Association, including its influential president Gordon Pullar, the new hire of veteran Karluk archaeologist Rick Knecht to direct the Alutiiq Culture Center (precursor of the Alutiiq Museum and Archaeological Repository), presentations of our discoveries to Karluk and Kodiak residents, working side by side in the trenches with eager Kodiak youths, and the general enthusiasm expressed by Kodiak Islanders—all of these and similar experiences gave me an understanding of the importance of engagement with resident communities. My career was forever molded by these formative months working on the Karluk One site in 1987.

Everyone participated in the daily work of the excavation: digging, carrying buckets, mapping house floors, collecting artifacts, and caring for objects. To uncover the prehistoric deposits, the field crew worked in 2 by 2 meter units, digging and taking notes in individual squares to track the complicated arrangements of boards and trenches and to map the location of artifacts as they were found. With the exception of the disturbed uppermost layer of the site, which was shoveled off, the massive excavation was done entirely by hand. Excavators used trowels and dustpans to uncover each floor, placing dirt in buckets for dumping. The dirt was wet and mucky. Moreover, much of what came out of the excavation was not dirt but wood chips, grass, and boards. It was impossible to conventionally screen this matrix for small objects. Often, excavators needed saws and hatches, tools seldom used by archaeologists, to remove boards. Pieces of wood that extended into the excavation walls were a particular challenge. Pull out a board and you might pull down the excavation wall with it. Chop the board and you might damage an object beneath it.

The crew worked six days a week, with Sundays off to sleep, do laundry, write letters, hike, and fish. Fishing was a constant activity, as the crew relied on fresh salmon for dinner most nights. Everyone lived in Karluk Village, in houses rented from the Kodiak Island Housing Authority. These houses provided a warm place to sleep, cook, and shower, and opportunities to socialize with community members. The crew walked the 3 km to and from the site daily, following the beach or climbing the gravel road that led to the airstrip and the river mouth. They left with peanut butter and pilot bread sandwiches (fig. 3.20) and returned with bags of ancient artifacts. Many objects were stored in the plastic camping coolers used to ship groceries to Karluk. The most delicate items, however, were placed in water-filled plastic bags and set into a stream-fed pond near the village to keep them cool.

In addition to sharing finds informally in Karluk, KANA helped to organize end-of-the-season presentations. Crew members laid artifacts on tables in the Karluk School, posted maps on the wall, presented short talks on their finds, and visited with villagers. These presentations were open to all, and KANA staff members often attended with representatives from other communities. The presentations not only provided community members with a chance to understand the finds but assisted archaeologists in learning about the use and manufacture of traditional objects from Karluk culture bearers. What began as a Karluk tradition expanded to include well-attended end-of-season lectures in Kodiak and provided a valuable spark for the growing Alutiiq heritage movement.

The final excavations at Karluk One took place during the summers of 1994 and 1995, when teams led by Rick Knecht worked rapidly to salvage artifacts from the advancing Karluk River. For an additional eight and half weeks, crews excavated an area north of earlier excavations (see fig. 3.16). Funded by Koniag, Inc., this work sought to recover a larger sample of the unique artifacts from Karluk One before they were washed out to sea.

The Destruction of Karluk One

The six-hundred-year history of Karluk One began its final chapter in 1978. Until this time, New Karluk, and the ancient deposits beneath, were protected from storms by the large gravel spit forming the northern bank of the Karluk River. This spit absorbed the damaging force of storms, protecting the lagoon and its shores beyond. The river flowing beside the site, and foot traffic up and down the bank, caused some erosion. Yet, the

Figure 3.20. Crew members eat lunch on the beach beside Karluk One, 1985. From left: Rick Knecht, Marie Shugak, Philomena Hausler, Frederica de Laguna, Patrick Saltonstall, Jennifer Krier, and Brian Panamaroff. Alutiiq Museum archives, AM193:86a.N.

peninsula made entirely of house remains, animal bones, and artifacts remained relatively stable.

On January 8, 1978, an unusually severe storm coupled with a monthly high tide (Mason et al. 1997) caused the river to breach the spit and form a new mouth directly opposite New Karluk. Without the buffering influence of the spit, the site and adjacent areas of the lagoon began to experience more intense annual storm damage (Rogers 1989). Around the lagoon, banks began to slough and erode more rapidly. Karluk One experienced the most intense erosion because it lay directly opposite the breach. This erosion began on the northeastern tip of the site, the portion of the deposit that stretched out toward the lagoon.

By 1983, the year archaeologists began to study Karluk One (fig. 3.21), a portion of the tip

Figure 3.21. Karluk One in 1983. The main excavations (1983–1987) were to the right of the largest building visible on the spit, which was the former fishing cooperative. Alutiiq Museum archives, AM193:11.S.

of the site had eroded. However, comparisons of old photos with the 1983 site map indicate that the damage was modest. Furthermore, as the river created a new channel, gravel bars re-formed in the lagoon, providing some protection for its inner shores. Today, the shoreline of the lagoon is largely stable. However, the same forces that stabilized shoreline erosion were starting to threaten the integrity of Karluk One.

As the river found its new channel, it began to turn south. The rapidly flowing water arced toward Karluk One before turning west and

Figure 3.22. Map showing the migration of the Karluk River channel across Karluk One from 1983 to 2008. Diagram based on a 1983 map on file at the Alutiiq Museum. Until 1983, most of the site erosion had been caused by winter storms, but in 1995, the river channel started to cut into the site. This fluvial erosion eventually destroyed the entire deposit and now threatens the Karluk Chapel. Illustration by Patrick Saltonstall and Amy Steffian.

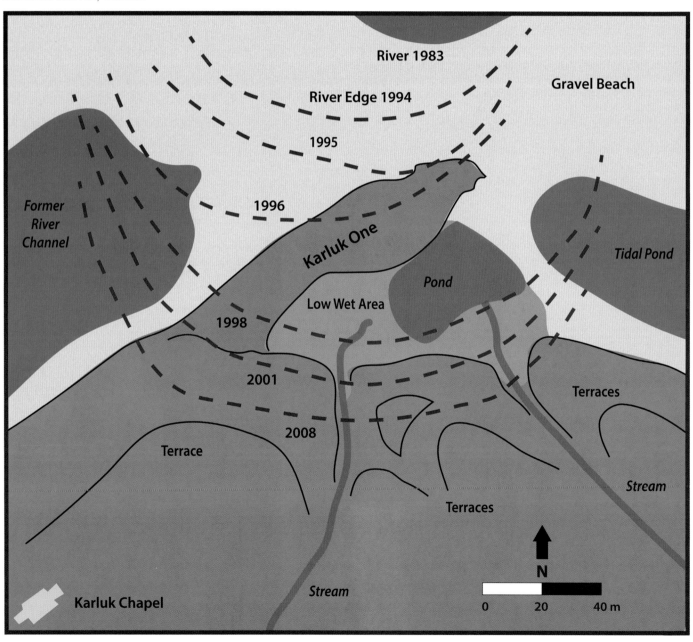

Figure 3.23. Rick Knecht and Libby Pontti Eufemio collect artifacts from the high-tide line in Karluk Lagoon, 1995. Alutiiq Museum archives, AM193:1092.S. Photograph by Patrick Saltonstall.

entering Shelikof Strait. Every year, this arc grew deeper, cutting farther into the shoreline and migrating south (fig. 3.22). This is the process that eventually destroyed the site. The migrating river channel ate away the deposit cutting from the tip of the peninsula back toward the bluff and the chapel above. The site did not erode from the ocean-facing bank, as it had previously, but from the tip of the deposit inward.

In the early 1990s when the destruction of the site began to escalate, Knecht recognized that there was little time left to sample its contents. With help from Koniag, Inc., he led two seasons of salvage excavations. By this time, the site had been eroding severely for several years, and with each storm, wooden artifacts floated into the lagoon

on the incoming tide. Prehistoric wood from the site lined the high-tide line encircling the lagoon. There was literally a ring of artifacts strewn about the shore. In addition to excavating the site, archaeologists spent hours collecting artifacts from the lagoon's shore (fig. 3.23). Scuba divers even investigated the bottom of the pond behind the site and the floor of the lagoon in attempts to recover artifacts.

After 1994, the pace of erosion accelerated as the river started to actively cut into the site (fig. 3.24, 3.25). By 2001, the Karluk One site had been completely destroyed by the migrating river channel (fig. 3.26). Today, the same process threatens Karluk's Russian Orthodox chapel and the historic deposits that surround it. In 2002, the

Figure 3.24. By 1995, the Karluk River had eroded Karluk One deposits back to the location of the bulldozer. Note the wooden posts associated with one of the earliest houses at the site sticking up through the beach gravel. Alutiiq Museum archives, AM193:1092.S. Photograph by Patrick Saltonstall.

Figure 3.25. Houses at the very back of the site eroding into the river channel in 1998. Note the old suspension bridge abutment on the beach in the foreground. Alutiiq Museum archives, AM725. Photograph by Patrick Saltonstall.

river was cutting into the bluff at an estimated rate of at least 1 m meter per year and had opened up a 122 m cut into the 46 m high bluff beside the chapel (United States Army Corps of Engineers 2007). By 2008, the river had eaten away most of the hillside between the chapel and the former location of Karluk One. The old boardwalks and stairs that once connected the chapel with the village lead to empty space. And the river continues to migrate south (fig. 3.27).

Figure 3.26. The Karluk River channel in the former location of New Karluk and Karluk One, May 2001. Alutiiq Museum archives, AM725. Photograph by Patrick Saltonstall.

Figure 3.27. Former location of Karluk One in 2008. The river continues to cut into the hillside below the chapel. Alutiiq Museum archives. Photograph by Jill H.H. Lipka.

Chapter Three Notes

1. A sazhen is 7 feet long.

2. A compartment or quarter with a barracks for housing Russian hunters.

3. The head overseer of an artel.

4. A storage shed, often for fish.

5. Air-dried salmon.

6. Russian term for Alutiiq sod houses.

7. Alutiiq name for a large grass cooking basket.

8. Starchy roots of the Kamchatka Lily.

9. Crowberries.

10. Cloudberry.

11. Community house.

12. Native people taken from settlements and made to work at artels.

13. Large open skin boats and kayaks.

14. Archimandritov's map likely informed Teben'kov's map.

15. In later years, students attended school at Old Karluk (Shugak 1978b).

16. In 1986, Bryn Mawr College crews excavated at the Crag Point site, near the town of Kodiak (Jordan 1992).

The Karluk One Collection

As Marnie Leist tugged gently, the metal drawer glided open in the stillness of the Alutiiq Museum's collections room. New to Kodiak and the care of archaeological collections, she was not expecting what appeared inside the sterile beige environment of that drawer. Thousands of small wooden artifacts were jumbled together, some shimmering as overhead lights reflected off their painted surfaces. She never imagined the quantity of extraordinary material that could be recovered from a single ancient settlement. In this drawer, one among 202 drawers and shelves that shelter Karluk One's treasures (fig. 4.1), Marnie eventually identified more than a thousand objects.

As Marnie came to know the collection, she realized that first drawer of Karluk One objects, their functional diversity, varying sizes, and amazing

---

Figure 4.1. Karluk One storage areas at the Alutiiq Museum, 2013. Carrie Barker (L) and Marnie Leist (R) working with bentwood vessel bottoms. Photograph by Sven Haakanson Jr.

preservation was a microcosm of the site's extensive contents. Sharing the development of the collection and the history of its care is part of preserving Karluk One for future generations. It helps us understand how materials from the past arrived in the present, and the stories they can tell.

Collecting in Karluk

As the essays in this volume attest, Karluk residents have long known about Karluk One. Until the end of the twentieth century, community members lived at the site, adding recent material to the deposit. Karluk One is one of a few archaeological sites in the Kodiak region whose occupation has not faded from living memory. Residents still talk about living at the river's mouth and how artifacts eroded with winter storms or surfaced when people dug into the ground (Lind essay Chapter 2). There is also a history of local collecting from the settlement (Gammon 1984:37; Hrdlička 1944:102–103; Tiffany 1995). Lucille Davis (1997b) recalled searching for artifacts during school recess and trading the objects she found for candy. "We would have fifteen-minute break, we'd go down the beach to find these old beads. And they'd go send us down there, and they'd always give us a piece of candy bar." Collecting intensified in the final decades of the site's history as erosion dramatically dismantled the deposit (Knecht 1995, Steffian 1996).

Community response to collecting from Karluk One has been mixed. Some Karluk residents are avid artifact collectors, enthralled by site finds and the connections they feel to ancestors.

Others believe that disturbing old objects disturbs their spirits and can be harmful to people. This is a long-held belief. Chechenev, an Alutiiq man interviewed around 1872, reported that people were afraid to touch old spear blades, fearing both hunting poisons and the sacred nature of the tools (Black 1981:5). During Karluk One excavations, Alutiiq youth were noticeably shaken when dolls were found. Some would leave the site for a time, and most refused to touch human figurines. Despite such cautions, many Karluk families are drawn to the beauty of ancestral objects and have artifact collections that include items from Karluk One. The changing course of the Karluk River causes continual bank erosion, spilling the contents of the region's many shoreline sites into the lagoon. Karluk residents have long encountered

Figure 4.2. Patrick Saltonstall standing in the incoming tide beside Karluk One deposits, September 7, 1995. Alutiiq Museum archives, AM193:1029.S.

Figure 4.3. People looking for beads on the beach below Karluk One, low tide, September 1, 1995. Alutiiq Museum archives, AM193:961.S.

and collected the tools of ancestors. Some report combing Karluk beaches after winter storms (fig. 4.2). Others talk of digging into deposits, often in search of historic glass beads (fig. 4.3).

Over the past century, artifacts from these private collections have made their way into museums. For example, there are two ground-slate ulu blades attributed to Karluk in the Alaska Commercial Company's collections at the University of California's Hearst Museum (Graburn et al. 1996:Plates 958, 959; Heizer 1952:12–13, 15). Although slate ulu blades are common finds and may have come from other sites in Karluk Lagoon, the presence of an Alaska Commercial Company store on top of Karluk One suggests their likely provenance (fig. 4.4,

4.5). Sitka's Sheldon Jackson Museum holds 114 artifacts attributed to Karluk (Steffian 2000). Although this collection lacks the wooden objects common at Karluk One, salmon harpoons made of antler and slate endblades from the late prehistoric era hint at a connection to the site. Similarly, the University of Alaska Museum of the North holds forty-four objects attributed to Karluk, including both archaeological and ethnographic pieces. Given to the museum by anthropologist Charles V. Lucier in 1953, the collection contains wooden artifacts likely from Karluk One. Information on this small collection's origins is limited (University of Alaska Museum of the North Accession Number 568). However, Lucier taught school in Karluk from the fall of

Figure 4.4. Alaska Commercial Company store in Karluk, built on top of archaeological deposits, late nineteenth century, Erskine Collection, University of Alaska Fairbanks archives. UAF-1978-28-1188,

Figure 4.5. Interior of the Alaska Commercial Company store, late nineteenth century, Erskine Collection, University of Alaska Fairbanks archives. UAF-1978-28-1188,

1952 to the spring of 1953 (Territory of Alaska Department of Education 1952) in a schoolhouse that rested atop Karluk One. Warren Tiffany, a Karluk School teacher who preceded Lucier, reports that there was a local collection of artifacts in a shed beside the teacher's quarters, which residents called the "museum" (Tiffany 1995). It seems likely that Lucier took these artifacts to the University of Alaska Museum. More recently, the Alutiiq Museum has been the recipient of numerous avocation collections from Karluk, including many items from Karluk One (fig. 4.6).

Other materials from the site remain in the care of Kodiak Island families.

Caring for the Karluk One Collection

Archaeologists began collecting from Karluk One in the mid-twentieth century. Supported by the University of Alaska, Frederick Milan studied two large settlements in Karluk Lagoon in August of 1952—Karluk One (KAR-00001) and Old Karluk (KAR-00031) (Milan 1953). Milan, a

Figure 4.6. Avocational collections from Karluk are often used in museum exhibits. 2013. Photograph by Marnie Leist,

friend of recently assigned Karluk teacher Charles Lucier, came to Karluk following his undergraduate studies at the University of Alaska Fairbanks. He was headed to the University of Oregon's graduate program in anthropology and investigating places for research (Milan 1952). In Karluk, Milan dug a narrow, 3 m trench into Karluk One's deposits, noting that the active community on top of the site made finding a suitable location difficult (Milan 1953:15). Working behind the old schoolhouse, he excavated a narrow trench but was not able to identify distinct cultural layers. We now know that Milan tested one of the least well-preserved areas of the site (Rick Knecht pers. comm. 1995). Despite this disappointing result, Milan recovered five artifacts: a wooden female figure, a wooden shaft fragment, a wooden gorge, a stone adze blade, and a chert core (Milan 1953:15).[1] These objects foreshadowed future finds, reflecting major categories of objects and raw materials that would be found in the site.

Although Milan chose not to pursue Karluk archaeology, Karluk One's well-preserved layers led him to recommend further exploration (Milan 1974). It was not until 1980 that interest in the area resurfaced. Visiting with Ronnie Lind, an Alutiiq resident of Karluk, Dr. Richard Jordan of Bryn Mawr College spied a beautifully carved wooden spool (Lind essay Chapter 2; Lazenby essay Chapter 1; see fig. 6.89). This prehistoric artifact—a spool for holding thread—featured a bird and a human figure standing back-to-back on top of a cylinder (Jordan 1983:29). Jordan, who was in Kodiak identifying archaeological sites in advance of the Terror Lake hydroelectric project (Righter and Jordan 1980:156), recognized the enormous potential of Kodiak archaeology and sought to learn more. Simultaneously graduate students Glenn Sheehan of Bryn Mawr College and Kevin Smith of the University of Michigan

began looking for opportunities to study the prehistory of Alaskan Eskimo societies. After a brief visit to Karluk in 1982, they too recognized the wealth of the region's sites. Working with Jordan, they created a proposal to document the archaeology of the Karluk River drainage and explore the evolution of Alutiiq societies.

In the summer of 1983, with funding from the National Endowment for the Humanities, Jordan, Sheehan, Smith, and a team of Bryn Mawr graduate students embarked on a survey of the Karluk Lake, River, and Lagoon (Smith essay Chapter 2). In the lagoon, crews combed the shores, studying embankments to locate, map, and test numerous settlements. Cleaning the erosion face at Karluk One, and collecting from the badly eroded face of the site, crewmembers recovered 655 historic and prehistoric objects (table 4.1; fig. 4.7). The prehistoric collection included many remarkably preserved wooden artifacts, spurring great interest in further study. Jordan returned to Pennsylvania and developed research proposals for additional work.

Figure 4.7. Kevin and Marianne Smith study the eroding bank at Karluk One, 1983. Alutiiq Museum archives, AM193:20.S.

Table 4.1 Development of the Karluk One collection

YEAR	COLLECTOR	SOURCE	ITEMS	PERCENT
1952	Frederick Milan	4.5 cubic meters of testing	5	‹0.1%
1983	Bryn Mawr College	3 cubic meters of testing, site profiling, surface collecting	655	2.5%
1984	Bryn Mawr College	39 cubic meters of excavation	2052	7.9%
1985	Bryn Mawr College	127 cubic meters of excavation	4602	17.8%
1987	Bryn Mawr College	279 cubic meters of excavation	5605	21.6%
1994	Kodiak Area Native Association	92 cubic meters of excavation, surface collecting	5492	21.2%
1995	Kodiak Area Native Association	23 cubic meters of excavation, surface collecting	2029	7.8%
Unknown	Unknown	Unknown	97	.4%
1994–2006	Various	Community collections (see Table 4.2)	5375	20.7%
		TOTAL	25912	

Item counts include artifacts and samples currently curated at the Alutiiq Museum. These do not include several hundred samples of animal remains currently held by the University of Washington's Burke Museum of Natural History and Culture. All figures are estimates.

In 1984, with funding from KANA, Jordan and Smith embarked on the first excavations of Karluk One (Jordan and Knecht 1988:256). The small crew included a mix of Karluk School and Bryn Mawr College students (Appendix II), who recovered 2,052 items. Jordan organized additional excavations in 1985 and 1987 with funding from the National Science Foundation (Jordan 1986, 1987). This support allowed larger crews and more ambitious goals. In 1985, a crew led by Bryn Mawr College graduate student Rick Knecht excavated 127 m3, recovering more than 4,602 items. Many of the artifacts were mapped in place to record their three-dimensional position in the site. In 1987, crews studied 279 m3 of the site and recovered more than 5,605 items. Over four years of study, the combined total of items recovered was more than 12,900, about 50 percent of the current Karluk One assemblage.

Table 4.1 summarizes the extent of excavation undertaken by Bryn Mawr College archaeologists and the size of the resulting collections.

The number of items from each year's research reflects everything collected—artifacts, manufacturing debris, samples, and some animal remains. However, it does not include the large number of bulk samples. The site's well-preserved layers produced a wealth of data not usually available to archaeologists. In addition to the wood charcoal commonly collected from Kodiak sites, crews filled bags with animal remains. Also known as midden, these samples contained the remains of fish, shellfish, birds, and mammals from ancient meals. They also saved botanic materials—seeds, grass; collected tufts of animal fur, feathers, and clippings of human hair; and sampled boards and posts from the remains of houses. At times, researchers had to use saws to remove protruding boards and posts, so well preserved were the site's contents (fig. 4.8).

In the field, crewmembers placed samples in zip-top plastic bags carefully labeled with their location in the site. Items too large to bag were wrapped in aluminum foil and labeled with aluminum tags, the type that landscapers use to label trees. Film canisters provided safe storage for very small objects. Notes taken for each excavation unit marked the precise location where nearly all of these materials were uncovered.

Following each season of fieldwork, Jordan shipped the excavated items back to his Dalton Hall laboratory in the Bryn Mawr College, Department of Anthropology. The Karluk One excavation was not the only research Jordan and his students undertook. Surveys of the Karluk and Sturgeon Rivers; site testing; excavations of Nunakakhnak (KAR-00037; Knecht and Jordan 1985), Old Karluk (KAR-00031; Jordan and Knecht 1988) and the Uyak Site (Steffian 1992b); and survey and testing in Uyak Bay (Crowell 1986) were part of a larger research strategy aimed at understanding the evolution of Alutiiq societies. These studies generated large collections as well. Some of the materials traveled by US mail, packaged in Karluk, mailed at the tiny local post office, and then shipped out by the commuter air taxi that flew over the site daily. Others traveled across the country in green metal camping coolers. These containers proved to be a convenient size and sufficiently sturdy to hold heavy stone objects or cradle delicate wooden artifacts. Duct-taped closed, they accompanied crewmembers on jet planes headed to Philadelphia for cleaning, conservation, and study.

At Bryn Mawr, Jordan hired work-study students and recruited volunteers to process the collections (fig. 4.9). The work began in his laboratory, but as the volume of materials expanded, it grew to encompass a second large laboratory in Dalton Hall. Here, undergraduates supervised by experienced graduate-student archaeologists Rick Knecht and Colleen Lazenby washed, conserved, and inventoried collections. It was an enormous job.

Figure 4.8. Karluk One's remarkable organic preservation. Storage box with owl mask (UA84.193:1044) and water scoop (UA84.193:1045) in place, 1984. Alutiiq Museum archives, AM193:93.S.

Figure 4.9. Undergraduates Nurit Goldman, Daniel Albrecht, and Nancy Downes work with Karluk artifacts in Richard Jordan's Dalton Hall laboratory, Bryn Mawr College, 1985. Courtesy Colleen Lazenby.

Processing the stone collections was relatively simple. Students washed objects, dried them on top of their collection bag, and then cataloged each piece by transferring information on the location of the find from its bag. Similarly, students dried, bagged, and numbered samples. Caring for

Karluk One's organic objects was a bigger challenge. The site preserved wooden objects due to the stable, cool, wet conditions in which they were buried. Once removed from this setting, deterioration was a serious threat. Jordan was very careful to keep wooden objects in sealed bags, sheathed in plastic wrap, or even refrigerated in cool, clean water until they could be soaked in a protective bath of polyethylene glycol (PEG). Wood absorbs this waxlike solution, which replaces water in its cells and reduces the chance of splitting and cracking as the material dries. Like wooden objects, a portion of the bone and antler objects required stabilization. Baths of Acrysol, a water-based acrylic adhesive, helped to fill the spongy pores of wet, boney tissues and provide support for these objects.

A professional conservator, Christine Del Rae of the University of Pennsylvania Museum, provided guidance on the care of organic materials. To process the enormous number of delicate wood and bone objects, students paired like-size objects together for soaking. This required

Figure 4.10. Conservation card documenting an unknown artifact type—dubbed a "clam decoy." As wood artifact preservation is so rare, many of the artifact types were unfamiliar to archaeologists, who invented names to help track the pieces. Elder Larry Matfay recognized this type of artifact as a throwing disk for a traditional game called *kakangaq*.

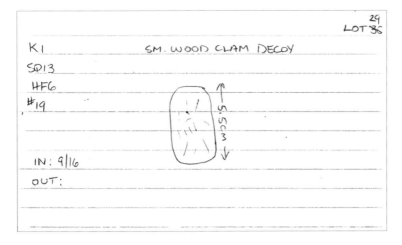

tagging each object to preserve its unique provenience. Students made tags from plastic flagging tape, wrote artifact information on the tag, then tied the tag to the object with dental floss before immersing the object in the appropriate chemical bath. To further guard against the loss of locational data, students filled out a conservation card for each object—a file card with a drawing, description, and measurements of the item (fig. 4.10).

Jordan anticipated that the Karluk collections would eventually be curated at the University of Alaska Museum. At the time, there was no repository in Kodiak, and Alaska's central storage for archaeological materials was in Fairbanks. As such, he obtained a set of accession numbers from the University of Alaska. Each site collection received a distinct number based on its year of collection. From 1983 to 1987, the number 193 was reserved for Karluk One, so that objects collected in different years could share a portion of their catalog number. As such, items from Karluk One received University of Alaska accession numbers that read, UA83.193, UA84.193, UA85.193, or UA87.193 followed by a unique catalog number (e.g., UA84.193/1234). The individual catalog numbers climbed each year, starting with a number beyond the last one used in the previous year's catalog. Students handwrote these numbers in black or white ink, in most cases on a base layer of clear acrylic. A top layer of clear acrylic sealed the number.

To describe objects, Jordan and Knecht developed a functional typology, a list of object names based on comparisons with ethnographically known artifacts (Knecht 1995). Using this typology was a difficult process. Since organic preservation is so rare, many of the artifact types were unfamiliar. As such, student interpretations of the specimens varied greatly. This created many inconsistencies in the catalog, particularly between different years of study. Moreover, as the computer technology of the day was limited, each entry in the catalog—catalog number, artifact location data, object type, raw material, and condition—had to be represented by a Fortran code: a number assigned to represent that piece of information. Catalogers filled out catalog sheets in pencil, creating rows of code that were typed into a computer. This process generated the first catalogs of the collection.

Collections processing at Bryn Mawr College supported the development of a variety of publications on Alutiiq history. Jordan and Knecht (1988) compared the technology of Karluk One to older tools from Old Karluk, a site on the opposite side of Karluk Lagoon. Their analysis of the 1983, 1984, and 1985 assemblages illustrated continuities in materials culture and the in place evaluation of Alutiiq culture. Up to this point, archaeologists had argued that Alutiiq culture was the result of a late prehistoric migration of people to the archipelago from the Alaska mainland to the west (Clark 1974; Dumond 1971, 1988). However, the exceptionally preserved technology suggested a different view. Alutiiq culture was the result not of an incursion but of the adaptation of local hunting, fishing, and gathering societies to an increasingly populated and competitive social environment. In short, Alutiiq societies grew in place, harvesting from the region's biological abundance with increasing efficiency. This new view, centered on the Karluk One assemblage, stimulated an abundance of additional research and anthropological debate.

Jordan (1994) also penned an article on feasting and ceremonialism in Alutiiq culture, sharing photos of forty-six items from Karluk One in an essay published by the Smithsonian Institution. Graduate student Chris Donta studied the site's ceremonial items as well, writing both a master's

thesis and a doctoral dissertation that considered the archaeological evidence for social inequality (Donta 1988, 1992, 1993, 1994). Rick Knecht (1995) charted cultural responses to environmental change across the Koniag tradition.

In 1988, Jordan accepted the position of Chair at the Anthropology Department of the University of Alaska Fairbanks, and the Karluk One collection moved north with him. He negotiated the shipping costs as part of his contract with the university. When it was time to leave Philadelphia, work on the 1987 assemblage was still underway. In Fairbanks, Jordan stored the collection in his laboratory on the third floor of the Eielson Building. It was much smaller than the Bryn Mawr space, and, like the Pennsylvania lab, lacked climate control. Cataloging work continued, however, again with the aid of students. The entire collection catalog was reentered into a database that a personal computer could read. Research on the collection also continued in Fairbanks. Dominque Desson (1995), a University of Alaska graduate student, studied the site's masks and figurines. As part of her doctoral research she compared these prehistoric pieces with masks collected on Kodiak in 1872 by French anthropologist Alphonse Pinart (Haakanson and Steffian 2009). Her work, which included translating some valuable historic accounts of ceremonialism, revealed the antiquity of Kodiak Alutiiq spiritual culture by linking historic collections and observations with the materials recovered from Karluk One.

In 1991, Jordan died suddenly, leaving his Karluk studies unfinished and the collections in need of a home. By this time, graduate student Rick Knecht was writing his doctoral thesis summarizing Karluk One (Knecht 1995) and working as the director of the Kodiak Area Native Association's (KANA) Culture and Heritage Department (Knecht 2000:148). Knecht contacted Koniag,

Inc., the owners of Karluk One, and secured funds to transport the artifacts and site documentation home to Kodiak. A contingent from Kodiak traveled to Fairbanks and packed more than seventy camping coolers full of Alutiiq cultural materials. Professional movers shipped the coolers south.

In Kodiak, Knecht stored the collections in KANA's Culture Center, an office, meeting space, and laboratory set up on the first floor of the former Kodiak Daily Mirror building on Rezanof Drive. The Afognak Native Corporation, renting the building at the time, generously shared the use of the first floor to KANA for cultural programming. KANA provided support for a collections assistant and Kodiak Alutiiq student Alana Tousignaut continued caring for the materials from Karluk. By this time, the artifacts were disorganized and in some cases battered from poor storage conditions and cross-country travel. Some of the first displays of Karluk One artifacts were made at this time, sharing a small portion of the collection in glass-fronted cabinets in the Culture Center's offices.

The grounding of the Exxon-Valdez oil tanker on Prince William Sound's Bligh Reef in 1989, and efforts to mitigate the effects of the disastrous ensuing oil spill, brought new opportunities for collections care. In 1993, after recognizing an increase in site looting, KANA applied for oil spill restoration money to create a Native-governed museum, a place where artifacts recovered during spill cleanup could be housed and where Alutiiq people could explore their heritage. KANA's efforts resulted in a $1.5 million grant to build the Alutiiq Museum and Archaeological Repository (Knecht 2000:151–152). In consultation with museum professionals, Knecht designed the new 5,000 ft² facility with Karluk One in mind. Climate control and professional shelving would provide the right environment for collections storage and ensure the long-term preservation of delicate artifacts. An exhibit gallery would allow Karluk One to be shared with the public, and a laboratory with an enormous sink would help staff members to care for large artifacts.

However, as museum construction began, the course of the Karluk River shifted. In the winter of 1993–1994, erosion began ripping the site apart. Although erosion had gradually been eating away at Karluk One, the scale of destruction accelerated rapidly. The fast-flowing river mouth, ocean waves, and daily tides now collided with the site. With support from Koniag, Inc., Knecht led salvage excavations, inviting volunteers to help him retrieve information and objects from the site and surrounding beaches. Community members chipped in, and a number of the students who participated in the Bryn Mawr College excavations returned to help. Excavations in the summers of 1994 and 1995 salvaged an additional 7,521 items, or 29 percent of the total collection as it exists today (Steffian 1996; Steffian and Knecht 1998).

Although impressive by museum standards, the volume of artifacts recovered from six seasons of research proved a small fraction of the materials the enormous settlement held. This became grossly apparent when a flotsam of ancient artifacts began ringing the lagoon. Torn apart by the advancing river, the site's layers deflated rapidly and their contents spread. Stone items littered the beaches around the site, but lighter, well-preserved wooden objects floated. For a couple of years, people walking Karluk beaches could find everything from wooden shaft fragments to art pieces mixed into the debris along the water's edge. Karluk residents and community visitors picked up countless objects. A number were given the Alutiiq Museum, adding an additional 5,375 items to the site collection (table 4.2). These salvaged objects represent nearly 21 percent of the total collection, a quantity equivalent to that obtained during the most prolific season of excavation. People also carried objects away. Sadly, rumors suggested that some objects were locally sold and traded. Tens of thousands more washed out to sea.

In the spring of 1995, as the new Alutiiq Museum readied to open, Knecht hired graduate student archaeologists Elizabeth Pontti Eufemio and Amy Steffian to oversee the museum's collections. They moved Karluk One into the repository,

Table 4.2 Avocational collections from Karluk One

COLLECTION NUMBER	DONOR	RECEIVED	ITEMS
AM13	Philip McCormick	1995	2
AM14	Ronnie Lind	1995, 2008	2,176
AM15	Arthur & Frieda Panamaroff	1995	638
AM20	Ronnie Lind	1995	1
AM38	Jerry Sheehan	1995, 1997	1,831
AM39	Karluk School	1995	256
AM48	Joe Kelley	1995	1
AM101	Catherine Reft	1995	2
AM102	Darren Malutin	1995	1
AM103	Clifford Sheehan	1995	84
AM175	Rick Knecht	1995	37
AM217	Wilfred Pavlov	1997	7
AM220	Unknown	1996	1
AM229	Teacon Simeonoff	1996	4
AM230	Herman Malutin III	1996	35
AM231	Clifford Sheehan	1996	101
AM240	Annie Hochmuth	1996	6
AM241	Nickolai Shugak	1996	2
AM251	Shanane Ernest	1996	1
AM269	Dale Reft	1996	2
AM270	Lydia Malutin	1996	5
AM274	Jeff Brown	1997	1
AM319	Jimmy Charliaga & Jackie Malutin	1997	2
AM341	Gordon Pullar, Max Dolchuk, & Maggie Knowles	1997, 1998	42
AM425	Larry Shugak	2001	1
AM450	Karluk School	2002	55
AM465	Frieda Reft	2003	8
AM466	Kristen Panamaroff	2003	2
AM546	Marie Jones	2006	1
AM551	Lydia Malutin	2006	59
AM560	John Johnson	2006	10
AM561	Frances Cater	2006	1
		TOTAL	5,375

where it was housed with the original field notes and photographs from the excavations. For the first time, it was possible to sort the materials by type and lay them in adequate storage. The museum's large laboratory also provided facilities to care for recently salvaged collections. As Steffian unpacked and organized collections, Eufemio tackled the cleaning and conservation of recently acquired artifacts. This time, artifact-catalog numbers followed the Alutiiq Museum's numbering system, using AM193 as the base number, followed by the year collected, and an object number (e.g., AM193.94:1234).

Caring for Karluk One

Elizabeth Pontti Eufemio, Archaeologist

"I can't believe I'm getting paid to do this!"

This thought often ran through my mind during the early days at the Alutiiq Museum and Archaeological Repository. It was mind boggling to get paid for doing tasks that I had done repeatedly in graduate school for free.

I was lucky enough to have moved to Kodiak at the very right time, in 1994, and to fall in with Rick Knecht at the old KANA Culture Center about a year before the opening of the brand new Alutiiq Museum. Rick roped me into working with the collections (of which I had plenty of experience) and leading the first membership drive (of which I had none). When we moved into the beautiful new museum building, endless cardboard boxes filled the lab and collection room shelves, much of the material from the famous site at Karluk.

At the University of Alaska Fairbanks, I'd learned about the Karluk One site from my professors, heard about it's fantastic and rare archaeological preservation of organic objects, and been amazed by a very long map of a village site spread across the hallway floor by Dr. Richard Jordan. I remember wondering what kind of place Kodiak must be with such riches in natural resources and cultural remains. Little did I know that my life path would lead to Kodiak, with an honest to goodness job in my field of study, focusing for many years on Karluk One.

Of the vast amount of material from Karluk, a large part was organic: wood primarily, but also bone, ivory, baleen, spruce root, and even human hair. In most archaeological sites, stone is the sole survivor of time, so the riches preserved at K-1 were stunning (fig. 4.11). I spent many hours unpacking these treasures onto shelves, labeling and cataloging individual objects, stacking bags of faunal remains, exulting in the riches and amazed at the level of preservation. I also keenly felt the weight of responsibility as we tried to determine *what to do with all of it*.

And it didn't stop arriving at the museum's doorstep. The Karluk One collection grew each year as folks heard about the museum and brought in what they'd been storing in their closets or under their houses, what they found eroding each year as the Karluk River undermined the site, or what museum staff excavated during salvage work (fig. 4.11). Fresh material from the site posed new challenges in preservation;

how should we wash a wooden bowl covered in black, greasy soil? What about that spruce root basket with shells still inside it? And baleen, how to keep it from splitting as it dried?

I spent many hours researching preservation chemicals and techniques. I learned about PEG (polyethylene glycol) and Acrysol, and by trial and error, how long to soak an object in each before mold engulfed the liquid; I learned how to best dry each piece and how to *not* inhale the noxious fumes that some of the processes released.

I felt the weight of responsibility deeply, not knowing if what we were doing was going to stand the test of time. These objects had come to us from the deep past—could we be ruining them in our efforts to save them for the future? When I really doubted our conservation efforts, however, I would remember an ancient wooden mask from Kodiak recovered by Dr. Donald Clark. He preserved the mask by soaking it in motor oil. That mask was still intact and available for people to study and see with their own eyes, albeit with a distinct smell—certainly our endeavors in preservation were probably going to be OK too.

Now there is this book about Karluk One, which shares a rare and special glimpse of the past, preserved in fragile materials. It gives me great pleasure to know that these objects are safely resting in the storage room at the Alutiiq Museum, waiting to inspire and amaze any who wish to visit them.

Figure 4.11. Libby Pontti Eufemio standing beside a layer of boards in the excavation, 1995. Alutiiq Museum archives, AM193:1137.S.

Knecht also entered into an agreement with the Smithsonian Institution's Arctic Studies Center that allowed a selection of the most spectacular objects from Karluk One to be incorporated into *Crossroads of Continents,* a traveling exhibit and publication on the cultures of Alaska and Siberia (Fitzhugh and Crowell 1988:134–135).

Improved storage at the Alutiiq Museum made objects from the collection readily available for display and study. Many of the Alutiiq Museum's first exhibits featured Karluk One artifacts. Artists began searching the collection for inspiration. Jerry Laktonen studied paddles and masks. Jacob Simeonoff investigated bentwood technology. As years followed, Alfred Naumoff looked at kayak parts, Coral Chernoff studied dolls and basketry, Jim Dillard scrutinized fire-starting technology, and Sandee Drabek examined oil lamps. Researchers also took advantage of the improved accessibility. Grace Egeland and a team of scientists (Egeland et al. 1999) studied the chemicals preserved in hair samples from the site. Amy Steffian and Patrick Saltonstall (2001) completed a detailed study of the labrets in the assemblage. Ben Fitzhugh (2003) considered Karluke One in modeling the evolution of Alutiiq societies. Amy Margaris (2009) studied the use of bone and antler in tool production. Catherine West used samples of twigs to obtain a new series of radiocarbon dates from the site (West 2011).

Between 1997 and 2001, Alutiiq Museum staff members worked with Aron Crowell of the Smithsonian Institution's Arctic Studies Center to develop a traveling exhibition featuring Karluk One objects. *Looking Both Ways: Heritage and Identity of the Alutiiq People* combined a selection of prehistoric Alutiiq artifacts with Alutiiq ethnographic items from the Smithsonian Institution's Fisher Collection (Crowell et al. 2001) to create a multivocal story of Alutiiq history (Clifford 2004). Karluk One artifacts featured centrally in the displays, and Alutiiq Elders studied and interpreted the pieces as part of exhibit development (Crowell essay Chapter 7). More than a million people saw the exhibition during its display in Kodiak, Anchorage, and Washington, DC. A book sharing the exhibit's title accompanied the show, making seventy-two (.0027 percent) of the objects from Karluk One widely accessible.

In 2005, care of the collection advanced once more. With funding from the M. J. Murdock Charitable Trust, the Alutiiq Museum hired its first museum professional, a registrar, to document and manage collections. Marnie Leist joined the museum's team. One of her first tasks was cementing curation agreements with collections owners. Consulting with Koniag, Inc. she created a long-term loan agreement for the collection, establishing the Alutiiq Museum as Karluk One's caretaker. She also worked with museum volunteer Patricia Kozak to enhance the storage of Karluk One objects. They added foam padding to drawers, created storage mounts, and continued to arrange the contents of this very large collection.

Volunteering with Benefits

Pat Kozak, Tribal Member and Alutiiq Museum Volunteer

I began volunteering at the Alutiiq Museum in 2001 and was put to work cleaning items from that summer's community archaeological dig. I think someone may have noticed that I was pretty darn particular about washing and sorting those endless totes of "rocks." I was soon asked to work in the inner sanctum of the collections room with the Karluk collection.

There was so much! It was overwhelming, and because I like things tidy and in order and I didn't have a lot of time to donate, I was really a little frantic in the beginning. My aim was only to get as much done as possible each time I worked. Drawers were practically overflowing and needed to be divided into two and three or more drawers, and I was finding pieces that were incorrectly numbered or not numbered at all, and often I had to stop what I was doing and research the items (fig. 4.12).

I was totally ignorant of my culture, and it took a while before I started having feelings for these people, ancestors of mine, who chipped, honed, carved, and wove all of these amazing items!

I would imagine them as I worked. I thought of the women and the hardships they endured. Yet they saw the beauty in their surroundings and translated it into the intricate patterns in their gorgeous baskets.

I struggle with words to describe my feelings about my work with the Karluk collection— admiration of course, but mostly awe.

My thoughts return to a particular simple, utilitarian, wooden bracelet that was used to secure the wrist of a seal-gut rain parka. I search for the perfect words to describe the beauty of this unembellished and practical piece. I picture him, the carver, in a snug barabara [sod house] on a cold winter day with the wind howling and *zhernicks* [oil lamps] providing dim light. And from a small and lovely piece of driftwood that he had probably spied washed up in the kelp at the high-tide mark weeks ago, he slowly, patiently carved this most stunningly simple yet elegant bracelet.

Figure 4.12. Pat Kozak organizes items from the Karluk One collection at the Alutiiq Museum, 2010. Photograph by Marnie Leist.

Today, though, I talked with my eighty-nine-year-old father about my feelings for the items in the collection and how I imagine the people as they created them. He was born in the old village of Afognak and lived his entire life outdoors hunting, trapping, and fishing around Afognak, Shuyak, and Kodiak islands.

Let me share what he said when I told him about some of the beautiful items in the Karluk collection: "Those people didn't waste their time, so I think the man who carved that bracelet was a hunter, and he was sitting on a point of land carving and watching for seals or maybe whales."

This evening I discussed both thoughts with my husband, and he feels that Dad and I are both correct. I am smiling as I type. He wasn't just being a diplomat, he admires these people as much as my father and I do.

And so I dream that these beautiful islands that we have inherited from those who came before us will one day be loved, respected, and revered in the way that the original creators of the Karluk collection did; by never taking more than what we need and leaving it unblemished by our passing.

Figure 4.13. Carrie Barker inventorying gaming balls, Alutiiq Museum, 2012. Photograph by Marnie Leist.

Despite advances in the collection's care at the Alutiiq Museum, the Karluk One assemblage presented staff members with a number of challenges. The most serious was the artifact catalog. Many items remained uncataloged. Portions of the site catalogs were not computerized, some catalog numbers had been used twice, and there were numerous inconsistencies in object identification. What one cataloger called a shaft fragment another might have recorded as a handle. In short, there was no single, comprehensive, systematic, computerized account of the enormous collection's contents. The museum's largest and most used assemblage needed to be better documented. There were also storage and conservation issues. Storage drawers were overfilled and in need of reorganization. Some of the rare organic objects were showing stress, forming precipitants, oozing conservation chemicals, and even cracking. A large batch of objects lost their catalog numbers due to smearing or chipping, and some were simply illegible. A professional conservator was needed to plan the next set of treatments.

In 2009, the Alutiiq Museum began a series of projects that would transform the care and interpretation of Karluk One. A 2010 grant from the Institute for Museum and Library Services (IMLS) supported *Picturing the Past*—a project that cataloged more than fifty thousand physical photographs in the Alutiiq Museum's collections. During this effort, Leist and collections assistant Valerie Maden numbered and inventoried more than three thousand slides, photographs, and negatives related to Karluk One, organizing and enhancing records of the site's graphic documentation.

In 2010, the focus turned entirely to Karluk One. A second grant from IMLS funded *Carlia'arluku— To Care for Karluk One*. This project addressed the major documentation and storage issues and supported a conservation assessment. Leist began the project by creating a single comprehensive catalog for Karluk One. She combined all the existing catalogs into a single Excel file and standardized terminology throughout the whopping 656-page document. To complete an inventory and better document the artifacts, Leist and collections assistant Carrie Barker organized artifacts by class, researched artifact types, developed definitions within the catalog, identified artifacts, weighed objects, and noted object condition where applicable (fig. 4.13). Alutiiq Museum Curator Patrick Saltonstall assisted with artifact and raw-material descriptions and the development of typological classes. Together, staff members identified 138 unique artifact classes (table 4.5), inventoried all of the objects in 131 of these classes, and partially completed the inventory of the remaining seven classes. In total, the project looked at about sixteen thousand excavated objects, all of them from the site's prehistoric layers. This represented about 78 percent of the archaeologically collected assemblage. The collections summary presented below is based on this data.

Working with Twenty-Six Thousand Pieces

Marnie A. Leist, Curator of Collections, Alutiiq Museum

One of the major steps in creating Kal'unek was inventorying the Karluk One assemblage. To write about the site and its remarkable contents, we had to be able to share the collection in meaningful ways. We had to have accurate object counts. We had to identify the major types of artifacts and raw materials. We had to photograph representative pieces. At the heart of this work was an inventory—a piece-by-piece accounting of all the objects in the collection. The job of looking at every artifact, more than twenty-six thousand pieces, fell to me. It was an amazing opportunity to learn about Alutiiq technology and an enormous challenge.

Figure 4.14. Finished stick labrets and stick labret preforms. AM193.87:9333, AM193.95:1501, Pullar, Knowles, and Dulchuk avocational collection, AM341:6.

The process was like a giant game of concentration—sorting objects into like groups. Yet, with every major task, there were boundless rewards. In the course of inventorying an artifact class, I would make discoveries, learn, use what I just learned, use it again later when more of that artifact class turned up in another drawer, match up pieces of objects that had broken prehistorically (and which often had been collected in different years form different parts of the site), all the while getting to work with amazingly intriguing objects. I can't tell you that the numerous bins of "worked wood," a.k.a. sticks, were enthralling to behold, but I can tell you it was fun to go through them to search for artifacts not yet identified or to sort like types into categories. For example, there are short fat pieces of worked wood that have angle-cut ends. These appear to be discarded objects—pieces left over from making some other object. I can't be certain what their distinctiveness represents, but I did find one piece that may provide a clue. A single whittled stick with carved ends: I looked at this piece on more than one occasion, finally realizing that both ends are labret preforms. The carver worked both ends of the whittled wood in making finished pieces (fig. 4.14). There were lots of surprises as well. I did not expect to see so many objects that had multiple uses. Nor did I expect to find so many examples of reuse. One banya scoop was split and repaired with baleen ties, used as a cutting board, then, once broken beyond repair, turned into clam knife. We often indicated in the catalog this transformation of an object's function.

Many times, the process of identifying objects was difficult. Patrick Saltonstall and I would often debate artifact functions. While we didn't often agree, and while we couldn't say for sure whether or not we got the identification right, we did use consistent terminology. This means that, if future discoveries are made, we can easily change the catalog. It is 656 pages, so consistency is important.

I could easily say that the most profound discovery I made was the number of antler artifacts in the collection—many of which had been identified as sea mammal bone. However, I think what is most important to me is learning about everyone else's experience with the collection. Working with the many researchers, artists, students, and educators that use Karluk One has opened my eyes to the very broad importance of this assemblage. The collection has been studied by many, has impacted many, and will now be preserved so others in the future can be a part of Karluk One. It has also impacted my work. The museum's next big project is an inventory of the Old Karluk collection. We will build on the knowledge gained by studying Karluk One to investigate the contents of this sister site, a quick paddle across the lagoon.

Figure 4.15. Patrick Saltonstall holds bifacial abraders, Alutiiq Museum, 2012. Photograph by Marnie Leist.

One significant discovery during *Carlia'arluku* was that many of the tools identified as bone are in fact antler. About 74 percent of the 341 antler tools in the assemblage were once classified as bone. Looking at the collection in its entirety also revealed new information. For example, Saltonstall and Barker also found an entirely new artifact type—a bifacially shaped abrader (fig. 4.15). Saltonstall surmises that these tools were used in woodworking, perhaps to scrape bark from pieces of wood.

Carlia'arluku also allowed the Alutiiq Museum to work with professional conservator Ellen Carrlee of the Alaska State Museum. Carrlee completed a collections assessment and hosted a community workshop on the care of archaeological organic materials. As part of this effort, she interviewed staff members to understand the complex history of the Karluk One excavation and conservation treatments. She also examined conservation records and literature about the site and its contents. Then, she surveyed the collection drawer by drawer, assessing artifacts, taking representative object photographs, and matching select artifacts to conservation-treatment records. This thorough documentation not only identified specific improvement projects that will help to ensure the long-term preservation of the collection but also outlined the complicated conservation history of the collection. It was the first time that this information was recorded in one place. As such, Carrlee's report (Carrlee 2011) will serve as a lasting, important record of the collection's care. It will help to guide future conservation work.

Based on Carrlee's recommendations, Leist and Barker rehoused most of the collection in archival boxes better suited to the size of objects. Many of these boxes are now lined with tissue to absorb any excess conservation chemicals (PEG—polyethylene glycol). Additionally, tissue has been used to separate stable and nonstable objects and as padding to support oddly shaped objects. Leist also made individual specialty boxes for fragile or extraordinary pieces. Many of these custom boxes have clear polyethylene sections or are mounted in ways to make the objects more accessible and easier to handle.

Intrigued by the collection, Carrlee also undertook a personal research project. In the summer of 2011, she worked with the Alutiiq Museum to analyze three fur samples, three baskets possibly made of baleen, and two samples of troubling accretions taken from labrets. From her analyses, Carrlee confirmed the pieces of basketry are baleen and identified the fur samples as fox, river otter, and wolverine. Fox and otter remains were not surprising as both animals are indigenous to Kodiak, but wolverines are not locally available. This animal pelt must have been brought to Kodiak from the mainland. Similarly, Carrlee determined that the yellow and blue accretions found a variety of wooden artifacts in the collection are mineral deposits, not a dangerous fungus. We now know that the accretions are a not a threat to the preservation of Karluk One's contents.

Conservation of Karluk One Artifacts

Ellen Carrlee, Conservator, Alaska State Museum

A conservator is a museum professional with training in chemistry, studio art, and art history/anthropology whose job is the preservation and treatment of artifacts. In 2011, I traveled to Kodiak to evaluate the Karluk One collection and provide recommendations for its future care. To assess condition, a conservator first asks: "animal, vegetable, or mineral?" Archaeological collections are typically made of inorganic materials such as stone, ceramic, or metals.

The Karluk One collection is unusual for its high percentage of organic materials made from plants and animals. Around three-quarters of the artifacts are made from wood, bark, antler, ivory, bone, fur, leather, feather, or baleen. Correct identification of materials is important for preservation because knowledge of the chemical structure and mechanisms of deterioration associated with a particular material aid in planning appropriate preservation strategies. For example, Alutiiq Museum staff noted mysterious blue and yellow accretions on some of the collection's wooden artifacts. It looked like biological growth, such as mold. But microscopy and X-ray fluorescence spectroscopy by the Alaska State Museum revealed the substances to be mineralized deposits, likely from contamination during burial and not a threat to the ongoing stability of the collection.

Material identification also provides information to help scholars and artists interpret the significance of the artifacts. For example, we discovered that baleen was widely used in the Karluk One collection. Baleen is composed of the protein keratin (similar to hair, hoof, horn, claw, and beak). Under the microscope, baleen has many characteristics similar to hair. Most hair has three main structures, all made of keratin: an outer cuticle of scales, an innermost pattern of cells down the center called the medulla, and a cortex in between them. The fibrous parts of baleen are similar to animal hair in their diameter, medulla, and scale pattern. The microscopic structures of baleen are different from plant materials, which have a distinct layered cellular appearance. Microscopy was one of three methods used to identify baleen. The other two methods involved analysis to confirm the presence of sulfur, an important element in the keratin molecule. A burn test of a tiny loose fragment yielded a distinct "burnt hair" smell characteristic of sulfur. Sulfur was further confirmed with a portable X-ray fluorescence spectrometer. With this knowledge, baleen was identified as the material used to lash together wooden containers, weave openwork twined basketry (fig. 4.16), and even construct a small model kayak frame. The ability to conclusively identify baleen on specific artifacts expands our understanding of its prehistoric use on Kodiak.

While the survival of the Karluk One organic materials in burial is remarkable, the collection is also special because of successful preservation efforts after excavation. Artifacts were damp when excavated and were immediately soaked in changes of deionized water to remove salts and contaminants that could cause ongoing deterioration. Most artifacts were treated with *impregnants* (substances that microscopically bulk up fragile artifact structures from within) or *consolidants* (thinned down adhesives to bind and strengthen internal structures). Organic materials made from plant and animal sources are much more delicate and difficult to treat than inorganic stone, metal, ceramic, and glass artifacts. Archaeologists also have far less experience treating organic materials because they are less common in archaeological sites. The most common impregnant used on the Karluk One collection was the water-soluble wax polyethylene glycol (PEG), mainly used on wood and basketry to replace the physical support of water molecules as the waterlogged material dries. The most successful consolidant was a water-soluble acrylic resin called Acrysol WS-24, used for the worked bone and antler artifacts.

Figure 4.16. Twined baleen baskets are among the many notable organic artifacts preserved in the Karluk One collection. AM193.87:19051.

Following treatment, access to the artifacts is balanced with long-term preservation in the museum environment. The Alutiiq Museum created custom storage housings and display mounts to safely support the artifacts while still allowing them to be examined and studied. Controlled temperature, humidity, light levels, pest-control protocols and handling procedures are also in place to balance preservation needs with continued study and viewing of the collection. Collections care is always ongoing, but the Karluk One materials are well preserved for future generations to study.

In 2011, a third IMLS grant supported the development of this manuscript and a key piece of collections research. Grant funds allowed the museum to work with the Kodiak Alutiiq New Words Council (NWC) to identify and develop Alutiiq terms for artifacts. The NWC is a group of Alutiiq speakers who meet to remember and create words for the Alutiiq language (Counceller 2010). About fifteen council members attended meetings to consider the appropriate Alutiiq terms for Karluk One's major artifact types. Saltonstall and Leist brought artifacts to two of the gatherings, showing members how tools worked. The memories of these local Elders helped Leist and Saltonstall better understand how objects were assembled into tools, and assisted the council in choosing the Alutiiq tool names that appear here (Counceller essay in Glossary).

Most recently, the Alutiiq Museum collaborated with the University of Washington's Burke Museum to find a permanent home for the animal remains collected at Karluk One as a more economical means of supporting their frequent study. This portion of the site collection traveled a very different route. The bulk samples of animal bones and shellfish remains from Karluk One were originally sent to Hunter College in New York, where arctic archaeologist Tom McGovern agreed to house them in his laboratory. Here, graduate student Tom Amorosi completed initial processing and review (Amorosi 1986, 1987). However, much of the impressive volume of material remained to be studied.

In 2000, archaeologist Bob Kopperl gained permission from collections owners to move the animals remains to the University of Washington, where he was a graduate student. He flew to New York City, rented a U-Haul, packed up all the samples of animal remains from Jordan's Karluk River studies, and drove them to Seattle. This included twenty-five boxes of samples from Karluk One. Although Kopperl ultimately choose not to study Karluk One, fellow student Catherine West incorporated fish remains from the site into her doctoral research (West 2011; essay Chapter 3). Eventually, the University of Washington Department of Anthropology sought a permanent home for the Kodiak faunal collections and approached the Burke and Alutiiq museums for assistance. The Burke Museum had the resources to care for the material, and the Alutiiq Museum had connections to its owners. Together, the organizations worked to have Karluk One faunal materials donated to the Burke. Now they are stored with the massive collection of similar materials from other Kodiak sites, enhancing their accessibility for research. Investigations of the materials continue today.

The Karluk One Collection

The activities described above resulted in the recovery of 25,912 items from Karluk One (table 4.1). Collections made by archaeologists account for 79 percent of the material and are the focus of the summary provided below. The remaining objects are from collections made by Kodiak residents and given to the museum (table 4.2). Many of these collections remain to be inventoried.

The objects from Karluk One can be divided into historic and prehistoric materials. While the prehistoric settlement of Karluk One is the focus of this publication, the site's historic objects tie the ancient collections to the present day. They illustrate both the endurance of the settlement and the collision of cultures that typify the last two centuries of Kodiak history.

The historic materials from Karluk One come from the uppermost level of site. This uneven layer extends from the site's grassy surface up to about 50 cm below (Knecht 1995:140). Due to the continued occupation of the site into the twentieth century, and the construction of buildings, gardens, a suspension bridge, and other features, the historic layer is mixed. More than six hundred objects are assigned to this layer. These materials include items of Alutiiq manufacture as well as European and Asian goods. For the purpose of this publication, we include all items of Alutiiq manufacture in the broader prehistoric Alutiiq collection, and all items of European or Asian manufacture in the historic collection. While arbitrary, this choice reflects both the nature of the site and the development of its collection. First, it is very difficult to separate historic and prehistoric Alutiiq materials at Karluk One, due to the complexity of the site's layers. Digging into the prehistoric layers in recent times mixed ancient artifacts with younger items (Knecht 1995:140). Moreover, researchers and community members salvaged a large portion of the collection from the beach. We do not know the age of the recovered objects, although most are assumed to be from the site's prehistoric layers. For these reasons, we consider all objects of Alutiiq manufacture separately from those of European or Asian manufacture.

The historic period represents about a third of the site's total history, more than two hundred of the six hundred years of occupation (West essay Chapter 3). Despite this fact, the historic layers of the site are relatively thin and the historic portion of the collection is small. Just 3 percent of the materials represent this era. In part, this reflects our choice to include items of Alutiiq manufacture in the broader prehistoric assemblage. However, it also reflects excavation strategy. Archaeologists were primarily interested in the deep, well-preserved prehistoric layers of the deposit. The upper disturbed layer was often removed quickly with few objects collected (Steffian 1996).

A brief review of the historic materials reveals a variety of objects of both European and Asian manufacture from both the Russian (ca. 1741–1867) and American (1867–1980) eras. European objects from the Russian period include glass beads, ceramics, iron axe heads, samovar spigots, and gun parts (fig. 4.17). Familiar American-era pieces include the remains of a pocket watch, buttons, dory knees, gun parts, spent shell casings,

Figure 4.17. Items reflecting the Russian era at Karluk One: axe blade, samovar spigot, bronze harpoon point, musket ball, flintlock musket action, spoon, Russian and British ceramics, button, and glass beads. Sheehan avocational collection, AM38:197; Lind avocational collection, AM14:132, AM14:226, AM14:1824, AM14:1730, AM14:200; AM193.94:1861, AM193.94:161, AM193.94:1953, UA84.193:1819, AM193.94:1954, AM193.94:170, AM193.94:1955, AM193.87:11017; Sheehan avocational collection AM38:85, AM38:86, AM38:88–92; AM38:100; UA83.193:947.

Figure 4.18. Items reflecting the American era at Karluk One: roof tile, ceramic plates, lock, burlap fragment, pocket watch, fox trap prong, weasel trap parts, soldering point, kaolin pipe, and buttons. Karluk School avocational collection, AM39:190; UA83.193:174, UA83.193:210, UA84.193:1747; Sheehan avocational collection AM38:251, AM38:242; Panamaroff avocational collection AM15:292, AM15:531; AM193.87:11380, AM193.95:533; Lind avocational collection AM14:1734; Karluk School avocational collection AM39:199.

Figure 4.19. Items from Karluk One reflecting the presence of Asian cannery workers in the community: Stoneware jar, stoneware w/stamp, porcelain, glass vial, and mahjong pieces. State of Alaska collection, AM247:2; AM193.87:11659, AM193.87:11619; Shugak avocational collection, AM425:1; Sheehan avocational collection, AM38:501, AM38:729, AM38:986.

Figure 4.20. Handmade lead icon from the historic level at Karluk One. Lind avocational collection, AM14:329.

ceramic roof tiles, fox-trap prongs, and deadfall-trap trigger parts for harvesting weasels (fig. 4.18). Stoneware jars, Mahjong game pieces, and tiny glass medicine vials reflect the influx of Asian cannery workers at the end of the nineteenth century (Roppel 1985:145) (fig. 4.19).

The historic portion of the collection also includes items that span both time periods: worked leather, nails, glass fragments from bottles, windows, lamps, and a variety of metal objects and ceramics. The ceramics are largely fragments of stoneware, as well as Chinese and British porcelains traded to Alutiiq people. The most unique historic piece is a handmade lead icon (fig. 4.20).

In short, the historic materials from Karluk One illustrate the influx of goods manufactured outside of Alaska. These items represent the addition of not only new tools but also new people and perspectives to the landscape of Karluk. This is particularly evident when the variety of historic objects and materials is compared to the assemblage of materials represented by the site's older layers.

Analytically, the remainder of the assemblage falls within the late prehistoric period, the roughly four hundred years from the founding of the site until the arrival of Russian entrepreneurs. For the purposes of summary, we divided these nineteen thousand items into three broad categories—samples, debitage, and artifacts. A summary of each category appears below.

Samples

Samples are items collected to study the age and environment of a site. Materials like animal remains and wood charcoal can provide essential information on site age, the character of the surrounding environment, and patterns of human activity. The Alutiiq Museum houses 1,005 samples from Karluk One (table 4.3). The most commonly sampled material was wood, collected to aid in dating the site's many layers. These samples represent minimally modified lengths of wood in all size—from sizeable logs and branches to twigs.

Animal remains are another broad category of samples. The Burke Museum at the University of Washington stores several hundred samples in this category. In contrast, the Alutiiq Museum holds individually collected animal remains, often from large mammals. Whalebones, especially vertebrae and ribs, are easily identified. Land mammal remains include caribou bones from

Table 4.3 Karluk One samples

TYPE	DESCRIPTION	NUMBER	% SAMPLES
Botanical	Bark, grass, floral, leaves, moss, seeds, twigs	121	12.0
Charcoal	Carbonized wood collected for radiocarbon dating	40	4.0
Faunal	Baleen, bone, claws, feathers, insects, octopus beak, shells, teeth	205	20.4
Fur	Fox, land otter, wolverine, and unidentified samples	177	17.6
Human Hair	Clippings of human hair	158	15.7
Mineral	Copper oxide, mica, ochre, unidentified blue stone	4	.4
Soil	Soil, site matrix, house floor, clay	54	5.4
Wood	Assorted logs, branches, twigs	246	24.5
	TOTAL	1005	100.0

This table does not include several hundred samples of animal remains curated by the University of Washington's Burke Museum of Natural History and Culture.

Figure 4.21. Individual fauna elements: killer whale tooth, sea lion tooth, dog-digested ivory and antler, dog tooth, bear tooth, burnt clam shell, octopus beak, bird cranium, albatross cranium, and eagle claw. AM193.94:5382, AM193.87:10072, UA85.193:4929, AM193.94:5324, AM193.95:1126; Karluk School avocational collection, AM39:157, AM39:156; AM193.95:1512, UA85.193:3979, AM193.94:2156, AM193.94:4618, Lind avocational collection, AM14:346.

the Alaska mainland. Mike Etnier of Western Washington University recently identified several dozen teeth from Karluk One, including those from fox, dog, bear, whale, shark, seal, sea lion, and sea otter. Remarkably, a single octopus beak also survived (fig. 4.21).

Animal fur and human hair samples are also surprisingly common. The clumps of fur found at Karluk One were probably shed from clothing or from hides worked into the great array of clothing, bags, bedding, and boat coverings that would have been manufactured in the village. In contrast, human hair samples appear to be clippings from ancient human haircuts. Researchers collected numerous short, evenly cut clusters of black

hair. Scientists studied the levels of trace metals preserved in the hair to better understand changes in exposure to substances like mercury between the past and present. Unfortunately, the wet conditions that preserved the hair also appear to have leached away its mineral content (Egeland et al. 1999), erasing clues about the minerals absorbed from foods.

Small collections of botanical remains—grass, bark, seeds, and even moss are also part of the assemblage reflecting the site's remarkable preservation and opportunities to study Karluk's ancient natural environment through the collection (fig. 4.22).

Figure 4.22. Samples of birch bark. Birch bark was used in multiple ways. There are three nearly complete vessels stitched from large cut and folded pieces of bark as well as fragments of birch bark vessels and numerous pieces of cut bark. Bark was used as a support material for the rims of spruce root baskets, as wrapping around net sinkers, and probably as kindling (Knecht 1995:558).

Debitage

Debitage is waste produced during artifact manufacture. Debitage can be used to understand how objects were made, to identify tools used, material preferences, manufacturing techniques, and stages of production. This broad category of Karluk One objects includes pieces of stone, bone, wood, and even fiber and leather debris. It also includes chunks of raw material—items collected by site residents (fig. 4.23). These items, whether modified or not, are not recognizable objects. They are manufacturing refuse. Debitage is common but not abundant in the Karluk One collection. Site residents manufactured a great variety of implements, leaving evidence of chipping, grinding, pecking, carving, twining, and sewing. Each of these activities represents an industry, a way of making tools (table 4.4).

Not surprisingly, pieces of worked wood and bone are the most common form of debitage. These carved organic materials make up more than half of all the worked materials in the site. Discarded pieces of chipped and ground stone were also a common find. Less common was evidence of sewing and weaving debris. Although wood was well preserved in the site, more delicate organics like fiber and leather are rare. Additionally, we know from ethnographic accounts that Alutiiq people employed these materials very efficiently,

Figure 4.23. Quartz crystals. These crystals may have been used as amulets, perhaps as part of a hunter's charm bundle (Knecht 1995:573; Merck 1980; Desson 1995). A rattle in the Fisher collection has a quartz crystal inside of it (Crowell and Leer 2001:208). AM193.95:821, AM193.94:4964, UA85.193:4321.

Table 4.4 Karluk One debitage

INDUSTRY	MATERIALS	NUMBER	%
Chipped Stone	Chert, metatuff, silicified slate, basalt, greywacke, chalcedony, obsidian, shale, coal	1254	25.5
Ground Stone*	Slate, metatuff, shale, limestone, siltstone, granite, basalt, mudstone	613	12.4
Pecked Stone	Greywacke, granite	6	.1
Unmodified Stone	Beach pebbles, quartz crystals, other raw materials	121	2.5
Carved Organics	Wood, antler, bone, ivory	2894	58.7
Worked Fiber	Grass, spruce root, baleen	34	.7
Worked Skin	Leather	6	.1
	TOTAL	4928	100.0

*Includes flakes exhibiting both chipped and ground surfaces, likely from adzes

using scraps for decoration and repurposing old items. Old boat covers became wraps for the dead (de Laguna 1956:233). Calico flour sacks were sewn into undergarments (Vlasoff 2007:44). The Karluk assemblage itself provides many examples of reuse: items whose function changed. We identified at least 350 pieces reworked from other objects. For example, two broken kayak paddles were fashioned into work boards. A harpoon dart butt was sharpened and used as an awl. Clam knives were often carved from discarded shafts, kayak stringers, and even bentwood vessel bottoms. In short, cultural practices altered the amount and type of debitage that entered the archaeological record. Collecting methods also influenced the types of debitage in the collection. For example, although excavators collected pieces of carved wood, the wood chips that littered the site's house floors were not saved.

Artifacts

Most of the Karluk One objects, more than 13,500 pieces, fall in the artifact category. This includes finished objects as well as preforms:

items in the process of being manufactured. For example, the collection includes slate lance points but also pieces of slate shaped into lances but not yet ground to a smooth finish. These preform pieces are included in the artifact category as it is possible to identify the type of object they represent (fig. 4.24). To manage the variety of objects, at least 138 types, we divided the assemblage into three broad categories: economic artifacts, household objects, and items related to social and spiritual life (table 4.5).

This summary should be considered preliminary. It is not intended as a detailed analysis but to provide a broad, generalized picture of the items excavated from the site. Artifact counts may be deceptive for a number of reasons. First, we do not differentiate between whole and fragmentary pieces in the assemblage. This means that each complete basket and basket fragment is counted once in table 4.5, although a number of the fragments might have been part of one basket in the past. Similarly, a close review of the seventy-nine pieces of gravel-tempered pottery suggests they represent one broken pot (fig. 6.68), not seventy-nine complete pots! Excavation strategy

Figure 4.24. *Canasuuteq*—thing for making (tool). While many artifacts are readily identifiable, there are many types of objects whose purpose remains unknown. Of the 424 unidentified tools, there are at least twenty-six distinct types. UA85.193:5624, Lind avocational collection, AM14:1920.

Table 4.5 Numbers of Karluk One artifacts by category and type

ECONOMIC LIFE (4,515)	HOUSEHOLD LIFE (5,913)	SOCIAL & SPIRITUAL LIFE (3,027)
Collecting (156)	**Building & Wood Working (1,112)**	**Warring (102)**
digging stick 14	splitting adze 63	armor 78
clam knife 142	planing adze 298	club 2
Fishing (714)	adze handle 29	shield 22
fish harpoon[a] 134	wedge 661	**Gaming (2,063)**
leister side prong 26	maul 6	kakangaq disc 252
leister center prong 16	plank[b] 15	kakangaq target 29
leister socket 1	**Cooking & Storing (2,453)**	augca'aq dart 175
fishhook shank 70	vessels (bentwood & other) 658	gaming ball 743
fishhook barb 43	basket 85	dice/game piece 8
line weight 39	vessel lid 50	tally stick 626
spacer bar sinker 30	vessel handle 111 (and others)	incised pebble 230
rig spreader 52	gravel-tempered pottery 79 sherds	**Personal Adornment (474)**
snood 10	box panel 60	labret 410
lure 6	mortar 4	labret-hole stretcher 35
stunning club 20	pestle 3	bead 7
net sinker 208	spoon 27	pendant 4
net float 54	fire-starter hearth 31	fastener/button 11
anchor 6	fire-starter drill 52	caribou tooth belt 1
line leader 1	fire-starter drill handle 15	nose pin/ring 6
Hunting (2,372)	fire-drill bow 1	**Festivals (388)**
ground lance (bayonet) 25	oil lamp 53	feast bowl 41
point sheath 26	ulu (including ulus w/handles) 1,050	mask 28
chipped point 13	ulu handle 141	maskette 74
chipped knife 4	plug 13	mask hoop 15 (and parts)
ground knife 84	tube 20	mask bangle 141
knife handle 5	**Sweat Bathing (404)**	drum handle 5
ground point 213	rock paddle 44	drum rim 25
end blade 89	rock tong 317	drum stick 1
gorge 2	water scoop 43	amulet box 1
toggling harpoon point 7	**Playing (324)**	rattle hoop[c]
non-toggling harpoon point/dart 83	children's doll 20	rattle cross brace[c]
arrow point 68	miniature/toy 142	dance wand 2
socket piece 58	kayak carving 38	shaman's doll 34
foreshaft 46	kayak figurine 26	story rock 2
shaft 1,119	angyaq carving 15	zoomorphic figurine 19
dart butt 37	model kayak part 72	
finger rest 5	model angyaq part 11	
throwing board 13	**Manufacturing (1,662)**	
throwing board pin 1	awl 94	
bow 41	needle 2	
arrow shaft 400	spool 5	
sinew twister 4	work board 83	
gutskin jacket-cuff clip 4	gut scraper 43	
drag handle 16	rodent-incisor carving tool 9	
wound plug 3	tool handle 108	
net 1	drill 5	
Trapping (118)	drill handle 5	
snare pin 118	chisel/tool bit 26	

Table 4.5 continued

ECONOMIC LIFE (4,515)	HOUSEHOLD LIFE (5,913)	SOCIAL & SPIRITUAL LIFE (3,027)
Boating (1,155)	net gauge 23	
kayak part 895	peg 94	
angyaq part 201	stake 18	
paddle 59	cordage/lashing 44	
	biface 9	
	flake tool 31	
	cobble scraper 540	
	chipped scraper 7	
	U-shaped abrader 19	
	hammerstone 194 (23 used as hones)	
	hone 104 (7 used as awls)	
	abrader 65	
	burnishing stone 72 (41 used as hones)	
	whetstone 63	
	flaker 1	

NOTE: This table does not include 359 finished artifacts of unidentified types (see Figure 4.24, Figures 4.32–4.35).

a. Some artifact types include multiple subtypes; e.g., fish harpoons may be socketed, scarfed, or spurred.
b. Planks were very common at the site; these fifteen represent the sample collected.
c. Artifacts identified in field notes but not in museum collection inventory.

also influenced the structure of the collection. For example, planks were a very common find at Karluk One but not typically collected. There was far too much wood to save every worked board (fig. 4.11). The fifteen planks in the collection reflect a sample of those encountered during the dig not a complete set. Thus artifacts related to home building are underrepresented in table 4.5. Additionally, many items could be assigned to multiple functional categories. Recycling is hallmark of Alutiiq culture and evidence of this practice appears throughout Karluk One. A variety of implements are made from worn or broken objects of a different type. Rather than discarding valuable material, craftsmen reused it to create another item. In short, many more studies of the collection are needed to fully understand its contents. Detailed reviews of artifact classes, investigation of manufacturing techniques, and comparison of the artifacts found in different areas and levels of the site are just beginning (see Knecht 1995; West 2011).

Table 4.5 illustrates that breadth of the collection: the objects found reflect activities that span the seasons—from summer and fall subsistence activities to winter manufacturing work and celebrations. The collection supports the view from settlement data (see Chapter 2) that the site was inhabited through much of the year. It also contains tools typical of ethnographically documented men's, women's, and children's activities. Hunting gear, house-building materials, and objects associated with warfare and masked dancing signal the presence of men, while gathering tools, food-processing items, and sewing gear suggest women's tasks (Merck 1980:106). Objects that helped children learn Alutiiq customs include dolls, miniature tools, and toy boats.

Figure 4.25. *Kakangaq* gaming disks as uncovered in the excavation. Alutiiq Museum archives, AM193:58.S.

In short, this is not a specialized assemblage typical of a specific season or task but a collection that broadly represents the activities of late prehistoric Alutiiq culture.

Not surprisingly objects associated with indoor activities are the most common. Excavations focused on a stack of superimposed floors, capturing the main living space and side rooms of large sod houses. Items related to food preparation, cooking, and storage abound in the collection, as do manufacturing tools and gaming pieces. When they were not handling food or creating the tools needed for daily living, the residents of Karluk One competed in *augca'aq* and *kakangaq*,

throwing games still played around Kodiak today (fig. 4.25).

Hunting gear is also common, particularly in comparison with fishing gear. There are three times as many objects related to hunting as there are to fishing. As the mouth of the Karluk River is one of the very best places in the entire North Pacific Ocean to intercept salmon, this find is intriguing. Site studies elsewhere in the Kodiak region illustrate that fishing nets were stored outdoors, along the edges of riverbanks where they were used. As Karluk One excavations focused on revealing houses, they may not have captured fishing gear stored elsewhere. Fishing gear may simply be underrepresented in this sample. Alternatively, this pattern may reflect the nature of settlement use. Items associated with the seasonal progression of fishing activities are all present—winter ice fishing, spring marine fishing, and summer and fall riverine fishing. Yet, this gear may reflect tool manufacture and not tool use. The large amount of manufacturing debris in houses suggests that tools for use throughout the year were made at Karluk One. People may have moved in and out of the settlement during the salmon season, taking tools manufactured at Karluk One to family fish camps. Settlement data from the Karluk River suggests that such camps are present (see Chapter 2). Additional studies of the Karluk assemblage and late prehistoric villages in the Karluk drainage are needed to explore this question.

Perhaps the most stunning part of the Karluk One assemblage is its small collection of festival gear. In addition to the great assortment of objects reflecting daily life, wet site conditions preserved rare objects reflecting the spiritual lives of villagers. Masks, drums, rattles, feast bowls, dance wands, animal figurines, and shamanic pieces extend the antiquity of ethnographically recorded practices and provide stunning examples of artistry. The winter festivals recorded by Davydov (1977) and Pinart (1872, 1873) are firmly reflected in the ceremonial gear from Karluk One.

Material Use

Another important dimension of the collection is the way materials were used. In addition to identifying the types of artifacts found in the site, researchers identified the materials used to make each object and piece of debitage. This information illustrates patterns of harvesting, trade, travel, and manufacture (Steffian 1992a), and it can show cultural and technological preferences (Margaris essay Chapter 5).

The Kodiak Archipelago has a unique geological and biological history, distinct from that of the adjacent Alaskan mainland. While Kodiak is rich in sedimentary rocks like slate and sandstone, it lacks the volcanic rocks—basalts and obsidians—common to the Alaska Peninsula. Similarly, the archipelago has fewer native land mammals. Only bear, fox, river otter, ermine, ground squirrel, bat, and vole are indigenous to the islands (Clark 2010; Rausch 1969). Notably absent are ungulates (moose, caribou, deer, sheep) and large rodents (beaver, marmot, and porcupine)[2] widely available in neighboring areas of the mainland.

These distinctions help archaeologists to identify the general source of materials used to make Kodiak artifacts (Steffian et al. 2006). For example, as no type of antler is available in the Kodiak region, any antler artifact must be made of material harvested on the Alaska mainland. This does not mean that the artifact came from the mainland, only that the material used to make it is from this distant source. The artifact may have been manufactured in Karluk, somewhere else on Kodiak, or on the mainland. By comparing the types of materials used to make artifacts with the materials represented in manufacturing debris (debitage), archaeologists can understand which materials were worked at Karluk One and which may have been brought to Karluk as finished objects.

Table 4.6 summarizes the raw materials used to make Karluk One objects. The table separates materials found in the archipelago from those available from more distant sources and illustrates which materials were used in artifacts and which appear as debitage or as supplemental material (secondary construction materials in object manufacture—e.g., for lashing or decoration). It is important to note several points about these groupings. First, these material identifications are preliminary. There are still a number of materials classified as stone or bone that require further identification. Other material identifications need to be confirmed. In short, the information presented here is intended to provide a general summary of the materials in the collection and broad patterns in their distribution.

Second, Karluk lies in a treeless landscape. Here, much of the wood used to manufacture artifacts grew in forests far from Kodiak and was transported to Kodiak by the ocean. Here, people harvested alder and willow brush on surrounding hillsides, and red cedar, pacific yew, hemlock, spruce, and cottonwood from Kodiak beaches where winds and tides delivered drift logs to the shore (Russell 1991). The same is true of pumice, a gritty volcanic stone that floats, is abundant on the Alaska Peninsula, and can be collected along Kodiak's coasts today. This doesn't mean that exotic woods and pumice were never obtained on the mainland, only that they are available on Kodiak and often harvested locally.

Third, materials found on Kodiak are not necessarily available near Karluk. The rocky beaches fronting Karluk and the bedrock cliffs nearby

Table 4.6 Raw materials used to make Karluk One objects

	KODIAK ARCHIPELAGO MATERIALS	ARTIFACTS	DEBITAGE	SUPPLEMENTAL	TOTAL
ORGANIC	Baleen	9	22	128	159
	Bark (cottonwood, unidentified, drift—e.g., birch, cedar)	485	371	8	864
	Bear claw	1	0		1
	Bird bone	31	27		58
	Fish bone (halibut)	0	1		1
	Grass	22	2	5	35
	Hide	1	7		8
	Land mammal bone (brown bear, fox, land otter)	9	9		18
	Sea mammal bone (harbor seal, porpoise, sea lion, sea otter, whale)	137	170		307
	Unidentified bone	147	15		162
	Shell	1		1	2
	Spruce root	66	11	39	111
	Tooth (bear, seal, sea lion, fish, unidentified, etc.)	1	3	2	6
	Wood (alder, cottonwood, willow, driftwood—spruce, cedar, pacific yew, hemlock)	8,284	2,161	1	10,445
INORGANIC	*Kodiak Batholith—widely available*				
	Granite	675	4		679
	Tonalite	20	0		20
	Quartz	2	10		12
	Kodiak formation—widely available				
	Black slate	1,757	1,016	4	2,777
	Silicified slate	266	223		489
	Greywacke	703	115		818
	Quaternary deposits—widely available				
	Amber	2	0		2
	Glacially transported pebbles (e.g., banded chert)	6	0		6
	Clay	24	1		25
	Gravel-tempered clay	79	0		79
	Iron oxide (red ochre)	0	0	166	166
	Pumice	38	0		38
	Uyak formation—western Kodiak accessible from Karluk				
	Metatuffs	176	237		413
	Radiolarian chert (red, gray, green)	7	176		183
	Schists (green & blue facies)	2	0		2
	Prince William terrane—eastern Kodiak far from Karluk				
	Sandstone	16	0		16
	Siltstone	30	2		32
	Tuff	1	0		1
	TOTALS	**12,999**	**4,583**	**354**	**17,935**

Table 4.6 continued

	NONLOCAL MATERIALS	ARTIFACTS	DEBITAGE	SUPPLEMENTAL	TOTAL
ORGANIC	Mussel shell	3	0		3
	Antler	338	129	1	468
	Fossilized ivory	13	1		14
	Ivory	20	6	1	27
	Land mammal bone (caribou)	0	1		1
	Tooth (beaver, marmot or porcupine incisors, caribou)	9	0	2	11
INORGANIC	*Volcanics—Alaska Peninsula*				
	Andesite	13	0		13
	Basalt	124	38		162
	Obsidian	1	2		3
	Rhyolite	0	1		1
	Scoria	28	0		28
	Unidentified black volcanic	8	0		8
	Other				
	Coal	12	15		27
	Chalcedony	1	111		112
	Copper oxide	0	1		1
	Exotic cherts—various colors	5	10		15
	Limestone	13	4		17
	Metal (copper and iron)	0	0	1	1
	Red shale	1	3		4
	Steatite	2	0		2
	TOTALS	**591**	**322**	**5**	**918**

	UNKOWN ORIGIN	ARTIFACTS	DEBITAGE	SUPPLEMENTAL	TOTAL
INORGANIC	Argillite	1	0		1
	Diorite	4	0		4
	Galena	0	1		1
	Hematite	0	1		1
	Molybdenite (pigment)	0	0	36	36
	Mudstone	8	1		9
	Nephrite	1	0		1
	Pigments (e.g., gray, black, white, green)	0	1	58	59
	Quartz crystal	23	0		23
	Unidentified stone	302	60		362
	TOTALS	**339**	**64**	**94**	**497**

NOTE: Supplemental materials are secondary materials—lashing, pigment—used in the manufacture of an object.

Table 4.7 Origin of Karluk One materials

ORIGIN	ARTIFACTS	DEBITAGE	SUPPLEMENTAL	TOTAL
Karluk region	12,891	4,570	315	17,776 (94%)
Kodiak region	108	13	39	160 (1%)
Mainland	629	322	5	956 (5%)

NOTE: Supplemental materials are secondary materials—lashing, pigment—used in the manufacture of an object.

provided hard stone including granite and greywacke. Other stone suitable to pecking, grinding, and chipping—red chert and slate—can be mined in outcrops along the western coast of Kodiak in Uyak and Uganik Bays, relatively near Karluk (Farris 2009:71). However, fine gritty siltstone and sandstone occur along the eastern coast of Kodiak, several days travel from Karluk. Similarly, spruce trees—a source of roots for weaving—do not grow in Karluk but are found at the northern end of the archipelago on Afognak and Shuyak Islands. In short, some Kodiak materials are not readily accessible from Karluk. Their presence at Karluk One reflects movement around Kodiak in the hands of people.

Materials available in the Kodiak Archipelago dominate the Karluk One collection (table 4.6). The collection contains an abundance of locally available wood, stone, and bone. Wood is the most common material for both finished artifacts and debitage. More than 55 percent of the Karluk One objects are made of wood, a result that illustrates the uniqueness of the collection. Most Kodiak sites of this age lack wood preservation, leaving archaeologists to study Alutiiq traditions without many common cultural objects.

Slate, granite, greywacke, silicified slate, metatuff, bark, and sea mammal bone are also widely present, illustrating the use of immediately available materials throughout the assemblage.

Eighty-nine percent of the collection is made of just eight materials.

Despite these preferences, the collection contains notable quantities of nonlocal materials (table 4.7). A small number of these reflect trade and transport across the Kodiak region—spruce root from the northern archipelago and abrasive sandstone and siltstone from eastern Kodiak. However, most are from the Alaskan mainland. Items from neighboring regions include glassy volcanic stones, colorful cherts, hard black coal, red shale, ivory, caribou bone, and caribou antler.[3] Many of these materials appear both as finished objects and as debitage, indicating the craftsmen worked the materials in Karluk (fig. 4.26). This pattern is particularly evident among the large number of antler artifacts. Although antler is not available on Kodiak, this spongy, resilient material was preferred for harpoon points, leisters, and other harvesting gear designed to withstand an impact (Margaris 2009). Antler objects represent over half of the nonlocal materials found at Karluk One (51 percent), and of these, more than a quarter are pieces of manufacturing debris. People worked antler regularly on the site, and residents must have made frequent trips to the Alaska Peninsula to collect antler or trade with neighbors to maintain a supply of the material. Some of the nonlocal materials are truly exotic, coming to Kodiak from very distant places. The

Figure 4.26. *Yaamam ilakuall'raa*—debitage; *yaamam ipgaa*—flake tool. Chalcedony core, flake, and utilized flake. Archaeologists found 112 pieces of chalcedony debitage at Karluk One. Craftsmen created these flakes using bipolar percussion. They placed a piece of chalcedony on a hard surface and knocked flakes off of it with a stone. This process created sharp shards for cutting or incising. UA85.193:2445, AM193.95:1441, AM193.94:1837.

Figures 4.27a,b. *Nuusiq*—ground knife. This mussel-shell knife is 8 cm long with one finely sharpened edge. UA85.193:3162.

chemical composition of a piece of obsidian from Karluk One indicates that it is from the Okmok volcano on Umnak Island in the Aleutian Island chain (Rasic 2011:7). A piece of copper oxide may be from Prince William Sound or the Copper River basin. Three pieces of worked mussel shell may be from Kodiak, but at least one resembles mussel-shell knife blades made and used in southeast Alaska (fig. 4.27a,b; cf. Emmons 1991:173), and two soapstone artifacts may be from the far north. The presence of these exotic materials and objects indicates that Karluk One residents participated in far-reaching trade networks. Trade was not just with neighbors but with a network of communities though which goods moved over great distances in the Gulf of Alaska and beyond. The nonperishable materials preserved at Karluk One likely represent a small fraction of the clothing, food, and raw materials that once made their way to Karluk and other communities.

Finally, our review of raw-material use indicates that Karluk One residents used a variety of pigments to paint objects. About 250 objects, most of them wood, have indications of painting. These include items from the sacred to the secular, dolls, mask parts, vessel handles, harpoon shafts, model kayak and *angyaq* parts, war shields, and work boards (fig. 4.28, 4.29). Red and black pigments are the most common, although the collection also has examples of green and white pigments. A sparkly, charcoal-grey mineral (possibly molybdenite) was often applied over or mixed with black pigment. The sources of these pigments are not known, though Russian accounts suggest that they are both local and distant (Davydov 1977:187). The red color on Karluk One objects may be from ochre, a pigment made from iron oxide available around Kodiak. Other pigments may be ground from materials like copper or limestone obtained in trade. In the eighteenth century, Alutiiq people baked and crushed pigment materials, then mixed them with binders of blood, fish eggs, and water (Davydov 1977:150, 153).

This brief summary illustrates the uniqueness of the Karluk One collection. The massive, well-preserved assemblage holds an array of objects not usually found in ancient Alutiiq sites and, therefore, offers an exceptionally rich picture of the past. It illustrates the skills of Karluk crafts-men who ingeniously transformed a great variety of materials into complex tools. The collection advances understanding of these tools by providing multiple parts of intricate technologies. We don't have to imagine how tools were manufactured or assembled, pieces from Karluk One demon-strate techniques. Slate ulu blades, so common in Kodiak sites, are hafted to wooden handles, lashed in place with split and knotted spruce root. The Karluk One artifacts are also a testament to the artistic talents of the Alutiiq people, who create exquisite works. Finely carved and finished ob-jects are not only beautiful but inspiring when you see the tools with which artists worked—stone adzes, chisels, and drills, animal-tooth knives, and gritty stone abraders. And when you step back

Figure 4.29. Marnie Leist holding a painted shield fragment from the Sheehan avocational collection, 2013. AM38:845. Photograph by Sven Haakanson Jr.

Figure 4.28. Unidentified painted piece of wood with black pigment and a sparkly substance that appears to be molybdenite. UA85.193:4495.

Figure 4.31. *Qalutaq*—water scoop. Detail of water scoop handles with bird carvings. UA85.193:4816, AM193.94:354.

Figure 4.30. *Agaa*—tool handle. Tool handle featuring a carved face. Sheehan avocational collection, AM38:56.

Figure 4.32. *Canasuuteq*—tool (thing for making). Tool type of unknown function, curved tapered tool with thin, flat polished end. UA85.193:6734, AM193.87:11348, AM193.95:1018.

and look at the assemblage as a whole, an Alutiiq worldview shines through. Tiny faces carved on the surfaces of implements—from tool handles to gaming pieces—represent the spiritual awareness in all objects in the Alutiiq world (fig. 4.30, 4.31). These small faces, the careful manufacture of objects, the attention to beautiful decoration all show a respect for the world that provided for Karluk people (Haakanson and Steffian 2004).

The remainder of this book looks at the Karluk One artifacts from a cultural perspective. Using

historic information, the knowledge of Elders, clues from the site and its collection, and environmental observations, the following chapters describe life in the village in prehistoric times. The discussion illustrates how the objects briefly summarized here functioned in the daily lives of Karluk residents, providing a rare look at Alutiiq traditions four hundred years ago, less than two centuries before the conquest of Kodiak by Russian traders.

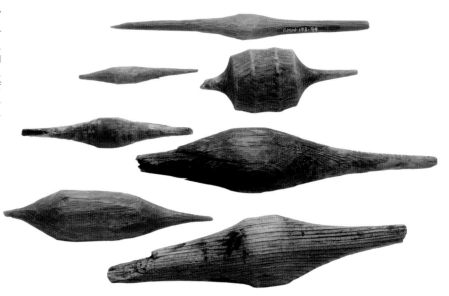

Figure 4.33. *Canasuuteq*—tool (thing for making). Tool types of unknown function, possibly darts, awls, or tool handles. Lind avocational collection, AM14:94; UA84.193:2069, AM193.87:19069, AM193.87:8477; Panamaroff avocational collection, AM15:22; AM193.94:957, AM193.94:5090.

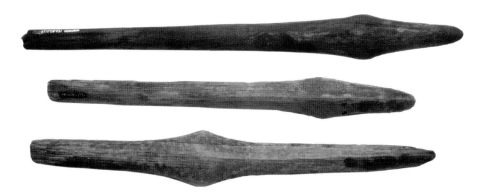

Figure 4.34. *Canasuuteq*—tool (thing for making). Tool types of unknown function. The middle piece is painted red. AM193.87:8128; Lind avocational collection, AM14:136; Sheehan avocational collection, AM103:77.

Figure 4.35. *Canasuuteq*—tool (thing for making). Tool types of unknown function. The small slate piece on the left may function as a pendant or represent a female figure. A similar piece is in the Kodiak Historical Society's collection at the Baranov Museum (accession number 86-20-19). UA85.193.3473, AM193.87:10762, UA85.193:5463.

Chapter Four Notes

1. Clark (1974:81) studied Milan's collections from Karluk sites at the University of Wisconsin Madison. In 2007, the US Fish and Wildlife Service transferred some of the artifacts to the Alutiiq Museum for curation.

2. Reindeer, Sitka black-tailed deer, elk, mountain goat, beaver, and hare are among the animals introduced to the Kodiak Archipelago in the first half of the twentieth century (Tennessen 2010:34).

3. Based on size and shape, pieces of partially worked antler in the collection appear to be from caribou. However, we cannot rule out the possibility that moose antler is also present.

5

Economic Life

Along the weather-beaten coast of southwestern Kodiak Island, a series of small lagoons punctuate steep, rocky headlands and long, wave-pounded beaches. Karluk Lagoon is the most northerly of these estuaries. In this shallow, triangular waterway, the river stalls and mixes with saltwater before escaping through a narrow channel into Shelikof Strait (fig. 5.1). A shifting sand and gravel spit separates the lagoon from the ocean, providing a protective barrier from the turbulent marine waters beyond. From an ecological standpoint, this small lagoon is part of a remarkably productive landscape.

Figure 5.1. Karluk River Lagoon, 1983. View west toward the Alaska Peninsula, visible in the distance. Bryn Mawr College Archaeological project, Alutiiq Museum archives, AM278:172.

The resources important to Karluk residents occur throughout the environment surrounding Karluk Lagoon, from the near-shore marine waters and the coastal fringe to the river and rolling hills that form the Karluk River valley. The Karluk One village was centrally located in this landscape. Perched on the beach and bluff at the southern edge of the lagoon, the community was equally well positioned to exploit resources from the ocean and the land, and to maintain control over the waterway and its wealth of food and raw material. Rounding the corner from Cape Uyak to the north, or Cape Karluk to the south, the village appeared to travelers a sentry at the mouth of the lagoon.

Ethnographic studies indicate that Karluk residents range broadly along the coast of southwestern Kodiak Island (Alaska Department of Fish and Game 1985; Davis 1986; United States Department of the Interior 1987). People hunt, trap, fish, and gather foods around the shores of area lagoons: Karluk Lagoon, Sturgeon Lagoon, Grants Lagoon, Halibut Bay, and Gurney Bay. Marine fishing occurs in the waters fronting Karluk. The kelp beds immediately offshore hold an abundance of rockfish. Sea mammal hunting took people farther from shore, and farther from home. Residents report traveling from Middle Cape to inner Uyak Bay in pursuit of prey (United States Department of the Interior 1987). A brief review of these environments illustrates the resources available and the likely sources of foods and raw materials harvested in each by the residents of Karluk One (table 5.1).

Table 5.1 Alutiiq names for economically important plants and animals in Karluk

ENGLISH NAME	SINGULAR ALUTIIQ NAME	DUAL ALUTIIQ NAME	PLURAL ALUTIIQ NAME
Sky Animals (Birds)—Qilam Unguwallria'i			
Cormorant	Agasuuq	Agasuuk	Agasuut
Ducks	Saqul'aaq	Saqul'aak	Saqul'aat
Eagle	Kum'agyak	Kum'agyak	Kum'agyat
Geese	Lagiq	Lagik	Lagit
Gulls	Qatayaq	Qatayak	Qatayat
Pigeon guillemot	Cuu'raq	Cuu'rak	Cuu'rat
Ptarmigan	Qateriuk	Qateriuk	Qateriut
Puffin	Tunngaq	Tunngak	Tunngat
Swan	Qugyuk	Qugyuk	Qugyut
Land Mammals—Nunam Unguwallria'i			
Brown bear	Taquka'aq	Taqukaraak	Taqukaraat
Fox	Kaugya'aq	Kaugyaraak	Kaugyaraat
Ermine/Weasel*	Amitatuk	Amitatuk	Amitatut
Ground squirrel	Qanganaq	Qanganak	Qanganat
River otter	Aaquyaq	Aaquyak	Aaquyat
Ocean Fish—Imam Iqalluarua'i			
Cod	Amutaq	Amutak	Amutat
Halibut	Sagiq	Sagik	Sagit
Herring	Iqalluarpak	Iqalluarpak	Iqalluarpat
Rock fish	Cilupuuk	Cilupuuk	Cilupuut
Starry flounder	Waa'uq	Waa'uk	Waa'ut

Table 5.1 continued

ENGLISH NAME	SINGULAR ALUTIIQ NAME	DUAL ALUTIIQ NAME	PLURAL ALUTIIQ NAME
Plants—Naut'staat			
Alder	Uqgwik	Uqgwik	Uqgwit
Birch	Qasrulek	Qasrulek	Qasrulet
Blueberries	Cuawak	Cuawak	Cuawat
Cottonwood	Ciquq	Ciquk	Ciqut
Driftwood (small)	Pukilaaq	Pukilaak	Pukilaat
Driftwood (medium)	Kapilaq	Kapilak	Kapilat
Driftwood (full log)	Tep'aq	Tep'ak	Tep'at
Grasses	Wek	Weg'ek	Weg'et
Greens	Naut'staaq	Naut'staak	Naut'staat
Bull kelp	Nasquluq	Nasquluk	Nasqulut
Kelp	Kapustat; Nuya'it	Kapustat; Nuya'it	Kapustat; Nuya'it
Lily bulb	Laagaq	Laagak	Laagat
Lowbush cranberry	Kenegtaq	Kenegtak	Kenegtat
Red cedar**	Qar'usiq	Qar'usik	Qar'usit
Rockweed	Kahngik	Kahngik	Kahngit
Salmonberries	Alagnaq	Alagnak	Alagnat
Sea lettuce	Kapuustaq	Kapuustak	Kapuustat
Spruce	Napaq	Napak	Napat
Willow	Nimruyaq	Nimruyak	Nimruyat
River Fish—Kuim Unguwallria'i			
Chinook salmon; King salmon	Aamasuuk	Aamasuuk	Aamasuut
Chum salmon; Dog salmon	Alimaq	Alimak	Alimat
Coho salmon; Silver salmon	Qakiiyaq	Qakiiyak	Qakiiyat
Dolly varden	Nanwam Ancia	Nanwam Anciatek	Nanwam Ancii
Pink salmon; Humpy salmon	Amartuq	Amartuk	Amartut
Rainbow trout	Anciq	Ancik	Ancit
Sockeye salmon; Red salmon	Niklliq	Nikllik	Nikllit
Steelhead trout	Mayuwartaq	Mayuwartak	Mayuwartat
Sea Animals—Imam Unguwallria'i			
Dolphin	Mangaq	Mangak	Mangat
Fur seal	Aatak	Aatak	Aatat
Harbor seal	Isuwiq	Isuwik	Isuwit
Killer whale	Arlluk	Arlluk	Arllut
Porpoise	Mangaq	Mangak	Mangat
Sea lion	Wiinaq	Wiinak	Wiinat
Sea otter	Arhnaq	Arhnak	Arhnat
Whale (grey, humpback, minke, sei)	Ar'uq	Ar'uk	Ar'ut
Shellfish—Mamaayaruat			
Blue mussel	Qapilaq	Qapilak	Qapilat
(Butter) Clam	Qahmaquq	Qahmaquk	Qahmaqut
Chiton	Uriitaq	Uriitak	Uriitat
Limpet	Sawak'iitaq	Sawak'iitak	Sawak'iitat
Octopus	Amikuq	Amikuk	Amikut
Sea urchin	Uutuk	Uutuk	Uutut
Snail	Ipuk	Ipuk	Iput

NOTE: This table does not include species introduced to the Kodiak Archipelago in the twentieth century.

*Available in archipelago, but not near Karluk.

**Available as driftwood only.

How the Animals Came to Be Created

A legend collected in Karluk, Alaska, February 7, 1872, by Alphonse Pinart

Translated by Céline Wallace

From the papers of Alphonse Louis Pinart
Hubert Bancroft Library, University of California, Berkeley

There were two Elders on a large strait, living there with a niece. By chance, the niece from Russia became pregnant. And when the time came for her to give birth, they took her into the jupan [side room—from Russian] of their barabara [sod house—from Russian]. After some time, they supposed that the birth had taken place and entered the jupan. They found that she had given birth to a sole. They took the animal and threw it immediately into the sea. As soon as they had seized the fish, she gave birth to more animals (fig. 5.2). When the Elders asked her where they came from, she said that she had become pregnant with the питтать.[1] Once she had recovered, she left the old men's place and ran away. She wandered for a long time and finally reached a large river. There she found a large number of animals and finally her husband, Mit'ak.[2] The latter told her that since he could not kill anything for food, they would have to eat their children. After that, they went back to the place where the old men lived. But they did not find anyone there, as they had died. They settled down in this place and lived there.

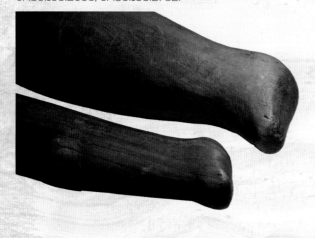

Figure 5.2. Wood tool handles with seal carvings. UA85.193:2556, UA85.193:2762.

Karluk One villagers had a commanding view of Shelikof Strait. On a clear day the snow-topped mountains of the Alaska Peninsula are visible from this spot, about 37 km (20 mi) to the west. Although notoriously rough and current riddled, the deep waters of Shelikof Strait are home to a variety of marine mammals. Harbor seals, sea lions, sea otters, porpoises, dolphins, and resident fin whales frequent the strait, and fur seals and other whales pass through on their seasonal movements to and from the Bering Sea. Cow-calf pairs hug the shoreline, bringing grey, minke, and humpback whales within reach. From Karluk One, sea mammals can be both spotted and heard as they surface to breath. Closer to the shore lie kelp beds, thick forests of marine plants that shelter black bass, cod, and halibut, fish that move shoreward in spring and entice sea mammals to feed.

In contrast with the ocean, Karluk One residents found relatively little on local beaches. The surf continuously reworks the narrow cobble-covered coast of southwestern Kodiak. Few places along this active shore harbor shellfish, although waves deliver valuable kelp and driftwood, and the brackish lagoons have modest populations of clams and mussels (Jordan 1983: Plate 1). Behind the beaches rise precipitous cliffs. Towering walls of Kodiak granite form the headlands flanking the entrance to the Karluk River valley and provide shelter to hundreds of marine birds (fig. 5.3). Glaucous-winged gulls, pigeon guillemots, and both tufted and horned puffins nest in rocky crevices, with different species found predictably at different heights above

the shore (Sowls et al. 1978: Map 35). Bald eagles also frequent these cliffs.

Moving inland, Karluk residents encountered a thickly vegetated landscape (fig. 5.4). In the Kodiak Archipelago, wet soils and long summer days encourage rapid plant growth. Filled with grasses, herbs, and shrubs, Karluk's low, rolling mountains are brilliantly green in the summer and difficult to hike. The plants they hold are those common to the Pacific coast of Alaska. Stands of cottonwood and black birch grow on the hillside of the nearby Sturgeon River valley and flank portions of Karluk River and Lake. Alder, willow, elderberry, and salmonberry brush thrive along terraces at lower elevations and choke the courses of fresh water seeps draining the hillsides. Grasses,

Figure 5.3. Cliffs facing Shelikof Strait and flanking the entrance to the Karluk River, 1987. Bryn Mawr College Archaeological Project, Alutiiq Museum archives, AM278:172. Photograph by Rick Knecht.

Figure 5.4. Panoramic view of the lower Karluk River Valley, spring 2010. Alutiiq Museum archives, AM620. Photograph by Patrick Saltonstall.

ferns, and herbs surround the tall brush, forming dense, waist-high meadows. On the hillsides, thickets give way to tundra muskeg and subalpine meadows with low brush and easier walking.

Studies of plant pollen from the Karluk and the neighboring Sturgeon River valleys suggest that the composition of plant communities on southwestern Kodiak Island has been stable for roughly four thousand five hundred years (Heusser 1960:178; Nelson and Jordan 1988). As such, the modern vegetation of Karluk resembles the vegetation present when people lived at Karluk One. In this landscape, the residents of Karluk One harvested a wealth of foods and raw materials—fibers for weaving; fuel for fires; wood for carving and construction; roots, greens, and berries to eat; and plants with medicinal qualities (Gideon 1989:52–53; Russell 1991).

Karluk's meadows and hillsides also shelter mammals and game birds. Although the introduction of wild game species to Kodiak in the twentieth century expanded the animals available to rural communities (Tennessen 2010), Kodiak was home to just seven land mammals in late prehistoric times: brown bear, ermine, river otter, red fox, ground squirrel, northern vole, and little brown bat (Clark 2010; Rausch 1969). As such, bears were the only large land mammal and one of the few local sources of large hides. Bears are known to den in the hills surrounding the Karluk River valley and are particularly common along the upper stretches of the river and the shores of Karluk Lake. As bears and people use many of the same resources, Karluk One residents likely encountered them in berry patches, beside salmon streams, and along habitually used trails (fig. 5.5). Maps of bear sightings around Karluk Lake (Troyer 1962) resemble maps of prehistoric site locations (Jordan and Knecht 1988) and reflect mutual use of salmon. Habitual behavior and habitat overlap made these animals easy to locate and perhaps even hard to avoid. Nearby Karluk

Lake has one of the highest recorded densities of brown bears in the world, with forty bears per 100 km² (Barnes and Smith 1995). Karluk bears also have a reputation for their size. The world-record Alaskan Brown Bear was taken in the Karluk Lake area (Dodge 2004:297) (fig. 5.6).

Fur-bearers are also predictable in their movements, and fox, river otter, and ermine were likely intercepted at regularly used dens, slides, resting areas, eating sites, and trails throughout the river drainage. Similarly, both rock and willow ptarmigan occur broadly in the valley, with willow ptarmigan in low, wet brushy habitat and rock ptarmigan in the subalpine and alpine meadows. Both varieties disperse in summer but congregate in flocks in wintertime, making them a predictable target for hunters' arrows.

Figure 5.6. Mark Rusk with a large brown bear skull found near Karluk Lake, spring 2009. Alutiiq Museum archives, AM620. Photograph by Patrick Saltonstall.

Figure 5.5. Well-used animal trail along the shore of Karluk Lake, spring 2009. Alutiiq Museum archives, AM620. Photograph by Mark Rusk.

More productive than its land or ocean environments is Karluk's freshwater system. The lagoon, the river, and their headwaters in Karluk Lake are home to an abundance of waterfowl and fish. Ducks, geese, grebes, loons, and swans stage and feed throughout the drainage and are plentiful in fall. The brackish water of the lagoon is also a good place to catch sculpin, saffron cod, and flounder, small marine fish that use the relatively warm, shallow waters as a nursery. The lagoons of southwestern Kodiak are also home to modest quantities of invertebrates particularly blue mussels and clams, although shellfish are largely absent from Karluk Lagoon today (Alaska Department of Fish and Game 1985:519, 531).

Far more productive and predictable are Karluk's massive anadromous fish runs. The

Karluk River is one of Kodiak's most productive salmon streams: a megasystem that supports all five species of Pacific salmon—chinook, pink, sockeye, coho, and chum. This makes the Karluk unusual. Only one other system on Kodiak, the Ayakulik River, has indigenous runs of all five salmon species. This Karluk system is so productive that it self-fertilizes. The bodies of dead salmon decompose, providing essential nutrients for the next generation of fish (Finney et al. 2000).

The magnitude of this resource is hard to imagine, but it represents a nearly inexhaustible supply of food and raw material for the region's animal and human residents. Accounts of the bounty provide some perspective. Fred Roscoe, who visited Karluk in 1895, said, "At the mouth of the river, just before the tide turned to come in, the salmon were packed so thick that a man could have walked across the river on their backs—their backs literally stuck out of the water" (Roscoe 1992:187). In the late 1970s, Nick Alpiak (1983:114) reported, "A few years back there were so many fish in the river at Karluk that people would have a hard time getting around with their skiffs."

Biologists believe the river's salmon runs were well established and increasingly productive six thousand years ago (Misarti 2007). Scientists estimate that the average number of all fish returning to the Karluk River has been between three hundred thousand and two million per year over the last five centuries (Finney 1998:392). Commercial fishing at the river seriously damaged fish runs at the end of the nineteenth century (Barnaby 1944). Tarleton Bean reports that 2.5 million sockeye salmon were harvested in 1888 (two hundred thousand cases with thirty sockeye salmon per case) and 3 million in 1889 (250,000 cases) (Bean 1890:20). Although some of these commercially caught fish were delivered to Karluk canneries from neighboring areas (Porter

1895:72, 79), Karluk salmon were being harvested at an unsustainable rate. Before this activity, more than seven hundred thousand fish returned to the Karluk River annually (Finney 1998:392). Studies of stable oxygen isotopes preserved in cod otoliths recovered from Karluk One indicate that the waters around Kodiak Island cooled notably about five hundred years ago (Foster 2009; West et al. 2011) during an era known as the Little Ice Age. While this cooling probably had an adverse effect on some subsistence resources, it strengthened salmon runs (Finney et al. 2000, 2002). Based on the abundance of salmon bones found in the site, these fish were increasingly important to the village economy (West 2011). The Karluk River had large quantities of salmon, harvested in great amounts by its residents.

The structure of the salmon resource in the Karluk River is important to understand. Different species of salmon are available at different times and in different quantities, influencing the ways that people harvest fish. Moreover, each species uses the river system in a distinct way (table 5.2). For example, chinook salmon arrive in small numbers in the spring. Chinook salmon use the entire river when many fish return but spawn mostly in lower river areas, below the portage to Larsen Bay in years with lower numbers of fish. Chum salmon are a fall arrival, spawning only in Karluk Lagoon in modest numbers. In contrast, huge numbers of coho, pink, and sockeye salmon use the entire watercourse, including Karluk Lake. Pink salmon return predictably in June and July, but the size of runs varies dramatically from year to year. Every other year, the pink run is very large, and only in these years do fish reach Karluk Lake. In low-return years, pink salmon can be found in the lagoon and throughout the course of the lower river. In contrast, sockeye salmon return in two distinct seasonal runs, one in spring and

Table 5.2 Availability of salmon, trout, and char in the Karluk River

SPECIES	AVERAGE QUANTITY	PRESENT	SPAWNING LOCATION
Chinook salmon (king)	2,000 to 15,000	May–September	Whole Karluk River (but in low-return years mostly lower river).
Humpback salmon (pink)	50,000 to 3,000,000	July–October	Entire system but only into lake and tributaries on high-population years. Today, high numbers return on even years—far less on odd-numbered years.
Sockeye salmon (red)	50,000 to 1,500,000	June–December	Karluk Lake outlet, tributaries & beaches. In general, early-run spawn in lake tributaries while late-run spawn in beach gravels and upper river.
Coho salmon (silver)	Not counted, but at least 5,000 to 75,000	September–March	Entire system—but spawning habits and specific locations not studied.
Chum salmon (dog)	Not counted but small population ca. 500 to 5,000	August–October	Karluk Lagoon
Steelhead	500 to 7,000	September–May	Lake and Portage area: October–April River: September–October & April–May
Arctic char		Year round	Entire system—mostly lake
Rainbow trout		Year round	Entire system
Dolly varden trout		August–June	Entire system

NOTE: Table produced with assistance from Matt Foster, Alaska Department of Fish and Game, 2013.

one in fall. Spring-run fish generally spawn in the small streams feeding Karluk Lake, while fall-run sockeye salmon prefer the upper river just below the lake and the small gravel beaches along the lakeshore. Importantly, although the peak season of fish return is from late summer through fall, fish enter the Karluk for months, and live salmon can be found in the lake and river in winter and early spring.

In addition to salmon, the Karluk River supports migrating populations of Dolly Varden and steelhead and resident populations of arctic char and rainbow trout. These fish are available throughout the system, although their season of availability varies (table 5.1). Dolly Varden are absent in the summer months, while steelhead winter in the lake, and rainbow trout and char are present year round. Although they are available in

much smaller quantities than salmon, steelhead, rainbow trout, and arctic char are valuable sources of fresh winter food.

This picture of the Karluk environment illustrates the key importance of fish. Fish are by far the most abundant, predictable resource in the region. They are available in enormous quantities and easy to locate at predictable times of the year. Although the exact timing and size of individual salmon runs varies from year to year, the sheer volume of fish provides a very stable foundation for area economies. Fish have fueled Karluk communities for millennia.

Birds and small furbearers—fox and otter—are also relatively abundant given the reliability of fish for food. Plant resources also abound. By contrast, sea mammals and shellfish are less predictable, less abundant resources. This view of the natural environment matches historic accounts of the goods Karluk residents provided annually to the Russian American Company. These included three hundred thousand dried salmon, two hundred baskets of lily roots, twenty-two barrels of berries (each barrel holding twenty-five buckets), modest amounts (three vats) of whale oil (Gideon 1989:39), three hundred fox and twenty-six river otter, and hundreds of bird skins (enough to make thirty-five parkas, Black 1990).

While the resources found around Karluk are broadly characteristic of the Alaskan Gulf coast and common to other areas of the Kodiak Archipelago, the relative abundance of individual resources, and their availability in space and time, vary. Different regions of Kodiak have unique sets of resources. To better understand the economic opportunities at Karluk One, as well as the potential for trade around the archipelago and beyond, it is useful to consider broader patterns of resource availability. The foods and raw materials available in Karluk reflect both local abundance and scarcity, patterns that residents took advantage of to feed their families and promote trade.

Within the Kodiak Archipelago, there are notable differences in vegetation and the availability of fish and sea mammals. When Karluk One was occupied, the forests of northern Kodiak were developing (Heusser 1960:55). Karluk was not forested, but trees were colonizing Shuyak and Afognak Islands, with spruce, devil's club, and tree mosses advancing from the edge of Alaska's coastal rainforest. Forest resources—wood, bark, root, and sap—were abundant at the northern end of the archipelago but only available to Karluk residents as flotsam (driftwood) or through trade.

Additionally, the east side of the Kodiak Archipelago has a different maritime environment than its western coast. Whales and fur seals migrating past Kodiak move predominantly along the island's eastern coast, then south through the Trinity Islands and on toward the Aleutian Islands. Although some animals pass through Shelikof Strait, the largest, most dependable populations of animals are found in the waters accessible from Chiniak Bay, Sitkalidak Island, and Alitak Bay. In contrast, cod populations are particularly rich along the southern and western coasts of the archipelago, and the largest, most productive salmon streams occur amid the rolling, treeless landscapes of southwestern Kodiak. In short, Karluk One not only lies in an area rich in fish but also enjoys exceptional fish resources in comparison to the archipelago's northern and eastern coasts. Fish are not only a source of food but a resource so abundant that they can be stockpiled and traded.

Farther afield, comparisons of Kodiak with the Alaskan mainland illustrate some of the greatest differences in economic potential. First, Kodiak has a unique geological setting. The archipelago is rich in sedimentary and metamorphic rocks like slate and greywacke, while the neighboring Alaska Peninsula holds valuable deposits of igneous rocks: volcanic scorias, obsidians, and basalts (Raisic 2012; Saltonstall et al. 2012), as well as deposits of cannel coal (Steffian 1992a). Kodiak's hard black slate makes excellent knives, spear points, and lances, while the Alaska Peninsula's volcanic rocks are preferable for flint knapping; its cannel coal can be beautifully shaped and polished into jewelry.

Similarly, the set of land mammals found on the neighboring Alaska and Kenai peninsulas is much larger than that found on Kodiak. Moose, caribou, mountain goat, black bear, wolf, beaver, marmot, and wolverine represent sources of hide, antler, tooth, and hair not available on Kodiak. In contrast, Kodiak's abundant fish and sea mammals are potential trade items. These resources are available on the Pacific coast of the Alaska Peninsula but not in the abundance found on Kodiak.

Karluk's proximity to the Alaska Peninsula also suggests that resources like nonlocal stone, birds, and animal materials were imported from here. Shelikof Strait is just more than 37 km (20 mi) wide at the entrance to nearby Uyak Bay, meaning that southwest Kodiak Island would have had better access to the products of the mainland than many other areas of the archipelago. Historic sources confirm the Kodiak people hiked and paddled great distances to socialize, raid, and trade. People from Karluk walked to Larsen Bay to socialize (Alpiak 1983:116). Larsen Bay residents hiked to the Karluk River in winter, crossing the portage trail on foot and then skating down the frozen river channel to Karluk (Davis 1997a). Residents of southern Kodiak Island describe traveling the length of Kodiak Island to attend a winter festival in Ugak Bay (Holmberg 1985:60). Bolotov (Black 1977:86) reports that prior to the arrival of the Russians, "the Kad'iak inhabitants maintained constant conflict with Unalashka Aleuts and the Americans of the Kenai and Chugach Bays." Gideon (1989:57) notes that communities in different regions of Kodiak traded with different areas of the mainland. Villagers from the northern and western coast of the island traded largely with communities on the neighboring Alaska Peninsula, while those from the southeast coast of Kodiak traded on the Kenai Peninsula and in Prince William Sound. Log books from nineteenth-century trading posts in Katmai and Douglas support Gideon's observation. Alutiiq communities on the Alaska Peninsula document traded with Afognak Island people (Partnow 2001:114).

Whether they traveled to the mainland or welcomed mainland visitors to Kodiak Island, the diversity and common use of nonlocal materials found at Karluk One (see Chapter 4) indicate that villagers had regular access to items from the Alaska Peninsula. Karluk residents likely acted as middlemen in the trade of such products, exchanging some materials from the mainland with residents of Kodiak's eastern coast.

Tough Tools: Bone and Antler Implements from Karluk

Amy V. Margaris, Assistant Professor of Anthropology, Oberlin College

As an archaeologist, I am particularly fascinated by "artifact underdogs"—the everyday objects of bone, wood, and fiber that are seldom preserved in archaeological sites. It was a dream come true when, as a graduate student, I had the opportunity to study Karluk One's exquisitely preserved array of bone and antler tools. Objects of great beauty and practical function, these tools offer insights into past Alutiiq society and spur important questions for future research.

Many of the bone and antler artifacts found at Karluk formed the high-impact "business end" of multipart tools: harpoons for taking marine mammals, arrows for stunning birds, and salmon-fishing harpoons with tips ingeniously designed to hold their prey by piercing and then turning in the wound. Other types of bone tools include woodworking wedges and a variety of pointed implements used for skin sewing and fiber working. Oral and written histories indicate that both men and women conducted tasks with such tools, so it is likely that all Alutiiqs were skilled in crafting objects from bone and antler.

Close inspection of Karluk One artifacts reveals that their makers selected carefully among the available bony materials, including marine mammal, bird, and land mammal bone, choosing certain materials for certain jobs. Karluk residents shaped many wedges from the porous bones of marine mammals and carved nearly all of their salmon harpoon tips from caribou antler. One of my objectives has been to understand why Alutiiqs so consistently matched specific materials to certain tasks.

Figure 5.7. Arrow point made of antler. At 8 cm long, this arrow is an average size. AM193.87:9916

Laboratory tests conducted on the raw materials reveal part of the answer. Both animal bone and antler are more pliant and tough than stone (which ancient Alutiiq people preferred to fashion into other types of tools), and antler in particular is extraordinarily good at withstanding impacts (Margaris 2009). Impact tolerance would be an invaluable quality for tool parts like harpoon tips which, if broken, could mean the loss of prey and a hungry family. Thus, it is no coincidence that Alutiiq toolmakers selected among nature's hardest-wearing materials to create tools that needed to be very durable (fig. 5.7).

The science of materials sheds light on some of the innate qualities of the raw materials found in archaeological sites, which carvers in many cultures have employed for similar purposes. However, the tools found at Karluk One also represent the unique history, culture, and experiences of Alutiiq peoples. After studying this collection, I am left with many new questions about late-prehistoric Alutiiq society: Was it prestigious to own tools crafted from caribou antler, a trade good that was perhaps costly for Karluk residents to obtain? Was there special meaning associated with carving the bones of whales—creatures that were dangerous to capture and laden with spiritual significance? There is much more to learn about Alutiiq views of bone technology.

A curious paradox also accompanies these fascinating artifacts. While they rarely survive in archaeological sites, their fracture-resistant qualities lend bone and antler tools the potential to survive years, even generations, if cared for by human hands. Indeed, while the types of tools described above were certainly utilitarian, many were also beautifully crafted in heirloom fashion. Modern attempts to replicate these and similar tools (e.g., see Stewart 1996) reveal the painstaking work required to carve a precisely barbed harpoon edge or the delicate curve of a fishhook. Thus, when dulled or broken, many of Karluk's organic tools were resharpened or recycled into different tools—in stark contrast with much of today's technology, designed for disposal (fig. 5.8a,b). While the antler and bone instruments recovered from Karluk One were used for a range of everyday tasks, the lessons and inspiration they offer to new generations of students, artists, and scientists make them anything but common.

Figures 5.8a,b. Fish harpoon valve made of antler (bottom), reworked valve of a salmon harpoon made into an arrow point (top). UA85.193:6469, UA83.193:822.

Seasonal Harvesting

According to Uri Lisianski (1814:209), who visited Kodiak in 1804 and 1805, in the summer Alutiiq people hunted, in the winter they feasted, and in the spring they starved. This is an overly simple picture. Historic accounts, including Lisianski's own, provide many additional details on seasonal activities, and scarcity was not always present. Yet, this brief characterization captures Alutiiq life at its most basic. Each Kodiak year has a predictable rhythm, a set of reoccurring

environmental conditions that presented economic opportunities and challenges.

Across the north, changes in weather and daylight drive the cyclical availability of resources. Long summer days and abundant resources give way to dark winter days with poor weather and limited sources of fresh food. Northern peoples expect these changes and prepare for them in a great variety of ways. In the populous village of Karluk One, likely occupied throughout most of the year, residents harvested the wealth of summer foods and preserved them for winter use. Much of

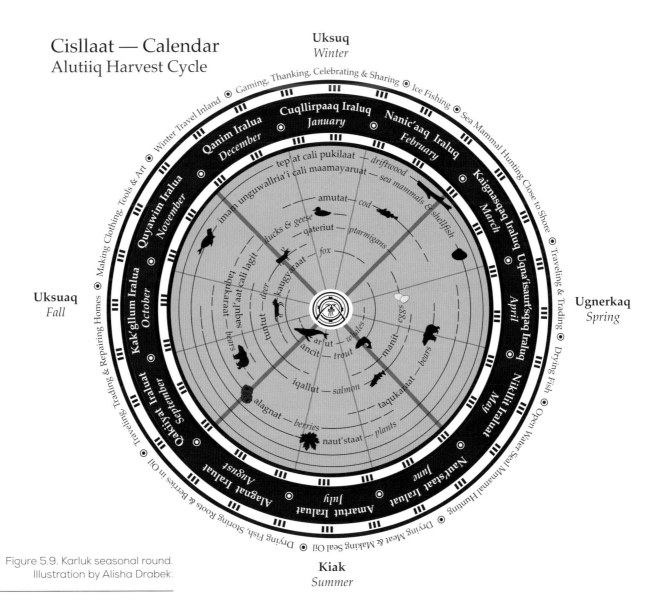

Figure 5.9. Karluk seasonal round.
Illustration by Alisha Drabek.

the village's economic life focused on extending the availability of fish, mammal, and plant foods beyond their season of harvest (fig. 5.9). The following discussion examines the subsistence cycle at Karluk One. It combines information on the availability of local resources, historic accounts of harvesting, evidence of subsistence practices preserved in ethnographic collections, and information from Karluk One artifacts to illustrate the likely yearly activities and show the ingenious ways that residents prepared for predictable changes in the availability of foods and materials. According to Lucille Davis (2000), who was born and raised in Karluk, its villagers "weren't hungry people."

Winter

In Karluk, the economic cycle began in late winter, as residents worked to collect fresh foods following the end of the festival season (see Chapter 7). This was the most difficult time of the year. In the cold months, salmon and trout are present in the Karluk River but in much smaller quantities. Similarly, marine fish and sea mammals disperse, spreading into deeper waters farther from shore. Here, they are harder to locate and retrieve. In late winter months, stormy weather and freezing of the river also limits boat travel and ocean hunting (fig. 5.10). Add to this situation dwindling stores from the previous summer's harvest, and the need for

Figure 5.10. Karluk Lagoon in winter, ca. 1960. Alutiiq Museum archives, Clyda Christiansen collection, AM680:316.

Figure 5.11. Men ice fishing for flounder in Karluk Lagoon, ca. 1955. Alutiiq Museum library. Courtesy Marie Jones.

fresh foods is apparent. At this time, Karluk residents looked to the lagoon, beach, river, and surrounding hillsides for food. While they waited for spring, people likely subsisted on starry flounder, saffron cod, sculpin, old salmon, trout, intertidal foods, ptarmigan, and the occasional cod or seal.

Flounder, a small oily fish, were a sought-after source of late-winter food in Karluk (Davis 1997a; Knagin 2013; Taylor 1965:215). Elder

Larry Matfay, who fished for flounder though the ice in Karluk Lagoon, shared the techniques in an interview (Kelly 1998). After cutting a 45 cm hole in the ice, he would sit and cover himself and the hole with a blanket. This helped him to see the fish in the dark water below. Matfay noted that it was helpful to sit on something for protection from the chill of the ice. Ice fishing required patience. Matfay learned to wait for the fish to swim by the hole, so its head was just under the edge of the ice, before spearing the animal. This kept the fish from seeing him and being spooked. At times, the water was so muddy that Matfay fished by sound. He would listen for flounder swimming under the ice. Two types of spears were used for ice fishing: leisters and lances. Family photographs from Karluk show both men and women ice fishing with lances—pointed sticks—in Karluk Lagoon and illustrate the large number of flounder that could be caught (fig. 5.11). Lucille Davis (1997a) recalled fishing for trout through the ice of Karluk Lagoon, using a bent pin as a hook and a piece of red yarn as bait.

Artifacts from Karluk One indicate that this practice is hundreds of years old. The site produced many wooden shaft fragments, wooden socket pieces, and a variety bone and antler prongs, the parts of effective leisters (fig. 5.12, 5.13). To a wooden shaft, fishermen attached a wooden socket piece, with multiple holes for

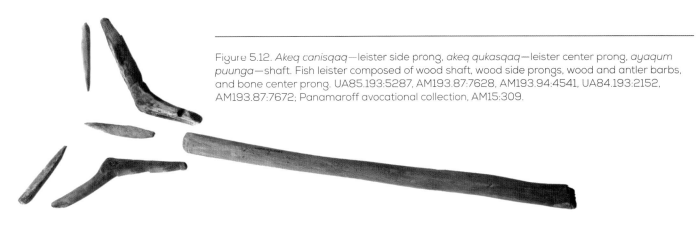

Figure 5.12. *Akeq canisqaq*—leister side prong, *akeq qukasqaq*—leister center prong, *ayaqum puunga*—shaft. Fish leister composed of wood shaft, wood side prongs, wood and antler barbs, and bone center prong. UA85.193:5287, AM193.87:7628, AM193.94:4541, UA84.193:2152, AM193.87:7672; Panamaroff avocational collection, AM15:309.

securing side and center prongs. Some prongs were barbed. Others were fitted at the far end with a small pointed piece of bone or wood that pointed inward. This created a barb that was difficult for a fish to escape.

These complex spears were likely assembled in different ways to form spears for fishing or arrows for bird hunting (Korsun 2012:74–75, 151; Lisianski 1814:Plate 3). The Alutiiq had two different words for fish spears, *kapsuun* and *ayaquq*. One of those words probably referred to a fish leister while the other referred to a toggling fish spear. The fish leister was more likely used when ice fishing. The Alutiiq also have a word for ice fishing—*anlluarluni* (literally, to fish with a spear through ice) (Leer 1976:57).

Small carved fish, about the size of a thumb, may have been used as lures, dangled in the water to draw flounder, cod, or sculpin to a fishing hole (fig. 5.14). Examples from Karluk One are carved of ivory, antler, and bone, and include a small, drilled hole for attaching a line.

On land, Karluk villagers hunted ptarmigan in winter. Alutiiq Elders continue to enjoy this food, which is believed to have medicinal qualities (Mishler 2001:163). However, there are few accounts of harvesting methods. Flocking birds could have been taken with small wooden bows and blunt-headed arrows, speared with bird leisters, or captured in snares. Wooden pegs for securing snares to the ground are common Karluk One artifacts. Snares designed to trap birds' feet, wings, or necks could have been set in the hills, left for several days, and then checked (fig. 5.15). Kodiak Alutiiq people hunted geese in this way (Davydov 1977:227), and the Smithsonian Institution's Fisher collection contains a goose snare with wooden pegs similar to those recovered from Karluk One (Crowell and Laktonen 2001:180).

Ayaquq
Leister

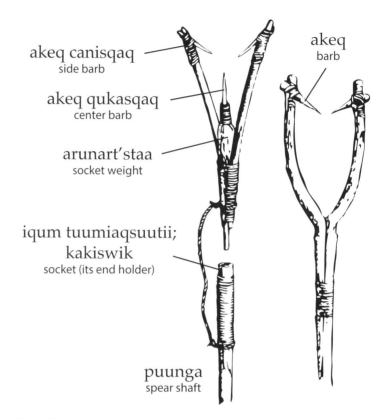

akeq canisqaq
side barb

akeq qukasqaq
center barb

arunart'staa
socket weight

iqum tuumiaqsuutii;
kakiswik
socket (its end holder)

akeq
barb

puunga
spear shaft

Figure 5.13. *Akeq*—leister. Illustration by Alisha Drabek, adapted from Lisianski 1814 and Stewart 1982:74.

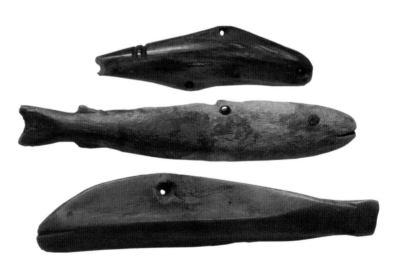

Figure 5.14. *Narya'aq*—fish lure. At just 6 to 8 cm long, these ivory and antler lures are carved with intricate anatomical details. UA85.193:2617, UA85.193:5003, UA85.193:1227.

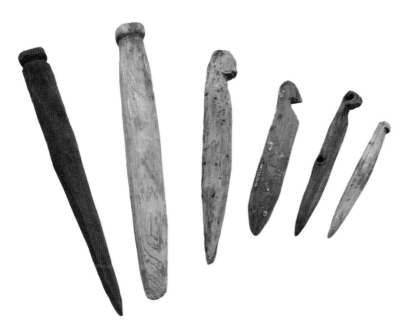

Figure 5.15. *Negam ilakua'a*—snare pin. Snare pins range in size from 10 to 26 cm long. Panamaroff avocational collection, AM15:416; AM193.95:343, AM193.87:10340, AM193.95:16, AM193.94:5160, AM193.95:754.

differ from some of the more robust ethnographically collected specimens identified as mammal-hunting tools and weapons of warfare (Korsun 2012:110–111). The Karluk One examples also lack evidence of backing, strands of animal sinew designed to provide reinforcement common to ethnographic pieces (e.g., Crowell and Laktonen 2001:Figure 169). However, the collection contains a few sinew twisters, a tool used to tighten these reinforcing strands, and a sinew-backed bow was collected in Karluk historically. This piece features a reinforcing cord made from a bundle of ten, braided sinew strings decorated with tuffs of colored thread (Graburn et al. 1996:Plate 118; Heizer 1952:13). As such, Karluk residents used several types of bow.

Recent studies of Alutiiq bowery suggest that distinct styles may reflect regional differences in manufacture or differences in intended prey (Krech 1989:100–101; Lepola 2013). Generally speaking, Alutiiq hunters used at least three different types of bows—sinew-backed recurved bows, long bows, and small bows. Some of these bows were used horizontally rather than vertically, as demonstrated by an Alutiiq hunter painted in 1817 (Korsun 2012:xxviii). This was a technique used in hunting from kayaks. The recurved sinew-backed bows were mostly used for warfare or hunting bears (Korsun 2012:110–111), while other bows were used to hunt seals and birds,

Bow and arrow parts were also common finds at Karluk One. Although these tools were likely employed in a variety of hunting activities, they are lightweight and easy to carry—ideal for pursuing ptarmigan in the uplands. Some Karluk One bows are relatively small: short and slender with diamond-shaped projections at both ends for attaching a string (fig. 5.16). These tools match historic bow descriptions (Davydov 1977:204) but

Figure 5.16. *Qitguyaq*—bow, *ruuwaq*—arrow. Painted bow fragment, bow and arrow. Malutin avocational collection, AM230:1; UA85.193:3693, AM193.94:5230, AM38:492.

often from kayaks. Karluk One's small, lightweight bows seem ideal for bird hunting (fig. 5.16).

No complete arrows were recovered at Karluk One, although the U-shaped nock found at the end of slender shaft fragments identifies these objects in the collection (fig. 5.17). Fragments of the business end of arrow shafts are also present and feature holes for inserting the stem of an arrow (fig. 5.16). Arrow points in the collection include both barbed and unbarbed points with a slender cone-shaped base (fig. 5.18). Many of these are made of flexible antler and show evidence of reworking. The use of unbarbed arrows supports the idea that bows were important for bird hunting. Specifically, blunt, unbarbed arrows are less likely to damage delicate bird skins commonly harvested for use in clothing (fig. 5.19).

The habits of ptarmigan in the Kodiak region are little studied. However, biologists note that their populations tend to fluctuate dramatically, and they are susceptible to overhunting (Alaska Department of Fish and Game 1985). In 1985, Barsh reported that Karluk residents had hunted out the ptarmigan within a 3 km radius of the village. Nick Alpiak (1983), writing about the same time, notes that Karluk hunters would hike into the neighboring Sturgeon River valley to hunt ptarmigan and duck. This information suggests that past hunters traveled widely in the mountainous uplands of the river valley to find ptarmigan.

Winter is the ideal time for hiking on Kodiak Island as swampy areas freeze, the vegetation is less dense, and snow cover can provide an easier surface for walking. In cold years, the Karluk River freezes, providing a highway into Kodiak's interior (Bean 1890:20). Elder Larry Matfay habitually walked between Akhiok and Karluk in winter, crossing more than 74 km (40 mi) of southwest Kodiak Island in the span of about three days. As Matfay notes, no matter what the weather, walking

Figure 5.17. *Ruuwaq*—arrow. Painted arrow shafts with U-shaped nock on proximal end. Arrow shafts taper from round in the center to oval at the proximal or nock end. The longest arrow shaft fragment is just 36 cm long. UA85.193:6402, Sheehan avocational collection, AM38:2701.

Figure 5.18. *Ruuwaq*—arrow. Arrow points have a distinctive tapering conical base that fit snugly into the ends of wooden shafts in the collection. While many have a uniform conical shape, some are oval or square in cross section. A couple were refashioned from salmon-harpoon valves. They range from 5 to 15 cm long. UA85.193:2726, AM193.95:5230; Lind avocational collection, AM14:75; AM193.87:11285, AM14:177.

Figure 5.19. *Ruuwaq*—arrow. At 8 cm long, these blunt wood arrows were designed to stun birds, not to penetrate. This preserved bird skins for use in clothing. UA85.193:6424; Sheehan avocational collection, AM38:59; AM193.94:3128.

Figures 5.20a,b. *Inartaq*—basket. Spruce root basket containing clamshells, top and bottom view. This basket has a unique oval shape constructed differently from other baskets in the collection that feature a circular base. It is similar to an oblong Alutiiq basket collected in Cook Inlet in the eighteenth century (Lee 1981:67). AM193.87:9665.

was always possible (Rostad 1988:88). Snow, wind, and other conditions might keep boats on shore but not hikers from the hills.

Intertidal foods are another type of resource available from land. While Karluk Lagoon holds few shellfish resources, chitons, whelks, periwinkles, and mussels can be collected around rocky headlands between Cape Karluk and Cape Uyak. Similarly, the neighboring Sturgeon River lagoon south of Karluk, as well as Uyak Bay to the north, both have clam and mussel beds where shellfish could have been harvested for use in Karluk. Moses Naumoff, who grew up in Karluk, recalled eating mussels and limpets (Naumoff 1979:91). Larry Matfay and Shorty Azuyak, who

lived in Akhiok, "thought nothing of walking over thirty miles to Halibut Bay to go clam digging" (Rostad 1988:88).

Prehistoric villages site on the upper Karluk River and the shore of Karluk Lake feature shell dumps, deposits of marine shells transported inland for food and discarded. A sample of these from Karluk Lakes includes mussels, surf clams, little neck clams, and butter clams (Morrison 2009). Similarly, shellfish remains were recovered from Karluk One (Amorosi 1987), including a basket filled with clamshells (fig. 5.20a,b). The most likely sources of clams and mussels are the neighboring Sturgeon River lagoon or the Uyak Bay region. Recent subsistence studies suggest that Karluk residents consume shellfish in quantities similar to other Alutiiq villages, despite the fact that they are not immediately abundant (Alaska Department of Fish and Game 1985:519, 531). Karluk residents could have reached Uyak by boat, following the coast of Shelikof Strait north, or they could have paddled or walked up the Karluk River and crossed into Uyak Bay via a short, flat portage trail. It is about 4.5 km from the Karluk River across this passage to the head of Larsen Bay, an arm of larger Uyak Bay. Historically, the portage was an important point of access between the Karluk River area and Uyak Bay, and people commonly moved food, gear, and boats across it (Davis 1997a; Dodge 2004:128, 185; Mulcahy 1986: 64).

In addition to shellfish, villagers gathered octopus, eels, and marine algae (seaweeds) from the rocky coast. One octopus beak found at Karluk One indicates that residents likely probed the surrounding rocky shore for animals hiding in intertidal areas, a widespread practice across Kodiak Island. A long stick with a sharpened or hooked end is an effective tool for pulling animals from their hiding places (Mishler 2001:167). According to

Moses Naumoff (Naumoff 1979:91), "octopus we used to use just a stick to get those things, just take and poke the stick in a hole where the octopus lived until he come out the other side." Although no octopus sticks were specifically identified at Karluk One, the large number of pointed lengths of wood suggests that a variety of artifacts could have been employed in this task.

Marine algae were probably the most important intertidal food as they are abundant, nutritious, and easily harvested. Unlike most intertidal foods, marine algae are a source of carbohydrates (Nobman 1993:3)—an important addition to the high-protein, low-fat foods typical of winter around Kodiak. Today, Alutiiq people primarily harvest rockweed, which is eaten raw. Importantly, people recognize rockweed as a source of food

for those who are lost, stranded, or otherwise in need of emergency food (Russell 1991). Alutiiq people also continue to harvest kelp, which is made into pickles (Alutiiq Museum 2013:11), and sea lettuce.

Winter collecting included harvesting driftwood when powerful storms deliver logs to Kodiak beaches. In 1808, Campbell noted that wood was plentiful in Karluk (Campbell 1816:99). As there are only a few stands of cottonwood, birch, and alder trees near the lagoon today, he was likely referring to driftwood. The abundance of driftwood at Karluk One—used in house construction and the manufacture of numerous household objects—seems to corroborate this observation, as do recent photos of the village, which show piles of driftwood logs (fig. 5.21). In recent times, Karluk

Figure 5.21. Picnickers sit on driftwood logs, Karluk Spit, ca. 1960. Alutiiq Museum archives, Clyda Christiansen collection, AM680:387.

Figure 5.22. *Laakarsuuteq*—digging stick, *mamaayam nuusaa*—clam knife. The few digging sticks in the collection are made of curved pieces of wood and sea mammal bone. They feature a blunt, rounded digging end. Digging sticks were used to harvest a variety of resources, including shellfish and roots. AM38:132, AM193.87:8202, AM193.87.8888, AM193.95:1946, AM19.94:1386.

residents lined up on the shore in winter, watching for wood and claiming individual logs as they appeared in the waves. Logs that landed at a distance from the village were towed home behind boats or formed into rafts and paddled across the lagoon (Russell 1991). When driftwood was not available or winter weather prevented travel beyond the lagoon, villagers harvested mountain alder, and probably willow, from local hillsides (Russell 1991). In ancient times, driftwood was probably more valuable as a material for house building and tool manufacture, and brush a key source of fuel wood.

Collecting from the beach required relatively simple technologies; a container, a digging stick, and a knife to pry open bivalves. Digging sticks from Karluk One are made from sturdy lengths of

wood or sea mammal bone, fashioned to a gentle point (fig. 5.22). Baskets of many sizes are present in the Karluk One collection. These lightweight, durable containers, fitted with woven handles, would have been ideal for carrying shellfish. Narrow, oval knives with thin, rounded tips were common as well (fig. 5.23). People used these implements, carved from wood or sea mammal bone, to open clams or to pry chitons and limpets from rocks. Many feature a tattered edge, the part of the knife used for prying (Knecht 1995:298).

Access and visibility are other important considerations for intertidal collecting. Although shoreline resources are easily harvested, they are

Figure 5.23 *Mamaayam nuusaa*—clam knife. Despite the relative scarcity of shellfish near Karluk One, there are quite a few clam knives in the collection, suggesting that people traveled to harvest this resource. Of the approximately 140 clam knives, ranging from 10 to 20 cm long, 56 display wear on both ends from prying. As with many tools at Karluk One, some of the clam knives were created from other objects—reworked from bentwood vessel bases, kayak parts, and wedges. A few have decorative painting or decorative carving. AM193.95:1946, AM19.94:1386.

not always accessible. Midwinter is actually the most difficult time to harvest shellfish. Minus tides are needed to access lower intertidal species and those that burrow. However, winter's stormy weather alters tidal height, pushing ocean water against the shore. Moreover, the minus tides of winter often coincide with darkness. On clear nights, moonlight and snow can enhance visibility. On cloudy nights, a source of light is helpful. Today, residents of Akhiok and Ouzinkie harvest shellfish by lantern light (Mishler 2001:156; Teacon Simeonoff pers. comm. 1996). Karluk villagers may have carried torches or stone oil lamps when collecting along the beach. Lamps from Karluk One come in many sizes, including small, portable examples (see fig. 6.23).

Though the stormy weather of late winter and early spring makes ocean travel unpredictable, calm days do occur. Karluk hunters would have taken advantage of such weather to launch their kayaks, hunting for seals or fishing for rockfish and cod in near-shore kelp beds. The technologies associated with these activities are described below. However, opportunities for such activities are unpredictable. In some years, the calm weather of spring arrives early, borne by high-pressure systems that disperse storms and permit ocean foraging. In other years, persistent low-pressure systems hurl storms at Kodiak every few days (Wilson and Overland 1986:90), prolonging heavy winds and waves and making boating difficult.

This unpredictability of late winter and early spring weather sometimes led to shortfalls. Russian eyewitnesses repeatedly report late winter as a time of scarcity and even starvation in Alutiiq villages (Davydov 1977:176; Gideon 1989:67; Holmberg 1985:41; Lisianski 1814:195, 202; Sauer 1802:170). In May 1805, Lisianski wrote, "In times of scarcity, which seldom fails to occur in winter, and is almost unavoidable during the spring, the islanders live entirely on shellfish" (1814:209–210). Such historic accounts must be understood in context, however. The horrifying loss of Alutiiq lives, the enslavement of Alutiiq people, and the changes to economic and social systems caused by the Russian conquest of Kodiak contributed significantly to periods of deprivation (Davydov 1977:175; Gideon 1989:66; Pullar 1992). Starvation was common in the historic era. Other classes of archaeological data support the idea that late winter was also a lean time in the more distant past. Archaeological sites filled with shellfish remains, and analyses of clam shells that indicate winter and spring harvesting, show an intense focus on these lean shoreline resources in the cold season (Fitzhugh 1995). Similarly, studies of ancient human skeletal remains from the central Gulf of Alaska provide broad evidence of periodic dietary stress (Lobdell 1980, 1988; Steffian and Simon 1994). Growth-arrest lines and defects in the formation of tooth enamel in men, women, and children suggest that periods of nutritional insufficiency occurred.

For Karluk residents without easy access to substantial shellfish resources, late-returning salmon and trout were likely key winter resources. Karluk Elder Herman Malutin reported to archaeologists studying settlements on the shores of Karluk Lake, "They stayed there all winter, there are fish in that lake in the winter" (Sheehan 1983:51–52). Elder Larry Matfay noted that such fish, like flounder, could be taken through the ice with spears (Kelly 1998). This included aging salmon, wintering steelhead, and other species of trout.

There is a common misconception that salmon are inedible once their bodies begin to decay. Alutiiq Elders report that this is not true (Steffian and Counceller 2012:110). Although the texture of salmon flesh changes as fish deplete their energy stores, these fish are still a good source of food.

Elders report that old fish have a crumbly, white flesh. Their meat contains less oil, but it is very good to eat raw, baked, boiled, or dried. Davydov, a Russian Naval officer who traveled around Kodiak in 1802–1803, noted that "Rotting or, as the local expression goes, bitter fish . . . is more popular in Kad'iak than fresh fish" (1977:174). The presence of such fish, and the relative ease with which they can be harvested, likely made the Karluk region a good place to spend the winter.

Spring

With the lengthening days of spring, men began to spend more time on the ocean in their kayaks. At this time, halibut and cod return to nearshore waters and are easier to catch. Writing in 1854, Finnish mining specialist and naturalist H. J. Holmberg described ocean fishing technology, noting a difference between rigs used for halibut and for cod (1985:47):

> Halibut is caught with the aid of a wooden hook, as with the Tlingits. But the fishing line which is used to catch cod, found throughout the year around Kodiak, also deserves mention here. It consists of two

un-evenly long bones, which are tied together with whale sinews to form an angle of 45 degrees. The longer piece is connected by a foot-long rope with one end of a stick, on the other end of which is tied a similar length of rope containing a weight (usually a roundstone). The fishing line is tied at the middle of the stick. The whole apparatus is let down 50 to 60 fathoms until the weight touched the bottom of the sea. When the hungry cod tries to devour the baited line, it naturally gets caught on the protruding barbed hook and pulls on the line so that the weight lifts every time, thereby showing the Koniag in the boat that a fish has taken his bait.

Artifacts from Karluk One include pieces of cod-fishing gear that closely resemble Holmberg's description. These rigs have two-piece fish hooks made from a small, single-barbed hook and a curved shank designed to be lashed together (see Korsun 2012: Figure 224). There are also rig spreaders (long slender pieces of wood from which the hooks were suspended), snoods (line enforcers of baleen and wood that kept lines from

Figure 5.24. *Canamasqaq*—rig spreader, *kicauteq*—line weight, *iqsam ilakua'a*—fishhook shank, *iqsam iqua*—fishhook barb. Ocean fishing rig assembled with Karluk artifacts and artificial sinew. For procuring ocean-dwelling bottom-feeding fish, such as halibut and cod, Alutiiq fishermen tied barbed hooks to rig spreaders fitted with line weights. In 1890, Mont Hawthorne, a cannery worker in Karluk, recalled watching people fish with such tools: "I used to stand up there on the point above Karluk when we were waiting for the bark 11 *Hope* [small sailing ship] to take us out for the winter and I'd watch the Indians fishing out there on the Shelikof Strait. The wind was sweeping down on them from Cook's Inlet and the spray was splashing clean over their boats and still they seemed so much more at home than they did when they got back on the island" (McKeown 1948:59–60). Sheehan avocational collection, AM231:63; Hochmuth avocational collection, AM240:6; AM193.87:8075, UA85193:2826, UA85.193:2352, AM193.94:26.

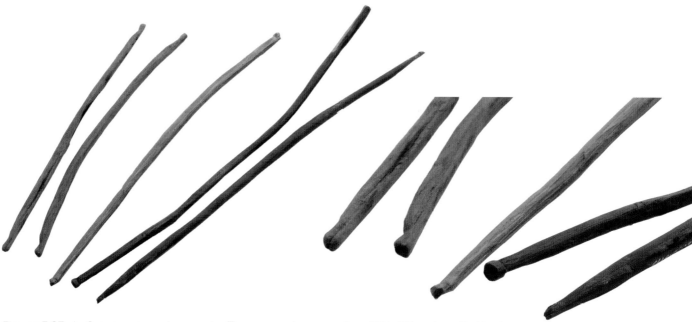

Figures 5.25a,b. *Canamasqaq*—rig spreader. These spreaders range from 20 to 36 cm long. End knobs occur on a variety of artifact types, including snoods, fishhook shanks, leister side prongs, composite ulu handles, tool handles, mask parts, and vessel handles. The types of knob ends vary throughout the Karluk One collection, but there are five basic forms: full knob—a groove goes all the way around to make a full knob (like a door knob); half-knob—the knob protrudes on top side, other side is flat; flat-knob—end of knobs are flat or blunt instead of rounded; two-notch knob—a notch on either side of a rounded shaft; step-knob—vessel handles occasionally have a knob end that is stepped (the bottom is lower so that the handle rises away from the vessel). UA85.193:5793, AM193.94:4182, UA85.193:6759, AM193.94:5316, UA85.193:5262.

Figure 5.26. *Iᴙafkum kupuraa*—snood. There are just fifteen examples of this type of tapering wood fishing rig component. They were used to reinforce the line and to keep different parts of the rig from tangling. Karluk One snoods range from 15 to 31 cm long. AM193.95:1304; Panamaroff avocational collection, AM15:616; UA85.193:4240, AM193.87:8407.

Figure 5.27. *Iᴙafkum tuumiaqsuutii*—line leader. The only line leader in the collection, made of baleen, is 18 cm long. One end has been bent while the other has a tiny knob for attachment. Like a snood, this leader would have protected fishing lines from sharp teeth and rocks. AM193.94:3225.

Figure 5.28. *Iqsam ilakua'a*—fishhook shank, *iqsam iqua*—fishhook barb. Fishhook parts—large fishhook shank and barb, various barb styles, and shanks. Made of wood or bone, fishhook barbs range from 5 to 10 cm long, and shanks range from 6 to 24 cm long. To make a complete hook, craftsmen tie a barb to the shank. Some shanks are curved while others are straight. Curved shanks were often manufactured from animal ribs or curved braches. In both cases, craftsmen took advantage of the natural shape of the material in manufacturing a hook shank. Shanks typically feature a knob at the top for attaching a line and a small carved recess at the other end in which to seat the barb for lashing. AM193.95:1511, AM193.87:9357, UA85.193:5035, UA85.193:5531, AM193.87:8182, AM193.95:1137, UA84.193:1131, AM193.87:9216.

Figure 5.29. *Kicauteq*—line weight. Pecked into granite cobbles, shallow grooves help secure a line to the weight. The groove often circles the length of the weight, but sometimes a second groove pecked around the width of the tool forms a set of *T*-shaped grooves. These weights range from 400 to 800 gm. Karluk School avocational collection, AM39:235; AM193.95:162; Sheehan avocational collection, AM38:29.

Figure 5.30. *Kicauteq*—line weight, *iRafkuq*—lashing. The grooved cobble and spruce root lashing pictured here were found separately. However, they are nearly identical to an example of a lashed line weight collected from Kodiak in the nineteenth century (Korsun 2012:156). Karluk school avocational collection, AM39:238; UA85.193:4522.

tangling), and granite cobbles for weighting gear to the ocean floor (fig. 5.24–5.30; Birket-Smith 1941:Figure 23). These cobbles feature hand-pecked grooves designed to help secure a line. One example from Karluk has a thin strip of kelp or bark wrapped around the groove to keep the line from rubbing against the stone (fig. 5.29).

A small number of hook pieces feature straight shanks and unbarbed pointed hooks. It is possible that different hook styles were designed for different types of fish, as suggested by the quote above from Holmberg (fig. 5.28). Historically, Alutiiq people are known to have fished for halibut with V-shaped hooks similar to ornately carved specimens made by Tlingit fishermen in southeast Alaska (Alutiiq Museum 2013:20; Birket-Smith 1941:147; Crowell and Laktonen 2001:177; Petrof 1884:233). Karluk One produced no hook components of this type, suggesting that V-shaped hooks may be a historic introduction. Composite rigs, perhaps with hooks styled for specific species, were the primary tools for capturing marine fish at Karluk.

To lower their gear to the ocean floor, Alutiiq fishermen fashioned lines from baleen (Billings in Merck 1980:207) or partially dried lengths of bull kelp, some long enough to reach depths of 70 m (Golder 1903a:20; Shelikhov 1981:54). People preferred kelp line to sinew line. Kelp was stronger than sinew when wet, less apt to stretch and break under the weight of a struggling fish (Lisianski 1814:206). An example of a Kodiak Alutiiq fishing assembly, complete with kelp line, is part of the collections of the Kunstkamera, the Russian Museum of Anthropology and Ethnography. Notes collected with the piece indicate that

people prepared kelp lines by soaking the kelp in fresh water then drying it in the sun or over a fire (Korsun 2012:156).

A club was another essential piece of fishing gear. Fishermen used small, wooden billies, about the length of their forearms, to dispatch struggling fish (fig. 5.31). A strike to the nose killed a hooked fish before it was pulled into a skin boat, and if well directed, left the head intact for eating (Davydov 1977:172). An Alutiiq-style kayak model in the British Museum's Lonsdale collection shows a kayaker in the act of clubbing a fish (Krech 1989:Figure 47, Model 184).

Figure 5.31. *Piqrutaq*—stunning club. Alutiiq people used clubs to dispatch fish caught on a hook, as well as small game trapped in a snare. Many tools from Karluk One have a decorated or stylized end. A few clubs, like the example pictured here, have animal carvings on the ends. Stunning clubs from the site range from 35 to 40 cm long. AM193.M:791.

Learning from Fish Bones

Catherine F. West, Research Assistant Professor, Boston University

Among the houses, artifacts, and animal remains at the Karluk One site were tens of thousands of beautifully preserved fish bones (fig. 5.32). I learned to be a zooarchaeologist by sifting, sorting, and identifying these fish remains. This long process gave me hours to think about what the bones could reveal. In the garbage from hundreds of fish dinners lay information about how past residents of Karluk One harvested food, and I just needed to decode it. People living at the site were uniquely situated to harvest fish from both the deep ocean waters of the Shelikof Strait and from the fresh waters of Karluk River. As I looked through the remarkably preserved fish bones, I wanted to know what types of fish people were eating and if there were changes in harvesting patterns over time. Kodiak's region is known to have cooled and warmed during the last five hundred years, during the time the site was occupied. Did these climate changes affect fishing around Karluk One?

When I examined the site's fish bones, I found that people were fishing in the ocean for Pacific cod, Pacific halibut, greenling, Irish Lord, starry flounder, and even the occasional salmon shark! From the rivers, they harvested huge numbers of Pacific salmon. Like today, salmon were a major source of food at

Figure 5.32. Exceptionally well preserved fish bones uncovered on the floor of a house, Karluk One, 1984. Alutiiq Museum archives, AM193:62.S.

Karluk and the most abundant fish in the archaeological record (Foster 2009). The ethnographic record and artifacts from the Karluk One site tell us that, much like today, salmon were pulled from the river using nets and weirs; they were fileted, then dried or smoked for winter storage to feed the village (Knecht 1995). This information was not surprising, but there was also a bigger story.

Some fish bones can also record the temperature of the ocean. As Pacific cod grow, they record water temperatures in the chemical composition of their otoliths or "ear bones." Like a tree, otoliths grow rings each year the fish lives. When the temperature turns cold, the rings contain more heavy oxygen atoms; when the temperature becomes warm, the rings contain more light oxygen atoms. When I analyzed the otoliths from Karluk One (West et al. 2011), the oxygen record told me that cod experienced periods of both colder and warmer temperatures during the last five hundred years. But how did this affect Karluk residents? Did changing ocean conditions alter the fish available and did people have to adjust their fishing?

A close examination of the different kinds of fish found in each layer of the site showed that when people first settled at Karluk One about five hundred years ago they were harvesting equal numbers of cod and salmon. However, as time passed, they began to harvest more and more salmon, until salmon almost completely dominated the fish remains. By the time Russian traders arrived in the eighteenth century, more than 80 percent of the remains were from salmon. Because the Pacific cod otoliths recorded variable climate conditions while people were living at Karluk, I expected that the change in fishing activity through time would reflect changing climate. However, in answer to my question, I found that variable climate conditions during the last five hundred years could not explain which fish people harvested—there was little relationship between climate conditions and the increase in salmon fishing. Instead, the Alutiiq people at Karluk likely focused on salmon to provide reliable food for the large village. They were creating winter stores for a growing population and perhaps building a commodity for trade (Foster 2009).

The spectacular preservation at the Karluk One site provides a rare, direct glimpse into the past subsistence practices of Alutiiq people through the animal bones they discarded, as well as their resilience amid changing climate conditions in the Gulf of Alaska.

Spring is an excellent time to hunt sea mammals around Karluk. Seals and sea lions return from the open ocean to rookeries for the pupping and breeding. Whales begin to pass through Shelikof Strait on their annual migrations west. This brings animals close to shore and on land in predictable locations. Harbor seals are probably the most commonly pursued sea mammals along the southwestern coast of Kodiak, as they range broadly, enter lagoons in search of fish, and rest on the area's long cobble beaches. In contrast, sea lions have no known rookeries in the area. Karluk hunters likely pursued these larger, coveted animals at sporadically used haul-out locations, perhaps on the rocky shoals of nearby capes. Joseph Billings, who visited Kodiak between 1790 and 1792, recorded that seal hunting around southern Kodiak Island began as early as February and continued until April (see Korsun 2012:58). Billings may be referring to open ocean hunting of fur seals, a practice recorded in animal remains preserved in archaeological deposits from eastern Kodiak (Clark 1986; Etnier 2011), Larsen Bay (Hrdlička 1944:478), and Karluk Lagoon (Amorosi 1986). As fur seals are typically found in deep ocean waters off Kodiak's eastern coast, however, they were not likely accessible in reliable numbers to the residents of Karluk.

Seals and sea lions provided both meat and fat and were an essential source of large hides for making boat covers (Davydov 1977:221). Alutiiq hunters pursued these animals in the water and on land. Historic sources indicate that hunters used harpoons and clubs to harvest animals resting on the shore (Lisianski 1814:205). Gideon describes seal hunting with decoys (1989:56–57). Hunters placed an inflated sealskin on the shore, hid behind it, and made seal calls. This attracted animals, which were speared or harpooned as they approached. Hunters wore wooden helmets carved

Figure 5.33. *Qayangcuk*—kayak carving, *suaruangcuk*—kayak figurine. Detail of miniature bark kayak with bark figurine wearing a seal decoy helmet. The small boats were probably children's toys. "From their very early years the children begin building baidarkas and launching them" (Davydov 1977:164). AM193.87:9360.

with the face of a seal for this activity (Black 1991:23). Although no seal helmets were found at Karluk One, a small bark figurine designed to fit in a model boat, features a paddler wearing a seal decoy helmet (fig. 5.33).

Nets were also employed in seal and sea lion hunting. Men stretched nets across the entrances to narrow bays to capture sea lions (Davydov 1977:220). The ends of the net were held in kayaks, which were sometimes dragged a long ways by entrapped animals. Gideon (1989:56) describes hunters stretching nets in the water near sleeping seals. The nets featured wooden floats and stone sinkers designed to keep the mesh open in the water. The hunters would then startle the seals, causing them to rush for the water and become tangled in the net. Billings collected one such net on Kodiak (Korsun 2012:158). It included slender wooden pegs for anchoring the net and mesh tied from sinew. While netting is rare in the Karluk One collection, floats carved of bark and wood and sinkers made from palm-size beach cobbles of greywacke illustrate the presence of these tools (fig. 5.67–5.70). The collection also includes wooden stakes that could have been used in securing nets in a variety of settings.

At other times, seals, seal lions, porpoises, and dolphins were harpooned from kayaks (Davydov 1977:220; Merck 1980:105). Hunters hurled harpoons at animals, often using throwing boards or bows, chasing them as they attempted to escape and propelling additional harpoons each time they surfaced to breathe. When the animal became exhausted and could no longer evade the hunter, it was dispatched with a spear. Model kayaks in museum collections show sets of ocean hunting gear tied to boat decks, illustrating the suite of common tools and their assembly (Korsun 2012:151, Plate 188–198). These include a bow, arrows, at least two varieties of harpoons (barbed and toggling), extra harpoon shafts, and leisters.

Holmberg (1985) describes six types of Alutiiq sea mammal hunting implements, and Lisianski (1814) depicts five, omitting whaling lances. The array of harpoons, lances, darts, and arrows the Alutiiq used to hunt sea mammals is impressive. Alutiiq sea mammal hunting technology is highly specialized with a different set up for every animal or situation a hunter might encounter. And, yet, due to its composite nature, the gear is also versatile. By simply switching projectile points, a single shaft could be used for multiple species. In general, the Alutiiq used arrows for shooting smaller, quicker game like sea otters, weapons propelled by throwing boards for medium-size game and whales, and hand-thrown or -thrust lances for the seals and sea lions. However, there was a lot of variability in hunting technique. For example, both bows and throwing boards were used to project bird leisters. While the situation and animal pursued often warranted a particular type of weaponry, weapon choice also depended on the hunter's particular preference.

The primary type of harpoon points from Karluk One is a stationary barbed point, also known as a non-toggling harpoon (fig. 5.34). Most are carved of antler, although there are a few bone examples, and at least three are carved of wood. These points are always unilaterally barbed, meaning they feature barbs on one edge of the point. The number of barbs varies from one to four, but they always fall in a single line along one edge of the weapon.

Village hunters also used toggling harpoons, likely for pursuing seals. A small, sleek, triangular-shaped weapon, toggling harpoon points were designed to pierce the skin of an animal and then turn sideways in the wound as the animal struggled. This helped to ensure that the harpoon stayed in place. This style is rare at Karluk One. In general, toggling harpoons are not common

Figure 5.34. *Qalugyaq*—non-toggling harpoon point. Non-toggling harpoon points and a composite wood socket. The principal type of harpoon point from Karluk One is a unilaterally barbed, non-toggling style made of antler. These projectiles have from one to four barbs. Often, the harpoon point was tied to a socket piece through a line hole near the point's base. Complete examples of these projectiles range from 4.5 to 20 cm long. AM193.95:504, AM193.87:9255, AM193.87:8639, AM193.87:10997.

Figure 5.35. *Paiktuq*—toggling harpoon point. Made of antler and sea mammal bone, this style of harpoon is rare in the Karluk One collection. Of ten likely examples, two have an end slot, an opening at the tip designed to hold a slate blade. Two varieties are shown here. The example at the top of the photo has a barbed tip. The specimen in the middle is made of antler. It is short because it has been reworked, carved to reform the end. Lind avocational collection, AM14:343; UA85.193:4846; Karluk School avocational collection, AM39:152.

in late prehistoric sites or ethnographic collections from Kodiak (Knecht 1995:222; Korsun 2012:66). There are just seven in the Karluk One collection, and only two are complete (fig. 5.35). This is a very small number, even in comparison to other sites of this age.

Both types of points were part of ingenious harpoon assemblies, complex tools expertly designed to kill and retrieve sea mammals. Karluk One included many parts of these assemblies (fig. 5.36). The site's stationary barbed harpoons sat in socket pieces. Conical bone sockets feature an oval opening on the top, into which the wedge-shaped base of the harpoon point fit. The bottom of the socket piece was split, carved like an old fashioned clothespin, for lashing to a wooden shaft (fig. 5.37). At Karluk One, wood socket pieces are present also. Composite wood sockets come in two sizes—short and long. Short examples are stepped on one side for tying together. The other side is scarfed, probably to secure the socket piece to its wooden shaft (fig. 5.38). Long slender single-piece wood sockets have oval openings with tapered proximal ends (fig. 5.39).

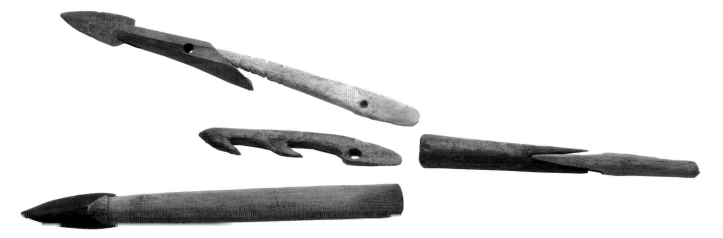

Figure 5.36. Montage of harpoon types. There are multiple ways a harpoon can be assembled. *Left*, shaft fragment with a sea mammal bone socket piece; *top*, a foreshaft and toggling harpoon with a slate-end blade tip; *center*, a non-toggling harpoon made of antler; *center and bottom*, a wood socket with an end blade. Lind avocational collection AM14:260; AM193.87:19070; Panamaroff avocational collection, AM15:594; UA87.193:9256; Lind avocational collection, AM14:257; AM193.95:1174; Panamaroff avocational collection, AM15:340; AM193.95:209.

Figure 5.37. *Ayaqum arunart'staa*—harpoon socket piece. A central part of harpoon assemblies, these heavy sea mammal bone socket pieces acted as a weight for harpoons and connect the weapon's different parts. At the far end of the socket, hunters inserted a barbed harpoon point (non-toggling), fitting the base of the point into an oval opening in the top of the socket. Then, they used small slivers of bone, wood, or skin to shim the base and create a tight fit. Similar bushings are seen in historic Kodiak Alutiiq sea otter darts (Heizer 1952:13). The opposite ends of socket pieces are bifurcated, split like a clothespin to fit the end of a double-scarfed wood shaft. The socket and the shaft were lashed together. Complete examples of these sockets range from 4.5 to 19 cm long. AM193.95:340, AM193.87:9479.

Figure 5.38. Two-piece wood socket pieces. Some socket pieces have two parts, designed to fit around the base of a point and be lashed together. Many are notched and scarfed on one end to assist in attaching the socket to a shaft. These types of sockets range from just 3 cm to more than 30 cm long. AM193.87:8481, AM193.87:9795, AM193.87:9796, UA85.193:6711, AM193.94:993; Sheehan avocational collection, AM38:1043.

Figure 5.39. Wood socket pieces. This style of wood socket piece featured an oval socket and a tapered end. Wood socket pieces range from 8 cm to more than 30 cm long and are most often ovoid, unlike their bone counterparts, which are round. UA85.193:4223, AM193.94:1506, AM193.87:8432.

Toggling harpoon points had one additional piece of gear, a foreshaft that suspended the point above the socket. Toggling harpoon points feature a small indentation in their base. The point of a wooden foreshaft fit into this hole, supporting the point. The foreshaft, with its wedge-shaped base, then sat in the socket piece. In these assemblies, both the foreshaft and the harpoon head had a hole for a line securing them to the harpoon shaft (Korsun 2012:66) (fig. 5.40).

When a hunter impaled an animal, harpoon assembly pieces below the point fell away but remained attached to each other, and thus his prey. These parts of the weapon acted as both a drag on the animal and a flag for the hunter. The animal pulled the pieces through the water, slowing it down and showing the hunter its location. An air-filled float, made from an animal's bladder and tied to the harpoon shaft, aided this process (Korsun 2012:91). A nozzle was used to let air in and out of such a float.

Karluk One contained more than eight hundred shaft fragments of varying sizes and widths and with round and oval cross sections. It is difficult to identify the types of weaponry these fragments represent. There are size and shape groupings within this class of objects, but extensive additional research is needed to better understand these groups. Generally speaking, however, shafts were made with great care. They are remarkably straight, consistent in diameter, and nicely finished. In fashioning an arrow, harpoon, leister, or lance shaft, craftsmen worked to create a highly uniform piece, and thus a well-balanced weapon (fig. 5.41). To some shafts, craftsmen tied finger rests, triangular wedges of bone, antler, or ivory that helped the hunter grip his harpoon (fig. 5.42).

Throwing boards helped hunters propel their harpoons, as well as a variety of intricately designed darts. Throwing from a kayak bobbing in the ocean requires a great deal of skill. Hunters improved the speed, force, and distance of their throws by using throwing boards. This device was about the length of a man's forearm and carved of wood. It had a handgrip on one end, a long central body with a groove for a harpoon shaft, and a small hook at the far end. A hunter laid a

Figure 5.40. *Ayaqum pegsuutii*—foreshaft, *paiktuq*—toggling harpoon point. There are a variety of foreshaft types. All have a squared-off base designed to fit into a socket piece at the end of a shaft. The other end of the foreshaft tapers to a point and is designed to fit into the base of a toggling harpoon point. Other foreshafts act as their own point and are often slotted to hold an endblade. The purpose of a foreshaft is to both facilitate the release of a toggling harpoon point and to provide an easily replaced segment at the end of a dart or spear, the part of the weapon most commonly damaged in use. Wood foreshafts, such as the ones pictured here, range from 8 cm to 25 cm long, while those made of antler and sea mammal bone range from just 5 cm to 23 cm long. AM193.87:11108, AM193.94:250; Karluk School avocational collection, AM39:152; Panamaroff avocational collection, AM15:407.

Figure 5.41. *Ayaqum puunga*—shaft. In assembling a harpoon, craftsmen created scarfs, carving designed to join pieces together. There are several possible reasons for scarfing. First, a craftsman doesn't have to have a single long piece of material to create a tool, but can join short or even or even broken pieces. Scarfing also adds flexibility to a projectile, helping the implement absorb the force of an impact. There are different types of scarfing in the Karluk One collections. The middle piece shown here features a step-scarf. In contrast, the top piece is double scarfed, or scarfed on both sides. The pieces of a scarfed joint were fitted together and then lashed to secure them. For example, the scarfed object pictured second from bottom retains a spruce root wrapping. Other materials, such as baleen, were also used to lash scarfed joints. AM193.94:4492, UA85.193:5844, AM193.87:8763, AM193.87:11898, UA85.193:2795.

Figure 5.42. *Suawik*—harpoon finger rest. Carved of bone, ivory, and antler, these pieces were made to fit a hunter's finger and lashed to a harpoon shaft to aid the hunter's grip when throwing the weapon. AM193.94:3919, AM193.95:771; Panamaroff avocational collection AM15:331.

harpoon in the thrower and then held the complete assembly behind his shoulder. When ready to throw, he simply swung his arm forward and snapped his wrist to launch the harpoon. The leverage provided by the thrower acted as an extension of the hunter's arm, creating a faster, more powerful throw. Karluk One produced a number of throwing board pieces and one complete board (fig. 5.43a,b).

This object is about 45 cm long and made of wood. The grip at the base is carved to fit the individual thrower's hand with a deep hole above the handle at the back for the pointer finger, as demonstrated by an Afognak Island Elder in an 1818

Figures 5.43a,b. *Nuqaq*—throwing board. From kayaks to clothing, a hunter's gear was design to fit his unique proportions. This complete throwing board is 46 cm long and made of wood, with an ivory pin and a bone or antler finger peg. On this peg, the board's user rested his index finger. His thumb and three other fingers wrapped around the board's handle. UA85.193:2814, UA85.193:4722.

Figure 5.44. *Nuqam kuuliangcua*—throwing board pin. Like this example, the pins in Kodiak Alutiiq throwing boards are most often made of ivory (Korsun 2012:84). Inset at the back end of the board, the pin rested at the end of a long narrow groove designed to hold a dart shaft. The pin fit snugly into the indentation on the end of the dart, stabilizing it for throwing (see Figure 5.46). UA85.193:2814.

watercolor (Korsun 2012:xxvi). Alutiiq throwing boards are typically round or triangular shaped in cross section (Korsun 2012:76–84), as compared to Unangan throwing boards, which are flat and boardlike. While most of the Karluk One specimens are of the triangular Alutiiq shape, the collection contains one fragment of a flatter, Unangan-style throwing board. Additionally, a number of the shaft fragments from Karluk One feature a dimpled end designed to link with a throwing board pin (fig. 5.44 – 5.46).

Figure 5.46. *Ayaqum nullua*—dart butt. Detail of painted dart butt. The dimpled end of the dart butts fits into the pin at the end of a throwing board to prevent the dart from slipping. UA85.193:2834.

Figure 5.45. *Ayaqum nullua*—dart butt. Carved from wood, many dart butts have a stepped-scarf joint for attachment to a shaft. Most are about 10 cm long. UA85.193:6143, AM193.95:1419, AM193.94:1796.

Figure 5.47. *Takesqat iquit*—ground lances. Eight cm long, these projectile points have a medial ridge and a rectangular stem. These slate points likely tipped wooden handles, forming lances for dispatching wounded sea mammals. UA85.193:3805, UA85.193:6521, AM193.87:10672.

Figure 5.48. *Amit neng'rsuutait*—work board (with painted sea otter). Just 15 cm long, this miniature work board is made from wood and painted with red pigment. The painting shows air bubbles flowing off the otter's coat, one of the signs hunters used to follow otters as they moved underwater. Marks on the back of the board suggest it was used as a cutting surface. AM193.87:19087.

Figure 5.49. *Qalugyaq*—dart. Darts like these bilaterally barbed pieces were used to hunt sea otters (Korsun 2012:60–72). A line was attached to the bottom of the dart and tied to the dart shaft. The dart was then inset into a socket piece at the end of a shaft. Once separated from the spear shaft, the dart remained attached to the line and shaft, helping the hunter to retrieve the animal. Made of bone and antler, these darts are uniformly about 5.5 cm long. UA85.193:3335.

Figure 5.50. *Mallarsuuteq*—wound plug. These wooden plugs filled the wound created by a hunter's weapon, retaining the animal's blood for later use. The holes in the end of the plugs indicate that hunters kept a set of these tools on a string. The wound plugs pictured are the only examples from Karluk One. They are 9 and 13.5 cm long. UA85.193:5059; Panamaroff avocational collection, AM15:417.

Once an animal was impaled, the final step was to dispatch it. Historic sources suggest that slate-tipped spears were a common part of a hunter's equipment. The short, slate lances found at Karluk One were likely used in this way. Ground to a sharp point, these tools feature a thick ridge in the center, perhaps used to strengthen the weapon, as well as a carefully squared base, designed to sit in a socket piece (fig. 5.47).

Sea otter hunting followed spring seal and seal lion hunting. Groups of men working together hunted the animals on the water from kayaks (Lisianski 1814:204), with as many as eight to fifteen boats participating (Gideon 1989:56). Hunters traveled quietly, so as not to alert otters of their presence. When an otter was spotted, a hunter used a throwing board to hurl a specially designed bone dart at it and then raised his paddle to signal the presence of an animal (Huggins 1981:15). The other paddlers then circled the area. When the animal surfaced to breathe, hunters hurled specially designed bone darts at it with a throwing board. This process continued each time the otter surfaced until it died or weakened and could be dispatched with a club or a lance. In calm water, bubbles from the otter's coat would indicate the animal's course, allowing hunters to follow. In rough waters, hunters knew that otters would swim against the wind and followed in that direction (Lisianski 1814:204). A small painted-work board from Karluk One shows a swimming otter with air bubbles streaming off its body (fig. 5.48).

Historic examples of sea otter darts points are bilaterally barbed (Birket-Smith 1941:135; Korsun 2012:68–71). Made from bone, these projectiles are similar to non-toggling harpoons used in seal hunting but smaller (Korsun 2012:67–73). Russian accounts and ethnographic collections indicate that there were also sea otter

Figure 5.51. *Nuusiq*—ground knife, *nuusim puunga*—knife handle. Slate knife blades in the collection have both single and double edges, pointed and rounded tips. Nineteen of the seventy-eight identified knives have stems. Eleven pieces have drilled holes where handles were attached. There may be many other ground-slate knife fragments in the assemblage, but they are hard to differentiate from fragments of ground ulus (Knecht 1995:519). Panamaroff avocational collection, AM15:51; UA85.193:5044, UA84.193:1450, AM38:2322, UA84.193:1588.

arrows, propelled with a bow. Dart points from Karluk One resemble historic examples, including an example collected in Karluk (Graburn et al. 1996:Plate 201). They feature a trapezoidal base, designed to fit in a bone socket shaped like a clothespin, which was in turn lashed to a wooden shaft designed for launching from a throwing board (fig. 5.49). Historic examples have a fletching, a feathered shaft typical of an arrow. However, the end of the shaft has a dimple designed to accommodate the pin of a throwing board. Dart heads from Karluk One are both unilaterally and bilaterally barbed. While common in historic collections from Kodiak, dart and arrow points are relatively rare in the Karluk One collection. This observation suggests that prior to the conquest of Kodiak by Russians fur traders, sea otters were not intensely hunted at Karluk. Preliminary studies of animal remains from Karluk One support this

idea. Researchers identified river otter bones, but not sea otter (Amorosi 1987:5).

Once dispatched, hunters employed a different set of tools to tow and butcher sea mammals. Karluk One includes examples not typically found in ethnographic collections. Collectors focused on obtaining weaponry but not the utilitarian tools used to care for a hunter's catch. Conical plugs of wood were used to fill the wounds created by harpoons, spears, and arrows to stem the flow of blood (fig. 5.50). Similarly, minimally carved, hand-size lengths of wood fitted with a central groove appear to be drag handles. A line secured between the handle and the seal, helped hunters move their heavy prey. Hunters butchered sea mammals with single- and double-edged knives. Example from Karluk One are ground from leaves of dense black slate and hafted in wooden handles (fig. 5.51).

Kodiak's brown bears are another valuable spring resource (Mishler 2001:164). Bears forage within individual territories, use distinct seasonal habitats connected by a well-developed series of trails. Many animals even maintain predictable daily schedules. This makes them easy to locate and intercept. Bears around southwest Kodiak Island leave their dens in April, two to three weeks earlier than bears in northern regions of the archipelago (Van Daele 1990:259). Despite their winter fast, these animals are often in remarkable condition. Although Kodiak brown bears loose up to 30 percent of their of body fat during hibernation, most animals retain a considerable supply of fat. Single adults may have more than 2.5 cm of back fat in spring. Similarly, although shedding may begin in the den, early spring hides are often in excellent condition (Roger Smith, Kodiak Office, Alaska Department of Fish and Game pers. comm. 1995). In the nineteenth century, Karluk men typically hunted brown bears in spring while waiting for the salmon-fishing season to begin and then again in the fall when the fishing season ended (Alpiak 1983:115).

In spring, bears move in and out of dens at the top of the alder line on the north- and east-facing hillsides. This movement leaves tracks in the rapidly melting snow that make dens easy to spot. At this time of year, animals are still groggy from hibernation. Karluk men took advantage of this situation, hunting bears in their dens and along habitually used trails. Moses Naumoff would smoke animals out of their dens with a fire built in front, a practice recorded historically as well (Davydov 1977:209). Other Karluk men were legendary for crawling into bear dens to spear animals (Dodge 2004:278–280; Tunohun 1987) or hunting bears in the dark (Naumoff 1978:62). More commonly, however, hunters patiently watched the hillsides for bears, spending days learning the

habits of individual animals, which they eventually intercepted and killed (Davydov 1977:209; Dodge 2004:275; Rostad 1988:144; Steffian and Counceller 2012:135). Others followed bears by kayak, watching their movements along the shore (Naumoff 1978:62). The reward was a wealth of meat, fat, gutskin, fur, tendon, and hide. The fresh hide of an adult Kodiak brown bear weighs more than 45 kg (99 lb) (Dodge 2004:131).

Karluk hunters were well known for their expert knowledge of bear behavior and Karluk-area terrain. Alutiiq men typically hunted bears in small groups (Black 1981:6), with experienced hunters teaching younger men how to track and kill. In the village, Nick Malutin taught Griska Nikolali, a hunter ten years his junior. Moses Naumoff learned from his uncle (Dodge 2004:276, 279; Naumoff 1978:62). When guided sport hunting became popular in the 1930s, Karluk men also acted as paid guides for sportsmen and are acknowledged for training the outfitters who employed them (Dodge 2004:245) (fig. 5.52). In short, Karluk was known for the great number and enormous size of its bears, as well as the skill of community bear hunters. Like salmon fishing, bear hunting was a Karluk specialty and an activity that extended throughout the lake and river valley.

Prehistorically, bows and arrows and spears were used to harvest bears. According to Davydov (1977:209), "On Kad'iak sometimes two or three people in a group creep up on an animal and fire arrows at it, and if it attacks them they fight it off with spears." Davydov adds that stone-tipped arrows were very damaging.

The heavy, hand-thrown or thrusted spears used in bear hunting were an important class of general weaponry. Lances were used for the largest of animals, such as sea lions and whales, or wounded animals close to a hunter, such as bears

Figure 5.52. Charles Madsen and assistant guides with trophy bear hide, south end of Karluk Lake, 1935. From left: "Walker," Charles Madsen, Fred Kvasnikoff, and Coleman Jonas. Courtesy Roy Madsen.

(Black 1977:85). In addition to throwing spears at bears, hunters sometimes braced their spears, causing a charging bear to impale itself on the end.

The tools Karluk bear hunters used were likely those common to other pursuits: slate-tipped spears, wooden bows, and arrows armed with stone points. There are two broad categories of stone arrow points in the Karluk One collection. A very small number of these are chipped-stone points—small, stemmed pieces of red chert and basalt (fig. 5.53). More common are slate end blades: sharp-edged, triangular pieces of ground slate designed to fit into the tip of a bone or antler arrow or in the end of a wood socket (fig. 5.54).

There are also slender slate lances. Ground to a sharp point, these weapons have a short, square stem and a raised ridge down the center of both faces. This gives them a diamond-shaped cross section, distinct from the flatter slate lances used in early time periods (fig. 5.55) (see Chapter 2).

To protect their stone arrows, boats, and fingers, hunters employed point sheaths. Historically, these covers were fashioned from wood or dried wild-celery stalks (Crowell and Laktonen 2001:167; Korsun 2012:109). Examples from Karluk are finely carved, triangular pieces of wood, a pair of which formed the cover (fig. 5.56). Each sheath piece has series of small side notches

Figure 5.53. *Nuusiq*—chipped knife, *kukeglugaq*—arrow point. Chipped stone technology is not common in Koniag tradition sites. These pieces may represent beach finds brought back to the site or obtained from neighboring peoples. The knife on the left is the only chipped knife identified in the collection. Complete, the knife measures 9 cm long and 4 cm wide. The two points on the right are examples of the few chipped projectiles in the collection. They each measure about 3 cm in length. AM193.94:3528, AM193.94:2486, AM193.87:8881.

Figure 5.54. *Iquq*—end blade. These triangular pieces of ground slate feature bifacial facets, areas of thinning on the point base that allowed the blade to slip into a slot at the end of a harpoon. End blades are the most prominent type of slate point in the collection. AM193.87:8832, UA85.193:2147; Lind avocational collection, AM14:257.

Figure 5.55. *Takesqat iquit*—ground lances. Slate lances with a diamond cross section. Averaging 10 to 12 cm long, these stemmed and barbed points have a thick medial ridge down the center, forming a diamond-shaped cross section. These points are characteristic of the early Koniag tradition. Many have tips battered from use. Panamaroff avocational collection, AM15:1785; Lind avocational collection, AM14:269; UA85.193:5060.

along the edge for lashing. This lashing secured the two sides of the cover over the point. Some of the Karluk examples retain stains from this lashing. The Karluk examples are remarkably similar to a point sheath lashed with sinew collected on Kodiak in the nineteenth century (Korsun 2012:109).

Like marine fish and sea mammals, birds return to Kodiak's coast as the weather warms. Sea birds nest on cliffs, waterfowl rest briefly in Kodiak waters on their way west, and songbirds fill the brushy hillsides. The rocky cliffs surrounding Karluk are good places to collect nutrient-rich eggs and capture sea birds. However, Russian sources note the Alutiiq people from Karluk also traveled to the Alaska mainland to harvest marine birds (Khlebnikov 1994:27, 37), where large populations of murres, puffins, cormorants, and gulls are still found today (Sowls et al. 1978:Map 35).

In areas with cliffs, Alutiiq hunters threw nets over groups of birds to entangle them. Some nets had a string that allowed the hunter to draw the net closed, forming a bag (Lisianski 1814:205). Other nets may have functioned as snares,

Figure 5.56. *Iqum patua*—point sheath, *ipegca'imasqaq iquq*—ground point. This two-piece point cover provided protection for both slate projectiles and the boats to which they were tied. Lind avocational collection, AM14:38, AM14:39; AM193.94:3818.

Figure 5.58. *Kugyasiq*—net. This small piece of baleen netting is just 8 cm across, with openings of only about 1 cm. AM193.87:9351

Figures 5.57a,b. *Inartaq*—basket. Thirty cm high and 30 cm wide, this large spruce root basket has a very tight weave and distinctive concentric circles on the bottom, a trait unique to Alutiiq basketry (Lee, 1981:69). AM193.87:19091.

entangling a bird's feet or wing (Merck 1980:95). Karluk residents may have climbed to the top of nearby cliffs and cast nets down the rock face to capture gulls, puffins, pigeon guillemots, and other birds. Karluk bird hunters also may have rappelled down cliffs to harvest birds and eggs, a practice recorded historically in the Kodiak region (Lisianski 1814:205; Pratt 1990). A sturdy rope and a collecting basket (fig. 5.57a,b) are the primary tools for this dangerous activity, although ladders were sometimes propped against rock faces to help hunters reach birds (Gideon 1989:65).

Karluk One produced a fragment of a net tied from baleen. The small openings in this net suggest it was used to harvest small fish or birds (fig. 5.58). Tiny stone sinkers may have been tied to the edges of such nets to act as weights (fig. 5.59).

Figure 5.59. Mary Pearce holds a tiny stone weight found in a Karluk River site, 2009. Small weights may have been attached to nets thrown over or set to entrap birds. Alutiiq Museum archives, AM620. Photograph by Patrick Saltonstall.

Other birds were harvested on the water with special spears tipped with leister prongs and launched with the aid of a throwing board. Bird-hunting gear from Karluk One includes a great many leister parts. Lisianski (1814:Plate III) shows the two types of leisters used by the Alutiiq. Bird leisters had multiple, curved and barbed side prongs, while fish leisters had just two, short, un-barbed, side prongs and a center prong. Bird leisters were designed as darts and arrows, propelled by throwing boards or bows, while fish leisters were used as spears and thrust by hand. Most leister parts in the Karluk One collection are of the variety used to hunt birds (fig. 5.60). However, the fishing variety may be under represented because it is harder to recognize (fig. 5.61). Still

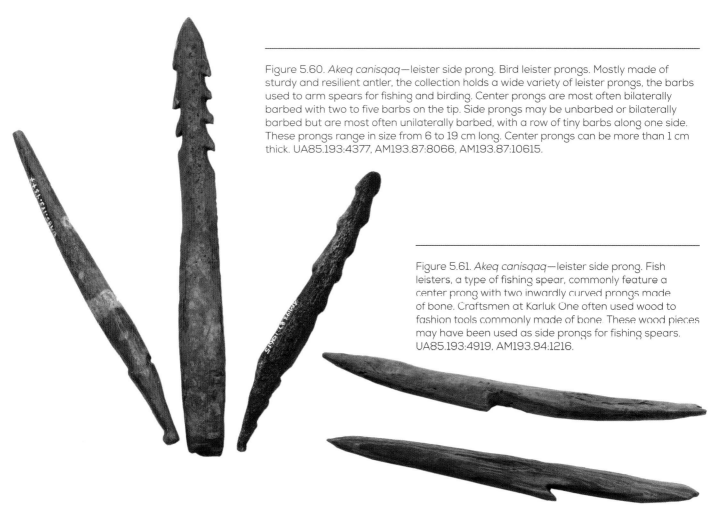

Figure 5.60. *Akeq canisqaq*—leister side prong. Bird leister prongs. Mostly made of sturdy and resilient antler, the collection holds a wide variety of leister prongs, the barbs used to arm spears for fishing and birding. Center prongs are most often bilaterally barbed with two to five barbs on the tip. Side prongs may be unbarbed or bilaterally barbed but are most often unilaterally barbed, with a row of tiny barbs along one side. These prongs range in size from 6 to 19 cm long. Center prongs can be more than 1 cm thick. UA85.193:4377, AM193.87:8066, AM193.87:10615.

Figure 5.61. *Akeq canisqaq*—leister side prong. Fish leisters, a type of fishing spear, commonly feature a center prong with two inwardly curved prongs made of bone. Craftsmen at Karluk One often used wood to fashion tools commonly made of bone. These wood pieces may have been used as side prongs for fishing spears. UA85.193:4919, AM193.94:1216.

other birds were taken with bow and blunted arrow, as described above.

Alutiiq hunters also used gorges to harvest birds. These simple but ingenious tools feature a short piece of wood, sharply pointed at each end and tapered in the center to hold a string. A hunter baited the gorge then unraveled the string and waited for a bird to take the bait. When the gorge stuck in the animal's gullet, the hunter could pull it to him and dispatch it. The gorges in the Karluk One collection are carved of wood and 6 cm long. They resemble ethnographic examples from western Alaska (Fitzhugh and Kaplan 1982:110).

In late spring, steelhead trout move down the Karluk River and out to sea. Historic sources indicate that Karluk residents occasionally caught and dried trout, but their contribution to the diet was minor in comparison with salmon (Bean 1890:37; Taylor 1966:215).

Small quantities of herring bones from Karluk One (Foster 2009:115) suggest that people also harvested this spring resource, although herring are not typically available around Karluk. These small oily fish spawn in large quantities in Kodiak's protected bays and were probably taken with nets. Karluk people also likely harvested herring spawn. Fish lay their eggs on marine algae, eelgrass, and even branches, making it easy to collect. Herring roe is a popular spring food on Kodiak today.

Greens are also an important source of spring food. Karluk's plant resources reflect the grassy habitat of southern Kodiak Island and include species found along the shoreline, in shrub thickets, and in alpine tundra (Russell 1991). As daylight increases, plant growth commences, beginning along Kodiak's shores and progressing up the hillsides until the island is emerald green. Harvesting begins at the shoreline in spring and moves uphill as plant growth and the season progresses. Along the shoreline, people pick young plants—tender

goose tongue leaves, beach lovage, lamb's quarter (beach spinach), seabeach sandwort, nettles, cow parsnip, and fireweed shoots (Russell 1991), among others. According to Russian observers, "There is virtually no growing plant, which they would not use in their food" (Davydov 1977:174). After a winter diet of fats and meats, these fresh foods were a welcomed change, a source of fiber and vitamins. Nettles are particularly nutritious with a high iron and protein content. Like shellfish and marine algae, people collected plant foods in baskets.

Summer

Elder Lucille Davis recalls that summer in Karluk began with the arrival of singing birds (2000). This was the signal that animals were returning to Kodiak and its near-shore waters and that fishing would start soon.

Historic accounts indicate that the whaling season began in early summer, following the spring sea otter hunt. June and July offer some of the calmest weather of the year and lots of daylight hours, a perfect combination for hunting in open water. Alutiiq whaling differed substantially from other sea mammal hunting practices (Crowell 1994, Desson 1995; Heizer 1943). Whaling was an individual pursuit, practiced by select hunters. Historic accounts indicate that only certain men inherited the right and the knowledge to harvest whales, an honor passed down through families (Lisianski 1814:209; Wrangell 1980:27). Whalers were not only skilled hunters but esteemed, elite members of society and ritual specialists trained in the art of physically and spiritually entrapping the largest sea mammals. Each whaler maintained a secluded cave where he stored his hunting gear and personal talismans—green stones, red stones, feathers, bear hair, and berries (Desson 1995: 94–97). Here, the solitary whaler undertook the spiritually powerful practice of preparing for the hunt (Demidoff 1962). This included mixing a potent poison from the roots of the Monkshood plant with a binder of human fat (Davydov 1977:215; Sauer 1802:178), applying the toxin to whaling lances and acting out the upcoming hunt with model boats. With the poisoned lance, the lone hunter speared the whale, preferably near the stabilizing fin, inflicting an injury that gradually paralyzed the whale and caused it to flip over and drown. Eventually, the carcass washed ashore and could be harvested (Heizer 1943). In 1831, Alutiiq hunters wounded 118 whales in the waters surrounding Kodiak and recovered 43 of these animals (Wrangell 1980:27).

Descriptions of whaling gear indicate that hunters used throwing boards to hurl 3 m long spears tipped with long, loosely fitted slate lances

Figure 5.62. *Takesqat iquit*—ground lance. The slate lances on the left is a preform. A craftsman formed this tool by sawing and snapping piece of slate to create a lance shape. He then ground the tools its final form and finish. The finished piece on the right features a maker's mark. The mark allowed a group of hunters to determine which man's lance had struck an animal. Karluk School avocational collection, AM39:120; UA85.193:6820.

(Birket-Smith 1941:138; Lisianski 1814:202; Wrangell 1980:27). This lance head was designed to detach or break off in the whale, leaving its poisoned point behind. The hunter could then retrieve his spear shaft and fasten on a new point (Demidoff 1962 in Desson 1995:109; Lisianski 1814:202; Merck 1980:105). French anthropologist Alphonse Pinart collected such a whaling lance point in Karluk in 1872. Made of hard black slate, this piece is more than 25 cm long and features a series of etched markings that likely identified its owner (Pinart 1872:12; Rousselot and Grahammer 2002:216). Given the danger of a thrashing whale, whalers targeted smaller animals. Alutiiq language terms for whales reflect the importance of animal size, with terms for whales reflecting both species and size (Wrangell 1980:28).

The Alutiiq residents of Karluk One commonly used whalebone and baleen. Wedges for working wood, mortars for grinding foods or minerals, gaming disks, digging sticks, and spoons are all made of whalebone material. Moreover, large pieces of cut whalebone occurred throughout the site, especially vertebrae. The site also held baleen. Many different artifact types found throughout the deposit have lashings of baleen, and strips of baleen prepared for use in lashing are also present. Evidence of whale hunting is less obvious in the collection, perhaps due to the spiritually powerful and secretive nature of Alutiiq whaling. However, several pieces of hunting weaponry may be whale darts. Items identified historically as the heads of whaling harpoons (Korsun 2012:102–104) match items found in the Karluk One collection: long, stemmed slate lances which fit into long wooden foreshafts with slotted ends (fig. 5.36). Like historic examples, some of the foreshafts are barbed, and one slate lance features an incised design (fig. 5.62). This may be the mark of an individual hunter. "Every whale hunter scratches his sign and marks into the clay slate, so there can never be a quarrel over possession, since the clay slate pieces in the wound identify the hunter who is the owner of the animal" (Holmberg 1985:48).

Another essential piece of sea mammal hunting gear was a bentwood hat. Carved from a single piece of wood and bent to shape with steam, each hat was a work of art, specifically designed for its owner with painted decorations and elaborate attachments of beads, ivory carvings, weavings, and animal whiskers (Black 1991). The functions of such hats were both practical and spiritual. They protected a hunter's face from rain, sea spray, and the glare of the sun. At the same time, they hid his face, transforming the hunter into a powerful being with the ability to kill sea mammals. In this way, they were a type of mask (Black 1994:138–139).

Like seal-hunting helmets, bentwood hats were not identified in the Karluk One collection. Hat parts may be present among the hundreds of bentwood fragments, but we have yet to identify them. However, small bark figurines from the site wear this style of headgear. The figurines were carved to fit into model kayaks (fig. 5.63). They indicate that bentwood hats were a part of Karluk's hunting culture and that the predominant style was a closed-crown variety (Black 1991:12). The absence of full-sized hats at Karluk One, in the presence of so many other wooden objects, may reflect the practice of storing hunting gear away from households and women. Additionally, at death, people were sometimes dressed in their best clothing and buried with possessions (Lisianski 1814:200; Petrof 1884:235; Shelikhov 1981:54). Bentwood hats may have been among the items interred.

In June and July, people harvested lily bulbs—the starchy, rice-like roots of the Kamchatka Lily (Merck 1980:106). The small flowing plant grows widely in Kodiak's meadows and is abundant in the Karluk area. Lilly bulbs were among the foods

Figure 5.63. *Suaruangcuk*—kayak figurine. Carved from bark, these small figures represent men in kayaks. Each has a peg-like base designed to fit into a small hole in a miniature bark kayak (see Figure 6.124). The figures range from 2.5 cm to 21 cm high, and each is uniquely designed. Panamaroff avocational collection, AM15:449; Pavlov avocational collection, AM217:3; AM193.94:4604, UA85.193:5609.

that Karluk residents collected for the Russian American Company artel in Karluk, putting up two hundred baskets of the roots a year (Gideon 1989:39). A digging stick and a basket were the only tools needed to collect this important source of carbohydrate, which was stored in water, brine, or oil (Petrof 1884:206), mixed with berries, or pounded and dried. "The bulbs are boiled, mashed and after a liberal supply of seal or whale oil has been thoroughly mixed therewithin, it is put away for winter use" (Fisher 1899:Entry 3).

By early summer, large fatty chinook and early sockeye salmon begin to arrive in the Karluk River, marking the start of the salmon-fishing season. In preparation, villagers repaired stone weirs built to trap fish in shallow areas of the river. The remains of such weirs are still visible in the upper

Karluk River. These long, V-shaped traps were made with river boulders (fig. 5.64). The pointed end of the stone alignment, at the upstream end of the trap, moderated the current by pushing water to either side. This created an opening with calmer water facing downriver. Alutiiq people report that they put boards along the sides, creating a fenced area into which fish could easily enter but not easily exit. Fishermen standing on the bluffs over the river watched for runs to arrive and waded into the river to spear fish diverted into the weir (Russell 1991).

Alutiiq ancestors used two types of fish spears. Like ice-fishing spears, leisters were employed to impale salmon. Curved and barbed side prongs and a barbed central project held the fish on the spear. Although leister parts were recovered at Karluk One, fish harpoons were more common. These tools featured a small, detachable point made from two or three pieces seated on a wooden shaft and attached to a line (fig. 5.65–5.67). When thrust into a fish, these harpoon points came off in the animal, securing it to the line. To catch another fish, the hunter simply rearmed his spear shaft with another harpoon point. Shelikhov

(1981:54) described this method of fishing. "In the rivers they catch fish by making stone weirs. They spear the fish with gaffs similar to spears, in the blunt end of which is a hollow into which is place a barbed point from bone, stone or iron, tied with sinew to the shaft."

Holmberg (1985:46) adds:

At a certain time of the year every one of these species moves from the ocean up to the rivers and streams in such numbers that they are easily speared with an iron nail or a rod with a point of bone, and this is the usual way of catching them. The inhabitants know exactly when every river is visited by a certain type of salmon, so that they seldom miscalculate the time even by a day.

Fish were also caught in shallow lagoon waters with nets crafted from whale sinews (Holmberg 1985:46). Net gauges in the Karluk One collection suggest that people constructed nets in the settlement. These tools help net makers to create a consistently sized mesh. Karluk examples have three distinct sizes (about 3 cm, 7 cm, and 15 cm), illustrating that residents tailored their nets for a

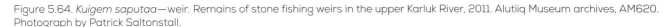

Figure 5.64. *Kuigem saputaa*—weir. Remains of stone fishing weirs in the upper Karluk River, 2011. Alutiiq Museum archives, AM620. Photograph by Patrick Saltonstall.

Figure 5.65. *Ayaqum iqua*—fish harpoon. Two-piece salmon harpoon with shaft, three-piece harpoon, and harpoon point part with spurred base. Fish harpoons are most often made of resilient antler. This reduces breakage, as antler withstands battering on rocky river bottoms better than stone or wood (Margaris 2009). The multiple-piece design also helped prevent the tips from breaking. AM193.94:3081, AM193.87:10718, AM193.87:8074, AM193.87:7704, UA85.193:6192, AM193.87:8108, AM193.87:1288.

Figures 5.66a,b. *Ayaqum iqua*—fish harpoon. There are three basic styles of fish harpoons: one-, two-, or three-piece. In most two-piece examples, the shorter component fits into the longer valve, and the two sides are wrapped together. In a three-piece configuration, a step-scarfed valve fits between the two other components. In this image, the top piece is a long component for a two-piece harpoon, the middle is step-scarfed for the long component of a three-piece harpoon, and the bottom is a short component with a spurred base. Valves range from just 3 cm in length to 12 cm in length, but most components are about 5 to 8 cm long. UA83.193:378, UA85.193:5202, UA84.193:714.

Figure 5.67. Drawing of a three-piece fish harpoon. Illustration by Alisha Drabek and Carrie Barker, adapted from Knecht 1995.

Three-Piece Fish Harpoon

a - step-scarfed long component
b - step-scarfed short component
c - small component

(a + b together make one "long component - as if one half of a 2-piece harpoon.)

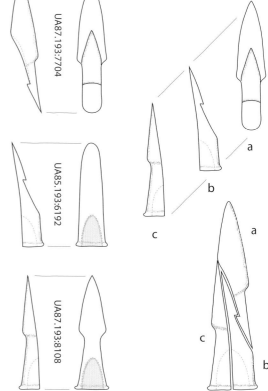

Figure 5.68. *Kugyasim uspersuutaa*—net gauge. When tying nets, craftsmen used these tools to measure the distance between their knots and create a uniform mesh. To do this you tie a knot and then use the gauge to measure from that knot to the spot where you will tie the next knot. Some of the Karluk One net gauges have multiple measuring devices, indicating the same tools were used to make nets with different mesh sizes. These prehistoric net gauges are very similar to the tool modern fishermen use to make or mend nets. Malutin avocational collection, AM102:1; UA85.193:3394, AM193.87:10409.

Figure 5.69. *Pugtaq*—net float. Some net floats were made from two pieces of wood, grooved and lashed together. Examples from Karluk One range from 10 to 26 cm long, but most are about 15 cm in length. AM193.94:1030, AM193.87:9750.

Figure 5.70. *Pugtaq*—net float. Smaller than two-piece net floats, these single-piece floats are only about 8 to 10 cm long and carved of bark. The presence of different sizes and styles of net floats in the collection suggests the use of nets designed for specific settings and types of prey. AM193.87:8744, AM193.87:8296, UA85.193:4637.

range of hunting and fishing tasks (fig. 5.68). To their nets, Karluk One residents attached a variety of objects. The collection includes some large, two-piece, wooden floats and smaller single-piece floats often carved from bark (fig. 5.69, 5.70). A variety of notched, water-worn beach pebbles were likely used as sinkers. These feature notches at either end of their long axis, where they were secured to the bottom edge of a net (fig. 5.71). There are also more carefully carved sinkers made from bone. Known as spacer bar sinkers, these long narrow pieces feature knobs at either end, or sometimes a small hole, to aid in attaching them to a net (fig. 5.72). Much larger, chipped and grooved stones from Karluk One functioned as anchors (fig. 5.73).

Nets equipped with floats, sinkers, and anchors may have been moored in the river to trap fish swimming upstream. Omit the anchor, and people wading in the river or working from boats could have surrounded fish with the net and pulled them to shore. Karluk residents commonly harvested fish with beach seines in the twentieth century (Taylor 1966:214) and continue this practice.

Fishing continued through the summer and into the fall months, as waves of fish arrived in the river. Men watched the river mouth from the village and the beach for signs of fish massing to run up the river (Shepherd 2010; Taylor 1965). During the salmon runs, Karluk was a busy place, with residents catching and processing many tens of thousands of fish. According to residents, the stronger the pink-salmon run, the better the fall harvest of salmon berries (Russell 1991:90).

Harvesting fish involved everyone able to help. Karluk men speared or netted fish, children carried them, and women cleaned them (fig. 5.74) (Alpiak 1983:114; Smith 2005). Splitting fresh fish is more difficult than splitting aged fish, so Karluk men filled their skiffs with salmon and let them sit overnight (Shepherd 2010). Nevertheless, Karluk women remember that cleaning fish took many days (Coyle 1983:113) and that they could each process two to three hundred fish a day during the fishing season (Shepherd 2010). Late nineteenth-century records indicate that the three hundred residents of Karluk harvested and dried about one hundred thousand fish annually (Goode 1887:94). Cleaning all this salmon required splitting each fish in half and removing its guts, head, and sometimes its spine (Gideon 1989:37). Each fish was also washed in the river (Shepherd 2010). Russian accounts indicate there were two varieties of processed salmon—one with the spine, known as *kachemas*, and another without the spine,

Figure 5.71. *Kitsuuteq*—net sinker. Water-worn cobbles of slate and greywacke were chipped at each end to create weights for the bottom edge of a net. On average, this type of sinker weighs 50 gm and is 6 to 8 cm in length. UA85.193:2700, 2801, 3090, 3544, 3686, 3698, 3948, 4906, 5815, 6008.

Figure 5.72. *Kitsuut'ruaq*—spacer bar sinker. Often made of sea mammal bone, these sinkers either have holes on the ends for securing to a net, or they have tapered ends with a knob around which a knot can be tied. They range in size from 10 to 20 cm long. Karluk School avocational collection, AM39:202; UA84.193:1813, AM193.87:9709; Lind avocational collection, AM14:149; AM193.87:8035.

Figure 5.73. *Kicaq*—anchor, *kitsuuteq*—net sinker. At 26 cm long and 2,060 gm (5.7 lb), this large anchor, made by chipping a cobble, dwarfs the approximately 5 cm and 27 gm (0.6 lb) greywacke net sinker. AM193.87:10390, AM193.95:634.

Figure 5.74. Beach seining in Karluk, ca. 1960. Alutiiq Museum archives, Clyda Christiansen collection, AM680:91.

Figure 5.75. Fish drying on the beach near Karluk Village, ca. 1980. Alutiiq Museum archives, Mike Rostad collection, AM539:560.

known as *iukola* (Davydov 1977:174). Villagers used every part of each fish, from the head to the tail, wasting nothing. In recent time, even fish guts were turned into fertilizer for Karluk gardens (Davis 2000).

Cleaned fish were laid on a cloth and then taken to a drying rack (Shepherd 2010). Drying took about three weeks. On dry days, people hung their fish with the flesh facing outward and the skin facing inward. On wet days they reversed the fillets, turning the meat inward to protect it from the rain (Shugak 1978a). Historic photographs of Karluk in summertime commonly show fish fillets, connected at the tail, hanging to dry from open-air racks (fig. 5.75).

Although villagers dried most of their catch, some fish were smoked. To start this process, people brined fresh salmon fillets. Mont Hawthorn, a Karluk cannery worker who visited Alutiiq families in 1890, described people digging holes in intertidal areas (McKeown 1948:51). Into this hole they placed a layer of grass, a layer of cleaned fish, another layer of grass, and covered it all with dirt. After five or six days of the tide washing over the hole, the fish inside were brined and ready for smoking. More recently, families soaked salmon filets in salted water for about eight hours, washed the fish several times, then hung them to dry for a day. After that, the fish were ready for drying over slow-burning, smoky fires often of cottonwood (Shepherd 2010) (fig. 5.76).

Not all of Karluk's stockpiled fish were for local consumption. Dried salmon were a valuable trade good. The summer weather that permitted long days of hunting and fishing encouraged travel. Russian entrepreneurs sent Karluk hunters to the Alaska Peninsula specifically to hunt birds (Khlebnikov 1994:27). In earlier times, men ventured across the Shelikof Strait to hunt and trade, pursuing birds and caribou on the mainland, and bartering with neighboring communities. Kodiak Islanders swapped whale oil, dried fish, and finished products like arrow shafts for caribou meat, hair, antler, and hides (Gideon 1989:57).

Boats were essential to summer travel. The Alutiiq at Karluk constructed two different types of skin boats—the *angyaq* (large open boat) and *qayaq* (kayak). Both had a wooden frame over which people stretched a cover of dehaired seal or sea lion skins (Black 1977:84). The *angyaq* was a large open boat with a flat bottom and benches for paddlers. In contrast, the kayak was a smaller, skin-covered craft with individual cockpits for paddlers. Each type of boat had a distinct function

Figure 5.76. Lawrence Panamaroff's smoke house, Karluk Lagoon, 1983. Alexander Dolitsky on left, Lawrence Panamaroff on right. Bryn Mawr College Archaeological project, Alutiiq Museum archives, AM278.

and pieces of both crafts are found in the Karluk One collection.

Angyat[3] were used to move substantial loads—people, gear, and goods—around the archipelago. These boats featured a distinctive discoid bow with an upturned stem, as well as benches to seat paddlers. The bow design enhanced speed and maneuverability as well as buoyancy (Anichtchenko 2012:173–174). In 1833, Kashevaroff reported that the village of Karluk had one *angyaq* with benches that seated seven paddlers each and that this boat transported a bird-hunting crew to the Alaska Peninsula each summer (Black 1990). Historic accounts mention up to one hundred people—even whole villages—travelling in such boats (Bancroft 1886:236; Campbell 1816:114; Huggins 1981:4; Sauer 1802:171). However, this may be an exaggeration (Lydia Black pers. comm. 2001). If three or four people occupied each bench, then the Karluk *angyaq* mentioned by Kashevaroff carried between twenty and thirty people and their gear.

Figure 5.77. *Angyam ilakua'a—angyaq* part. Thwarts, floor timbers, and ribs. The size of *angyaq* pieces depends on their location in the boat. Thwarts toward the bow and stern may have been just 30 cm long, while those in the middle were more than 65 cm long. One almost complete floor timber in the collection is about 95 cm long. Several complete ribs are 40 to 46 cm in length. AM193.94:230, AM193.94:3084; Lind avocational collection, AM14:3; AM193.87:11815, AM193.87:11814; Sheehan avocational collection, AM38:613.

Figure 5.78. *Angyam ilakua'a—angyaq* part. *Angyaq* stern post and board. This whale tail-shaped piece, placed at the stern or back of a boat, may represent the eyes of the *angyaq*. Like the all-seeing supreme being Llam Sua, the eyes of the *angyaq* guide the paddler's course (Anichtchenko 2012:171; Haakanson Jr., personal communication, 2011). Although the carving of the "eyes" is less distinctive in this piece, it is similar to historic examples that display this feature (Korsun 2012:144). AM193.94:1056; Sheehan avocational collection, AM38:1099.

Karluk One produced a wide array of *angyaq* parts, indicating that boat building was a common activity on site (fig. 5.77, 5.78). As *angyat* have not been made in living history, we identified their parts by comparing Karluk One artifacts with drawings of *angyat* and pictures of model boats, including a nineteenth-century model collected in Karluk (fig. 5.79; Anichtchenko 2012; Crowell and Laktonen 2001:154). These parts include fragments of a brace, chines, floor timbers, keelsons, ribs, sternpost, and many thwarts.

Kayaks were the crafts of individuals, the sturdy, flexible boats used for daily work. These boats were most often used to pursue fish and sea mammals in the ocean (fig. 5.80–5.83). On occasion, members of a family would travel in a kayak

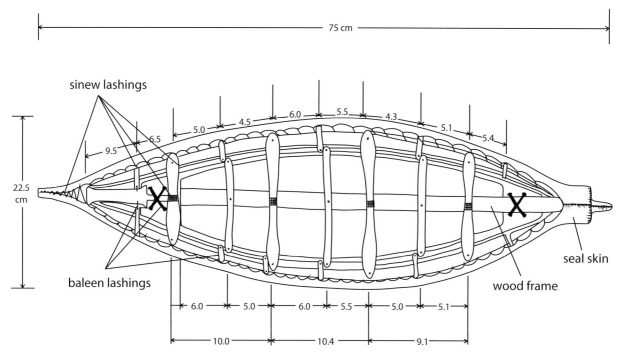

Figure 5.79. *Angyaq*—open boat model illustration, collected in Karluk, 1883. National Museum of Natural History, Smithsonian Institution. Catalog no. EO 90464. Illustration by Alisha Drabek from a drawing and measurements provided by Kathleen Skonberg.

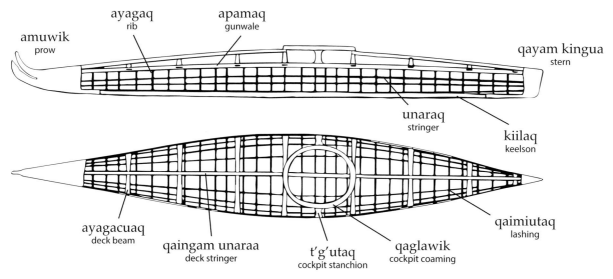

Figure 5.80. *Qayaq*—kayak illustration. This drawing illustrates the location of the kayak parts found in Karluk One collection and described here. Adapted from Zimmerly 2000, based on an Alutiiq kayak collected by Heinrich J. Holmberg in 1851, in the Danish National Museum, Copenhagen. Illustration by Alisha Drabek.

with people lying under the cover, between the paddlers. Larry Matfay remembers his mother and father paddling a kayak to fish camp while he and his sister huddled under the cover (Rostad 1988:45). Archibald Campbell, a mariner injured in a shipwreck off Kodiak's western coast, traveled to Karluk lying in the tight quarters inside a kayak. A gutskin garment, probably a spray skirt,

Figure 5.81. *Qayam ilakua'a*—kayak part. Deck beam, cockpit coaming, deck beam, stanchion, stern piece, keelson. Most of the kayak parts in the collections are ribs and stringers (Figures 5.82, 5.83), the common pieces of the framework. However, fifty-five artifacts in the collection represent other types of kayak parts. Clifford and Jerry Sheehan avocational collection, AM38:930; AM193.94:1022, AM193.87:11248; Clifford and Jerry Sheehan avocational collections, AM231:87; AM38:506, AM38:2707.

Figure 5.82. *Unaraq*—kayak stringer. There are over six hundred seventy kayak-stringer fragments in the Karluk One collection. Oval in shape and about 2 cm wide, they have variable ends. Most taper gradually. Others flare and then taper. A few are notched for lashing to a kayak prow, and a couple have designs carved in the ends, such as an *X* mark. AM193.94:237, AM193.94:3824, AM193.94:3769.

Figure 5.83. *Ayagaq*—kayak rib. Carved from wood, the kayak ribs from Karluk One are relatively small in comparison to ribs from historic kayaks (see Naumoff this chapter). They are a little more than 0.5 cm thick and about 2 cm wide. Many examples from the site are also broken. UA85.193:6333, UA87.193:7823, AM193.87:8000, UA85.193:6663.

covered the hole where he entered (Campbell 1816:98). *Angyat* faded from use in Alutiiq communities during the historic era. However, kayak use persisted in Karluk until the early decades of the twentieth century. Historic photos show men paddling kayaks in the lagoon and river (fig. 5.84), boats resting along the shore below Karluk One, and kayak frames stored on top of people's houses.

Alutiiq kayaks featured a wooden frame covered with de-haired seal or seal lion skin (Black 1977:84; Huggins 1981:4). Although similar to Unangan boats in design, Alutiiq kayaks tended to be shorter and broader than those used in the neighboring Aleutian Islands (Birket-Smith 1941:147). Karluk resident Moses Naumoff recalled that men carved kayak frames from red cedar but made boat ribs from cottonwood (Naumoff 1978:61). These boats had a bifurcated bow—split, upturned, and with a squared-off stern. This distinctive bow design is a hallmark of Alutiiq watercraft, and one that promoted both speed and efficiency (Crowell and Laktonen 2001:146). Model-boat pieces from Karluk One, perhaps used in teaching the art of boat building, demonstrate the use of the upturned bow by village mariners (fig. 5.85, 5.86). They also demonstrate the technique of using a single piece of wood with a curving grain to create a strong prow. Full-size kayak pieces from Karluk One include fragments of prows, as well as cockpit coamings and stanchions, deck beams, keelsons, gunwales, and many stringers and ribs. Importantly, some of

Figure 5.84. Men paddling a kayak near the entrance to the Karluk River, 1889. Albatross Collection, National Archives, Washington, DC, 22-FA-1154.

Figure 5.85. *Qayangcum ilakua'a*—model kayak parts. Paddles, prows, keelsons, and deck beam. Men practiced and perfected the art of kayak building by making model boats, a tradition that continued into the twentieth century. Very detailed model boats are common in ethnographic collections, constructed and equipped like full-sized boats (Korsun 2012:159, 143). Some model boats may have been used in ceremonies. Whalers prepared for the hunt by acting out pursuits with the help of model boats (Pinart in Desson 1995:89). The size of the model kayaks made at Karluk One are similar to those found in ethnographic collections. The miniature paddles pictured are 9.5 and 11 cm long, the longest prow 12.5 cm in length, and the deck beam 9 cm long. AM193.87:10157, AM193.95:1595, AM193.94:4321; Sheehan avocational collection, AM38:910; UA85.193:4245, AM193.94:1156, AM193.87:8214.

Figure 5.86. *Angyangcum ilakua'a*—model *angyaq* part. Ribs, deck beam, and floor timbers. Like the model kayak parts, *angyaq* parts from Karluk One mirror the full-size parts in the collection. The ribs, which would have been set into the chine and secured to the gunwale with lashing strung through the hole, are 10.5 and 13 cm long. The floor timbers are about 10.5 cm long. In the collection, one timber that would have fit toward the bow or stern is just 4 cm long (not pictured). The deck beam depicted in this image is 9 cm long. Again, another piece in the collection (not pictured) is just 4.5 cm long. Pullar, Knowles, and Dolchuk avocational collection, AM341:42; AM193.95:1254, AM193.94:5315, AM193.87:11374, UA85.193:3653.

these pieces appear to be preforms, partially finished kayak parts that reflect boat building in the village. Elders recall that men pulled their boats inside their sod houses in the wintertime to work on repairs (Matfay 1990). This may be why so many boat parts were found in Karluk One houses.

Historically, Alutiiq boat builders made kayaks with one, two, or three cockpits. Those with three cockpits are thought to be a recent adaptation of boat design, created to carry a Russian trader or clergyman (Crowell et al. 2001:147). Thirty-eight miniature kayak carvings from Karluk One all have a single cockpit (see fig. 5.33), suggesting that single-hatched kayaks were the primary form made and used in the village. Similarly, a painted box panel from the site shows people traveling in both *angyat* and single-hatched kayaks (see fig. 6.66).

To seal the kayak hatch and keep waves and rain from flooding the boat, paddlers wore long, waterproof jackets made of gutskin. The bottom of the jacket had a string that secured the garment tightly over the cockpit opening. The paddler seated himself in his boat and then tied the base of his jacket around the cockpit coaming. In Karluk, women typically stitched these jackets from

Looking at Kayaks

Alfred Naumoff Jr., Alutiiq Artist

Alfred Naumoff's family relocated to Kodiak from Douglas (Kaguyak village) after the 1912 Katmai eruption. The Naumoff family moved around the island eventually settling in Old Harbor. Alfred was born there, the child of Alfred Naumoff Sr. and Luba Kelly Naumoff. As a young man, Alfred was interested in carving and studied kayak building with high-school teacher Dave Kubiak and Elder Larry Matfay. This led to a passion for Alutiiq watercraft (fig. 5.87). In March of 2012, Alfred traveled to the Peabody Museum at Harvard University with Sven Haakanson Jr. and Susan Malutin to study an Alutiiq kayak. During their visit, he spoke to Sven about learning to build kayaks and the importance of museum collections to this journey.

Larry would tell stories of growing up with his dad taking him out in the kayak and how they used to do the sea otter hunting. Stories like that intrigued me. I was wondering why we didn't have anything left for our own people to use. Up north, people had kayaks of different designs, and they still used them. People in the southeast still had their red cedar canoes. It was kind of a lost thing for us. I was in search of more of our background. It was an interest of mine because everyone else knew where they belonged, and I didn't feel that we belonged anywhere.

I studied with Dave Kubiak and Larry Matfay. Larry coached us on building. Whenever we could we took out our history books and talked to Larry. He'd be telling a story on how to make things, and I actually got to see Larry's kayak bow. I didn't know what to think about this bifid bow. We didn't know how to put them together. He told us how things went together. It was just a big learning process. That was in about 1978.

Not long after that, we ended up having to build a two-man kayak. That was kind of disturbing in a way. We learned a lot and made a lot of mistakes. Understanding what Larry was telling us verbally was kind of hard. Not being able to see something physically was a little challenge to us. Being woodworkers, we figured things out and studied more.

In 1979, I built my single-hatched kayak, and that had a bifid bow, but we didn't know how to finish that up. There were no real pictures, no real studies on any of the top pieces. So, we kept on looking. It was probably about ten or twelve years later that we finally figured out how that bow had plates put on it and a stopper over the plates and exactly how the gunnels got locked up underneath that bow with a notch. Slowly, it all came back together to restore the original-style Kodiak bow. That was a real tough one to learn. The rest of it we figured out pretty good.

We are always still learning about things. I mean, anywhere I've studied, like the Alutiiq Museum, provided a lot more insights. Whatever I could dig up, I would—not only on my own but through the Alutiiq Museum and the Baranov Museum. I looked at models and whatever came my way. For example, the rib sizes on those [artifacts] in the Karluk One collection. The smaller ribs had me questioning things. I think they were probably alder wood or some possibly even willow.

During our studies, we bumped into a guy from Canada. He had written a piece about the measurements of the three-man or two-man kayak. That was similar to how Larry used to tell us about measurements, and it all started making sense. Everything was measured to fit the owner's body. You made sure it fit you and not anybody else, because

Figure 5.87. Boat builder Alfred Naumoff sanding a model kayak part during Alutiiq Week, Port Lions School, 2009. Alutiiq Museum archives. Photograph by Sven Haakanson Jr.

your life depended on it. It's a spiritual thing for a lot of people. It's like having you know, a part of you that really belongs, but you have to search for it.

I built like seven or eight kayaks, full size, and maybe seven or eight small ones. I also carve them all the time. They all have their own personality. That kind of gives you the idea of who really used them. What size they were. Maybe in the 1800s, some of the boat measurements add up to 15'2", 15' and a half. That gives you an idea of who was using the boat.

I never thought I'd come to a place like the Peabody Museum. I felt almost alone with that kayak when I first walked into the room. It was sitting there. I seen all the hair on the bow and the stitching. That kind of gave me a sadness, but yet I felt like I was at home because there was something left from home. This has been an eye-opener for me because of the construction, design, and quality. Just knowing where it came from was quite a big deal for me.

I learned a lot from the kayaks, but the people who came in to ask questions broadened my mind too. That's always good. When you are working with people they open your eyes to different questions. That broadens your mind, too, knowing that people from another place [have] the same exact feelings as kids at home. They are excited when they hear you talk about something. That just makes it all worthwhile—studying. You can teach [what you learn] to someone else, and its going be passed on. The knowledge I learn from teaching everyone on these trips is something I'll never forget. Its imprinted in my mind, and it will never go away. I just hope to pass it on. I talked to my boy, and he wants to build a kayak. He is excited about the things I'm telling him on the phone.

bear gut (Matfay and Matfay 1987; McKeown 1948:59; Pinart 1872:21).

Unlike other coastal-Alaska peoples, the Alutiiq propelled their boats with single-bladed paddles, often fitted with a short crosspiece that acted as a handle (Krech 1989:Figure 43). These long narrow paddles were well designed for stabilizing boats in rough water, allowing paddlers to reach below the waves. Double-bladed paddles, the type commonly used by modern kayakers, are known from historic collections (Korsun 2012:124–125). However, they appear to be a late introduction for Kodiak. Paddle fragments from Karluk One have two distinct blade shapes. One fragment is a long oval with a rounded end. Another has an hourglass shape with a triangular end (fig. 5.88). Both paddles are narrow, ca. 7–10 cm wide, with a flat oval –cross section. Knecht (1995:301–305) notes that the Karluk paddles are relatively narrow when compared with historic examples, a design which may reflect their use in the exceptionally windy waters of Shelikof Strait. A third paddle-like fragment has a broad, oval, leaf-shaped blade and a pointed tip (fig. 5.88). This may be an *angyaq* oar. Painted black, this artifact is similar to oar fragments held by the rowers seated in a model *angyaq* collected on Kodiak between 1860 and 1870 (Crowell and Laktonen 2001:152).

Another important part of a paddler's gear was a gutskin jacket. Stitched from the intestines of seals, sea lions, and bears, these jackets were lightweight, waterproof garments that protected their wearers from rain and sea spray. They also fit snugly over kayak cockpits, preventing water from entering. To secure the sleeves of the garment, hunters wore a baleen clip on each wrist. These bracelet-like objects featured an encircling groove for a line that secured it to the wearer's wrist. This kept water from running up a paddler's sleeves. Despite the remarkable preservation at Karluk One, delicate animal tissues like gut were not preserved, but baleen wrist clips are present (fig. 5.89a,b).

In late summer, Karluk women and children climb the hills around the lagoon to harvest berries, especially low bush cranberries and alpine blueberries (fig. 5.90). Elder Lucile Davis (2000) recalled that people waited until the first of September to begin harvesting, to ensure these berries were in prime condition. People from neighboring Larsen Bay will travel to Karluk to harvest

Figure 5.88. *Anguat*—paddles. Long, narrow paddles carved of wood helped kayakers steady their boats in rough water. The blades of these paddles range from 38 to 56 cm long. They are just 10 cm wide at their widest point. Sheehan avocational collection, AM38:658; Karluk School Sheehan collection, AM39:1; AM193.94:3560.

Figures 5.89a,b. *Kanagllum tayarnaa*—gutskin jacket cuff clip. Keeping water out of a kayak and its paddler dry was important. In the cold, windy waters around Kodiak, men risked hypothermia if they got wet. Clips that secured the cuff of a paddler's jacket to his wrist kept water from running up his sleeves. "A hoop is fastened around the top of the manhole, to which the bottom of a waterproof shirt is tightly bound. Upon seating himself in the boat, the native puts on this shirt, tying it at the throat and wrists, and thus becomes as it were an integral part of the boat" (Huggins 1981:4). Wrist clips in the collection are made of baleen. UA85.193:3540.

Figure 5.90. Boy with berries, Karluk, ca. 1960. Alutiiq Museum archives, Clyda Christiansen collection, AM680:257.

berries, and Karluk ladies report picking gallons of fruit each summer (Russell 1991). Historically, Karluk provided the Russian American Company with some of the largest quantities of berries in the archipelago (Black 1990). Women and children collected these foods in spruce root baskets designed for this purpose and more recently used old flour sacks (Coyle 1983:113). Berries were repeatedly poured between baskets or on a mat or blanket, using the wind to winnow out leaves and stems (Russell 1991). Berry collecting continued in the fall, when people picked fruit sweetened by the first frosts. Elder Julie Knagin recalled daylong trips into the hills behind the village to gather cranberries. Families picked together and packed a large picnic lunch to sustain themselves over a long day of harvesting (Alutiiq Museum 2013). Elder Mary Peterson (Smithsonian Institution Arctic Studies Center 1997), who lived in Karluk as a small girl, had similar memories of people berry picking together. "They were going behind

the mountain in Karluk. You know. Where the Church is but down. . . . From there they climb up. We pick cranberries back there. . . . I remember one time there was a whole bunch of people and . . . my dad was packing me, and my mom was carrying the pack sack—big five gallon can and other sacks."

Fall

The arrival of migratory waterfowl marks the beginning of fall in Karluk (Taylor 1966:215). At this time of year, subsistence activities turned toward the land. Although August and September are often characterized by fair weather, in October the weather turns stormy and boat travel becomes more difficult. High winds create large waves that can capsize a kayak or *angyaq*, and the combination of wind and colder temperatures can cause ocean water to freeze to boats making them unstable. Fortunately, the resources available at this time of year are those found around freshwater and on the land: waterfowl, late-run salmon, and fur bearers.

In the fall, thousands of ducks, geese, and swans migrate through Kodiak, moving south from summer nesting grounds on the Bering Sea coast. Although few migratory birds overwinter on Kodiak, flocks rest and feed in the marshy lowlands, rivers, and near-shore waters of southwest Kodiak. Karluk residents likely hunted geese with snares, a technology represented by the numerous snare pins found at Karluk One (see fig. 5.15). Ducks were taken with bows and arrows, leisters, and nets. Historic accounts describes Alutiiq kayakers firing a barrage of arrows at a flock of ducks on the water and dispatching wounded and tired animals with their paddles (Davydov 1977:228). Lawrence Panamaroff, a Karluk hunter, favored an onshore wind for this type of hunting, noting that an offshore wind pushed animals out to sea.

In this situation, a hunter might be able to kill an animal but not collect it (Mulcahy 1986:14).

Nets stretched across a narrow waterway, like a river mouth, were also common duck-hunting tools. Tied just above the surface of the water, such nets trapped low-flying ducks and were particularly effective around dawn and dusk, when animals move between resting and feeding locales (Davydov 1977:228). Late into the fall, ducks can be easily ambushed with bird leisters at small springs and at lake outlets that remain ice free.

At this time of year, salmon runs taper off, but fish remain in local rivers. This is an excellent time to harvest. Spawning fish are less fatty and can be smoked or dried more easily than fresh-run fish. Karluk residents likely fished along the river in early fall to harvest late-run coho and sockeye salmon and preserve them for winter use. People likely worked from streamside fish camps upriver, harpooning fish where they lingered.

As Kodiak's hillsides turned from green to brown, overland travel became easier, and the pelts of bear, river otters, and fox reached prime condition. Although bear hunting can be done throughout the warm season, fall hunting trips were a Karluk tradition and a way to stockpile food. In recent times, people stored bear fat for cooking and salted bear meat in the fall for winter use (Dodge 2004:293–294). These trips could also have been a time to set snares to capture smaller fur bearers, such as fox and otter. In the early nineteenth century, Karluk provided three hundred fox and thirty river otter pelts a year to the Russian American Company (Black 1990), and harvesting fox and otter pelts continued to be a lucrative activity through the end of the nineteenth century (Porter 1895:79). These animals were likely harvested with nooses made of braided sinew line set along habitually used tails (Davydov 1977:211;

Naumoff 1979:90). A collection assembled by the Alaska Commercial Company includes sets of snares collected in Karluk in the late nineteenth century. These snares feature loops of baleen or feather quills tied to a sinew line and held open by a small wooden knob (Graburn et al. 1996:Plates 453, 454).[4] One set contains twelve snares, the other sixteen.

In the early twentieth century, Alutiiq men living on southern Kodiak Island trapped from remote sod houses, located far from their villages. Trapping was typically done before heavy snows and hard freezes of winter (Rostad 1988:57–58). Moses Naumoff, who grew up in Karluk, trapped with his uncle, leaving the village for a month at a time. The two worked till their food supply ran low and they had to return (Naumoff 1979:90).

Children learned to trap by pursuing small game near home. Sophie Katelnikoff Shepherd set weasel traps made by her father. She placed these along the stream by her Karluk home and checked them on the way to school (Balisle 2010:45). As a child, Lucille Davis trapped near Karluk with her father. Together they set and checked snares, catching foxes. Lucille learned to stun animals with a blow to the head, then to break their necks. They carried their catches home in a gunnysack, and her father taught her to skin, hang, and dry a hide. A community celebration followed her first catch (Davis 2000; 1997a). Lucille hunted and trapped until she reached puberty, at which time it was inappropriate for her to continue. Menstruating women were thought to scare away animals (Crowell and Laktonen 2001:142; Davis 1997b; Demidoff 1962).

As winter approached and the land froze, the social scene began to thaw. People returned to the village to wait out the cold, dark season. Here, they began crafting tools, clothing, and boats from the materials collected over the summer. They also celebrated the abundance of the year with games, visiting, and festivals. And then as stores of summer food waned, the cycle of harvesting began again.

Life in Karluk had a predictable seasonal rhythm, a pulse of abundance followed by a period of scarcity. The warm season in the village was filled with activity. People watched for the return of fish, birds, and sea mammals; studied the weather; prepared for each harvesting opportunity; hunted, gathered, and fished; and cared for the catch. The entire community was involved, working diligently to not only harvest but preserve the wealth of summer resources for winter use. They were aided by long days and the relatively drier weather in Karluk, both essential to drying fish, meat, and hides.

While a similar seasonal pattern of harvesting can be found in any Alutiiq village, life on southwestern Kodiak, and in the village of Karluk, had a unique flavor. Here, the central resources were those available in the river and on the land, not along the ocean shore. While Karluk residents were skilled at hunting sea mammals and fishing in ocean waters, they were first and foremost salmon fishermen. More than anything else, Karluk is known for its abundance of salmon, a resource that represents both a source of food and a valuable commodity for trade. For six months of every year, from the early runs of May through the late runs of November, harvesting fish was a focus of community life. This was punctuated by opportunities to harvest other locally abundant foods—berries, lily roots, ducks, and bears. Like Karluk River salmon, the region's brown bears are legendary, as are the skill of its Alutiiq bear hunters. In this riverine environment, the quantities of fat, meat, bone, and gut harvested from bears provided a valuable supplement to those of sea mammals.

Chapter Five Notes

1. Unknown Alutiiq word written with Cyrillic characters (see Leer and Haakanson 2009:177), possibly referring to a powerful spirit.

2. Mit'ak refers to a star person, a spirit who looks down on earth from the sky world. The word come from the Alutiiq root for one that has landed.

3. *Angyat* is the plural form of the Alutiiq word *angyaq*, used to denote three or more boats.

4. These pieces are identified as snowshoe-hare snares. However, snowshoe hares were not found on Kodiak at the time the materials were collected. The Alaska Commercial Company Collection was made between 1868 and 1897, when the company operated trading posts in the region (Graburn et al. 1996). Snowshoe hares were introduced to Kodiak in 1930s (Tennessen 2010:33). As such, the snares may have been made elsewhere and taken to Karluk, or perhaps they were designed to trap other small game, such as weasels or foxes.

6

Household Life

The settlement pleased me . . . there was an air of order in it, and a supply
of everything necessary for a well-inhabited place.

—Uri Lisianski describing an Alutiiq village in 1804 (1814:180–181)

Like its beautiful wooden artifacts, Karluk One held many remarkably preserved features. As researchers peeled back the site's layers, the floors, rooms, tunnels, hearths, storage boxes, and drainage ditches that outfitted people's homes appeared. Much of the site excavation focused on uncovering and recording these features. While such objects are not a physical part of the museum collection, their documentation provides an abundance of information on life in Karluk and the ways artifacts were used. This chapter examines Karluk One's houses and their contents to illustrate daily life in the village.

The Village

Historic photographs of Karluk help us reach back in time to picture the village. An image from 1889, taken before residents adopted wood-framed houses, shows the community filling the hillside along the entrance to Karluk River (fig. 6.1; Bean 1890). Rolling mountains watch over a hamlet of sod houses. Dwellings, mounds of grass and lumber, line the riverbank and sit on the bluffs above. The buildings are closely spaced, particularly along the river's edge, with doorways facing the water. Some houses have multiple rooms, although it is difficult to determine the number from photographs. Boards, boats, and gear lean against the dwellings and rest on their roofs. Small buildings, laundry lines, and well-worn paths wind around the houses and up the hill to a Russian Orthodox chapel. On the beach below, wooden racks hold drying fish and animal skins, and boats are stored along the bank.

This image compares nicely with the character of ancient settlements documented by archaeologists around the Kodiak Archipelago. Large, late prehistoric Alutiiq villages, like Karluk One, held clusters of sod houses organized in rows. Settlements along the Karluk, Ayakulik, and Olga rivers, for example, have dwellings overlooking the water. Closely spaced houses line the very edge of river terraces and many have doorways

Figure 6.1. *Kal'ut*—Karluk Village, 1889. Albatross Collection, National Archives, Washington, DC. Photograph by Tarleton H. Bean.

opening directly onto the riverbank. The arrangement suggests a focus on the waterway, both for access to the river and to monitor the movements of fish. In these sites, the size and shape of houses varies considerably, from small dwellings with a single side room to enormous structures with as many as eight side rooms. Historic sources suggest that community leaders and their families lived in larger, more nicely outfitted houses (Golder 1903b:86; Golovnin 1979:24; Lisianski 1814:184), places where families amassed goods and community members gathered (cf. Fitzhugh 2003:128). In late prehistoric villages sites, the largest houses tend to cluster together in the center of a village or at one end. Here, people of

influence may have lived beside each other, perhaps even in neighborhoods (Jordan 1994:148).

In larger settlements, there is sometimes a second row of dwellings behind the first. Where space along a terrace was limited, people choose to build in dry areas behind their neighbors. This appears to be the case at Karluk One. Archaeological deposits on the riverbank were deeper and more extensive than those on the bluffs above. The village originated along the water's edge, eventually spreading to the bluffs. This expansion may even have occurred in historic times (see Chapter 3). Russian entrepreneurs built an artel, a provisioning station, above the site in 1785. The bluff overlooking the river's mouth is also the long-time location of Karluk's Russian Orthodox Chapel of the Ascension of Our Lord, a community focal point. Whatever the evolution of the community, historic images showing paths leading to the river and the presence of fish racks, boats, and gear stored in this location, show that the riverbank was an actively used part of the village (fig. 6.2).

Archaeological data suggest that the layout of prehistoric Karluk One was similar to that of the historic village shown in fig. 6.2. As people rebuilt their houses, a process that occurred repeatedly over the use of the site, the location and orientation of structures changed little (Knecht 1995:143–149). At least along the bank of the river, people built one house on top of the next, maintaining a very similar position in this prime

location. This likely reflects the limited amount of space. Residents built their houses close together in both the sod-house village and in later times when wood-framed homes were the norm. It also may reflect the use of the same household location by a particular family over generations, and the importance of maintaining access to the river and its resources. Writing about village locations, Russian Naval Officer Gavriil Davydov said (1977:155), "The islanders will not move away because, they say, that is where their fathers lived."

How many houses were in the village and how many people lived there? The construction of wood-framed buildings, gardens, and other features atop the prehistoric deposits made it impossible for archaeologists to see the configuration

Figure 6.2. Detailed view of the Karluk village, 1889. National Marine Fisheries Service. Photograph by Tarleton H. Bean. Image ID: line 1691, NOAA's America's Coastlines Collections.

of sod structure on the ground surface (Knecht 1995:140). Moreover, bank sloughing and erosion, a process visible in historic photos and underway during the archaeological studies, removed portions of houses. We do not know how many houses were present, how they varied in size, or what other types of buildings were part of the community.

Bean's 1889 photographs show at least seventeen structures (see fig. 6.1). However, they are difficult to count. It is not possible to see the entire village or to separate outbuildings from houses. Similarly, we do not know if every house was occupied at the same time. Alutiiq Elders report that old sod houses were often used for storage after their residents moved to new homes (Russell 1991). Moreover, while this number provides a rough estimate of the historic sod houses at Karluk One, it doesn't account for other areas of Karluk Lagoon occupied at the same time.

Throughout the life of Karluk One, people also lived in adjacent areas of the lagoon. Old Karluk, another extensive late prehistoric village site lies on the opposite shore of the lagoon (Jordan and Knecht 1988). Historic maps and accounts note several Alutiiq settlements in the lagoon and suggest that people moved between them (see Chapter 3). It is not uncommon in the Kodiak's archaeological record to find two similarly aged settlements on opposing riverbanks. For skilled mariners with dependable boats, crossing the Karluk River was a minor task and settlements on either side of the waterway were likely part of one large community. This has long been the case in Karluk. In the twentieth century, Karluk residents lived on both shores of the lagoon (Bean 1890:Plate LXXXI) and traveled back and forth over a suspension bridge originating at Karluk One (fig. 6.3). According to Kenneth Taylor, an

anthropologist who lived in the community in the early 1960s, this spatial separation of families has little impact on social cohesion (1965:32). All parts of the village maintained strong ties. Even in the 1980s, when the archaeological study of Karluk One was underway, community members

Figure 6.3. The Karluk River suspension bridge. "Before you could walk down the spit from our side of the river and cross on the bridge to the other village. There are two villages, one is called the Spit side and then there is Old Karluk which is across the lagoon on our side where I live."— Frieda Reft (Charliaga 1980:87). Alutiiq Museum library, Knagin collection, Karluk 58.

were living in Old Karluk, New Karluk (a name for the late nineteenth- and early twentieth-century village at Karluk One), and a new village site on the western shore of the inner lagoon—Karluk Village.

Whatever the configuration of settlements in Karluk Lagoon, the village was historically a "well populated spot" (Shelikhov 1981:47). Late eighteenth-century census figures suggest that 344 people lived in the Karluk area—173 men and 171 women (Langsdorff 1993:31). However, this figure likely includes people from neighboring regions like Uyak Bay, as Russian census data was taken for regions, not communities. Nineteenth-century accounts suggest that there were about thirty Native families in Karluk Village (Campbell 1816:98), with fewer than three hundred residents in the region (Luehrmann 2008:164–170; Tikhmenev 1978:413). These figures are likely lower than in prehistoric times, before forced labor, disease, starvation, and relocation dramatically impacted the Alutiiq population (Gideon 1989:69–71; Huggins 1981:3; Langsdorff 1993:29–31). Nonetheless, these statistics agree generally with historic accounts of other Kodiak Alutiiq villages, where two to three hundred people typically lived in ten to fifteen houses (Holmberg 1985:43).

In addition to houses, other features of the village likely included small outbuildings, storage pits, burials, and perhaps a community house. Based on archaeological data from the banks of Karluk River, small, one-room structures were sometimes built beside a larger multi-roomed house. Alutiiq Elders and historic sources suggest these sheds were used for both storage and seclusion. Dying people were sometimes moved into an outbuilding (Lisianski 1814:200), as families often abandoned a house in which a person died

(Davydov 1977:179). Likewise, a mother who lost a child was secluded for a number of days following burial (Lisianski 1814:200). Huts were also used to seclude menstruating and laboring women. According to Demidoff (1962), women and the sick gave off vapors that clung to the body and could upset animals. Elders describe women's seclusion huts as lean-tos; small, windowless structures built beside a house or even within a home (Hausler ca. 1990). Russian observers noted that these structures were less than a meter in diameter and a meter high, "built of reeds and covered with grass" (Davydov 1977:171; Gideon 1989:51; Lisianski 1814:184, 201; Petrof 1884:235). Men did not enter these structures (Gideon 1989:49).

While archaeologists did not identify seclusion huts at Karluk One, it is likely that they were part of the village. Menstrual seclusions continued well into the twentieth century on Kodiak and reflected strong beliefs in the reproductive power possessed by women (Crowell 1992:21; Drabek 2012:151). Elder women recall being isolated in their bedrooms and forbidden to look out a window for fear they would invite bad weather (Steffian and Counceller 2012:67). Lucille Davis, an Alutiiq Elder raised in Karluk, reports that menstruating women were not allowed to cross the suspension bridge over the Karluk River for fear the salmon would not return (Crowell and Laktonen 2001:142).

Storage pits, holes dug into the ground outside of houses, were not found in the Karluk One excavations. However, as the site eroded, archaeologists saw clay-lined pits in the face of the deposit. Ethnographic accounts indicate that Alutiiq people buried a variety of foods in such pits to enhance their taste and preservation. For example, Alutiiq people soured whale meat in pits, alternating layers of meat and greens, then covering the hole with a layer of clean grass followed by dirt (Merck 1980:106; Petrof 1884:231). Other pits were lined with grass, filled with food, covered, and marked with a stick. The cool earth kept the food fresh and prevented it from freezing in winter (Russell 1991).

The dead were also buried in villages (Merck 1980:107). Dressed in their best clothing, their remains were interred in plank-lined graves dug about three feet into the ground. The body was laid on its sides, often on a layer of grass, with knees bent and face covered (Merck 1980:107). A hunter might be wrapped in the skin cover from his boat (Black 1981:4). Over the remains, people might place a sealskin and layers of rocks and earth (Gideon 1989:54; Lisianski 1814:200). The deceased's tools—kayak, throwing board, net, instruments of warfare, or other gear were sometimes placed in or over the grave (Black 1977:86; Merck 1980:107). Other belongings were given away at death (Petrof 1884:235). Family members in mourning cut their hair, painted their faces, and visited the gravesite to cry, sing songs, remember the deceased, and console the departed person's spirit (Black 1977:86, 96; Black 1981:4).

Investigations at Karluk One encountered eight burials with the remains of thirteen people.[1] Two burials occurred in outdoor areas, beside the edge of a house. The remaining six burials were inside houses. The outdoor burials match historic descriptions of graves. Just beyond the wall of a house, a teenage girl was laid to rest. Placed on her right side, with her knees drawn to her chest, she was buried inside a plank-and-grass-lined grave (Feuerstein 1988). Another burial held the remains of an adult man, also surrounded by planks and lying on his left side with his knees drawn to his chest.

In contrast to the structures used and maintained by families, some communities had a *qasgiq*, a community house (Davydov 1977:154; Merck 1980:100). Built by a wealthy leader with the help of community members, these large buildings had one or two open rooms with benches lining the walls (Gideon 1989:40). Here, men gathered to talk politics, plan raiding and trading parties, and repair tools. These large buildings were also the location of winter festivals, annual wintertime celebrations of the year's harvest marked with feasting, gambling, and dancing. When young people were old enough to join adults in these activities, they were initiated into the *qasgiq* (Black 1981:5; Davydov 1977:184; Desson 1995:130). We don't know if there was a *qasgiq* at Karluk One, although artifacts associated with dancing and gaming abound in the site's artifact collection (fig. 6.4), indicating that celebrations were part of the rhythm of village life (Donta 1993; see Chapter 7).

Houses

Information on Karluk's prehistoric houses comes largely from the remains of two adjacent structures, rebuilt repeatedly in prehistoric times (fig. 6.5). Archaeologists studying the site worked in a large, horizontal excavation area. Over the first three years of excavations, this hole captured a portion of the main room in two adjacent houses, including their hearth features. It also revealed three side rooms, one associated with the southern house and two with its northern neighbor. In the top layers of the site, there were seven distinct house floors rebuilt in the same location. Beneath these seven consecutively built houses were portions of three additional house floors and two major midden deposits (Jordan and Knecht

Figure 6.4. *Cit'suutet*—tally sticks on house floor 4, excavated in 1985. These small, carefully formed sticks were used to track points earned in traditional games. Alutiiq Museum archives, AM193:275.S.

1988:257; Knecht 1995:141, 155). In later years, when the site was eroding rapidly, excavations captured other fragments of house floors. In 1995, archaeologists recorded a sequence of nine over-laid floors and sampled artifacts from their central rooms in an area surrounding a series of superimposed hearths (Steffian 1996).

None of these houses were complete. The large size of ancient dwellings and the presence of modern buildings on top of the site made excavation of an entire house difficult. Moreover, erosion had damaged Karluk One's houses. In all of the excavated structures, a portion of the central room had been washed away. While excavators were able to study central rooms, side rooms, and a great variety of household features, these came from a selection of houses spanning four hundred

Figure 6.5. Layout of squares excavated from 1984 to 1987, superimposed on the location of underlying sod houses (generalized). Illustration by Amy Steffian, adapted from a map by Catherine West.

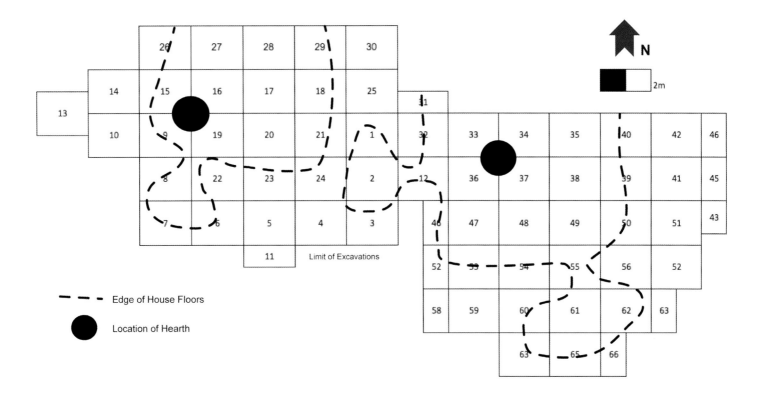

years, not one single dwelling. Thus, the following description provides a composite picture of Karluk houses based on finds from four centuries of house building.

House Building

Like Alutiiq homes built throughout the Kodiak Archipelago until the twentieth century, Karluk houses were made of wood, earth, and grass. These locally available, easily harvested materials were ingeniously combined to make warm, weatherproof dwellings. The house remains excavated at Karluk One provided many details on the style, construction, and features of ancient dwellings.

Alutiiq sod houses—known in the Alutiiq language as *ciqlluat*—began with a foundation (table 6.1). Builders dug a shallow hole into the ground to create a floor. This hole was about 60 cm deep (Lisianski 1814:214). Houses typically had multiple rooms—a large central room and small side rooms connect to the central room by narrow passageways. The house foundation mirrored the floor plan of the entire structure, with sunken areas for each room and passageway. In many areas of the Kodiak Archipelago, Alutiiq people dug through the soil into underlying gravel or glacial deposits to create a hard, durable living surface through which water would drain. Soil floors can get muddy and slippery with use, particularly in wet environments. As such, people preferred a gravel base. At Karluk One, the oldest houses, those at the bottom of the site, were built into beach gravel. Because the beach had no soil,

Table 6.1 Alutiiq terms for parts of a sod house

ENGLISH NAME	SINGULAR ALUTIIQ NAME	DUAL ALUTIIQ NAME	PLURAL ALUTIIQ NAME
House	Ciqlluaq*	Ciqlluak	Ciqlluat
Room (literally "inside location")	Qamnaq	Qamnak	Qamnat
Entrance (tunnel)	Siinaruaq*	Siinaruak	Siinaruat
Hearth	Kenirwik*	Kenirwik	Kenirwit
Smoke hole	Puyum Angwia	Puyum Angwiak	Puyum Angwiat
Smoke hole cover (literally "its cover")	Patua*	Patugak	Patui
Bench	Aqum'agwik	Aqum'agwik	Aqum'agwit
Door	Amiik	Amiik	Amiit
Post	Napataq	Napatak	Napatat
Plank	Qupuraq; Alasarnaq	Qupurak; Alasarnak	Qupurat; Alasarnat
Wall	Estinaq	Estinak	Estinat
Roof	Englum Qainga	Englum Qaingik	Englum Qaingit
Shed	Saʀayaq	Saʀayak	Saʀayat
Menstrual hut	Ayawik	Ayawik	Ayawiat
Steambath; banya	Maqiwik	Maqiwik	Maqiwit

*Word belongs to the modern Alutiiq lexicon.

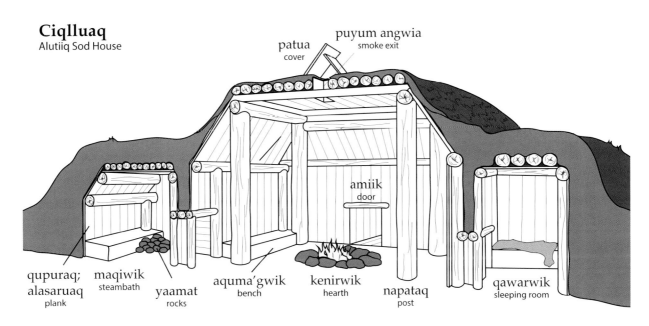

Ciqlluaq
Alutiiq Sod House

patua
cover

puyum angwia
smoke exit

amiik
door

qupuraq;
alasaruaq
plank

maqiwik
steambath

yaamat
rocks

aquma'gwik
bench

kenirwik
hearth

napataq
post

qawarwik
sleeping room

Figure 6.6. Interior of an Alutiiq sod house. Illustration by Alisha Drabek. Adapted from a drawing by Philomena Hausler (ca. 1990).

sod for building must have been cut and collected nearby and brought to the beach.

In the center of a house foundation, Alutiiq builders erected large posts—*napatat*—designed to support wooden beams (fig. 6.6). Builders first erected four main posts, creating a rectangle (Billings in Merck 1980:204; Gideon 1989:39; Matfay 1990). These post were not completely upright but leaned gently inward toward the center of the structure. This design crated a sloping roof that helped to funnel smoke up and out of the house through an opening in the roof. Additional posts were set in the corners of the rooms about 1.2 m from the central posts. Then, the tops of all posts were notched so that beams could be fastened to them. The resulting structure was up to 2 m tall in the center (McKeown 1948:54), allowing people to stand inside, but much shorter on the side, about 1.4 m high.

Archaeologists found the remains of some house posts at Karluk One. Often, fist-size rocks were wedged into the ground at the base of a post to keep it firmly in place. In many other cases, however, posts were missing (Knecht 1995:152). Large holes in house floors indicated where posts once stood and suggested that people purposefully removed these critical timbers when rebuilding their homes. When a house could no longer be maintained, people appear to have salvaged wood from its frame, collapsed the structure, and rebuilt on top.

Over the post and beam framework, Alutiiq carpenters secured planks, flat pieces of lumber that also sloped gently inward (Davydov 1977:154; Merck 1980:100). To make these planks, they split driftwood logs with the aid of large stone mauls, resilient wedges of wood, sea mammal bone and antler, and heavy stone splitting adzes (fig. 6.7–6.9). Alutiiq mauls and splitting adzes were made of beach cobbles. Craftsmen pecked grooves into the cobbles and sometimes shaped the stone. Historic examples are lashed

Figure 6.7. *Muʀut'uuruasinaq*—maul, *kliitaq*—wedge. The stone maul, or hammer, in the upper left was reworked into an oil lamp after it broke. Wedges were used for a range of tasks from heavy work like splitting driftwood logs to the creation of planks and small lengths of wood. The wood wedges on the left are triangular in cross section, while the two on the right are round and then cut to form an angled tip. The wedges on the far left and right have drilled pits in which fat was added to lubricate the wedge as it was hammered into a piece of wood (Knecht 1995:439). Wood wedges range from about 10 cm long and 3 cm wide to 40 cm long and 12 cm wide. Many have battered or chipped ends where they were struck. AM193.87:8782, AM193.87:8858; Karluk School avocational collection, AM39:227; UA85.193:2958, UA85.193:3133, UA85.193:6837, AM193.87:11558.

to sturdy wooden handles with strips of leather (Korsun 2012:180; Varjola 1990:248). Splitting adzes helped craftsmen break open logs (Knecht 1995:252). Then, with mauls, carpenters hammered a series of wedges into the logs, splitting the wood into rough planks (cf. Stewart 1984:41). Lengths of wood were then shaped and smoothed with smaller planning adzes. Heavy woodworking implements like these are a hallmark of late prehistoric Alutiiq toolkits. People began to make

and use these tools when they started to build large, multi-roomed homes.

House planks were often made of cedar (Matfay 1990), a rot-resistant material that splits easily. Builders placed these planks side by side vertically to form walls—*estinat* in the Alutiiq language—and cover the roof, thus creating a paneled interior. Short, roughhewn planks were common finds at Karluk One, both on floors and along the edges of room (Knecht 1995:152).

Figure 6.8. *Tupuuᴙuq*—splitting adze. There are two main shapes of splitting adzes in the Karluk One collection, the shoe form and the D shape (Heizer 1956:44). These D-shaped stone adzes have grooves for lashing to a handle and resemble a splitting maul collected on Kodiak in the historic era (Birket-Smith 1941:152). UA84.193:821, AM193.94:81.

Figure 6.9. *Tupuuᴙuq*—splitting adze. These shoe-shaped adzes (cf. Heizer 1956:44) have a single pecked groove on the ridge. Other examples have a double or, less commonly, a triple groove. Splitting adzes are generally 16 to 23 cm in length, with the longest from the collection being 30 cm long and the smallest 13 cm long. Karluk School avocational collection, AM39:162; Lind Sheehan avocational collection, AM14:313; AM193.87:8796.

Some prehistoric houses had narrow trenches along the walls where the bases of planks were set into the floor (Saltonstall 1997). Just as they salvaged posts, carpenters likely reclaimed wall and ceiling boards from Karluk houses when rebuilding.

Over the wooden planking, builders placed layers of grass, mud, and sod to create a waterproof, insulating cover. Matfay (1990, 1992) described this process in detail. Men worked from the bottom of the structure upward, covering the entire framework with a thick layer of freshly cut grass. Working in this direction prevented leaks, as did laying the grass so that it would shed water. Sometimes, builders packed a layer of dirt over the grass to help hold it in place (Gideon 1989:44). Sod blocks cut about half a meter (ca. 1 foot) square were the final addition. With the grassy side of a sod block oriented toward the house, builders stacked sods against the framework and pressed them into place. Work began on the inside the edge of the foundation. From here, men worked up the sides of the house, covering side rooms and a portion of the central room with sod. The result was a sturdy house that looked like a "ball of grass" (Matfay 1990).

Sorting Out the Sods

Patrick G. Saltonstall, Curator of Archaeology, Alutiiq Museum

I got my start in Alaskan archaeology excavating at the Karluk One site in 1985. Up till then, my archaeological experience consisted of studying shell middens on the coast of Maine. At Karluk One, the wood preservation amazed me. At this site, we weren't just finding fortuitously preserved bits of bone and stone, we were finding everything. It was an incredible experience to clear a cover of grass from intact floorboard, to discover the grass roll that edged the floor, or to find an upright corner posts that once held up a roof (fig. 6.10). These architectural details brought the site to life in three dimensions.

None of us had excavated houses of wood, sod, and grass before, and it was a chance for everyone to learn. At the time, lead researcher Dick Jordan looked to neighboring Yup'ik people for ethnographic examples of houses to help interpret the site's features. There was not yet a detailed record of Alutiiq houses, but Yup'ik peoples built sod and wood-framed structures. Jordan saw the dense layers of sod and grass at Karluk as roof layers and the intervening layers of boards, grass and wood chips as floors. This made sense. The floor layers contained the bulk of the artifacts and features like hearths that provided evidence of indoor activities. The sod layers contained few cultural materials.

A few years later, I excavated similarly aged houses at the Settlement Point site on Afognak Island. Here, there was no wood preservation. However, the houses had not been disturbed or built on top of by later site occupants, as was the case in Karluk. I was surprised to find that none of the Settlement Point houses had roof layers. There were thick floor layers, built up from lots of use, but no roofs. Where were the insulating earthen layers found repeatedly at Karluk? I also discovered that each side room had a unique tunnel; a box-shaped entry between the central room of the house and the side room designed to trap cold air. Why hadn't we seen something similar in Karluk where so many architectural details were preserved?

These questions baffled me until I returned to Karluk in 1994 and 1995 to help with salvage excavations. Here, my Afognak Island investigations proved illuminating. Some of the wood features first interpreted as storage boxes at Karluk One suddenly became clear as wooden frameworks for cold trap tunnels. And the ubiquitous sod layers proved to be reflooring episodes. The Karluk site lies between a pond and the ocean, at the base of a steep hill. It is a wet spot. Here, Alutiiq people built drainage ditches in the floors of their homes to direct water away from sitting and sleeping areas. Each time they rebuilt one of these large houses, they began with a dense clean layer of earth, a barrier against the wet deposits beneath. The sod layers weren't roofs but foundations.

Over two decades of study, we've learned that ancient Alutiiq houses were not built in the same way as Yup'ik houses. The larger Alutiiq structures dating after AD 1300 had sod roofs over their side rooms, but their spacious main rooms were thatched, covered in grass. This idea has been supported by survey data. Whenever we investigate depressions left by collapsed multi-roomed houses, our shovels quickly find the floor layer. Sometimes, we even see the stone slabs used to build a hearth showing right on the surface, but there are never the remains of a sod roof.

Figure 6.10. Richard Jordan and Patrick Saltonstall digging in the upper levels of the site, 1985, watched intently by village children. *From left*: Gladys Alpiak, Catherine Reft, Larry Shugak, and Cecil Charliaga. Alutiiq Museum archives, AM193:292.S.

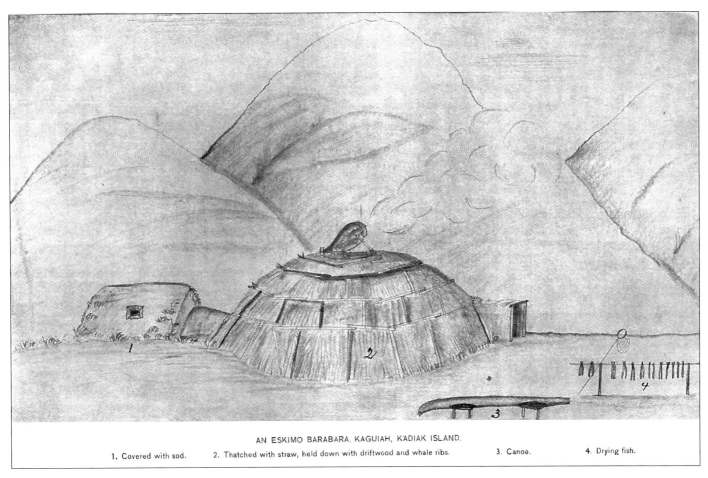

AN ESKIMO BARABARA, KAGUIAH, KADIAK ISLAND.

1. Covered with sod.   2. Thatched with straw, held down with driftwood and whale ribs.   3. Canoe.   4. Drying fish.

Figure 6.11. *Ciqlluaq*—sod house. Drawing of an Alutiiq sod house showing construction characteristics, including roofing styles. From Jackson 1894:96.

Although layers of sod separated the house floors at Karluk One (Jordan and Knecht 1988:257), these layers appear to be house foundations designed to provide a clean, dry living surface, not a roof layer. Archaeological studies of similarly aged houses throughout the Kodiak region show that sod roofs typically occur only over side rooms. Central rooms lack evidence of a sod cover (Saltonstall essay Chapter 5). An illustration of a historic Alutiiq house from Kaguyak also shows this roofing pattern. The house has a side room covered in sod and a central room covered in grass thatching (fig. 6.11).

At Karluk One, as cultural materials accumulated and the village became elevated above the beach, drainage became a problem. Water from the small pond behind the site seeped into the deposits. While this helped to preserve many beautiful objects, it also made the village wet. To channel water away from their homes, residents carefully engineered subfloor drainage ditches (fig. 6.12). These shallow trenches were up to 20 cm deep and, in places, both covered and lined with boards. The trenches often had narrow boards across them, pieces of wood placed at intervals along the trench to support a cover of planks. The planks typically ran parallel to the ditch, following its path across the floor. As these features aged, they filled with muck and people stacked more boards on top. The trenches often extended all the

Figure 6.12. Frederica de Laguna cleaning a subfloor drainage ditch, house floor 8, 1985. Alutiiq Museum archives, AM193:86f.N. Photograph by Rick Knecht.

way across a house floor and even intersected with other trenches, but they do not appear to have extended out of the houses. They seem to have been designed to catch water, and perhaps encourage it to drain down into the site, but not to channel it out of the house.

Drainage ditches were one short-term solution to wet houses. Villagers also solved the ongoing water problem by reflooring. People periodically added grass, sods, and even planks to Karluk One floors. This created dense floor deposits, some as thick as 30 cm. In other Kodiak area settlements, people used beach gravel to cover the floors of their homes. After repeated reflooring with gravel,

some houses contained as a much as 50 cm of gravel inside (Saltonstall 1997). At Karluk One, when a house floor got too thick or its wooden structure deteriorated beyond easy maintenance, inhabitants started afresh. At this point, people tore down the structure (removing the vertical timbers in particular) and rebuilt their house on a layer of clean, freshly cut sod blocks. This process created a layer of sod on top of each house floor and promoted the large accumulations of site deposits. When first measured, Karluk One's layers rose 4.2 m above the beach.

The final step in house construction was to weight the roof. People piled driftwood, kayak frames, paddles, and other gear on top of their houses to help keep the thick grass cover in place (Matfay 1990). Historic photographs from Karluk show large logs lying on roofs and discarded portions of seine nets covering houses (fig. 6.13). Matfay (1992) reports that from the inside of the house it was sometimes possible to see daylight through the boards and grass covering the roof but that, regardless, a well-constructed roof kept a house warm and dry.[2]

Roofs were sturdy. Russian observers note that people often sat on household roofs to track the weather and watch for fish and game (Lisianski 1814:181). At Karluk One, this would have provided an excellent view of fish entering the river, whales feeding in Shelikof Strait, or visitors approaching from the mainland.

Maintenance of the roof was critical. People never removed old layers of roofing grass but added to them. Cutting grass was a chore completed by older men and often done in the fall in preparation for winter (Gideon 1989:44; Matfay 1990). At this time of year, people cut and covered their houses with a fresh layer of grass. At other times, they reused grass. According to Matfay (1990), people cleaned their homes weekly during warm

Figure 6.13. *Ciqlluaq*—sod house, Karluk village, 1889. Note the driftwood used to secure the grass roof. National Marine Fisheries Service, fish7461. Photograph by Tarleton H. Bean.

weather, removing the grass used to cover house floors and depositing it on top of their homes.

A central feature of the roof was a cover or *patua*, designed to cover a centrally located, rectangular smoke hole or *puyum angwia* (Merck 1980:100). Residents oriented this square board toward the prevailing wind and propped it open with a stick. If the wind typically blew from the east, the hatch would open with the cover secured to the east side of the smoke hole, blocking gusts from entering the house. The hatch could be opened and closed as needed to let in light and fresh air and let out smoke from the fireplace below (Matfay 1990) or soot generated by oil-burning lamps (Black 1977:83). Researchers did not find any smoke hole covers at Karluk One. However, the village is known to be very windy (McKeown 1948:40; Tiffany 1995) and

photographs of sod houses in Karluk show these objects in use. Additionally, pieces of gutskin were fashioned into small windows (Davydov 1977:154; Gideon 1989:40), and in some cases, used to cover a smoke hole (Merck 1980:100). Early collections from the Kodiak Alutiiq, stored at the Kuntskamera in St. Petersburg, Russia, include four skylight covers made of gutskin. One is made from the membrane covering a whale's liver, another from whale intestines, and another features long baleen ties (Korsun 2012:169–172).

The result of these construction methods was a series of warm, weather-resistant dwelling. Historic sources indicate that each home accommodated a large, extended family. Here, groups of related women lived together with their families. Several sisters, their husbands, their children, and perhaps a grandparent occupied one house.

Families shared the central room and a side room designed for steam bathing, but each had its own sleeping chamber. Typically, a newly married coupled lived with the bride's family until they had a child (Black 1977:85; Gideon 1989:50). At that point, the couple moved into their own home. House building and maintenance were community activities. When a new house was completed or an existing home refurbished for winter, the owner provided a generous, celebratory meal for those who had assisted in its construction (Gideon 1989:44; Matfay 1990).

Parts of a House

People entered their houses through low, narrow passageways (Shelikhov 1981:56) known in Alutiiq as a *siinaruat*. The door to this entry tunnel was about a meter square, and archaeological studies illustrate that it was invariably placed in the middle of the central-room wall closest to the nearest adjacent waterway (Knecht and Jordan 1985:24; Saltonstall and Steffian 2006). A piece of seal or sea lion skin tied to one of the posts framing the doorway covered the opening, protected the interior from wind and rain, and could be tied shut (Billings in Merck 1980:205; Davydov 1977:154; Demidoff 1962; Golder 1907:297; Langsdorf 1993:32; Sauer 1802:175).[3] The doorway was either level with the ground or required visitors to step down into the home. Historic accounts indicate that people crouched or crawled to enter (Langsdorf 1993:32; Merck 1980:100) but that houses were warm. A low entrance helped to keep rising warm air inside. Entry passages led to the central room and in recent centuries were about a meter long. In contrast, entry passages seen in older multi-roomed houses were often longer and more elaborate (Saltonstall and Steffian 2006; Steffian and Saltonstall 2004).

Figure 6.14. Amy Steffian stands beside an entrance tunnel eroding from the beach at the base of Karluk One deposits, 1995. Alutiiq Museum archives, AM193:1016.S. Photograph by Patrick Saltonstall.

Dogs, a common resident of Alutiiq villages, often slept in the entry tunnel (McKeown 1948:54).

Researchers recorded one example of an entry passage at Karluk One, eroding from the beach at the very bottom of the site (fig. 6.14). This was one of the first houses built in the settlement. Here, a meter-wide passage extended over three meters out of a main room toward the water. Six large posts held up the superstructure, and the passage was lined with vertically placed planks. Researchers found a plank mask at the very bottom of the floor deposits, just inside the outer entrance of the tunnel. The mask may have been intentionally placed in this spot when the house was first built.

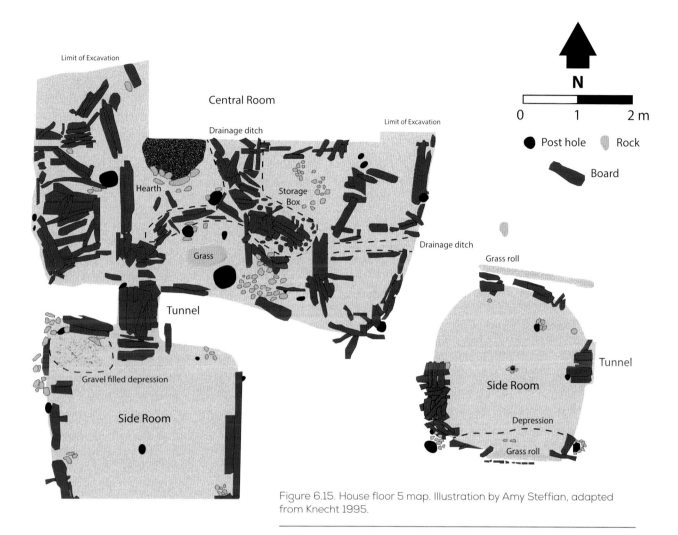

Figure 6.15. House floor 5 map. Illustration by Amy Steffian, adapted from Knecht 1995.

The central room was the heart of the house, where a great variety of activities took place. Here, people cooked, manufactured, played, slept, stored their food and belongings, and hosted gatherings (Huggins 1981:6). According to Matfay (1990), central rooms varied in size but were about 7.6 m across, large enough for a hunter to bring his kayak inside for repairs. A historic sod house from the village of Nunakakhnak, located on the shore of Karluk Lagoon just 2 km from Karluk One, had a small central room, about 5.5 m across. In some Alutiiq houses, earthen benches for sitting and sleeping lined the walls (Knecht and Jordan 1985:24). In others, people sat and slept directly on the floor (Matfay 1990). This seems to be the case at Karluk One, where sod benches were uncommon (Steffian 1996).

According to Matfay (1990), sod houses were carefully swept and maintained to keep them clean. Excavations of a historic sod house at Nunakakhnak match this description, as the structure's floor was largely free of debris (Knecht and Jordan 1985:23). This was not the case at Karluk One. Here, house floors were up to 30 cm thick, hard packed from use, and filled with dirt, charcoal, wood chips, grass, gravel, fish bones, boards, and objects (fig. 6.15). Grass was particularly common.[4] Within house floors, there were thin horizontal layers of floor matrix separated by discontinuous layers of sod just a few centimeters thick. These layers likely reflect cleaning and maintenance. In the twentieth century, people typically changed the grass on their house floors weekly—removing the old grass, sweeping the dirt or board floor, and recovering the floor with a fresh layer of grass (Matfay 1990). At Karluk One, people appear to have added layers of both grass and dirt to their floors, perhaps to manage the wet conditions. At the edges of houses, archaeologists often found long narrow rolls of grass. The purpose of these rolls is not known.

The main feature of the central room was a stone-ringed hearth, or *kenirwik* in the Alutiiq language. Rectangular cobbles lined the edge of a shallow depression in the floor (Lisianski 1814:212), creating a fire pit (fig. 6.16). The nineteenth-century house at Nunakakhnak had such a hearth. This feature was about a meter in diameter and 25 cm deep, with three rows of cobbles following its edge (Knecht and Jordan 1985:24). Matfay (1990) reported that hearths were sometimes lined with gravel and flanked by two small stakes designed to hold a pole for hanging a kettle over a fire. Small stakes and stake holes were present around a number of Karluk One hearths, sometimes in large numbers. One hearth was surrounded by seventeen of these small uprights, many with their tips burned (Steffian 1996). These were likely skewer sticks used to roast foods, a practice observed historically (Lisianski 1814:195). Langsdorff (1993:140), who visited an Alutiiq home in 1804, and shared a meal with its residents wrote, "Everyone sat around a fire burning in the middle of the hut. A kettle of fish was hanging over it. Several small salmon, spitted upon sticks stuck in the earth around the fire, were being roasted."

Figure 6.16. *Kenirwik*—hearth. Rock-ringed hearth from house floor 8, with an adjacent pile of cooking or heating rocks, 1995. Alutiiq Museum archives, AM193:1163.S. Photograph by Patrick Saltonstall.

Household hearths provided residents with both light and heat and were a center of activity. Karluk One hearths were often filled with charcoal and wood ash and the surrounding floor area stained black. Small piles of fire-reddened and cracked rocks were common finds in and around these features; the remnants of stones heated for warming side rooms, cooking, and steam bathing (fig. 6.16). Archaeologists found few artifacts in hearths or the immediately surrounding area. However, the broader area circling these features was often rich in objects.

Alutiiq people used friction to create fire, working with small, wooden drills to make sparks (Black 1981:3; Davydov 1977:187; Demidoff 1962; Merck 1980:106) (fig. 6.17). A wooden handle with a hole in the base (fire-drill bearing) held the top of a cylindrical piece of wood (fire drill). The fire builder rotated this piece rapidly with the aid of a string tied to a small bow. The bottom of the cylinder rested in a fire hearth, a board designed to catch fire. People held dried

Figure 6.17. *Nucuutaq*—fire-starting gear. Fire-starting hearth, drill, drill handle, drill bow. "They make fire by using a sharpened stick. . . . In the middle of this stick, the end of which is smeared with fat, a string has been twisted round several times. They take the end of the string in their hand, and turn it as quickly as they can in both directions, until smoke comes from the end of the stick which is poked into the woodchips. Then they pick up a smoldering chip and put it to some dry grass; this they wave in their hands until a flame appears" (Davydov 1977:187). UA85.193:4689, UA85.193:2871, AM193.95:1699, AM193.94:4327.

grass against the smoldering wood and then blew on the grass to create a flame. Fire drill pieces are common in the Karluk One collection, and many artifacts have small circular burn marks indicating they were used as fire-starting handles or hearths. Matfay (1990) reported that people selected the wood for their fires carefully, choosing alder and certain types of driftwood that did not spark. This prevented household fires, although not always. Archaeologists have uncovered late prehistoric houses where wooden structures appear to have burned (Hoffman 2009; Saltonstall and Steffian 2006:81; Saltonstall et al. 2012:61; Steffian and Saltonstall 2014:76).

People also gathered embers from neighbors' fires to start their own. According to Katya E., who grew up in a sod house in Karluk:

> We had a cooking place and no such thing as matches. We had to make fire going in the early morning. . . . And in the morning when my mother would get up, she'd tell me to build that fire, then when I got up I'd see another ciqlluaq's smoke and I thought

I'll run to that place. I ran to that place and they'd give me that fire thing "*uquRLumcirmek*" and told me to keep shaking it. I was running back shaking it as I was told. My mother would tell me right away to put it in there . . . all I had to do was put it in there and *who, whooh* (Reed 1962b).

In addition to fires, Alutiiq people lit stone oil lamps, called *naniq* in the Alutiiq language. These were another source of light inside relatively dark sod houses. A legend from Karluk indicates that lamps were common household items and that at least some of them were left at home when people traveled (Golder 1909:23). In this tale, villagers abandon Ughek, an annoying prankster, by sneaking away at night. Afraid to be alone and of a man-eating sea monster known to emerge at low tide, Ughek gathers oil lamps from the community's houses. After filling them with oil and lighting them, he sings and dances to console himself.

The lamps from Karluk One are made from naturally formed cobbles of granite, diorite, greywacke, and sandstone—stone that could be shaped by pecking. Craftsmen used a second rock to gradually peck and grind the object to shape, a laborious process. Tonalite, a hard, pale-green, granitic rock, was a common choice for lamps and may be from an outcrop at the entrance to Uyak Bay. A beach in this area is locally known as lamp rock beach (Knecht 1995:318). Karluk One lamps come in many sizes, from small portable

Carving Alutiiq-Style Oil Lamps

Sandee Drabek, Artist

"Where to begin?" This is what I asked myself as I began my journey learning to carve Alutiiq-style oil lamps, when there were no teachers left to instruct me. The answers had to lie in the beautifully crafted works of art left behind by the ancient Alutiiq master carvers, lamps that have endured for thousands of years.

I began my study with the stone oil lamps held in our family's care. With an open mind, I hefted their weight and felt their curved surfaces, noting their form, symmetry, structure, and balance, all elements essential to a seafaring people, even when constructing a lamp. I reflected on the strength of the curved shape and the selection of stone. These stone lamps had withstood generations of use and when finally abandoned, rolled in the surf for countless years on rocky beaches, remaining miraculously intact when rediscovered generations later.

I was particularly inspired by the decorative lamps from the Late Kachemak tradition, between 2,700 and 1,000 years ago. These lamps are great works of art. Their basins often contained diving whales, a bear head, raised platforms, or the head of a rising seal. The bases include gracefully carved whale flukes, seal images, and other traditional design elements, while the lateral sides were crisply beveled and grooved.

Thankfully, my efforts were encouraged, and I was offered an opportunity to learn from the wealth of knowledge stored in the Alutiiq Museum's collections of Kodiak lamps. I was invited to explore and photograph the lamp collections, many from Karluk One, and converse with the conservators of these treasures. Imagine my delight when I discovered a lamp that had been started but never finished. A lamp under construction! It had a carved base, straight sides, perfectly shaped symmetry and balance, but no basin. Such reassurance! Start with the base and balance, this had been my approach too (fig. 6.18). I truly felt led, taught by those that had gone before. It was as though I had somehow passed a test and been given permission to continue.

Recognizing my desire to learn as much as I could, the curator of the Alutiiq Museum gave me a copy of Robert F. Heizer's study of the lamps found by anthropologist Dr. Aleš Hrdlička in the 1930s at the

Figure 6.18. These two Alutiiq stone oil lamps are crafted in soapstone by Kodiak artist Sandee Drabek. A whale lamp excavated from Uyak Bay by Aleš Hrdlička in the 1930s provided inspiration for the larger lamp, although the modern work has deeply incised whale flukes on its base. It was carved for a Koniag Education Foundation fundraiser honoring the *Giinaquq: Like A Face* Alutiiq mask exhibit in 2008. The smaller lamp is based on a unique triangular bear's head lamp. Its base has an incised bear petroglyph found at Cape Alitak. Courtesy Don Mason Photography.

Uyak Bay site on Kodiak's western shore. Photos and drawings of this large collection include weights and measurements, thoughts on comparative age, and illustrations of the traditional designs used for bases, basins, bevels, and lateral decorative carvings. These notes, along with photos of lamps shared with me over the years and verbal descriptions of lamps held in the memories of friends and Elders have been, and continue to be, my guide. With them, I create new soapstone lamps with traditional designs. These are my teachers, and as I carve with rasps, power tools, and sandpapers, I marvel every time at the timeless treasures the ancient masters created using the simplest of stone tools, their imagination, and little else. It is a humbling experience to bear witness to such talent.

In addition to carving lamps, I frequently include petroglyph and other Alutiiq designs in my paintings. The notes and updates collected by archeologists and books suggested by the Alutiiq Museum staff assure me I am as accurate as I can be when sharing art with the public. It is my intent to honor the enduring journey of Kodiak's Alutiiq people, for the many images formed so very long ago still have the power to inspire, touch our hearts, unite generations, and remind us of the creative insight and respect the original artists had for this, their island home.

Figure 6.19. Karluk girl playing outside, ca. 1955. Note the very large stone oil lamp against the side of the house. Clyda Christensen collection, Alutiiq Museum archives. AM680:345.

lamps to very large examples weighing more than 15 kg (34 lb). Some truly enormous lamps are known from private Karluk collections, and one appears in a historic picture of the village (fig. 6.19). Whatever their use, Elders report that people often stored lamps upside down, a practice that kept the spirit of the lamp, its *sua*, from leaving (fig. 6.20). Lamps uncovered at Karluk One were often found this way (Knecht 1995:318).

Figure 6:20. *Naniq*—oil lamp. Oil lamp bases. Cater avocational collection, AM561; UA85.193:4833, UA84.193:668.

About two-thirds of the lamps from Karluk One are carefully shaped and finished (fig. 6.21, 6.22). They have purposefully shaped sides and flattened bases as well as a distinctive flat rim, similar to historically collected pieces from Kodiak (Birket-Smith 1941:149). This rim, often polished to a smooth finish, surrounds an oval or subrectangular bowl that tapers toward a wick shelf at one end. This shelf is typically blackened, stained by soot that accumulated as a wick burned the sea mammal oil used to fuel the lamp. Oils rendered from the blubber of seal, bear, sea lion, and whale were all used as fuel (Shelikhov 1981:54). Alutiiq families used stone oil lamps into the twentieth century, and Elders recall that people twisted pieces of moss, cotton grass, and other absorbent plant materials into short wicks (Petrof 1884:233; Steffian and Counceller 2012:90).

Other Karluk lamps were more quickly made (fig. 6.23). Some are simply cobbles with a pecked oil reservoir. Others have a shaped body

Figure 6.21. *Naniq*—oil lamp. Stone lamps were relatively common in the Karluk One collection. There are fifty-three oil lamps including three partially shaped pieces. Many are from the upper layers of the site, although lamps occur throughout the deposit. This may indicate that lamps were passed through families, cared for by each succeeding generation. The carefully finished pieces illustrated here show the variety of lamp sizes. There are four general sizes—small traveling lamps that are less than 10 cm in length, medium-sized lamps that are 10 to 20 cm in length, large lamps that are roughly between 20 and 30 cm in length, and large, communal-style lamps that are longer than 30 cm. AM193.87:8764, UA85.193:4833; McCormick avocational collection, AM13:1.

Figure 6.22. *Naniq*—oil lamp. Stone lamps from late-prehistoric sites, like Karluk One, are not typically decorated. However, one example from Karluk One—center above—has three, deep, vertical grooves below its prow. The flat rim on these lamps is characteristic of many late prehistoric lamps. UA85.193:6856; Karluk School avocational collection AM39:213; AM193.87:8770.

Figure 6.23. *Naniq*—oil lamp. People working outdoors or traveling would squat over a small lamp to warm themselves. "Combining the parka with a vest [kamlei] of intestines, an Aleut can withstand wind, cold and damp for a long time. Should he get very cold and the parka is damp, he either goes into a tent or remains outside, sits on his haunches, sets a lampion filled with oil at his feet, lowers his parka down to the ground, and wraps it tightly around himself, including his head. In an hour or even sooner his whole body is warm and at the same time his clothes are dry" (Khlebnikov 1994:26). UA85.193:4807, AM193.87:8769, UA84.193:667.

but lack the flat rim and smoothed oil reservoir. A few feature wick channels, a groove in the base of the reservoir. Still others are fortuitously shaped rocks, with a natural, bowl-like depression used to hold oil.

The distinction between the two varieties of lamps is unknown. However, large, carefully finished pieces may have served as centerpieces for gatherings. Historic sources indicate that lamps

were lit for winter festivals. At a festival held in Kodiak in December of 1802, "Two men holding drums sat in the middle of a room by a large lighted saucer (oil lamp) . . . on both sides of the lamp stood two girls in kamleika."[5] At another on Woody Island, "A large oil lamp burnt in the center of the kazhim and several smaller ones around the walls . . . here two men are sitting near an oil lamp holding drums" (Davydov in Desson 1995:162–163).

European visitors noted that Alutiiq homes were filled with both gear and food. People hung hunting implements on the walls, stacked tinder, dried fish, and dried plants in the rafters, hung seal-stomach containers filled with sea mammal oil from beams, and piled buckets, clothing, food, and other items along the walls (Billings in Merck 1980:205; Davydov 1977:154; Gideon 1989:40; Holmberg 1985:41; Russell 1991). Houses functioned as general storage areas. The corner of a central room at Karluk One had a 2 m^2 area covered with a layer of small branches (fig. 6.24). On top of the branches lay a thick layer of fish remains (Knecht 1995:154). This may be food set aside for winter use, or perhaps this particular house was no longer occupied but remained in use as a storage shed.

People also built formal storage features in their homes. In one Karluk house, planks lined a small nook in a sod wall where residents stored a stone

Figure 6.24. Alder branches in the side room of house floor 2, Karluk One, 1984. Alutiiq Museum archives, AM193.66.S.

oil lamp (Knecht 1995:159). In at least three oth-er houses, archaeologists found rectangular boxes built into the floor of the main room. These boxes were made from small posts driven into the floor to create a rectangular enclosure about 1.5 m long, 1 m wide, and 65 cm high. Short planks lined the bases of these boxes. Some boxes were sunk into the house floor. Others rested atop the floor. Most of these boxes were empty, but a storage box from House Floor Two produced four artifacts (fig. 6.25a,b). Beneath a covering of boards, and sev-eral large stones, excavators found a full-size mask with the face of a bird, a mask hoop, a water dip-per, and a maul (Knecht 1995:153).

In contrast to the all-purpose nature of the central room, smaller, low-roofed side rooms had specific functions. Some were sleeping quar-ters, others were steam baths, storage areas, and, at times, places for burial (Davydov 1977:154; Gideon 1989:40; Knecht and Jordan 1985:Figure 6; Lisianski 1814:213; Merck 1980:107). Like the central room, side rooms were roughly rect-angular with plank-covered walls. Some of these smaller chambers had a deeper foundation than the adjoining central room (Holmberg 1985:44; Knecht and Jordan 1985:25), others had a raised floor. Houses with raised side rooms are common in late prehistoric settlements along the Karluk River (Saltonstall and Steffian 2010) and have been seen in excavations on Kodiak and Afognak Islands (Saltonstall 1997). Side rooms at Karluk One were roughly square, with an interior area between 4 m² and 24 m², and one large side room at Karluk One appears to have had a small hearth.

People entered these small chambers through narrow tunnels connected to the central room. Historic accounts indicate that the tunnels were tight, just wide enough for one person to crawl through (Gideon 1989:40; Shelikhov 1981:56).

Many examples of side-room tunnels were uncov-ered at Karluk One. These features are generally 1.5 m to 2 m long by .75 m to 1 m wide, although there was at least one much longer tunnel. The tunnels resembled a box and were surrounded with a set of narrow, closely spaced planks with a post at each corner of the box. The posts support-ed beams that held up the tunnel's roof. Typically, the floor of the tunnel was deeper than the level of the house floor and lined with boards at a right angle to the tunnel. As such, tunnels often had a gentle U-shape—higher on the ends and lower in the middle. This purposeful design, also seen

Figure 6.25a,b. Storage box in house floor 2, Karluk One, 1984—before and after opening. Courtesy Colleen Lazenby.

in entrance tunnels associated with more ancient Kodiak houses (Steffian 1992b), acted as a cold trap. Cold air would sink into the tunnel and not flow into the house. During recent excavations of a later prehistoric sod house in the Kodiak Alutiiq community of Old Harbor, archaeologists uncovered a side-room tunnel built below the level of the main-room floor. This tunnel had a step up into a side room whose floor was a meter higher than the floor of the main room. Similar changes in elevation between main rooms, tunnels, and side rooms may have been present at Karluk One but were difficult to recognize due to the deeply stratified nature of the site and intensity of prehistoric rebuilding. However, not all late prehistoric houses had cold-trap-style side-room tunnels. Some tunnels were level, a flat crawl space with a path of planks that connected the main room with a side room. Indeed, house depressions studied in late prehistoric sites along Kodiak's major rivers suggest that U-shaped, cold-trap, side-room tunnels were more common before about four hundred years ago.

Sometimes, underground tunnels connected houses. Archibald Campbell (1816:99), a sailor who visited Karluk in 1808, noted that people moved between homes in the village via underground tunnels. While no examples were uncovered during the excavations of Karluk One, surveys of late prehistoric sites on southwest Kodiak Island indicate that occasionally, closely spaced, neighboring houses had connecting tunnels (Saltonstall and Steffian 2006).

Many side rooms functioned as family sitting and sleeping areas (Merck 1980:100). Here, parents, their young children, a grandparent, or even a dog might curl up together (Davydov 1977:154).[6] Young adults, however, typically slept in the central room (Matfay 1990). Covered in sod and

separated from the main room, side rooms were both warm and dark. Some featured a tiny window covered in gutskin that let in light (Gideon 1989:40). Stones heated in the central room were sometimes carried into these rooms to provide heat, a practice seen in many of the side rooms excavated at Karluk One.

Russian visitors to Alutiiq homes report that the walls of side rooms were filled with items. "In these sleeping chambers, spears are hung on the walls as ornaments, and, to commemorate the animals taken in the hunt, thoracic vertebrae or bladders of seals and sea otter heads; beneath are stored platters of various sizes, cups and porringers, spoons and *kaluzhki*, that is elongated vessels for water" (Gideon 1989:40). At Karluk One, the floors of side rooms tended to be thinner and cleaner than those of central rooms, with fewer artifacts. This find reflects both the function of these rooms and perhaps the use of floor coverings. Here, people slept on the floor in their clothing, often on bear hides, seal skins, or grass mats (Matfay and Matfay 1987; Sauer 1802:175). During the day, these hides were rolled up or hung to dry (Demidoff 1962; Matfay 1990).

The smallest side rooms were used as steam baths. Known as a *maqiwik* in the Alutiiq language, or by the Russian-derived term *banya*, similar baths remain popular today. Described as tight, *maqiwit* were typically less than 3 m² (Matfay 1990), with a raised floor (Saltonstall 1997), and a low roof. Here, residents splashed water on hot rocks to create steam for both physical and spiritual cleansing. People bathed often for relaxation, medicinal purposes, and in preparation for hunting or warfare. Bathing also helped to mark special events like the celebration of a marriage, the introduction of a mother and her newborn baby to the household (Gideon 1989:50; Lisianski 1814:199,

201), and in recent centuries, church holidays (Huggins 1981:10).

Like other rooms, the floor of the steam bath had a layer of boards covered in grass (Matfay 1990). A pile of hot rocks was placed in a corner of the room. In studies of late prehistoric houses, archaeologists often find this pile to the right of the steam-bath entrance (Saltonstall 1997). This helped people escape the steam without burning themselves on the extremely hot rocks. The small size of the room, its low roof, a skin or wood door at the room entrance, and the hot rocks combined to make a highly effective steam bath. Matfay (1990) described these rooms as uncomfortably hot, so hot that it could be hard to breath. The doorway opened outward, preventing bathers from being trapped inside.

Preparations for steam bathing included laying fresh grass on the floor, filling containers with fresh water, collecting alder switches and beach grass roots for scrubbing (Russell 1991), and heating rocks in the central-room hearth. Heating

rocks was an art. Young men competed for this job, which was thought to please the spirit of the steam bath and ensure hunting luck (Bobby Stamp in Knecht 1995:328). People selected certain types of stone to avoid dangerous explosions when the hot rocks were splashed with cool water. Rocks containing iron pyrite were also avoided, as they can give off noxious fumes when heated (Donald Clark pers. comm. 2014). Today, Alutiiq people consider quartz, slate, and granite poor choices, opting for Kodiak's abundant greywacke cobbles (Knecht 1995:329). In prehistoric houses, however, slate rubble is very common in steam baths (Saltonstall 1997). In part, the choice of steam-bath rock may reflect the stone immediately available. At Karluk One, the beach below the site is filled with granite and greywacke cobbles.

According to Matfay (1990), to heat the rocks men began by creating a half-meter high pile of stones over a carefully laid fire. The builder stacked his firewood in a cone and laid stones over it (Knecht 1995:328). If correctly arranged,

Figure 6.26. *Qalutaq*—water scoop, *yaamat tuumiaqsuutait*—rock paddle, *yaamat tuusuutait*—rock tong. The water dipper on top split and was repaired with baleen lashing. Burn marks from hot rocks are evident on the rock paddle. Rock tongs were frequently created by reworking discarded kayak stringers. Banya water scoops and paddles are generally about 35 cm long and 11 cm wide, but like all objects in the Karluk One collection, there are very small to very large versions. One rock paddle has a very long handle and is 108 cm long. AM193.94:10, UA85.193:4816, AM193.94:995.

Figure 6.27. *Qalutaq*—water scoop. Large water scoop showing tool marks on the interior from its manufacture. UA84.193:1045.

the wood used to fuel the fire would burn in the middle, causing the stones to fall into the hot coals, and not to roll outward on to the house floor (Knecht 1995:330; Matfay 1990).

Once heated, men passed the hot rocks from the central room, through the passageway, and into the steam bath. One man worked with a pair of tongs to remove hot rocks from the hearth. In the tunnel, he passed the rocks to a second man equipped with a rock paddle. This man took the rocks into the steam bath where he placed them into a pile (Matfay 1990). Pieces of these tongs from Karluk One are lengths of wood with blunt, flattened oval ends (fig. 6.26). Two pieces would have been lashed together to form a pair of tongs (Knecht 1995:331). Rock paddles from Karluk One are shaped like scoops, except they are flat. Both tools feature burn marks from handling hot rocks. Other steam-bath tools included water scoops (fig. 6.26, 6.27) and wooden water containers. The remains of containers of many different sizes and shapes were very common at Karluk One. This included hundreds of fragments of wooden vessels, buckets, and bowls, made with a carved wooden bottom and a rim bent from a single piece of wood. Some of these vessels served as buckets for hauling and holding water.

Although none of the side rooms excavated at Karluk One were clearly used just for sweat

bathing, many had piles of fire-cracked rock suggesting this practice. It appears that in some prehistoric homes one room functioned both as a sleeping chamber and a steam bath (cf. Lisianski 1814:213–214). Or perhaps a steam-bath room simply wasn't encountered at Karluk One. Based on the size of the site, researchers examined a small fraction of the deposit through excavation and only portions of houses.

Six of the burials encountered at Karluk One were inside houses. Historically, Alutiiq people buried the dead in a variety of ways. Spiritually powerful people might be mummified and their remains placed in a cave (Davydov 1977:233). Others were laid to rest in graves dug in or near a village (Davydov 1977:179; Demidoff 1962; Gideon 1989:54; Merck 1980:106; Sauer 1802:177). In winter, when digging was difficult, side rooms functioned as graves. The dead were placed in a room, the tunnel sealed, and the roof collapsed (Billings in Merck 1980:206; Merck 1980:107; Gideon 1989:53). People were typically buried in their best clothes, sometimes with a selection of their tools in or on top of the grave (Billings in Merck 1980:205; Black 1981:4; Lisianski 1814:200).

Burials inside Karluk One's sod houses were found only in the upper layer of the site, in the latest prehistoric houses (Feuerstein 1988;

Utermohle 1988). Four of these burials were in side rooms, while the other two, an adult woman and an adult man, were laid to rest along the edge of a house's central room. One side room held the remains of a woman and an infant. Another had an adult male. A third held the remains of four men and a male child, buried at roughly the same time. One of these men, an older individual, had a bone arrow point near his pelvis, possibly the cause of his death. Residents buried this man with a full size wooden mask, a stone gaming ball, a bear canine, and a cobble spall (a cutting and scraping tool). In all of these burials, people were placed on their sides or back, with their knees bent at least partially toward their chest. The tight position of some people suggests that they were wrapped in a skin. Several people were found with labrets, decorative plugs of wood, bone, or stone worn in the face.

Household Activities

Daily life inside the houses at Karluk One generated many of the artifacts preserved in the site's collection. As people worked and played, objects were created, used, broken, reworked, and discarded, leaving abundant evidence of indoor activities. The following sections consider cooking, manufacturing, and recreation to paint a picture of household life and share artifacts from this setting.

Cooking

Preparing food was one of the most common daily tasks. As discussed in Chapter 5, Karluk residents harvested an array of fish, sea mammals, birds, plants, and shellfish. Together Russian accounts, Karluk artifacts, and the knowledge of Elders illustrate how villagers transformed these resources into meals. Information on food is a common part of historic accounts of Kodiak, as visitors to

Alutiiq communities were uniformly "received kindly" (Gideon 1989:35). Offerings of food and water were typical (Billings in Merck 1980:206; Huggins 1981:26; Lisianski 1814:176; Sauer 1802:78), a tradition visible in Alutiiq legends (Golder 1903b:96) and maintained in Karluk. In the historic era, villagers offered visiting cannery workers tea and lumps of dried brown sugar (McKeown 1948:54). In the 1980s, community members offered visiting archaeologists smoked fish, salmon baked in seal oil, and cookies.

In classical Alutiiq society, visitors arrived with food for their hosts, who in turn provided food to eat during their stay and to take as they departed. Visitors were expected to leave with a supply of food that included leftovers, any food they had not finished consuming (Billings in Merck 1980:206). Moreover, it was customary to place dried fish in the center of your home when leaving, to care for guests who might arrive in your absence (Gideon 1989:55).

Common dishes included dried fish; dried, boiled, and roasted fish and meat; pieces of blubber; lily roots and berries preserved in oil; a paste of lily roots mixed with water; steamed plants mixed with fat; sorrel[7] cooked to a porridge-like thickness and mixed with whale meat; salmon roe pounded and mixed with fat; and a number of raw and fermented foods (Fisher 1899:Entry 3; Gideon 1989:35, 38, 52; Lisianski 1814:178, 195; Shelikhov 1981:55). Whale meat, blubber, shellfish, fish, fish heads,[8] and plant foods were all enjoyed raw, while fish, fish eggs, whale meat, eggs, and a variety of other foods were aged in pits and containers before eating (Billings in Merck 1980:206; Davydov 1977:174).

Meals varied by season, depending on the availability of foods and their preparation. In summer, for example, people enjoyed boiled or roasted freshly caught fish, while in the winter, they ate dried fish. Similarly, people ate whale meat, a highly prized food, raw or roasted when in season. At other times of year, they enjoyed aged meat preserved in pits (Billings in Merck 1980:206; Petrof 1884:231). Oil was a particularly important part of every meal, and dried foods were served with a dish of sea mammal oil for dipping (Black 1977:85; Petrof 1884:231). People drank water and a mildly fermented juice made from aged berries (Davydov 1977:174).

Although the Alutiiq are known for their large, lavish feasts, meals in daily life were small and frequent. People ate throughout the day (Black 1977:85). Lisianski (1814:182) describes an evening meal on Sitkalidak Island in April of 1805, where family members gathered around the fire in their sod house:

> The cook having filled a wooden bowl with boiled fish, presented it to the master of the house, who, after eating as much as he could, gave the rest to his wife. The other dishes were served up in similar order, beginning with the oldest of the family, who, when he had eaten his fill, gave the dish to the next in age, and he again to the next; and thus it passed in rotation till it came to the youngest, whose patience, as the family was numerous, must have been a little exhausted.

The dish mentioned by Lisianski was likely a carved wooden bowl. Women served food to visitors and family members in a variety of differently shaped bowls (Gideon 1989:43) and bentwood containers. Carved wooden bowls from Karluk One vary from shallow, platter-like dishes to deeper bowls (fig. 6.28). Many have cut marks on the bottom, suggesting their use for both preparing and eating food. These dishes also likely served as grease bowls, containers for the oil served with dried foods at meals.

People often ate with their fingers, although they also used spoons (Gideon 1989:40; Shelikhov 1981:54). Spoons in the Karluk One collection are generally made of wood and resemble small scoops. They typically feature a short, cylindrical handle and a long oval or tear-shaped

Figure 6.28. *Yaasiiguaq*—vessel. Variety of wooden dishes—feast bowl fragment, feast bowl rim fragment, large rectangular bentwood vessel base, and an elongated vessel with a short handle. Pullar, Knowles, and Dolchuk avocational collection, AM341:16; Sheehan avocational collection, AM38.44, AM38.566, AM38.2036.

Figure 6.29. *Laus'kaaq*—spoon. The middle spoon was probably used for cooking as it has a burned bowl. AM193.87:11199; Lind avocational collection, AM14:196; AM193.95:1050.

bowl that tapers to a wide, thin, rounded end (fig. 6.29, 6.30). Some have decorated handles, including one featuring the snout of an animal carved at the end (fig. 6.31). A few spoons used in cooking have long handles and short, shallow bowls (fig. 6.29).

To store and cook foods, Alutiiq people used a great variety of containers. Visitors to Alutiiq homes described food stockpiled in large spruce root baskets, wooden vessels, and sea mammal stomach pokes—containers for liquids (Black 1977:85; Demidoff 1962; Gideon 1989:38). Container parts were one of the most common finds at Karluk One, illustrating their importance. In Karluk, people used wooden, fiber, bone, and ceramic containers. Gutskin pokes were also likely present, although none were preserved.

In recent centuries, people cooked in pots hung on a stick over the household hearth (Matfay 1990). Before the introduction of metal pots, cooks heated water, stews, soups, and medicinal teas by dropping hot rocks into watertight baskets or wooden boxes (Billings in Merck 1980:207). Large spruce root baskets from Karluk One and the bases of wooden boxes feature burn marks

Figure 6.30. *Laus'kaaq*—spoon. This spoon, which measures 12 cm long and 4 cm wide, has a teardrop-shaped bowl with burn marks. AM193.87:11121.

Figure 6.31. *Laus'kaaq*—spoon. Detail of a spoon with an animal carving on the end of the handle. UA85.193:3076.

Figures 6.32a,b. *Yaasiiguaq*—vessel. Bentwood vessel base (inside and out) showing burn marks from hot cooking rocks and cut marks on the bottom. Notice the carved side where a bentwood rim with overlapping edges would be secured. The baleen lashing visible here helped to secure the rim to the base. This base is 21 cm long and 15.5 cm wide. This small-to-medium-size base is common in the collection, but bases up to 60 cm long also occur in significant numbers. AM193.94:51.

from the hot rocks used to heat their contents (fig. 6.32). Archaeologists commonly found small piles of cooking stones next to the hearths at Karluk One (see fig. 6.16). Here and at other sites, these rocks are often smooth, water-worn beach cobbles made of material unlikely to fracture and leave pieces of stone in food (Saltonstall 1997).

Spruce root was the preferred material for basket construction at Karluk One. Of the eighty-six pieces of basketry in the collection, sixty-one are made of spruce root, fifteen of birch bark, six of grass, and four of baleen. Most spruce root baskets were woven in a conical shape, although one

basket is oblong (see fig. 5.20a,b), similar in shape to an eighteenth-century Alutiiq basket from Cook Inlet (Lee 1981:67). Tightly twined from split lengths of spruce root, conical baskets feature a round base and often a rim finished with sturdy three-strand twining (fig. 6.33, 6.34). Many of the conical baskets also feature bases with concentric rings of raised stitching, typically three or four per basket (fig. 6.34–6.36). Weavers applied this stitching to the surface of baskets, and it appears to be decorative rather than a means of reinforcement. This method of decorating bases appears throughout historic Alutiiq baskets and illustrates that the Karluk One examples are part of an ancient, distinctly Alutiiq way of weaving spruce root (Lee 2006:167).

Concentric-circle motifs occur in other forms of Alutiiq artwork. They are carved on the surface of labrets (Steffian and Saltonstall 2001), painted on box panels (see fig. 7.43), and painted on masks and mask coverings (Haakanson and Steffian 2009:4, 164). The circles may represent the layers of the Alutiiq universe, which included a series of five sky worlds (Crowell and Leer 2001:198). A story collected on Kodiak in the early twentieth century suggests a connection between baskets and the sky world. A young woman who marries a star man travels between her village and her husband's sky home in a large basket (Golder 1903:23–26). Travel to the sky world in a basket is a theme also found in Yup'ik stories (Lantis 1938:141).

Spruce root basketry stitches in the Karluk One collection range from a coarse weave of about 6 per cm² to a fine weave of 49 per cm², illustrating the use of differently sized weft strands for different baskets and different purposes. The three largest spruce root baskets in the collection are more than 100 cm in diameter and 40 cm tall. Large baskets likely functioned as containers for

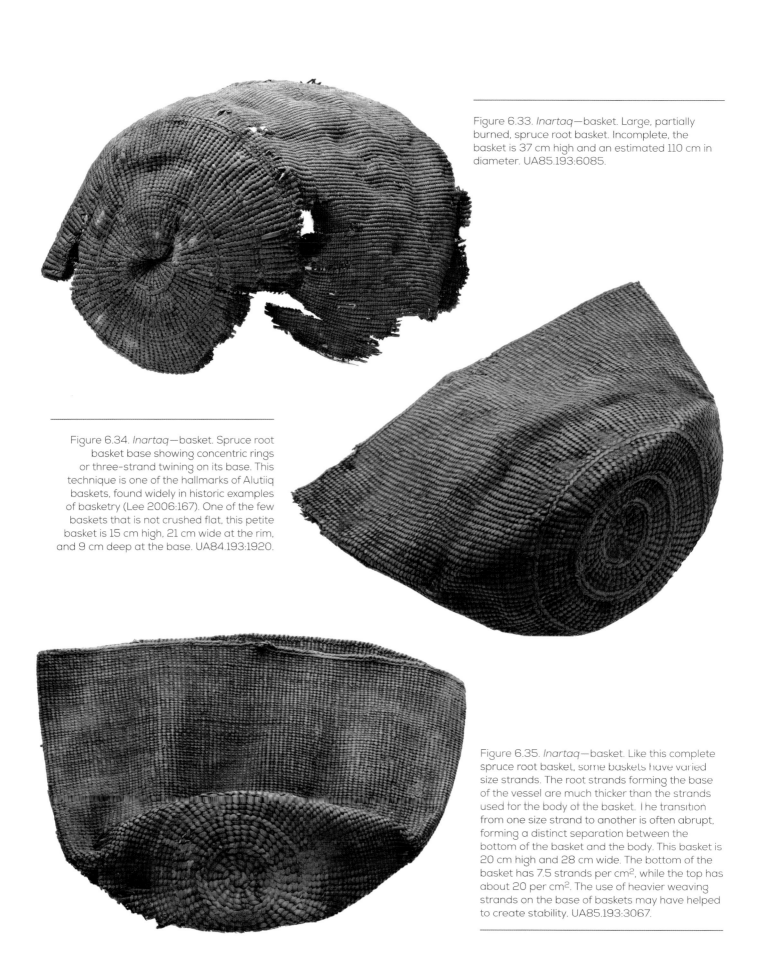

Figure 6.33. *Inartaq*—basket. Large, partially burned, spruce root basket. Incomplete, the basket is 37 cm high and an estimated 110 cm in diameter. UA85.193:6085.

Figure 6.34. *Inartaq*—basket. Spruce root basket base showing concentric rings or three-strand twining on its base. This technique is one of the hallmarks of Alutiiq baskets, found widely in historic examples of basketry (Lee 2006:167). One of the few baskets that is not crushed flat, this petite basket is 15 cm high, 21 cm wide at the rim, and 9 cm deep at the base. UA84.193:1920.

Figure 6.35. *Inartaq*—basket. Like this complete spruce root basket, some baskets have varied size strands. The root strands forming the base of the vessel are much thicker than the strands used for the body of the basket. The transition from one size strand to another is often abrupt, forming a distinct separation between the bottom of the basket and the body. This basket is 20 cm high and 28 cm wide. The bottom of the basket has 7.5 strands per cm², while the top has about 20 per cm². The use of heavier weaving strands on the base of baskets may have helped to create stability. UA85.193:3067.

Figure 6.36. *Inartaq*—basket. This small fragment of a spruce root basket is 17 cm wide. Lind avocational collection, AM14:338.

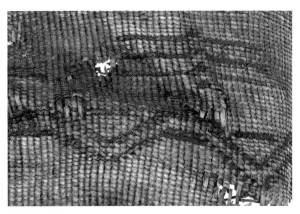

Figure 6.37. *Inartaq*—basket. Decorative false embroidery applied to the surface of a large spruce root basket in a series of parallel bars and zigzags. The zigzag pattern is also found in Tlingit basketry where it is known as a shark's-tooth pattern (Lee 2006:168). The black material used in false embroidery on the Karluk One baskets is plant fiber. It may be grass or maidenhair fern stems (Lee 1981:68). This design appears near the base of the basket, on the lower third of the object. AM193.87:19086.

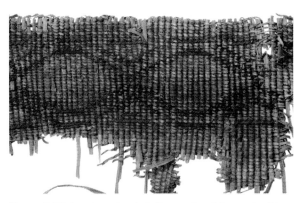

Figure 6.38. *Inartaq*—basket. Decorative false embroidery applied to the surface of very large spruce root basket in a pattern of bars and double-lined diamonds. This pattern is also found in Tlingit basketry where it is known as the mouth track of wormwood (cf. Lee 2006:168). The design appears just below the rim of the basket. AM193.87:19072.

collecting, storing, and cooking, while smaller baskets were used as dishes and cups or to hold small items.

Evidence of basket making is present in the form of basket starts and bundles of spruce root. Importantly, as spruce root is not available in Karluk, people obtained the material for these common, widely used vessels through travel and trade. All of the spruce root baskets from Karluk One were woven upside down, working in a circular pattern starting from the base of the basket. Weavers typically wrapped two rows of weft around vertical warp strands, a technique known as plain twining (Lee 2006:167). Some of the spruce root baskets also have attachment loops for a handle, and several have a handle of braided spruce root. Ladies carried baskets around their necks, hanging the container from a cord so it could rest on their chest or their back (Korsun 2012:146).

Some of the Karluk baskets are decorated. Many are twined with minimal ornamental stitching or surface embellishment. However, at least four baskets, two of them large, have contrasting, geometric patterns added to their surface through false embroidery (fig. 6.37, 6.38). In one case, this embroidery is just below the rim of the basket. In the other, it lies both below the rim and on the lower body of the basket. To create false embroidery, weavers worked with three strands of weft, using two strands of the body materials and a strand of different material or color as the third, decorative weft. By twisting this decorative strand around the weft in front of the work, weavers created patterns only visible on the surface of the basket (Lee 2006:170). The motifs used in the four examples of false embroidery from Karluk One resemble those found in historic Alutiiq baskets and known also in Tlingit basketry (Lee 2006:168).

Two other basket fragments have raised bands of decorative stitching starting just below the rim and repeating every eight to nine rows (fig. 6.39). Similar stitching appears in examples of historic Alutiiq baskets (Korsun 2012:174–176; Lee 1981) and on the bases of many of the conical baskets from Karluk One. More broadly, however, many of the Karluk One baskets lack the intricate designs and the use of primary and secondary design fields common to more recent Alutiiq baskets (cf. Lee 1981:70–71). While weaving techniques, false embroidery, decorative stitching, and even design elements link the Karluk basketry firmly to historic examples, the finely made prehistoric baskets are not as elaborately embellished as those from later collections.

In addition to spruce baskets, women may have woven mats for use as floor coverings, household partitions, or bedding (Korsun 2012:177–179). Although none were positively identified in the Karluk One collection, archaeologists uncovered fragments of ancient mats at the Uyak site in nearby Larsen Bay. Made from 2 cm, parallel bundles of grass stitched together in an open weave, these thick mats rested on several of the site's house floors (Heizer 1956:30; Hrdlička 1944:342). Two fragment of delicately woven material, probably

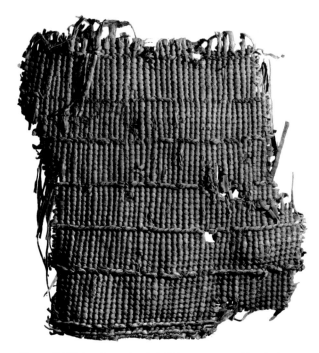

Figure 6.39. *Inartaq*—basket. This spruce root basket body fragment shows evenly spaced rows of decorative twining—spaced 2.5 cm apart. AM193.94:8.

the innermost portion of spruce roots, may be mat fragments (fig. 6.40, 6.41).

Although spruce root was a preferred material for basketry, Karluk ladies also made containers of grass, baleen, and birch bark. A grass basket start, fragments of tightly woven grass basketry, and four tiny, complete, open-weave grass baskets were preserved in the site (fig. 6.42, 6.43). This is not surprising given the widespread use of grass as a building material, but it highlights the excellent preservation at Karluk One and the antiquity of grass weaving on Kodiak. Three of the complete grass baskets feature a decorative braided rim, attached to loops of braided material, in turn attached to the basket's body. The smallest basket measures just 5.5 cm high and 5.5 cm wide. The rim style and the relatively loose stitch mirror the weaving seen in larger baskets from historic Aleutian Island collections (Lee 1981:72).

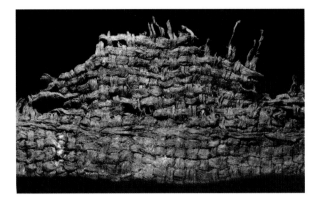

Figure 6.40. *Inartaq*—basket. The rim of this spruce root basketry fragment has been folded over and stitched down to make a thicker, 2 cm wide edge. AM193.87:10815.

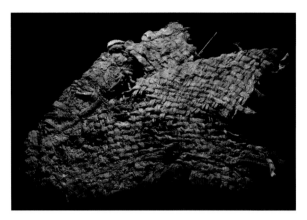

Figure 6.41. *Inartaq*—basket. Grass basket fragment. With even strands, the weaving of several grass baskets appears to have a checkerboard-like pattern. There are no complete pieces with this style of weaving. It is possible these fragments are from mats, rather than baskets. AM193.87:10819.

Figure 6.43. *Inartaq*—basket. Small open-weave grass basket with a braided rim. AM193.M:900.

Figure 6.42. *Inartaq*—basket. This delicate grass basket start is 15 cm long. AM193.87:10714.

Figure 6.44. *Inartaq*—basket. Small open-weave baleen basket fragment with a braided rim. On its own, this fragment is very similar in technique and size to the open-weave grass baskets; however, this is just one of twenty fragments that make up a larger, and sturdier, baleen container. AM193.87:19050.

The art of weaving baleen has faded from living memory on Kodiak, although craftsmen continue to carve baleen to make model boats. However, fragments of three baleen baskets from Karluk One indicate that weavers fashioned the materials into large open-weave containers, likely for collecting and storing (fig. 6.44). One baleen basket fragment is 52 cm wide (fig. 6.45). Another features a braided rim. The small sample indicates that craftsmen wove this tough but flexible material in ways similar to grass, twining it. On both objects, thick strands of baleen weft are secured with thinner strands of baleen warp woven through the material in bands spaced 1 cm apart. This style of weaving resembles that of fiber mats collected from Palutat Cave in Prince William Sound. These Chugach Alutiiq artifacts were made from thick strands of shredded bark weft secured by a warp of grass, woven in bands through the material at 4.5 to 6.5 cm intervals (de Laguna 1956:234–239). However, the Kodiak Alutiiq baleen work is

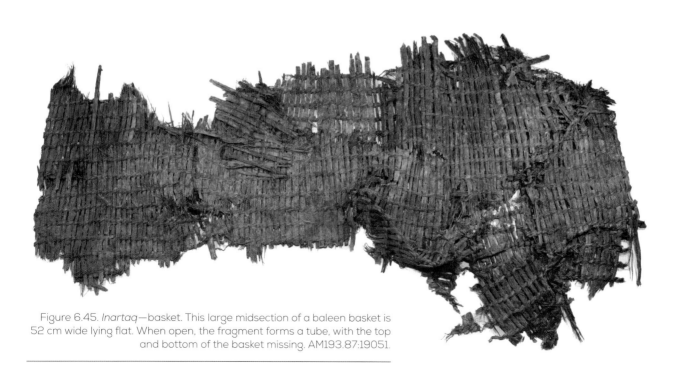

Figure 6.45. *Inartaq*—basket. This large midsection of a baleen basket is 52 cm wide lying flat. When open, the fragment forms a tube, with the top and bottom of the basket missing. AM193.87:19051.

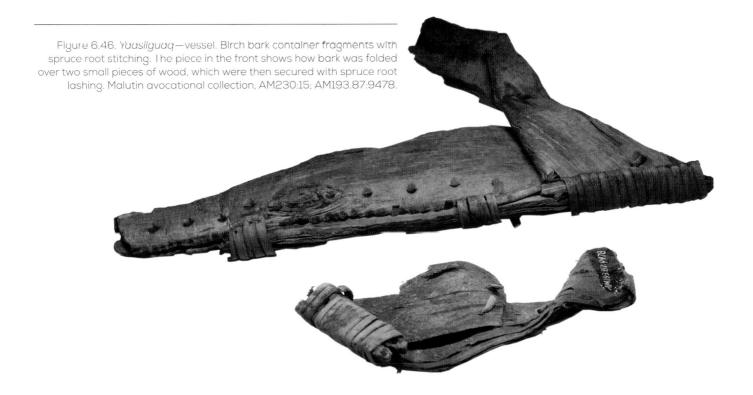

Figure 6.46. *Yaasiiguaq*—vessel. Birch bark container fragments with spruce root stitching. The piece in the front shows how bark was folded over two small pieces of wood, which were then secured with spruce root lashing. Malutin avocational collection, AM230:15; AM193.87:9478.

Figure 6.47. Birch bark container, folded in thirds like a sewing bag. AM193.95:917.

distinct from the bent baleen containers used by Inupiaq people, as well as the tightly woven, historically manufactured baleen baskets found in the far north (Fair 2006:47).

Birch bark containers from Karluk One resemble prehistoric examples found in Palutat Cave in Prince William Sound (de Laguna 1956:233), as well as those made by Athabaskan craftsmen (Fair 2006:106). These containers are fashioned from cut and folded pieces of bark stitched with strands of spruce root. There are fifteen examples in the collection. Most are very fragmentary, represented by carefully shaped pieces of bark with small even stitch holes or by a strip of bark edged with spruce root stitches (fig. 6.46). One of the birch bark objects folds into thirds, like a wallet, and is reminiscent of historic sewing bags (fig. 6.47). Ladies kept their needles, awls, thread, and other sewing notions in such a bag, call *kakiwik* in the Alutiiq language (Birket-Smith 1941:150; Crowell and Lührmann 2001:50). Another bark

Figure 6.48. *Yaasiiguaq*—vessel. Rounded birch bark container with spruce root stitching. This fragment is 14 cm high and 24 cm wide. The stitching on this piece creates a pocket-like opening. AM193.87:19045.

Figure 6.50. *Yaasiiguaq*—vessel. Rectangular bentwood vessel rims. The largest rim is 28 cm long, 23 cm wide, and 4 cm high. The small rim is 8 cm long, 7 cm wide, and 2.5 cm high. Both of these rims are held together with pegs only. There is no spruce root or baleen lashing or holes for such lashing. Pegs near the bottom of the rims, which once secured these artifacts to vessel bases, are present in all three pieces. Sheehan avocational collection, AM38:578; UA85.193:3504; Sheehan avocational collection, AM38:180.

Figure 6.49. *Yaasiiguaq*—vessel. Complete bentwood vessel. This midsize bentwood vessel is 17 cm long, 13 cm wide, and 7 cm high. The inside is caked with some form of residue, and the bottom is slightly charred and covered with cut marks. AM193.94:1434.

Figure 6.51. *Yaasiiguaq*—vessel. Ovoid bentwood vessel rims. The large oval rim is 32 cm long, 24 cm wide, and 6 cm high. The small rim is 15 cm long and 10 cm wide. Oval bentwood vessels slightly outnumber rectangular vessels in the collection. AM193.94:5153, AM193.94:6.

container has a rounded edge (fig. 6.48). As large birch trees are relatively rare in the Kodiak region, the bark used in these containers was likely harvested from driftwood logs or obtained from the mainland through travel or trade.

The collection also holds many different sizes and shapes of wooden vessels. Bentwood bowls and boxes are the most common type of container (fig. 6.49), made by attaching a thin, bent rim of wood (fig. 6.50, 6.51) to a sturdy, flat wooden base (fig. 6.52). Some had square bases, others oval bases. Some had short sides, like a tub or dish, others had tall sides, like a bucket or box. Some of these containers were fitted with handles— lengths of wood with grooved ends to which a cord was tied (fig. 6.53–6.55). Like boxes and

Figure 6.52. *Yaasiiguaq*—vessel. Bentwood vessel bases are either flat or carved with a deepened basin. Sheehan avocational collection, AM38:98; AM193.94:3595, AM193.94:51; Panamaroff avocational collection, AM15:448; AM193.94:1342.

Figure 6.54. *Agaa*—vessel handle. Variations in vessel handles include an undulating style (top), painted handles with a bird head (possibly ptarmigan) carved on the ends, and decoratively carved handles. AM193.95:3000, UA85.193:1663, AM193.87:8435.

Figure 6.53. *Agaa*—vessel handle. The top handle has stepped ends, so that the handle rises away from the vessel. Other handles have knob ends for securing the handle to the vessel. UA85.193:3690, AM193.87:9805, AM193.95:971, AM193.94:3674, AM193.87:8045.

Figure 6.55. *Agaa*—vessel handle. Several handles in the collection have ptarmigan carvings on the ends. One of these small bird carvings features insets of decorative hairs or very thin pieces of baleen. AM193.87:10155.

Figure 6.56. *Patua*—vessel lid. The two small lids shown here are made of bark. The round one is 7 cm in diameter. The small one is 5.5 cm long and has the remnants of a stick in the center hole. The small bark type is more common than the larger wood lid, which is 15 cm long and 13 cm wide. The shape and size of these pieces are similar to *kakangaq* disks, and they were initially thought to be tops, a child's toy. UA85.193:6441, UA84.193:785, AM193.87:11210.

Figure 6.58. *Yaasiiguaq*—vessel. This unbent vessel rim preform shows how corner areas were carved very thin before the rim was bent. Sheehan avocational collection, AM38:935.

Figures 6.57a,b,c. *Yaasiiguaq*—vessel. Complete bentwood vessel. AM193.95:1068.

Figure 6.59. *Yaasiiguaq*—vessel. Round bentwood vessel with a wide, stylized rim. The rims of bentwood vessels are sometimes scarfed, carved thin, or notched for joining them together. The thick lip on the rim of this vessel has been notched on one side to fit the two ends together. The vessel is approximately 20 cm in diameter. Sheehan avocational collection, AM38:2179-2181.

Figure 6.60. *Yaasiiguaq*—vessel. The overlapping ends of the vessel rim are pegged together and reinforced with baleen stitching. This elongated vessel is 28 cm long, 19.5 cm wide, and 8 cm high. Reft avocational collection, AM269:2.

baskets, vessel handles come in a range of sizes, some small and delicate, others large and sturdy, reflecting their use with different types of containers. Carved wooden lids, often with a finger hole in the top (fig. 6.56), may have covered the contents of bentwood vessels or a variety of small baskets and boxes. A Kodiak Alutiiq legend tells of a boy trapped by his uncle in a wooden box with a tight fitting lid. The boy was set adrift on the ocean in the box. However, as the box was water tight, he floated safely to land (Golder 1903b:92–93).

To create wooden containers, craftsmen carved a thin piece of wood into a rim and bent it to shape with the aid of steam. The precise method of steam bending is not known, but pieces of water-saturated wood were probably heated gradually, perhaps in the steam bath or in a pit designed for this purpose (cf. Stewart 1984:47). Craftsmen carved the corners of rims intended for square and rectangular vessels especially thin (fig. 6.57a,b,c). This eased the bending process and prevented cracking (fig. 6.58). Rim ends in the Karluk One collection are sometimes thinner than the body of the rim. This allowed the rim ends to overlap and create a thickness similar to that of non-overlapping areas (fig. 6.59, 6.60). Other vessels have a base with a notch designed to accommodate the thicker portion of the rim, where its ends overlap. An incomplete vessel from Karluk One illustrates that the next step was to glue the ends of the rim together. Craftsmen then attached the bent rim to the flat wooden base of the vessel, inserting small wooden pegs into holes drilled through both the rim and the base (fig. 6.61–6.63). Finally, the rim often was further secured by drilling

Figure 6.61. *Kuuliangcuk*—peg. Peg preforms. From roughly shaped pieces of wood, pegs were whittled to shape, stuck into the premade hole in the vessel, snapped off, and the end smoothed flat. AM193.87:8395, UA85.193:3004, AM193.94:3698, AM193.M:569, UA85.193:1934.

Figure 6.62. *Acaa*—bottom. Bottom of bentwood vessel. Wooden pegs help secure the bottom of the vessel to the rim. The notched rim fits snugly into the notched bottom. Reft avocational collection, AM269:2.

Figures 6.63a,b. Fragments of bentwood vessel rims showing peg holes and pegs. Pegs are conical in shape. The tapered, pointed ends secured the rim and the base. The visible pegs on the inside of the rim are smoothed flat. The diameter of the uniform pegs on the outside of the rim is 4 mm. The diameter on the inside of the rim is 3 mm. AM193.94:2831.

Figure 6.64. *lᴿafkuq*—lashing, *kuuliangcuk*—peg. Baleen lashing and wooden pegs on a bentwood vessel rim fragment. The lashing, often made of spruce root or baleen, was strung through predrilled holes, and then pegs were inserted into the holes to join of the rim ends. AM193.87:10496.

additional holes in its ends for spruce root or baleen lashing or additional pegs (Birket-Smith 1941:151) (fig. 6.64).

Similar to bentwood vessels, wooden boxes from Karluk One were pegged or lashed together (fig. 6.65). Boxes held people's belongings, including objects like knives and feathers (Golder 1903b:90). Typically small, these containers feature carved panels for both the sides and the bases. Karluk craftsmen fashioned these panels with beveled corners and drilled holes for joining (fig. 6.65). Interestingly, a number of small wooden box panels from Karluk One feature painted images. One shows a group of people in kayaks and *angyat* traveling together (fig. 6.66a,b,c), another shows an erupting volcano (Steffian et al. 1996:13), and two panels found together feature stylized faces surrounded by concentric circles (see fig. 7.43). These last two images may be depictions of the Alutiiq universe and the powerful

Figure 6.65. *Yaasiigem cania*—box panel. Box sides and box base. The small box side is intricately painted with alternating black and red sections and lines. This pattern is found on several objects in the collection, including the painted handle with bird carvings in Figure 6.54. AM193.95:1294, AM193.94:949, UA84.193:1088, and UA85.193:4771.

Figure 6.66a,b,c. *Yaasiigem caniia*—box panel. Side panel of wooden boxes showing people in *qayat* and *angyat*. This single panel depicts *angyat*, or open boats, with many travelers, and single-man kayaks. Although it is hard to see, as the pigment has faded, the styles of the kayaks seem to vary. Note the spruce root lashing run through holes drilled into the side of the panel, which would have helped to unite the sides of the box. Kelley avocational collection, AM48.

spirits that influenced life on Earth (Crowell and Leer 2001:198). Like storytelling, singing, or dancing, painting is a way to preserve cultural and historical information and pass it to others (Minc 1986). The painted box panels may represent scenes from Alutiiq history or characters from Alutiiq legends.

In addition to containers for storing, eating, and cooking foods, wooden vessels had many other functions. They held water (Gideon 1989:40), tools (Lisianski 1814:181), and urine. Families stationed tubs outside the entrance to their houses where men and children relived themselves. The urine was then used to clean animal hides and intestines (Davydov 1977:152). The ammonia in the urine broke down fats in the tissues, making them grease free and suitable for use in clothing, bedding, and boat covers.

Evidence for the use of stomach containers at Karluk One may be preserved in a variety of valves, stoppers, and tubes (fig. 6.67). To make a poke, people tied one end of a cleaned sea mammal stomach closed, filled it with oil, and then

Figure 6.67. *Mallarsuuteq*—plug, *cupllukaruaq*—tube. All of these plugs and tubes are wood, except for the ivory plug in the lower left. AM193.94:1104; Sheehan avocational collection, AM231:37; Malutin avocational collection, AM230:3; Sheehan avocational collection, AM103:46; AM193.87:10890.

tied the other end shut. One end may have been fitted with a valve or stopper—a wood, bone, or ivory plug designed to help people access the contents of the poke. Examples from Karluk One are oval, with an encircling groove where a cord could be secured. Some plugs have holes in the top, perhaps for inserting a tube to help pour or drain the liquid inside. In addition to oil, Alutiiq people preserved berries, plant foods, fish roe, and even shellfish in oil-filled pokes (Billings in Merck 1980:206; Campbell 1816:99; Davydov 1977:173; Demidoff 1962; Fisher 1899:Entry 3).

Historic accounts indicate that people used ceramic pots to melt sea mammal blubber and produce oil (Davydov 1977:187; Lisianski 1814:195; Merck 1980:106). Archaeological examples of these pots come in two general shapes (Clark 1966a:160). The most common form, and the one found at Karluk One, is large and cone shaped. These pots have a wide, flat collar and a body that tapered to a flat base (cf. de Laguna 1939). Although the art of pot making has not survived, examinations of prehistoric pots indicate that people mixed clay with gravel, sand, or grass, shaped the vessel with the aid of a small paddle, applied a wash of clay to the outside, and then fired the pot to a hard finish (Clark 1966a, 1974). Although they were easily broken (Merck 1980:106), these pots had an important quality absent in other containers. They were fireproof. They could be set directly in a hearth.

Pottery is a common find in late prehistoric village sites located along the eastern coast and southwestern end of Kodiak Island, but it is rare in sites along the western and northern shores of the archipelago (Clark 1966a; Heizer 1949). Researchers recovered just seventy-nine ceramic fragments from Karluk One, pieces that appear to be part of a single conical pot (fig. 6.68). This contrasts with sites on the eastern shore of Kodiak,

Figure 6.68. *Qikumek canamasqat*—gravel-tempered pottery sherds. The pieces of this reconstructed pot indicate that it was approximate 25 cm in diameter. The base is 13 cm in diameter. The walls of the pot are about a centimeter thick and built of clay tempered with small pieces of unmodified gravel, probably by shaping the sides with a hand-held paddle. The surface of the pot has exfoliated in many places, but where the original finish is present, it has been smoothed, perhaps with the addition of a paste. The inside of the pot is encrusted with debris from use. AM193.M:825, AM193.M:826.

where archaeological investigations at three different settlements recovered fragments of more than fifty unique pots each (Clark 1966a:160). The presence of just one pot suggests that pottery was seldom used in the village. Here, residents likely rendered oil from blubber by aging the blubber slowly in pits or by chewing pieces. According to Davydov (1977:175), older people and children "cut the blubber into strips, chew it, and spit it out into some kind of receptacle. Then they cook it with berries and add several ground roots to this mixture."

Ingenuity in Artifacts

Sven D. Haakanson Jr., Curator of Native American Anthropology, University of Washington, Burke Museum

first saw pieces from the Karluk One collection sitting in vats of water at Karluk School. It was 1984, and I was seventeen. The archaeologists working at the site had laid the artifacts on tables for community members to see, placing fragile wooden items in water to keep them from drying and cracking. The Kodiak Area Native Association flew a planeload of cultural leaders to Karluk to see the finds, and I traveled along with Larry Matfay. The Elders looking at the objects were excited. I was not! I did not understand the value of the site or its contents. What did these artifacts mean to me? I suspect many young people today have the same question.

My perceptions have changed. I have studied the collection for nearly two decades, and I am never done. Each time I examine the pieces, I discover something new. From masks to bentwood bowls, spruce root weavings, and bark toys, I am struck by the skill of our ancestors. Each object records how it was made and how it was used. I imagine the person who created the artifact. With a piece of wood and a marmot tooth, obtained in trade from the mainland, they fashioned knives sturdy enough to carve everything from tools to toys, from objects essential for survival to works of art. Their story is carried on even now. This perspective reminds me how clever our ancestors were at making tools. They solved problems without a hardware store or advice from the Internet.

In the past, young people learned to make tools by experimenting with toys. Building a miniature kayak or a toy bow helped children learn the skills necessary to not only operate important tools but create them as adults. This way of learning remains important to our people, and the Karluk Collection provides an avenue for traditional ways of education.

There are over 150 faces carved into stone, bone, and wood in the collection. The majority are maskettes and dolls. When I first started learning about them, I studied their shapes and lines, the way carvers designed each face. I experimented with the designs in my own carving. Then, I used this knowledge to teach youth to carve in the same way (fig. 6.69). When you share an old tool with a modern teen, they often laugh or scoff at the idea that such an object could have had such an important job. But when you show them how the tool worked and how it was made, they want to learn more. When you teach them to make the tool, they become respectful. By exploring

Figure 6.69. Sven Haakanson Jr. at Petroglyph Camp, Cape Alitak, July 2012. Courtesy Marcus Lepola.

ancestral technology, we all learn an entirely different story about the past. Youth, adults, Elders, and scholars learn that we are descendants of smart, capable people. This creates a sense of pride and spreads dignity through our community. It's a transformative experience.

When the students ask me which mask is my favorite I tell them all of them, because they are. When you look at each piece and know it is the only one like it in the world, you realize how important the Karluk One collection is to Alutiiq history and Kodiak. Being able to compare this ancient collection with historic collections shows the deep roots of our traditions. We see the endurance of our culture and the consistency of its traditions, as well as its beauty and complexity.

The central importance of the Karluk One collection is its potential to teach. Every object tells a story relevant to the Alutiiq people today. The artifacts record our traditions, illustrate our technological sophistication, document our artistry, and fill us with a sense of dignity. Our people were not primitive. They thrived in Kodiak's unpredictable, dynamic environment with intelligence and what they could make with their hands. The Karluk One collection proves it.

Processing

To clean and slice foods, scrape hides, and cut fibers for sewing and weaving, villagers used ulus. Researchers found more than a thousand of these ground-slate knife blades at Karluk One, making them one of the most common tools in the village. This is not surprising given that ulus were the essential tool for splitting and cleaning salmon (Gideon 1989:37).

Karluk's ulu blades are fashioned from leaves of Kodiak's hard grey slate, a material that is not available around Karluk Lagoon. However, high-quality slate, suitable for tool making, is widely available in nearby Uyak Bay. The predominant ulu type at Karluk One has a thin, gently curved blade with a blunted top edge. Incomplete blades from Karluk One illustrated that craftsmen chipped leaves of slate to shape and then ground them to a smooth finish. Modern experimentation illustrates that with a flat, hard rock, some sand, and a little water, ulu blades can be easily ground to a smooth finish (Steffian and Counceller 2010:24).

In most cases, both faces of the Karluk One ulu blades were ground smooth, and the working edge of the knife was sharpened by grinding one or both faces at an angle. This produced a thin, beveled edge that could be easily resharpened.

Karluk One ulu blades were made in a variety of shapes (fig. 6.70). Some have a distinctively curved, crescent-shaped blade, while others are oblong with either a straight blade or an upturned tip at one end. Variations in the shape of Karluk One ulu blades match examples from other prehistoric and historic collections (Birket-Smith 1941:156; Clark 1974). According to Knecht (1995:492), Alutiiq Elders recognized knives with curved blades as cutting tools. In contrast, those with straighter blades functioned as scraping tools. Ulu blades of both shapes commonly feature a stem and or a hole to aid in attaching a handle.

Wooden handles were attached to the top, thicker, blunted edge of the slate blade (fig. 6.71, 6.72a,b). Moses Naumoff, who was raised in Karluk remembered, "They used to use stone

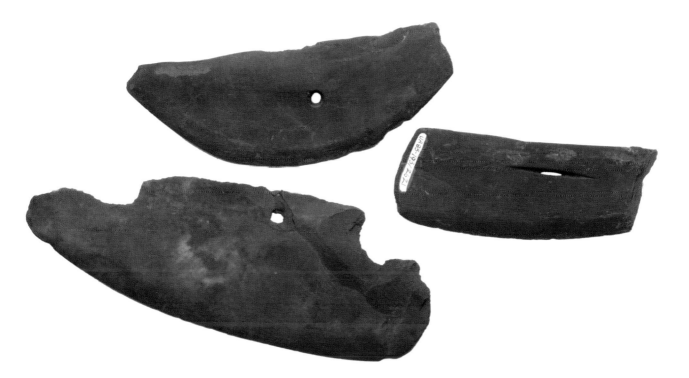

Figure 6.70. *Ulukaq*—ulu. Variations in ulu shapes and the three types of handle hafting holes appear in this image. The top ulu has a crescent-shaped blade and a drilled hole. The middle piece is oblong with a flat blade and a slotted hole formed by sawing. The bottom ulu is stemmed with a slightly tapered blade with a chipped hole. UA84.193:700, UA85.193:2621, AM193.M:849.

Figure 6.71. *Ulukaq*—ulu. The shape and size of this slate ulu is average at 10 cm high and 13.5 cm wide. Once dulled, a slate ulu blade could be re-sharpened. If an ulu blade broke, the handle was often reused. Many of the ulus with associated handles have been repurposed. For example, an ulu without a hole was shimmed into a handle made for an ulu with a hole. The handle has a groove for lashing, yet the ulu has no hole in which to secure the lashing. AM193.M:860.

Figures 6.72a,b. *Ulukaq*—ulu. Slate ulu with wooden handle. Note the cut marks on the handle. UA85.193:6884.

Figures 6.73a,b. *Ulukam agaa*—ulu handle. Semi-zoomorphic wooden ulu handles. Some ulu handles are shaped to resemble animals and have animal carvings on them. The handles pictured here have the same shape as zoomorphic ulu handles but do not have the carving of the animal's head on the end. Ulu handles are slotted or notched for blade insertion. A notch is partial groove, made for the insertion of a stemmed ulu. Slotted handles have a groove that runs the entire length of the handle. The top and bottom handles have a perpendicular lashing groove around the middle. AM193.95:1252, AM193.87:9244, AM193.87:9532.

Figure 6.75. *Ulukaq*—ulu. Large slate ulu with wooden handle lashed to blade with spruce root threaded through a drilled hole. The large size of this ulu and its long straight edge suggest that it may have been used to scrape hides. AM193.87:9250.

Figure 6.74. *Ulukam agaa*—ulu handle. Wooden ulu handles with beveled ends. The bottom piece shows how the slot was made. A preform reveals that notches were made in the bottom, and then the lengthwise section was carved out. UA85.193:6354, AM193.94:1379, UA85.193:6836.

knives, curved ones like a half moon. Those rocks they used to have sticks on the tops so their hands wouldn't get sore" (Naumoff 1979:90). Like ulu blades, handle shapes and methods of attachment vary in the collection. Some handles simply slid over the top edge of the blade (fig. 6.73,

Figure 6.76. *Ulukam agaa*—ulu handle. Two-piece, wooden ulu handles with carved recesses to accommodate the top edge of the ulu blade and grooved ends for lashing the handle together. UA85.193:6426, UA85.193:6478.

Figure 6.77. *Ulukam agaa*—ulu handle. Arched ulu handles of wood. AM193.87:11342, AM193.94:45.

Figure 6.78. *Ulukam agaa*—ulu handle. Crescent-shaped, wooden ulu handles with hand grips. AM193.87:9245; Sheehan avocational collection, AM38:2127.

6.74). These may have been attached with a glue made by boiling salmon skins (Merck 1980:106) or shimmed with small fragments of wood to hold them in place. Other handles were lashed to the blade with a length of spruce root or baleen passed through a hole in the ulu (fig. 6.75), a pattern also seen in many prehistoric and historic ulus from Kodiak (Birket-Smith 1941:155–156). There were also two-piece ulu handles (fig. 6.76). These sandwiched the top of an ulu blade between two handle pieces that were lashed together at the ends. Some handles in the collection are decorated: carved in the shape of animals or fitted with gentle grooves or a handhold to enhance the user's grip (fig. 6.77–6.80). A review of the different handles shows distinct styles. Perhaps ulus designed for specific tasks had unique handles, or perhaps each woman or a family of women used a distinct style to distinguish their knives.

Cobble spalls were another common all-purpose cutting, scraping, and sawing tool (fig. 6.81). At Karluk One, researchers recovered hundreds of these simple knives, made by knocking large

Figure 6.79. *Ulukam agaa*—ulu handle. Wooden ulu handles featuring animal carvings. AM193.87:11339, AM193.87:9974, UA84.193:1199.

Figure 6.80. *Ulukam agaa*—ulu handle. Detail of animal face carved on wooden ulu handle. AM193.87:9974.

Figure 6.81. *K'ligsuuteq*—cobble scraper. Flakes knocked off of greywacke cobbles were used as knives and scrapers. UA85.193:2850, UA85.193:1625, UA85.193:1476, UA84.193:751.

chips off greywacke beach cobbles. The result was a sharp-edged tool with a smooth back, a thick upper edge for gripping, and a thin, sharp, relatively straight, lower edge similar to that of an ulu. Cobble spalls are one of the most common tools in ancient Alutiiq sites, and their use dates back thousands of years (Steffian et al. 2006:114). These easily made tools are the Swiss Army knives of prehistory, effective for many tasks. Collectors recovered 540 cobble spalls from

Karluk One, many with edge damage from use (Knecht 1995:429).

Processing foods and plant medicines sometimes required mashing. People pulverized fish roe, berries, roots, and greens to create pastes and powders for both immediate use and long-term storage. Pounding was a particularly common way of transforming plants into medicines. People made healing poultices, plasters, gargles, and teas by breaking down plant materials (Fisher 1899:Entry 2; Gideon 1989:52). Berries were commonly mashed in cooking, and Karluk residents still make *ciitaq*, a dish that combined mashed berries with sugar and milk (fig. 6.82). People also crushed materials to make dye and paint. Craftsmen extracted colors from barks, grasses, and berries or created colorful powders

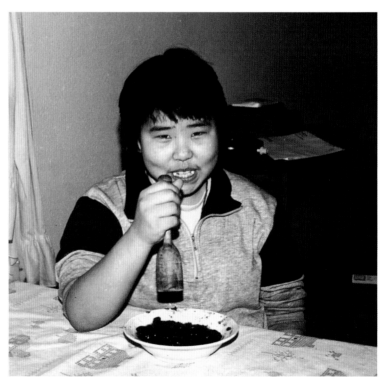

Figure 6.82. Marie Shugak mashes berries with a pestle and a bowl, Karluk, 1991. Kodiak Area Native Association Collection, AM4:196. Photograph by Priscilla Russell.

Figure 6.83. *Ciisuun*—pestle. Bentwood bowl and wooden pestle. UA85.193:6889, AM193.87:8844.

Figure 6.84. *Ciiwik*—mortar. Whalebone vertebrae mortars. The mortar on the left has been modified very little in contrast to the small mortar pictured in front. Besides the obvious basin, the large mortar's rim has been shaped, and there are deep cut marks on the bottom from butchering. This vessel is approximately 18 cm high and 29 cm wide. The small mortar is just 10.5 cm high and 11 cm wide; it has been carved to shape with a lipped base but not highly finished; the carving is rough. AM193.95:658; Sheehan avocational collection, AM38:248; Lind avocational collection, AM14:182.

by crushing red shale, iron oxide, copper oxide, graphite, charcoal, and other minerals (Merck 1980:103–104; Petrof 1884:230).

Two wooden pestles from Karluk One illustrate the antiquity of this method. One of these

funnel-shaped artifacts has a stout cylindrical handle and a cone-shaped base stained dark brown from use (fig. 6.83). Whalebone mortars are more common in the collection and include both simply carved and carefully worked pieces (fig. 6.84). Some are hollowed whale vertebrae, other pieces are carved from whalebone. One cup-like piece has a square wooden plug in its base, a repair that allowed people to continue using the piece. Another large fragmentary carving of whalebone resembles a bowl with thin, elegantly carved sides (Knecht 1995:369). The use of whalebone mortars continued into the twentieth century. Alutiiq Elders recall using similar vessels to grind *iqmik*, a form of snuff that combined pulverized tobacco, black tea, nettle leaves, and wood ash (Russell 1991; Steffian and Counceller 2012:46).

Tool Manufacturing

Inside the houses at Karluk One, people also made all of the items needed for daily life. Transforming natural resources into sustenance went far beyond cooking and included the manufacture of everything from boats and clothing, to the tools pictured in this book. Although manufacturing took place throughout the year, there was also a seasonal rhythm to this type of work. During the warm months, when daylight and resources were both plentiful, people focused on harvesting, traveling, and trading. At this time of year, they collected materials. During the cold season, when the weather was stormy and waning daylight limited outdoor activities, people focused on fixing and producing objects. Men repaired their boats, oiling the outer covering or removing it to rest and dry. They also worked wood, antler, bone, and stone to create new objects and tools. Women wove baskets, worked hides, made thread, and created clothing, bedding, and boat covers.

Many manufacturing jobs required special tools. According to Lisianski (1814:181), men and women stored such tools in baskets with small collections of raw materials. Men's toolkits included a variety of arrows, small pieces of workable wood and stone of different kinds, small adzes, a crooked knife, and teeth. In contrast, women's tool baskets held items related to sewing, including thread, rags, and beads. By rags, Lisianski is probably referring to scraps of hide. In the Alutiiq tradition, no part of an animal is ever wasted, even the tiniest scrap of hide. Instead, women save scraps, which become a palette for elaborate clothing decorations. It is also an Alutiiq tradition to show respect for the plants and animals that sustain human life by creating beautiful objects from the resources given to people (Haakanson and Steffian 2004).

Visitors to Alutiiq communities repeatedly noted the great skill of Alutiiq seamstresses (Lisianski 1814:207). A woman who could sew was considered a good wife (Gideon 1989:50) and sometimes presented a potential husband with an elaborately decorated cord to demonstrate her skills (Korsun 2012:256). The manufacture and repair of clothing was a continual job, one that women must have worked at nearly daily. The skill of seamstresses is particularly apparent when you consider that ladies sewed in the low light of their sod homes by firelight and lamplight.

Alutiiq people designed their clothing for wear in the Gulf of Alaska's maritime climate. It was lighter than the skin clothing found in more northern regions of Alaska (Fair 2006:76). The typical garment was a long-sleeved, hoodless robe stitched from bird or mammal skins (Black 1977:85). Women used cormorant, puffin, murre, goose, and swan skins to create clothing, as well as caribou, sea otter, ground squirrel, otter, fox,

bear, hare, marten, marmot, wolverine, lynx, and fish skins (Coxe 1780:116; Davydov 1977:149, 151; Hunt 2000:89; Langsdorff 1993:32; Merck 1980:102; Petrof 1884:230; Shelikhov 1981:53; Varjola 1990). These garments reached the shins or even the heals, with a narrow opening for the head and sometimes a low collar band (Davydov 1977:148; Huggins 1981:5; Korsun 2012:xx). They could be worn with the fur or feathered side facing toward the body, or reversed. Bird skins shed water well and Alutiiq people wore bird-skin parkas with the feathers facing outward on rainy days. Some parkas had slits along the sides. This allowed the wearer to slip his or her arms out of the sleeves and through the slits to move and work more freely (Korsun 2012:xxiv, xxxvii, xxxii). To retain heat, people belted their parkas (Huggins 1981:5), a practice shown in historic paintings (Korsun 2012:xxviii). Over their parkas, people wore a gutskin jacket, a waterproof, flexible, lightweight coat that protected from the wind and rain (Korsun 2012:xxv). Made from the intestines of sea mammals and bears, these jackets had a narrow opening for the head and a hood that could be tightened around the face.

In addition to robes and jackets, people wore simple undergarments made from soft skins, socks woven from grass, and sometimes skin boots (Huggins 1981:5; Korsun 2014:246; Lisianski 1814:194). People often went barefoot, especially in the summer, saving skin boots of sea mammal or caribou skin for the coldest winter weather (Coxe 1780:116; Davydov 1977:153; Merck 1980:102). This practice continued well into the historic era. On summer days in the 1890s, Karluk ladies walked barefoot to church services in fancy velvet dresses (McKeown 1948:53). Pants were uncommon (Coxe 1780:116). However, caribouskin trousers are part of historic collections from the Alaska Peninsula (Korsun 2012:34; Varjola 1990:258) and may have been traded to Kodiak or produced on the island. People often bartered for clothing and skins to make clothing (Billings in Merck 1980:205, 207; Coxe 1966:116; Davydov 1977:4, 27–28; Gideon 1989:85, 98; Shelikhov 1981:53, 77), and they took clothing from other communities as part of the loot obtained in warfare (Davydov 1977:9). Analysis of fur samples from Karluk One indicates that wolverine skin was present in the village though wolverines are not found on Kodiak (Carrlee 2011).

People, particularly the wealthy, had both everyday clothes and fancy garments for celebrations. Clothing for special events might be tailored differently (Korsun 2012:243) or made out of finer materials—the iridescent skins from the throat of a cormorant or plush sea otter fur carefully shaved with a stone tool to create a velvety texture (Coxe 1780:114). Whatever the materials,

Figure 6.85. *K'ligsuun*—gut scraper. "For the preparation of the gut, one method is always used. They are turned inside out and the fat and offal are scraped off with a sharp shell; then they are washed and rinsed in urine, squeezed in water, allowed to dry, and squeezed by hand" (Davydov 1977:152). The four scrapers on the left are made of antler, while the one on the right is wood. Each scraper has a different design and thus different edges—flat, rounded, elongated, sharp, and dull. AM193.87:9493, AM193.87:10246, UA84.193:1027, AM193.95:1764, UA85.193:3020, AM15:57.

all types of clothing were elaborately decorated. Alutiiq women were known for their skill at embroidery and appliqué work, and the cuffs, collars, hems, and seams of garments were adorned with fancy stitching, appliqué, tassels, and other striking embellishments (Varjola 1990).

Processing hides was the first step in making clothing, bedding, and boat covers. Women scraped, washed, and stretched hides to prepare them for cutting and stitching. The type of hide and its intended use dictated the way it was processed. For example, a sealskin destined for a kayak cover might be scraped clean, rolled with wet moss, and left for the hair to loosen before it was cleaned again. In contrast, feathered bird skins intended for parkas might be scraped, soaked for three days, washed, and wrung dry (Davydov 1977:151). Similarly, gutskin, animal intestines used to produce waterproof jackets, bags, hat covers, and spray skirts, were turned inside out, scraped, sometimes washed in urine, inflated, dried, and then split into long bands of material. Historic collections from Kodiak illustrate that Alutiiq people also worked with tissues found inside animals—stomachs, bladders, esophaguses, and the strong membranes that surrounded internal organs (Korsun 2012; Varjola 1990).

Scraping tools from Karluk One preserve evidence of hide working. The ulus and cobble scrapers, discussed above, were general-use tools likely employed in cleaning hides. On the other hand, more delicate spoon-shaped scrapers were used to work gut (fig. 6.85–6.88). Made of antler, wood, sea mammal bone, and in one case Dall sheep horn (Knecht 1995:343), these tools are smooth. They are designed not to nick or tear the delicate gutskin. As a person scraped a length of gut, the bowl of the scraper filled with tissue that was then discarded (Knecht 1995:468). Once the gut was scraped, it was inflated with air and left to dry. Although Karluk villagers used gut from a variety of sea mammals, bear gut was favored in the village for waterproof jackets (McKeown 1948:59; Pinart 1872:21), and Elders recall that Karluk hunters pursued brown bears in spring specifically for their gut (Matfay and Matfay 1987).

Thread was an essential ingredient of all clothing, and Alutiiq ladies "pulled" their own from baleen and animal tendons—especially those of whale, porpoise, and caribou. Russian observers noted that the thread-making process was time consuming (Davydov 1977:151) but compared the finest sinew thread to silk (Lisianski 1814:207). According to Moses Naumoff of Karluk, this thread was also strong. "To make that sinew, they dry it up, after that they just broke it into pieces and take it and tear it off then start to braid it and make thread and twine out of it" (Naumoff 1979:91). Ladies wrapped their thread around wooden spools. Examples from Karluk One are cylinders of wood, with marks left by tightly wrapped thread (fig. 6.89–6.91). Some spools have exquisite carvings on the top. One features a man and a bird standing back-to-back, another a carving of a ptarmigan.

After cleaning, women stretched hides to promote drying and prevent shrinking. Larger hides, those of seals, sea lions, and bears, may have been fastened to a simple frame or staked to the ground (Crowell and Laktonen 2001:159). Researchers recovered a variety of wooden stakes from Karluk One that may have served this purpose. These stakes average 20 cm long and less than 4 cm wide, and a number have damage on the top from pounding. Each stake has a pointed end, created by cutting opposing sides of the tool into a V shape. Some of the stakes are carefully carved and finished with knobs at the top. Others are informally modified branches.

Figure 6.86. *K'ligsuun*—gut scraper. The end of the middle scraper is shaped like a whale's tail. However, the narrow width of these wood gut scrapers suggests they were used to scrape seal intestines. Straight-edged ulus were likely used to scrape wider membranes, like bear gut, sea lion esophagus, and whale pericardium. The middle scraper is 11 cm long and 2.5 cm wide. Sheehan avocational collection, AM38:500; Lind avocational collection, AM14:1912; AM193.95:431.

Figure 6.87. *K'ligsuun*—gut scraper. At 12.5 cm long and 4.5 cm wide, the bowl of this spoon-shaped scraper made of sea mammal bone is very thin with relatively sharp edges. Lind avocational collection, AM14:158.

Figures 6.88a,b. *K'ligsuun*—gut scraper. Gut scraper made of antler featuring a seal flipper with a hole through the center. As seen in Yup'ik art, such holes could be interpreted as passageways designed to let animal spirits pass between the human and non-human worlds. This process supports reincarnation and helps to ensure a plentiful future supply of game. 11 cm long and 2.3 cm wide. UA84.193:1966.

Figure 6.90. *Qikarllum elgwia*—spool. Wooden spool with ptarmigan carving. The largest of the six spools in the collection, this one is not symmetrical. The overall length is 12 cm, but the barrel of the spool (below the ptarmigan) varies from 4 to 4.4 cm in diameter and from 7 to 8 cm in length. One of the other spools is also not perfectly round. AM193.94:16.

Figures 6.89a,b,c. *Qikarllum elgwia*—spool. Wooden spool with man and bird. Found by Ronnie Lind. UA85.193:6888.

Figure 6.91. *Qikarllum elgwia*—spool. Dimpled base of wooden spools. A dimpled end is a common feature among the six spools in the collection. All of the spools also have marks, striation for the thread wrapped on them. Most also have remnants of paint. AM193.94:3094, UA85.193:6888.

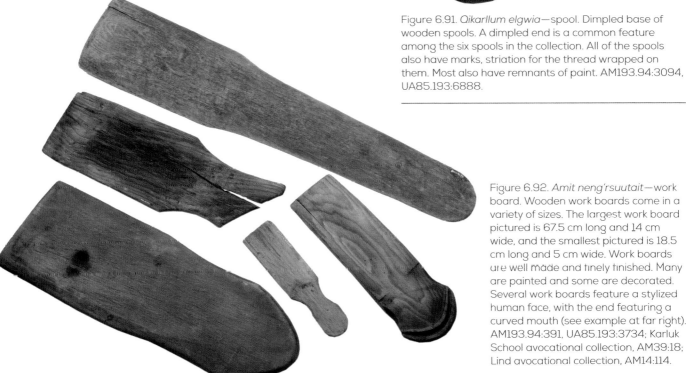

Figure 6.92. *Amit neng'rsuutait*—work board. Wooden work boards come in a variety of sizes. The largest work board pictured is 67.5 cm long and 14 cm wide, and the smallest pictured is 18.5 cm long and 5 cm wide. Work boards are well made and finely finished. Many are painted and some are decorated. Several work boards feature a stylized human face, with the end featuring a curved mouth (see example at far right). AM193.94:391, UA85.193:3734; Karluk School avocational collection, AM39:18; Lind avocational collection, AM14:114.

Figure 6.93. *Siilaq*—awl, *qikarllum elgwia*—spool, *mingquteq*—needle. Sewing tools. Sharp awls are made of a variety of materials. From left to right is an antler awl, a double-ended wood awl, a bird-bone awl, and lastly the 13 cm long finely finished and very sharp wood awl. The wooden spool shown is the smallest in the collection at 5 cm long to 1.5 cm in diameter. Two of the three needles in the collection, the top one is made of antler, while the bottom is made of bone and measures just 1.5 mm in diameter. AM193.94:5228, UA85.193.2944, AM193.87:8676, AM38:502, AM193.87:9678, AM193.94:1791; Panamaroff avocational collection AM15:567.

Small hides, those of otters, foxes, squirrels, and ermine, women stretched over finely made wooden work boards (fig. 6.92). These boards were tapered at one end, probably to hold the snout of an animal. Karluk seamstresses also cut their hides on work boards, perhaps using one board as a cutting surface and another as a straightedge (Knecht 1995:484). Examples from the village come in a variety of sizes and are heavily scarred with cut marks. Sewing tools included both awls and delicate bone needles (fig. 6.93). Women kept such tools in skin bags. An example, collected in Karluk in 1953, is made of cloth with lace and embroidery. Another is fashioned from bear lung (University of Alaska Museum of the North Accession Numbers 568-5555 and 586-5556).

Seamstresses used the awls to poke holes in a hide and a needle to pull the thread through the holes. Awls from Karluk One come in many shapes and sizes. Some are made by grinding one end of a long, otherwise unmodified piece of bird

bone to a point. Others are pieces of wood, antler, and bone purposefully shaped into hand-size, pointed tools. The one complete needle recovered during excavation of the site is made of ivory and features a tiny hole in the end. The method for drilling minute holes in delicate ivory needles remains a mystery, although Lisianski noted, "The needles were of bone: the instruments for boring the eye in them, are still found in almost every family" (1814:207). Other historic accounts indicate that bird bone was a preferred material for needle making (Merck 1980:103), a preference also found in more ancient collections from Kodiak (Steffian 1992b). Although women manufactured clothing, men were also adept at sewing

Figure 6.94. *Yaamam ilakuall'raa*—worked piece. Pieces of cut and grooved antler reveal techniques used to work antler, bone, and even wood. Craftsmen often created a desired length of material by carving a piece of antler around its circumference (see second piece from left and piece on the far right). This groove weakened the material, allowing it to be broken apart—by hand or with the aid of a tool. Other pieces of antler were scored lengthwise for splitting or have cut and drill marks. AM193.87:9240, UA85.193:5459, UA85.193:6013, UA85.193:4390, AM193.87:11100.

Figure 6.95. *Struusaq*—planing adze. Adzes were chipped to shape and ground to a smooth finish, especially on the working end. The ends of these adzes are double beveled, evidence of resharpening. Sheehan avocational collection. AM231:24, UA85.193:5816.

and traveled with needles and thread to make essential repairs to their boats and clothing (Merck 1980:105).

While women sewed, men manufactured tools and household objects. The floors of Karluk One's houses were filled with wood chips, whittled sticks, fragments of worked bone and antler, and flakes of stone (fig. 6.94). Researchers recovered more than 4,900 pieces of manufacturing debris (see Chapter 4), illustrating how materials were carved, ground, chipped, and pecked to make objects. Carving was one of the most common household activities. Around the light of the household hearth, men worked lengths of wood, chunks of cottonwood bark, and pliable pieces of bone and antler. Walrus ivory is present in the collection but appears to have been worked very little at Karluk One. There are just seven scraps of ivory, and several appear to be fragments of broken objects. Walrus are not found in the Gulf of Alaska. Their nearest source is Bristol Bay, on the northern coast of the Alaska Peninsula. As such, finished ivory objects were probably trade goods, obtained from residents of the Alaska Peninsula.

To transform pieces of wood or bone into tools, craftsmen used a variety of adzes, knives, chisels, and drills. Adze blades were chipped from a hard, green stone and their bits finely ground to create a smooth surface and a sharp beveled cutting edge (fig. 6.95). These blades were fastened to flexible wooden handles made from soft woods like cottonwood or alder (Knecht 1995:461). Craftsmen selected pieces of wood with both a portion of a tree trunk and a branch, taking advantage of the natural strength of an L-shaped piece of wood (fig. 6.96). The branch formed the tool handle, and a portion of the adjoining trunk provided a place to seat the adze blade, which was secured with lashing. Examples in the collection fall into three general size classes, suggesting their use for different tasks and differently sized objects. Large adzes were likely used to plane boards and for

Figure 6.96. Sтʀuusaq—planing adze, *tupuurum puunga*—adze handle. Three sizes of hafted adzes and wooden handles. Small adze blades are less than 7 cm long, medium size are 7 to 12 cm long, and adzes considered large are longer than 12 cm. "The ax-heads were made wedge-shaped from a hard black and green stone, and were attached to a short, curved handle and look like our large axes" (Davydov 1977:186). AM193.87:10510, AM39:174, UA85.193:4123, UA85.193:4158, AM193.94:3466, UA87.193:7158.

Figure 6.97. *Agaa*—tool handle. Side-slotted tool handles. The bottom two handles are similar in size. They are 13 and 14 cm long and 1.5 and 2 cm wide. The narrow slots on the side, which once held a thin blade of stone, are 3 and 4 cm long. UA85.193:3637, AM193.87:10577, AM193.87:7997.

Figure 6.98. *K'ligsuun*—rodent-incisor carving tool. Like crooked knives, the working edges of these tools are their sides, not their ends. AM193.87:10160, AM193.87:9356, UA85.193:6387, UA85.193:3151.

other rough shaping work, while smaller adze and adze-shaped chisels assisted with finer carving and work on smaller items.

For detailed carving, craftsmen worked with knives. According to Davydov (1977:187), "The Koniagas work very well with bone which they fashion with a small, bent knife. They always try to make the bone they use for arrowheads clean and smooth. They are constantly measuring it and checking it by eye. To cut the bone up, they simply use a small piece of metal which has been wetted or smeared with fat" (Davydov 1977:187). Several historic knives collected on Kodiak Island features a small piece of iron with a pointed tip and a gently curved blade fitted into a side slot in a bone or antler handles (Crowell and Lührmann 2001:41; Korsun 2012:181). These objects may indicate the shape of the blades used in handles of the same style from Karluk One (fig. 6.97). Although it was not commonly available, metal was sometimes salvaged from debris that

washed onto Kodiak's shores in prehistoric times (Davydov 1977:155, 186). As such, Karluk handles with narrow side slots were likely fitted with stone blades, perhaps thin pieces of sharpened slate or sharp flakes of stone.

Another type of carving tool also features a side-hafted blade. Short wooden handles hold rodent incisors hafted perpendicular to the length of the handle (fig. 6.98). Judging from their size, the incisors may be from marmots or porcupines, animals found on the adjacent mainland.[9] The width of the incisors matches the width of carving marks left on a variety of unfinished objects in the

Figure 6.99.
Ukit'suuteq—drill. The large
wooden drill on top is 59 cm
long and features two narrow open
sockets back-to-back that are 3 cm long
and 4 and 6.5 mm wide, to accommodate
a tool bit. Depending on the size of the hole
needed, perhaps bits could have been exchanged, or perhaps a bit
broke, and a new socket was carved to install a new bit. AM193.87:8084,
AM193.94:1229.

Figure 6.100. *Agaa*—tool handle. Narrow socketed and stepped tool
handles. The tool handle on the far left has an open socket on the end
(8 mm wide) where a carving bit would have been set, while the other end
was used for prying. The next two pieces also have a narrow open socket,
but also a lip on the end to better secure the lashing that held the bit in
place. The handle second from the right has a carving of a bird beak on the
end. The slender handle on the far right has a small off-center protruding
stem, possibly for lashing hair or fur to make a paintbrush. UA85.193:3361,
AM193.95:1532, UA85.193:3017, UA84.193:1778, UA84.193:825.

Figures 6.101a,b. *Agaa*—tool handle. This multipurpose
tool held two different carving bits. The large open socket
likely held a rodent incisor, while the narrow open socket
at the bottom probably featured a stone bit. The
round drill holes, charred black from friction, also indicate that
the piece was used as a drill handle. A human face is
carved in the side. UA85.193:2416.

Karluk One collection (see fig. 6.27), indicating
that the tools were used to shape objects by goug-
ing out material.

Other wooden handles have a socket for hafting a tool bit at their end (fig. 6.99, 6.100). These

U-shaped recesses are designed to hold a chisel,
gouge, or drill bit. Tools bits in the Karluk collection include a variety of small, adze-shaped chisels
that fit into some of these sockets. Other tool handles have multiple places to insert a tool bit (fig.
6.101a,b), illustrating the use of one handle to create a multipurpose tool. Like many other classes
of artifacts from Karluk One, some of the tool
handles were decorated. One has a face carved
into the side (fig. 6.101). Another is shaped like
an animal (fig. 6.102).

In addition to knives, stone tools assisted carvers in shaping objects. For example, small stone
bits likely tipped drills (fig. 6.103) and U-shaped

scrapers chipped from greywacke cobble spalls (fig. 6.104) were probably used to smooth and shape implements with shafts—harpoons, lances, kayak stringers, and paddles (Knecht 1995:523). Bobby Stamp (1987), an Alutiiq Elder from Chenega, recalled using sharp pieces of glass to shave bits of wood from the handle of a paddle, much the way a prehistoric craftsman might have used a U-shaped scraper:

> You'd take glass and you'd break it and get the sharp edge like this. This would be the sharp edge and here was the paddle handle, you wanted to make it round. You just shaved it just real, real fine shavings with that sharp glass part. If the glass got dull you broke it again and you used that shaving part. There was no sandpaper you know, and all of it was done [like] that. Little after you could whittle it down, as smooth as you can get it with a knife, you took that glass.

Pieces of pumice and sandstone also helped to shape items made from wood, bone, and antler. Theses gritty materials were used like sandpaper to grind objects to shape, remove tool marks, and create a smooth surface. The final step in preparing a wood or bone object was burnishing. By rubbing a smooth stone over a freshly carved object, a craftsman could flatten the wood grain, polish its surface, and remove scratches (Knecht 1995:431). Karluk One produced many waterworn pebbles of a distinctive, dark green, banded stone used especially for this purpose (fig. 6.104).

In addition to tools for working wood and bone, Karluk One held tools for chipping, grinding, and pecking stone. Flaked stone tools from the site included a small number of knives, bifaces, points, scrapers, and sharpened flakes of glassy stone, as well as a variety of adzes, and slate and cobble tools. Although finely chipped objects are

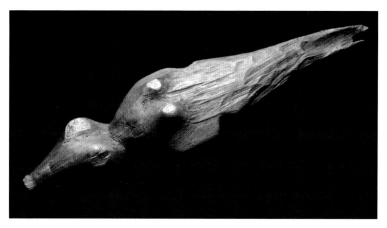

Figure 6.102. *Agaa*—tool handle. End-socketed tool handle carved into the shape of an animal. UA85.193:1752.

Figure 6.103. *Ukit'suuteq*—drill, *nuusiq*—knife. Drilling tools and slate knife fragment. The exact method for drilling holes is unknown, but slate tools demonstrate that holes were frequently drilled from two sides. Working with a stone-tipped shaft, craftsmen drilled into one side of the object, then flipped it and drilled on the opposite face until the holes intersected. The drill may have been rotated by hand or, more likely, with the aid or a small bow fitted with string looped around the drill handle (Davydov 1977:187). AM193.94:3793, UA85.193:5205, UA85.193:5158.

rare, Karluk One produced more than 1,200 pieces of chipped-stone debitage—flakes and chipped chunks of chert, metatuff, silicified slate, basalt, greywacke, chalcedony, obsidian, shale, and coal. Residents knew how to break stone and created

Figure 6.104. *Rasqaq*—abrader, *minguutaq*—whetstone, *k'liguasuuteq*—U-shaped abrader, *ipegcaisuuteq*—hone, *mulut'uuk*—hammerstone. Stone tools used in manufacturing. From left: a pumice abrader with a deep groove from sanding a thin bone tool like the arrow point featured here; two whetstones of gritty sandstone used to sharpen the edges of slate tools; two U-shaped abraders chipped from greywacke and likely used to shape wooden shafts; a slate hone, another tool for grinding the edges of tools; a hammerstone, and a burnishing stone used to flatten the grain on the surface of wooden objects and create a smooth finish. UA85.193:5236, AM193.87:8038, AM193.94:1878, UA84.193:916, AM193.87:10427, AM193.95:1082, AM193.87:9077, UA84.193:885, AM193.95:637.

tools for stone working. These tools include a variety of hammerstones, water-worn beach cobbles with damage on the end or the side. Many of the hammerstones are narrow water-worn cobbles that fit easily in the hand. They are typically made from granite or greywacke cobbles available on the beach below the site, although nonlocal basalt cobbles were also used. People used these cobbles to break apart other stones, knocking flakes off greywacke beach cobbles to create cutting tools, shaping cobbles into anchors, notching flat, water-worn pebbles to make net sinkers, shaping pebbles incised with designs, or working glassy chert into hunting and butchering tools. It is also likely that craftsmen used hammerstones to create pecked-stone objects. People shaped lamps, grooved cobbles, mauls, and splitting adzes by

pitting their surfaces with another stone. Recent experimentation at the Alutiiq Museum suggests that using two hammerstones works best, one as the pecking tool, the other as a hammer to drive the pecking tool (Alutiiq Museum 2011:1).

For finer stone working, craftsmen used resilient pieces of bone and antler to shape tools or chip a sharp tool edge. Karluk One produced a single flaker, a gently curved piece of antler, 10.2 cm long, with a rounded, blunted end. Other pointed pieces of bone and antler in the collection may also have been used this way.

To create ground-slate tools, men chipped pieces of stone into a rough shape and then ground them to a smooth finish. They made adzes, ulus, knives, lances, and the end blades that tipped harpoons this way. Tools documenting the

Table 6.2 Use of fibers in the Karluk One collection

MATERIAL	BASKETRY	OTHER OBJECT	CORDAGE	LASHING	WRAPPING	RAW MATERIAL	TOTAL
Baleen	4	7	1	133	1	12	158
Birch bark	15	0	0	1	7	180	203
Grass	6	0	10	0	0	2	24
Spruce root	61	0	6	45	0	3	109
TOTAL	86	7	16	180	8	197	494

NOTE: This table does not include seven objects carved from baleen.

Figure 6.105. *IRafkuq*—cordage. Three-strand braid of grass slightly more than 1 cm wide. This piece is very similar to a piece of cordage recovered at Palutat Cave in Prince William Sound (de Laguna 1956:240). AM193.87:10183.

Figure 6.107. *IRafkuq*—cordage. This piece of baleen cord is braided with a box stitch and is about 1 cm wide. AM193.94:1660.

Figure 6.106. *IRafkuq*—cordage. Four strands create these round braids of spruce root, about 1 cm wide. UA85.193:3654.

manufacturing process include hammerstones and a variety of whetstones and hones that functioned as grinders (fig. 6.104). The whetstones are gritty pieces of fine-grained stone against which tools were smoothed and sharpened. Flat, thin, irregularly shaped blocks of sandstone, siltstone, mudstone, and silicified slate are worn smooth from the objects rubbed against their surfaces. Similarly, hones, long narrow pieces of greywacke and slate, helped craftsmen sharpen the edges of knives and points. Some of the hones are unmodified, water-worn beach pebbles. Others are carefully shaped pieces of slate that resemble an awl

Figure 6.108. *Iʀafkuq*—cordage. Prepared bundle of fiber cordage about 2.7 mm in diameter. UA85.193:4459.

Figure 6.109. *Weg'et*—grass. Bundle of grass tied in the center. The strands of grass are not complete blades but portions of blades separated for weaving. AM193.95:1439.

or a pencil. Some hones also served as hammerstones or burnishing stones (fig. 6.104).

Ropes, cords, and lines were essential parts of many tools. Hunters secured harpoon points to harpoon shafts with lines (Birket Smith 1941:137; Korsun 2012:60–7, Lisianski 1814:204), towed sea mammal carcasses home with rope (Davydov 1977:121), hunted birds with braided nooses (Black 1977:850), tied their boats together (Davydov 1977:121), and retrieved fishhooks from the ocean floor with long lines (Birket-Smith 1941:147). In their homes, people suspended

gear from the rafters with line, carried containers with braided handles, and used cords as part of clothing, bags, and jewelry (Holmberg 1985:38). Making line was a job undertaken by women (Korsun 2012:256; Lisianski 1814:202), and one of the tasks little girls practiced (Gideon 1989:49). Historic accounts suggest that Alutiiq craftsmen preferred whale sinew for cord. Although sinew was not preserved at Karluk One, the site's artifacts include braided cords of grass, spruce root, and baleen (table 6.2, fig. 6.105–6.107). There are also bundles of fibers prepared for use (fig. 6.108, 6.109). Researchers recovered lengths of spruce root cleaned of its outer covering, split into strands, and bundled for later use. They also found strands of split and bundled grass and thin, uniform strips of baleen.

While cordage is relatively rare in the Karluk One collection, evidence of lashing is widespread. A variety of Alutiiq tools had multiple pieces tied together. Knots, ties, stitches, and even complete lashings appear on shields, pieces of slat armor, adzes, knives, handles, containers, boat parts, and toys. The ends of vessel rims are literally stitched together with thin flat pieces of baleen run through drilled holes (see fig. 6.64). Birch bark baskets were sewn together with spruce root, and a selection of ulus feature wooden handles secured with spruce root. Craftsmen ran strands of root through a hole in the slate blade, over a groove in a handle, and tied the ends to form a secure bond. Similarly, people tied broken objects back together. A hole drilled in each side of the break allowed craftsmen to rejoin cracked, split, and separated items and put them back to use.

Baleen is by far the most common lashing material, found throughout the collection and in all levels of the site. This material was an essential part of object manufacture. Pieces of baleen recovered from Karluk One illustrate that people separated strong, thin fibers from segments of baleen plates to create wiry lashing material. Some of these fibers were found in bundles, others were wound around pieces of wood for safekeeping (fig. 6.110). Baleen fibers were used both singly and in groups to create lashings. Fragments of kayak models from Karluk One show ribs and stringers lashed together with thin strands of baleen (fig. 6.111, 6.112). Spruce root and, in one case, birch bark were also used for lashing (table 6.2).

In contrast to braided, bundled, and lashed fibers, people used thin, flexible pieces of bark as a wrapping material. A reinforcing layer of bark helped to join some tool parts. Sea otter arrows collected from Kodiak in the early nineteenth

Figure 6.110. Iʀafkuq—lashing. Karluk One residents carved, wove, and lashed with baleen. Cut and polished pieces formed inlays in labrets, line leaders for fishing, clips for the wrists of gutskin jackets, and even toys. Thick flat pieces were woven into basketry, tightly twined strands formed cords and knots, and thin fibers joined delicate items. These artifacts demonstrate baleen working; top: segments of baleen; middle: baleen strands tied together; bottom: delicate baleen strands wrapped around a piece of wood. UA87.193:7730, AM193.M:761, AM193.94:1421.

Figure 6.111. Partial framework of a model kayak tied with thin strips of baleen. While the collection holds individual pieces of model kayaks, such as deck beams, prows, and ribs, this kayak model fragment survived intact because of its baleen lashing. The lashing of kayak parts is critical to a boat's function. Properly tied parts provide flexibility, allowing boats to bend in rough water and when landing, and protect wooden elements from breaking. AM193.94:3607.

Figure 6.112. This view of the kayak model fragment looks down on the center keelson, with the kayak stringers parallel on each side. The once curved ribs have been crushed open, but the baleen lashing running the length of the ribs securing each rib to the stringers and keelson is still intact. The lashing method is similar to historic examples (Haakanson personal communication 2012). AM193.94:4306.

Figure 6.113. *Kitsuuteq*—net sinker. Birch-bark-wrapped pebbles. The top pebble, which is shiny due to conservation treatment, is 14 cm long and 3 cm wide. AM193.94:3223, 3224.

Figure 6.114. *Inartaq*—basket. Spruce root basketry fragment with birch-bark reinforcement secured to its edge with baleen thread. AM193.87:10897.

century feature a layer of birch bark covering the point where the wooden arrow shaft joins the bone foreshaft (Heizer 1952:13; Varjola 1990:298). The maker secured the bark to the weapon with sinew lashing over the top. This use mirrors an example from Karluk One. Here, a stone fishing sinker features a narrow strip of bark, or perhaps kelp, fitted into its encircling groove (see fig. 5.30). Presumably, the material helped to secure a line, keeping it from slipping and fraying. Five other artifacts are pebbles wrapped in bark, like a

hard candy (fig. 6.113). These may be sinkers, tied in their wrapping to a line. Finally, small pieces of what appears to be bark are sewed to the edge of one spruce root basket with strands of baleen (fig. 6.114), again likely for reinforcement.

Decoration was a final step in making many objects. People carved, stitched, and wove with great care to create items that were both functional and beautiful. Cleanliness, fine work, careful use of materials, and embellishment showed respect for the plants and animals that sustained human life (Crowell and Leer 2001:192–193). People embroidered clothing and bags with delicate, ornate stitching, lined the edges of woven mats with sea otter fur, wove decorative designs onto the surface of baskets, dyed gutskin, and attached a great variety of tassels, beads, carvings, and even small weavings to hats and clothing (Billings in Merck 1980:201; Davydov 1977:153; Holmberg 1985:39; Merck 1980:102; Shelikhov 1981:55). The elaborate bentwood hats worn by hunters are some of the best surviving examples of intricately painted Alutiiq objects (Black 1991), but people also painted household objects and hunting gear.

Paint appears on at least 250 objects in the Karluk One collection, including everything from vessel handles to toys, model-boat parts, arrow shafts, work boards, war shields, and ulu handles. Many other objects were probably painted, but the pigment has not been preserved. A spruce root hat from Karluk, collected in 1884, illustrates the dramatic use of paint that may have once typified Karluk One objects. The hat is painted bright blue with a stylized animal face in red and black on its crown and decorative red paint along its brim (see fig. 7.57).

Historic accounts indicate that people crushed plants and minerals and mixed them with binders of fat, fish roe, blood or water to

Figure 6.115. *Ciisuun*—pestle. Grinding stones coated in iron oxide, a red pigment also known as ochre. One possible source of this material is on the shore of Cape Ayakulik, at the southwestern end of Kodiak Island (Davydov 1977:150). UA84.193:788, 717.

create paints and dyes (Davydov 1977:150, 187; Golder 1903b:102; Holmberg 1985:38) (fig. 6.115). According to a historic account:

They use a red paint, called *ktak*, to paint themselves. It is derived from a rust-red bolus. . . . They also use a white paint, *kut-khlioak,* made from a limestone, which they burn together with the red stone. Then they

grind it to powder on a rock, and store both kinds of powder in small soft bags, tied with tongs, until they need it for painting. They also use a blackish copper paint, *akh-sak*, which they grind to powder on a rock. They tie that into a piece of gut (Merck 1980:103–104).

At Karluk One, people used beach cobbles to pulverize iron oxide (fig. 6.115), and the mortars and pestles described earlier may have served this purpose too. Artifacts from the site feature the three paint colors noted by Merck. The most common that survives is a bright red paint, followed by black. Both colors appear in painted images on box panels and as geometric designs (e.g., stripes) and solid colors on other objects (fig. 6.116). Some of the black paint sparkles dramatically, perhaps from the addition of a ground mineral like molybdenite. Objects with white paint are the least common. Other colors may have been used. Green paint is common on historic collections from Kodiak, often in association with spiritually powerful objects like masks (Haakanson and Steffian 2009). Soft green stones are present, but green paint has not been recorded on the surface of any of the artifacts recovered from Karluk One.

To apply paint, people used small sticks (Holmberg 1985:38) and probably their fingers or a small brush. There are several examples of potential paintbrush handles in the Karluk One

Figure 6.116. *Mikt'sqaq*—miniature (toy). This miniature shield painted in red and black is 10.5 cm high and 9 cm wide. When waterlogged wood artifacts are recovered from an archaeological site they will crack and fall apart unless treated. In many cases, the wood objects from Karluk One were immersed in a waxy solution of polyethylene glycol (PEG). While this soaking preserved the objects from splitting, it also removed some of the delicate pigments preserved on their surfaces. This painted toy shield, not soaked in PEG, has cracked, but it reveals the original bright, and sparkly, pigments used to decorate its surface. UA85.193:3644.

Figure 6.117 *Yaamat tuumiaqsuutait*—rock paddle. This banya paddle displays decoration, reuse, and repair, characteristics found throughout the Karluk One collection. It is a household tool with a decorative bird carving on the handle. Burn marks indicate that the handle was used to stir or shift hot coals, while the back of the paddle was used as a cutting board. When the paddle split, it was repaired by drilling holes on opposite sides of the split and lashing between them. Panamaroff avocational collection, AM15:620.

collection (see fig. 6.100). Each is about the length of a pencil, with a small stem at one end. To the stems craftsmen may have tied bundles of hair. Knecht calls these tools stemmed hafted handles and notes that the small stem is delicate. It is not designed to withstand pressure (Knecht 1995:544–545) and must have been associated with fine work whatever its function.

Like decoration, both thrift and keeping one's tools in good condition Alutiiq people consider signs of respect. The artifacts from Karluk One demonstrate the antiquity of these beliefs, as many showed evidence of repair (fig. 6.117). For example, a craftsman rejoined the pieces of a feast bowl by drilling small holes and lashing the parts back together. Even stone tools were repaired. A finely made steatite oil lamp, likely a prized trade item, has drilled holes where its broken parts were rejoined.

Objects were also reworked and repurposed, recycling a broken item into a new and useful tool. For example, broken mauls were turned into oil lamps, fragments of the bases of bentwood vessels became knives for opening shellfish, and boat stringers and harpoon shafts were commonly reshaped into a variety of new tools. Some tools were repurposed numerous times (fig. 6.117). A kayak paddle became a skin-working board and then a tong for moving hot rocks.

Recreation

Life in Karluk was not all work. Models, toys, and gaming pieces were common finds in the ancient village and illustrate the importance of recreation in daily life. Elders who grew up in Karluk recall that when their chores were done—the beds made, dishes washed, sweeping completed, water carried, and wood chopped—they could play. Outdoor activities included *laptuuk* (an Alutiiq version of baseball), *ruuwarluni* (a bow-and-arrow shooting game), hoop rolling, swimming in the river, ice skating on flattened milk cans, sledding in the hills behind the village, and playing hide and seek, among many others (Anderson and Panamarioff 2010:23; Balisle 2010:46; Christensen 2010; Davis 1997b; Shugak 1978a) (fig. 6.118). Katya Chichenoff remembered, "When we were young we played with arrows. There were a lot of them, even old men, many played on the beach. While we were fooling, especially when the people would come from different places, we'd use the arrows. When we'd get tired we'd quit" (Reed 1962a:23–24).

Children learned the skills for adult life by observing adults, participating in the work of daily life, and listening to legends and stories (Drabek 2012:5). Young people also apprenticed with cultural experts, learning specialized jobs like whaling, healing, midwifery, or shamanism from experienced community members (Demidoff 1962; Gideon 1989:60; Lisianski 1814:207; Mulcahy 2001). Other specialists, known as wise men or *kas'aq*, were specifically charged with passing knowledge of Alutiiq history, religion, and ceremonial life to youth (Desson 1995:157). For example, these specialists taught ritual dances (Lisianski 1814:209).

As young as six, girls began leaning to sew and weave, making patterns for clothing, sewing bags, creating thread, and weaving hats and containers with instruction from the women in their homes (Davydov 1977:165). Boys began their training by making tools, throwing spears at targets, helping to put up fish, and practicing kayak building and paddling (Birket-Smith 1953:87; Davydov 1977:164; Gideon 1989:49):

> A father places his son when he is six or seven in a baidarka with him and teaches him how to paddle it. Shortly afterwards he makes him a small paddle and places the baidarka in the sea where large waves are breaking on the shore with noise and spray. To start with the father ties a rope to the baidarka so as to draw his son into the shore if it overturns, but later he does not even do that.(Davydov 1977:164).

Figure 6.118. Boys playing on Karluk Spit, ca. 1955. Alutiiq Museum archives, Clyda Christensen collection, AM680:166.

In the late nineteenth century, Karluk fathers purposefully trained small boys to tip and right their kayaks, an essential skill in the windy waters of Shelikof Strait (McKeown 1948:59).

There are many miniature artifacts from Karluk One—tools identical in detail to their full-size counterparts (fig. 6.119–6.123) Some may be useful tools, while others appear to be children's toys. Miniature artifacts are a common find in Kodiak's prehistoric sites, including settlements much older than Karluk One (Steffian 1992b). The Karluk miniatures reflect all areas of life, from tools used in hunting, fishing, and food preparation, to objects associated with warfare and ceremonial life. For example, tiny ulus and war shields

Figure 6.119. *Mikt'sqaq*—miniature (toy). Miniature bows, arrows, and harpoon parts. AM193.87:9364, AM193.87:11200; Sheehan avocational collections, AM38:281, AM231:33; UA87.193:7797, AM193.95:1000, AM193.87:9067, UA85.193:6709, AM193.87:9422, AM193.94:4009, UA85.193:6031, UA85.193:2334, AM193.94:1786.

Figure 6.120. *Mikt'sqaq*—miniature (toy). Miniature household tools—skin-working boards, ulu, banya scoops. UA84.193:1629; Lind avocational collection, AM14:166; AM193.87:9141, AM193.95:195; Panamaroff avocational collection, AM15:149; AM193.94:2031.

Figure 6.121. *Mikt'sqaq*—miniature vessels. Several of these small bark and wood vessels have burn marks from being heated over hot coals. Unlike toys, which are too small to be functional, these vessels may have had a unique purpose. The smallest one in the collection is just 2.5 cm in diameter, but the more average-size vessel (*front*) is 7 cm long, 5.5 cm wide, and 1.8 cm high. AM193.87:19068, AM193.94:702, UA87.193:7173, AM193.95:1041, AM193.87:9534.

Figure 6.122. *Mikt'sqaq*—miniature (toy). Miniature war shields. These miniature war shields are carved like full-size examples. The one on the right even has baleen lashing for attaching a handle. The smallest shield is just 4.7 cm high and 4 cm wide. The shield on the left is 10.5 cm high and 9 cm wide, while the middle shield is 21 cm high. Many of the miniature shields have cut marks, suggesting they were fashioned from discarded vessel bottoms or work boards. UA84.193:930, AM193.94:978, AM193.95:1766, AM193.87:11070.

Figure 6.123. *Mikt'sqaq*—miniature (toy). Miniature drum handles and drum rims. Miniature drum handles range from 6 to 10 cm long. The only miniature rim in the collection is 31 cm long and 8 mm wide. Panamaroff avocational collection, AM15:546; UA85.193:6094, AM193.87:10317, UA85.193:2964; Panamaroff avocational collection, AM15:131; AM193.87:8999.

were probably designed for imaginative play, and may even have been crafted by children learning to carve (Knecht 1995:604). Children may have used small skin-working boards and wooden bows designed for stringing (Knecht 1995:612) to practice skills like hide working or shooting. Elders fondly remember playing *ruuwarluni*, a target-shooting game that took place on Karluk beaches with bows and arrows (Christensen 2010; Crowell and Laktonen 2001:45). In short, toys from the site represent the range of activities in which young people could expect to participate as adults.

Figures 6.124a,b. *Qayangcuk*—kayak carving, *suaruangcuk*—kayak figurine. Miniature boats range in size from just 8 cm long to over 34 cm long. The smallest figurine in the collection—pictured at bottom (a) and middle (b)—is just 2.7 cm high, 1.2 cm wide, and 1.6 cm deep. Despite being tiny, details such as the mouth on the seal helmet are well-defined. Lind avocational collection, AM14:36; AM193.87:8835, AM193.87:11375, AM193.87:9360, AM193.94:5, UA85.193:3923.

Figure 6.125. *Angyangcuk—angyaq* carving, *qayangcuk—kayak* carving. Miniature kayak and an *angyaq* with a stabilizing pebble. Panamaroff avocational collection, AM15:19; Sheehan avocational collection, AM38:66.

Figure 6.126. *Angyangcuk—angyaq* carving. The small toy *angyaq* on top measures 13.5 cm long and 2 cm wide. This miniature boat features a split prow and stern, which is unique in the collection. Kayaks from the Kodiak region are known for their split-prow design, but the design is not typically found in open boats. AM193.94:1646, AM193.94:2020.

Miniature boats are another common find. Made from buoyant pieces of bark, these simple, one-piece carvings are shaped like *qayat* and *angyat* (fig. 6.124–6.126). Many of the kayak carvings feature a single hole in the center of the deck, a hatch into which small figurines from the site fit nicely. Also carved of bark, these figurines have detailed hats and faces. Some wear bentwood hats,

one wears a helmet shaped like seal heads, and one piece wears what looks like a top hat. Some of the kayaks also have a hole carved in the base. Into this depression people inserted a small beach pebble, designed to weight the boat and keep it upright in the water (fig. 6.125). While the presence of these models in households and the common use of toy boats by Alutiiq children (Knecht 1995:605) hint that these tiny boats are toys, some may have been associated with rituals designed to promote successful hunting (Jordan 1994:158). For example, whalers used model boats in private rituals preceding the hunt (Desson 1995:91).

Some of the miniatures are pieces of model *angyat* and kayaks or items designed to accompany these models (see fig. 5.85, 5.86). Boat-model construction helped craftsmen learn boatbuilding skills, from the shape and placement of pieces to their proper lashing. Alutiiq boat models in ethnographic collections often include tiny sets of hunting and fishing gear held by figures seated in the boats or fastened to the boat deck (Crowell and Laktonen 2001:147; Korsun 2012:151, Plates 188–198; Krech 1989:Figure 47, Model 184; Varjola 1990:244). The Karluk One collection has a tiny painted throwing board that may be an example of such a miniature.

Wooden dolls are also part of the Karluk One collection. Some appear to be shamanic pieces (cf. Lisianski 1814:178) (see Chapter 7), others children's dolls (cf. Davis 1997b). Toy dolls typically have a head, a torso, and legs but no arms (fig. 6.127, 6.128). They are carved with male or female anatomy and often have painted designs on the face and neck. These dolls represent men and women and may have been dressed in miniature clothing. In contrast, shaman's dolls often feature a head resting on a long trapezoidal body that resembles a stake. These dolls may represent specific people. The carvings lack detailed bodies

Figure 6.127. *Suaruaq*—doll. The female doll on the right is a typical size at 11.5 cm tall, 6.5 cm wide, and 2.8 cm deep. Sheehan avocational collection AM38:298; AM193.94:1.

but have unique painted faces fitted with labrets, which may represent the adornment of specific individuals (Knecht 1995:86; see fig. 7.54).

Although used as playthings, children's dolls were powerful objects associated with the rebirth of the year (Crowell and Leer 2001:45). Lucille Davis (1997b) shared that dolls were put away at Christmastime and not played with till Easter.

Sophie Shepherd remembered playing with her dolls in spring. "Spring time, when the birds come, we'd listen for the birds. They wouldn't let us take out our dolls until we heard this particular bird song, a golden-crowned sparrow . . . because if we did, there would be winter for summer" (Balisle 2010:50). The association between dolls and the rebirth of the year appears to reflect Alutiiq concepts of reincarnation, as dolls were seen as souls waiting to be reborn (Crowell and Leer 2001:195).

Adults also played games (Petrof 1884:235). Hundreds of darts, disks, throwing pieces, targets, dice, and tally sticks from Karluk One represent games still played in Alutiiq communities (Knecht 1995:575–604; Steffian and Counceller 2010:38–39). Many of these games involve throwing an object at a target and require excellent hand-eye coordination. They helped hunters both hone and demonstrate their skill. Elders recall that gaming was a social event, where people gathered to compete, gamble, and visit. We explore gaming, and its links to social life, in more detail in Chapter 7.

Karluk One's sod houses and their contents paint a picture of a busy community. Closely spaced homes suggest a tight-knit community, where families lived for many generations, watching over and harvesting from the mouth of the Karluk River. In this village, extended families lived together, sharing the daily work of preserving and cooking foods, making tools, teaching children, and caring for each other. Warm sod houses provided them shelter from wind, rain, and snow, areas to work and sleep, and a safe place to store food and personal belongings. Houses were also a center of social activity, where people shared meals, visited, played games, and celebrated the cycle of life. The social and spiritual aspects of village life are represented in hundreds of artifacts associated with personal adornment, games, warfare, and ceremonial life. These objects are considered in the following chapter.

Figure 6.128. *Suaruaq*—doll. In profile, this male figure has no neck. The mouth, with pronounced labrets, sits well below the shoulders. This is a smaller figure at just 10 cm tall, 4.5 cm wide, and 2 cm deep. AM193.95:774.

Chapter Six Notes

1. Following the wishes of the Karluk community, human remains excavated in 1985 were buried on the hill above the site (Panamaroff essay Chapter 1). Today, guidelines established by the Kodiak Alutiiq/Sugpiaq Repatriation Commission (2008) and the provisions of the Native American Graves Protection and Repatriation Act, require archaeologists to cease excavating when human remains are encountered so that tribal descendants can determine the best ways to proceed.

2. People continued to use grass as insulation in the twentieth century, stuffing it inside the walls of their wood-framed houses (Balisle 2010:46).

3. Wood-framed doors were a historic addition and typically opened inward to prevent residents from being trapped in their homes by deep snow.

4. Thick layers of grass were also found on the floors of prehistoric houses in the lower levels of the Uyak Site (Heizer 1956:30), suggesting that the practice of using grass as a floor covering is at least several thousand years old.

5. *Kamleika* is a Russian-derived term for a waterproof gutskin jacket.

6. Multigenerational sleeping continued into the twentieth century in Karluk. Sophie Shepherd remembers sharing a bed with her grandmother who told her Alutiiq tales at night (Balisle 2010:47).

7. Ethnobotanist Priscilla Russell (1991) suggests this plant was sour dock (*Rumex*).

8. During the cannery days in Karluk, villagers commonly salvaged salmon heads discarded by commercial fish processors (McKeown 1948:48).

9. Carving bits made from beaver incisors are also found on Kodiak (Donald Clark pers. comm. 2014), although they were not recovered at Karluk One.

Social and Spiritual Life

Studying the social and ceremonial practices of past societies can be challenging for archaeologists. Often the archaeological record preserves only hints of a society's rules and beliefs. Evidence of the social categories, political practices, and the spirituality fundamental to daily life often occurs in clothing or religious objects not typically preserved in ancient sites. Imagine Karluk One without any organic artifacts. Remove the wooden tools, the bone and antler carvings, and the weavings, and the view of community life would be quite different. The site collection would be a fraction of its current size and filled with stone tools used to harvest and process food. While these artifacts illustrate the ingenious way that people transformed raw materials into implements and help us to understand subsistence pursuits, they provide limited information on peoples' social lives and beliefs. The picture is incomplete.

Before the study of Karluk One, the typically poor preservation of Kodiak's late prehistoric village sites led some to believe that the Alutiiq culture was unsophisticated; that people were poor and used primitive tools. The objects from Karluk One provide a distinctly different view. The recovery of rare bone, antler, wood, and fiber objects demonstrates the tremendous skill, ingenuity, and artistry of ancestral craftsmen and the wealth of resources that flowed through Karluk. These objects also provide a unique opportunity to look beyond subsistence practices to consider the social and spiritual dimensions of the community. In jewelry, warriors' gear, gaming pieces, talismans, and ceremonial artifacts, a fuller picture of Alutiiq life emerges.

Society

Across the Gulf of Alaska, the coastal societies recorded by European traders lived in large, permanent communities led by wealthy chiefs. From the northwest coast to the Aleutian Islands, people from very different cultures organized their societies along a similar set of principles. A fundamental goal in all of these societies was the accumulation and distribution of wealth. In this pursuit, a village or a group of closely tied villages acted as a community and the central social unit (Davydov 1977:190; Townsend 1980:129).

Late prehistoric Kodiak Alutiiq villages, those of the Koniag tradition, followed this pattern. While members of different villages recognized shared cultural and linguistic ties, there was perhaps no overarching political system that joined communities together. Historic sources (Luerhmann 2008:75; Taylor 1965:40) suggest that each community was an independent world that managed its own business. Within communities, households were the basic social and economic unit. In each household, closely related people lived and worked together harvesting food, sharing resources, building boats, raising children, and celebrating life. Alutiiq Elders describe such communities as tight knit, cooperative, and unified (Taylor 1965:44) (fig. 7.1). Although each household typically had its own set of daily activities, people throughout communities assisted each other regularly and participated in deciding community affairs (Gideon 1989:95; Mulcahy 2003:81–82). "Each Koniaga considered himself a member of the village in which he lived, and as having an equal share in matters of general concern with all the others" (Davydov 1977:191).

Communities were also associated with land—the areas where members harvested resources. Communities were named after local landforms—for example, bays or capes (Davydov 1977:190). Here, individual families might use a specific fishing or berry-picking spot, but the shores, hills, and waterways surrounding a community were community resources (Mulcahy 2003:81; Porter 1895:77; Taylor 1965:42). We suspect that the settlements found in Karluk Lagoon and the lower course of the Karluk River prehistorically were part of one large community, with many related households across which people interacted with ease (see Chapter 2). This is the way Karluk functioned in the contemporary era, when portions of the village lay on opposite shores of the lagoon:

The geographic division of the village into two portions, on either side of the lagoon and separated by a 10 minute walk along

Figure 7.1. Karluk residents, ca. 1920. Alutiiq Museum library. Courtesy Alex Brown.

the 'spit', and by a bridge across the mouth of the river, has not resulted in a coincident political split. It is in fact remarkable the number of family, 'Church relationships', and friendships ties which 'cross the lagoon', and the complete absence of any signs of political cleavage (Taylor 1965:32).

Until the time of Russian conquest, a man from a wealthy family acted as a community leader. This person managed daily economic, social, political, and even spiritual activities (Davydov 1977:190). Today, Alutiiq people refer to this person as a chief, or *angayuqaq*, in the Alutiiq language. Chiefs organized community labor, settled disputes, and tracked the travels, harvesting activities, and the well-being of community members. They also oversaw public safety, interacted with strangers, managed diplomatic relations, owned an *angyaq* (large open skin boat), built and maintained the community men's house, led raids, organized winter festivals, and distributed food, tools, clothing, and valuables (Black 1977:84; Davydov 1977:108, 109, 188; Drabek 2012:101; Gideon 1989:40–41, 48; Lisianski 1814:173, 176, 196; Mulcahy 2003:82; Taylor 1965). The power of the chief lay in his ability to attract followers, accumulate resources, and uphold community ideals, not in his ability to compel support (Black 1977:84; Davydov 1977:190; Luehrmann 2008:75; Merck 1980:109; Taylor 1965:72; Townsend 1980:136). A respected chief was fair, considerate, and able to build consensus. Although chiefs could punish or banish those who acted badly, punishments were typically decided with plenty of community input. Moreover, those who disagreed with a chief could move to another community (Mulcahy 2003:83, 85). In short, people stayed in a community because it was advantageous to be affiliated with a successful chief.

In the distant past, chiefs came from wealthy families, inheriting the opportunity to lead. The position of chief was passed through families, and a number of male relatives could assume the role upon the death or retirement of a chief—a son, brother, uncle, nephew, or even a son-in-law (Gideon 1989:40). Where possible, the chief designated his successor in a meeting of men in his *qasgiq* (community house). Here, he announced the new chief. Once acknowledged, the new chief provided a feast for the whole community (Gideon 1989:41). While a chief could name his successor, community acceptance of the new leader was essential, and the chief's designate was not necessarily selected (Pullar 2009:54). More recently, chiefs were elected or appointed, although often from the extended family of the former chief (Mulcahy 2003:84–85; Taylor 1965:33, 34). Ideally, succession was gradual, with the old chief instructing and assisting the new one (Gideon 1989:40; Mulcahy 2003:85).

Historic accounts suggest that villages often had several wealthy families and that a number of people served as advisors to the chief. In recent times, political advisors included a second chief (*sakaasiik* in the Alutiiq language), Elders, and church leaders (Lisianski 1814:196; Mulcahy 2003:80; Pullar 2009:54; Taylor 1965:33). While a person's family background provided the opportunity to lead, success as a leader depended on leadership skills and the ability to build wealth. Chiefs are described as physically strong, intelligent, knowledgeable, and shrewd (Huggins 1981:29; Merck 1980:109; Mulcahy 2003:85). Russian traders who sought to harness Alutiiq labor often took chiefs as hostages or replaced a chief with a person of their own choosing. This was not always successful, as community members would not necessarily follow the Russian-appointed leader, or *tuyuq* in the Alutiiq language

(Black 1977:105; Davydov 1977:106, 162, 190; Gideon 1989:40). In time, the term *tuyuq* became widely accepted and is still widely used in referring to a tribal chief.

Wealth in Alutiiq terms included large accumulations of food, raw materials, and manufactured goods, as well as rare materials like amber, dentalium shells, pearls, mother-of-pearl, and slaves. Food, boats, animal skins, containers of oil, stocks of whale meat, baskets filled with berries or roots, and dried fish, were among the items a wealthy person amassed (Davydov 1977:149; Gideon 1989:41–42, 43, 46; Lisianski 1814:195; Merck 1980:103; Sarychev 1806:16). To accumulate wealth, chiefs relied on strong support from their families. A large, industrious family provided labor for activities and strong social backing. Family members supported large harvests of food and materials, construction and maintenance of a community house and large open boats, and the manufacture of goods that could be given as gifts. In return for their support, family members were ensured a comfortable living. Historic accounts indicate that some men had multiple wives, especially chiefs and other wealthy men (Golder 1903b:87; Lisianski 1814:198; Merck 1980:108). Presumably this practice resulted in larger families and greater economic and social support.

Trade was another way that families accumulated wealth. The Kodiak Alutiiq were centrally located on the coast of the heavily populated Gulf of Alaska, between the Unangan and Aglegmiut to the west, the Dena'ina and Chugach to the north, and the Eyak and Tlingit to the east. Trips to neighboring regions and social connections with peoples from other cultures helped community leaders acquire goods like caribou skins, antler, and walrus ivory that were not available on Kodiak. Leaders were able to make such trips because they owned large boats, could assemble men to accompany them, and had family members working to harvest resources and manufacture goods at home. Karluk leaders likely traveled to the Alaska Peninsula to hunt, collect, and trade. By AD 1500, when people were living at Karluk One, Alutiiq families had established communities across the Alaska Peninsula, inhabiting environments on both sides of its mountainous spine (Hoffman 2009; Saltonstall et al. 2012). This may have created new opportunities for visiting and exchange with people in Bristol Bay and areas beyond.

Slavery was also an essential part of this system. Slaves in Alutiiq society were orphans—people without close family ties—or those taken hostage in warfare (Davydov 1977:167; Merck 1980:109; Townsend 1983). Slaves were most often women, children, and teens, captured in community raids and taken to their captors' homes (Davydov 1977:190). Slaves were considered property and valued both as a symbol of prestige (Huggins 1981:30) and as means of generating wealth. Slaves provided additional labor for harvesting and manufacturing, and they could be traded, given as presents, left to one's heirs, killed at will, or sacrificed at their owner's death (Black 1977:86; Davydov 1977:180; Merck 1980:108; Townsend 1983:122). Slaves also freed their owners' from work. A wealthy man had slaves to carry water and chop wood, allowing him to travel, trade, and lead raids. A poor man had to do his own work (Huggins 1981:30).

Anthropologists describe such social systems as *ranked* and note that ranked communities were home to people with different social standings (Townsend 1980:130). Across the Alaskan Gulf coast, late prehistoric societies had free and slave classes. Within the free class, there were also a small number of wealthy families recognized as elite members of society with a high social position. Differences in social standing reflected access to resources. While all members of the free class had unlimited access to the foods and materials needed for daily living, only certain families had the ability to access and accumulate wealth by producing a surplus of food and objects, trading long distances, participating in warfare, and owning slaves (Townsend 1980:134). Those from nonelite families participated in this system because it provided security and assistance. Elite families were obliged to support others. They were expected to systematically reinvest their wealth in the community by giving to guests (Huggins 1981:30), sharing with the needy (Golder 1903a:16), distributing loot taken in war (Black 1977:92, 2004b:146), and hosting celebrations and ceremonies (Black 1977:85; Gideon 1989:43, 45–46). These activities demonstrated and reinforced the abilities of leaders, strengthened economic ties, and established social obligations. Through generosity, a chief built support for his position as a leader.

Evidence of this social system occurs through the archaeological record of the Karluk region. For example, researchers note differences in the size and design of structures in prehistoric villages along the Karluk River. Winter villages typically hold a small number of large houses with many side rooms, the type of structures we would expect large, wealthy families to occupy (cf. Golder 1903b:86; Desson 1995:514; Golovnin 1979:24; Lisianski 1814:184). Some villages also have a large single-roomed structure, similar to descriptions of a community house or *qasgiq*. Similarly, by the late prehistoric period, trade goods were streaming into Kodiak from both neighboring areas and great distances. In addition to materials

such as antler, likely obtained from the Alaska Peninsula and manufactured into hundreds of hunting and fishing tools in Karluk, the site held materials and objects from southeast Alaska, the Bering Sea, and possibly even northern Alaska. More broadly, evidence of regional warfare appears in Kodiak fortress sites (Knecht et al. 2002; Moss and Erlandson 1992:84), injuries preserved in human skeletal remains (Simon and Steffian 1994), and artifacts designed for battle in Kodiak's archaeological record starting about one thousand years ago.

Despite these broad indications of a ranked society, some of the best evidence for differences in social standing comes from the items of personal adornment found at Karluk. In addition to their elaborately decorated clothing, Alutiiq people adorned their bodies with tattoos, paint, piercings, jewelry, and haircuts. Historic accounts indicate that decoration was both an artistic and social practice (Donta 1993:206). Clothing, jewelry, and body modification were not only beautiful, they illustrated a person's social and spiritual connections. They helped others to understand a person's identity.

At the broadest level, dress and decoration reflected a person's cultural heritage. Explorers traveling between coastal communities in the Gulf of Alaska noticed broad cultural differences in everything from clothing designs to hairstyles (Sarychev 1806:18). Within the Alutiiq world, there were also regional differences in dress. While the Alaska Peninsula Alutiiq wore caribou-skin clothing, people from Kodiak and Prince William Sound wore bird-skin parkas (Hunt 2000:42). Although these differences partially reflect the resources available in different regions, they illustrate identifiable cultural preferences. Through dress and decoration people also displayed gender, family ties, passage through life events like puberty, achievements, occupations, social standing, and ancestry (Hunt 2000:37–38). Women and men wore differently styled parkas, tattoos, and hairstyles. Shamans had special clothing and gear (Crowell 1992:29; Hunt 2000:60). Women from wealthy families wore distinct hairstyles (Shelikhov 1981:53), and the rich wore select furs and elaborate decorations to illustrate their power, heritage, and ties to the spirit world (Gideon 1989:48; Lisianski 1814:194). In essence, Alutiiq people covered themselves with items that expressed social categories. The importance of clothing to a person's identity is underscored by reports that a person who failed to follow social rules could be stripped of his parka (Gideon 1989:55). This method of shaming not only exposed the person physically, it removed his or her social skin.

Although clothing was not preserved at Karluk One, evidence of clothing styles appears in the site's many incised pebbles (Donta essay Chapter 7). Researchers recovered 230 of these small pieces of stone from the site's lower levels, each with an ancient drawing. Scratched into the surface of the stones are images of faces, clothing, jewelry, and ceremonial gear (Donta 1993:132–133). The array of headdresses, decorative parka elements, belts, and jewelry shown indicate that prehistoric personal adornment was elaborate, creative, and varied. About a third of the pebbles studied show clothing, including bird-skin and possibly gut-skin garments (Donta 1993:252–256). A large proportion of these garments feature a V-shaped collar with decorative fringe hanging below. This style may be distinct to Karluk or perhaps southern Kodiak Island. A large collection of incised pebbles from Monashka Bay (Clark 1964; Donta 1993) on northern Kodiak Island has a number

of pebbles showing a different collar style. Here, V-shaped collars are also common, but they have small decorative triangles or squares on the upper edge (Clark 1964:127; Donta 1994:349–350).

Other evidence of adornment from Karluk One seems to indicate more personal displays of identity with tattoos, face painting, jewelry, and labrets. Alutiiq people made tattoos by pulling a soot-blackened needle beneath the skin (Davydov 1977:149; Merck 1980:103). "The tattooing was performed by lifting a small piece of skin with the point of a needle until blood showed. Ink, made of spruce charcoal mixed with blood, was applied, and on the body [against the skin] it assumed a dark-blue color" (Gideon 1989:58). Both men and women wore tattoos, though of different styles. Women tattooed their chins, cheeks, arms, and chests, and often had bands of tattoos running over their shoulders (Billings in Merck 1980:200, 205; Korsun 2012:xxiii; Merck 1980:103). For women, tattoos seem to have been associated with life-passage events. Some were applied when a girl reached puberty, illustrating her entrance into adulthood (Crowell 1992:21; Merck 1980:103). Others were added at marriage as a sign of love for her husband (Davydov 1977:149). Men also wore tattoos on their faces, necks, and torsos (Korsun 2012:xx; Shelikhov 1981:53), and at least some of these indicated personal wealth. The richest men had bands of tattoos on their shoulders (Gideon 1989:58).

Evidence of tattooing at Karluk may be preserved in wooden figures with incised lines and painted designs on their torsos. One female carving has nine delicately incised lines radiating from her lower lip across her chin and sets of four parallel, incised lines above each breast. These lines slope downward from the shoulders toward the sternum and match historically recorded patterns

Figure 7.2. *Samanam suarua'a*—shaman's doll. Female wooden figure with black painted lines on the chest. This doll is 8 cm high, 3.5 cm wide, and 2.5 cm deep. UA85.193:3508.

Figure 7.3. *Yaamaruaq*—incised pebble. Made from beach pebbles, cobble spalls, small pieces of roughly shaped slate, and even fragments of ground slate tools, these artifacts feature stylized drawings of faces and clothes. They provide a rare look at ancient clothing, decoration, and ceremonial gear. People used sharp tools to scratch designs into these pebbles and sometimes polished the surface before drawing on it. Often one side is incised, but a number of the Karluk One pebbles are incised on two sides (Donta 1993:235). This small slate pebble is just 4.3 cm high and 2.9 cm wide. UA85.193:6499.

Figure 7.4. *Yaamaruaq*—incised pebble. Water-worn greywacke pebble with a drawing of a face and feather parka. The side of the pebble with the etching has been polished. The face features a pair of lines below the mouth that could be chin tattoos. Most of the incised pebbles from the site feature depictions of human faces, particularly an arched brow, nose, and mouth (Donta 1993:235). UA87.193:7829.

of tattooing. Another female carving has a pair of painted black lines forming a V from the shoulders to the center of the chest and a red band around the bottom torso (fig. 7.2). The painting could represent body paint, clothing, or tattoos. Karluk dolls are typically carved naked, and we know that tattoos were typically black. As such, the painted black lines may reflect the bands of tattoos recorded historically. Incised pebbles from Karluk One also appear to show tattoos (Donta 1993:347–348). A large number of the faces depicted have lines drawn below the mouth interpreted as chin tattoos (Clark 1964:119; Donta 1994:133) (fig. 7.3, 7.4). Historically, this style of tattooing was associated with women (Merck 1980:103) and may indicate that a selection of the pebbles depict Alutiiq women.

Faces from the Past

Christopher Donta, Senior Principal Investigator, Gray and Pape, Inc.

Like a number of sites in the Kodiak Archipelago, Karluk One contained hundreds of small beach pebbles incised with faces. Stylized sketches of people appear on unremarkable bits of slate and greywacke found in a thin band across the lower layers of the site. These artifacts are always a treat to find because, at first glance, they look like ordinary beach pebbles. But because we know they are there, we clean off every small flat rock to look for the faces, and on some—*voila*—a face looking back at us from hundreds of years in the past! A quick dip in some water if handy, or maybe a lick or two with the tongue if not, and all the details become visible. It sounds unpleasant to lick a dirty rock, but at the time, it seems such a minor thing in order to know whether or not it is more than just a rock! Inevitably, then comes a shout of excitement and a passing around of the special artifact for all to see.

Over the years, archaeologists have been intrigued by the purpose of these artifacts. But their meaning is elusive. The tradition of drawing faces and clothing on stones did not continue to the present, and we have no direct knowledge of their use or function. However, because there are many hundreds of well-documented archaeological examples, and we now better understand their ages and locations from several sites, it is possible to make some interpretations about the role of these small pieces of graphic art.

The incised pebble drawings are consistently made up of a face, formed by eyebrow ridges descending into a nose, often with eyes drawn, and a box-like mouth. Around the mouth, nose, and eyes is a variety of decoration, including labrets, beads, and perhaps the carvings often attached to masks. Not all pieces have decoration, but most do. It is even possible to see that some kinds of clothing and adornment are more common at certain sites than at others. For instance, Karluk pieces often have fringed V-neck clothing and a single labret centered under the mouth (fig. 7.5). In contrast, pebbles from the Monashka Bay site on northern Kodiak Island often have multiple, small, beaded labrets under the mouth and a curved-neck parka. The eyebrows and nose elements are nearly identical at all Koniag sites, and almost all the stones were made during a short time period. The consistency and rule-bound nature of the stylized drawings point to an element of the sacred rather than some utilitarian purpose. So what were these little stones for? The fantastic preservation at Karluk One provides some clues. There are other examples of this same ancient imagery in Karluk One artifacts.

Identical faces have been found on a mask and two painted wooden box panels from Karluk One, complete with the eyebrow ridges, eyes, nose, and box-like mouth. The painted faces on the box panels show rays of light coming from the eyes. This ties into the traditional story of a powerful being who can see in the dark with supernatural sight. Rings around the face on the box panels mimic rings around masks and may be metaphors for the different levels of the Alutiiq universe. Therefore, the rule-bound, repeated figure on the incised stones may represent the central, supernatural being in traditional Alutiiq religion (as in Pinart 1873). Or it may reflect images of multiple different deities or celestial ancestors. The same stylized face has also been found on the tip of a slate spear point from Karluk One. Whoever drew it on the point was likely hoping that the imagery would assist the weapon. The power of such a strong figure, placed on a spear point or involved in a village ceremony, would be significant. This tradition of drawing faces on rocks may have arisen from similar drawings on seashore rocks, such as at Cape Alitak, and continued later in the form of masks and paintings such as the box panels.

Why are so many of these stones found throughout Alutiiq villages five to six hundred years ago? Houses from the centuries surrounding this time suggest major changes in Alutiiq culture were underway, accompanied by the emergence of more powerful leaders (see Donta 1994). The illustrations on the

Figure 7.5. Incised pebbles showing people in fringed V-neck garments. This style of garment appears commonly on Karluk pebbles and is distinct from garment necks depicted on incised pebbles from the northern Kodiak, suggesting the presence of regional clothing styles. Illustration by Amy Steffian from drawings by Chris Donta.

stones may reinforce new social statuses and leadership positions by linking people to high-status ancestors or ancestral spirits. The large numbers may be a result of their widespread distribution among community members who participated in ceremonies, with the imagery serving as an expression of ancestral power, available to all or many village members.

Body painting was a common part of preparing for events and performances, occasions when people interacted with members of neighboring communities. "When a Koniaga is about to embark upon some important undertaking, either hunting or rowing a long distance at sea, he paints his face with red graphite (found on Cape Iakolitsk and in other places), he does exactly the same thing when he is about to receive his guests" (Davydov 1977:150). People used black, red, and white paint, and the choice of color at least partially reflected the setting in which it was worn. For example, people in mourning painted their faces black (Lisianski 1814:200).

Historic accounts and illustrations describe many different types of body painting and suggest that variation in designs reflected personal choices, social standing, and affiliations (Korsun 2012:xxvi). Men painted their faces and bodies for festival dancing (Davydov 1977:110; Merck 1980:100; Sarychev 1806:18). Women painted stripes on their cheeks and colored portions of their faces—the nose, the forehead, or the eyebrows (Merck 1980:104). Some of this body paint had spiritual significance, helping performers to interact with the non-human world. Other body painting supported social signals, helping to display gender, age, rank, and social ties. For example,

Figure 7.6. *Agaa*—tool handle. This ergonomically designed tool handle was likely used as a paintbrush. The small knobbed end could have had fur or hair tied to it for bristles. UA84.193:750.

the portrait of a well-dressed Kodiak chief painted in 1818 shows red paint covering a band across the man's face, from the base of his nose to the tops of his eyelids (Korsun 2012:xxxii). In Prince William Sound, patterns of face painting differed by village, helping people determine the community from which a person came (Birket-Smith 1953:114).

While we cannot say for certain that Karluk One residents used body paint, it seems very likely that this form of expression was part of a larger pattern of illustrating personal identity. The pigment stones, mortars and pestles, and possible paintbrushes from the site (fig. 7.6) are artifacts that could have been used to make and apply such paint. Similarly, carvings of human figures with painted faces and bodies may illustrate past styles of body painting in the village. For example, one male figure carved of wood features a red forehead that matches historic description of face painting (fig. 7.7). This figure also has a pair of red bands on the chest that may represent body paint.

In recent times, jewelry included beaded items. Both men and women wore beaded earrings, and women wore beaded necklaces, bracelets, rings, anklets, and belts (Crowell and Lührmann 2001:50–51; Davydov 1977:110, 149, 150; Gideon 1989:58; Korsun 2012:xxvii, 258; Lisianski 1814:195). Jewelry was worn in daily life but also donned for special events to illustrate social information like wealth or availability for marriage. Beaded items became quite elaborate after

Figure 7.7. *Samanam suarua'a*—shaman's doll. This painted wooden figure has a red forehead and bands of red paint on the chest that could represent styles of body painting. It is 16 cm high, 5 cm wide, and 3.5 cm deep. UA85.193:3695.

Russian conquest, when glass beads manufactured in Europe were traded in large quantities to Alutiiq people and incorporated readily into jewelry and clothing (Crowell 1992:19; Davydov 1977:149). In contrast, prehistoric beads are relatively rare. There are just seven hand-carved beads from Karluk One, three pendants, and a handful of button-like fasteners (fig. 7.8, 7.9). Despite their small numbers, these decorative artifacts show great diversity. No two are identical. These are made in a variety of shapes and sizes and from an array of materials that include amber, ivory, coal, clamshell, a bear's tooth, and even a halibut vertebra. Beads are also relatively rare in portrayals of people on the site's incised stones, occurring on just 5 percent the drawings (Donta 1993:240). However, they appear to be represented on a few stones showing earrings (Donta 1993:250). Together the small number of beads in the collection and images of decorative collars, belts, and headdresses preserved on incised pebbles (Donta 1994:133) suggests that many ancient decorations were made of perishable materials not preserved at Karluk One.

Figure 7.8. *Pinguaq*—bead, *uyamillkuaq*—pendant. From top to bottom, left to right: crescent-shaped ivory pendant, bear tooth pendant, slate bead, ivory bead, amber bead, coal bead, modified halibut vertebra. AM193.87:10729, UA85.193:4737; Lind avocational collection, AM14:6; UA85.193:4507, AM193.94:5143, AM193.87:8854, UA84.193:1141.

Figure 7.9. *Puukicaaq*—fastener. These small carvings of wood, bone, and ivory were likely used for adornment and for practical uses like securing clothing. UA85.193:3934; Malutin avocational collection, AM230:19; UA85.193:4050, UA83.193:932, AM193.87.11311.

A necklace made of seeds, collected on Kodiak in 1818 (Korsun 2012:264), and ornaments like puffin beaks and fur tassels found on historic clothing support this idea.

One very unique decorative item found at Karluk One was a small fragment of a belt made from caribou incisors. Although no leather was preserved, neat, parallel rows of teeth, found beside a Karluk hearth, mirror women's belts worn in western Alaska. Yup'ik men cut the teeth from the lower jaws of caribou, carefully keeping the eight incisors connected. Sets of these incisors were sewn in rows on strips of leather to create narrow belts believed to have healing powers (Fitzhugh and Kaplan 1982:146). A woman who wore such a belt demonstrated that her husband was a good provider, someone who could harvest many caribou (Fienup-Riordan 2003:320). Caribou-teeth belts are not known in Alutiiq ethnographic collections, suggesting that the belt uncovered in Karluk was a trade item. This is another example of a rare and valuable object obtained from a distance and of a unique item of personal adornment.

Prehistorically, some of the most common forms of jewelry were nose pins and labrets, objects worn in facial piercings. People pierced their nose cartilage to hold a narrow pin, and slit the skin beneath the chin or near the corners of the mouth for one or more decorative lip plugs (Billings in Merck 1980:205; Gideon 1989:58). Nose pins are described as tubes of bone (Davydov 1977:110, 148; Lisanski 1814:195), and historic paintings of Kodiak Alutiiq people show them worn by both men and women (Korsun 2012:xxxii). Examples of nose pins from Karluk One are thin, gently curved pieces of wood, pointed on both ends (fig. 7.10). One features a small carving of a bird, perhaps a puffin based on the shape of its head (fig. 7.10 bottom). Researchers also recovered one nose ring, a U-shaped piece of polished coal designed to hang from the nasal septum—the piece of skin separating a person's nostrils.

Figure 7.10. *Paciiruam kulut'rua'a*—nose pin. There are five complete nose pins in the collection weighing between just .4 and 1.5 gm each. The bottom piece with a bird carving on the end is 9 cm long. Karluk School avocational collection, AM39:5; UA84.193:1665, AM193.94:5151.

Figure 7.11. *Qukaciq*—labret. A group of bowler-shaped labrets uncovered in the excavation, 1987. Alutiiq Museum archives, AM193:385.S.

Labrets were the most common pieces of jewelry at Karluk One. Researcher found 410 labrets, of which 34 were pieces in the process of manufacture (fig. 7.11, 7.12). Most Karluk labrets (87 percent) were made of wood and bark, as compared to 13 percent made of heavier antler, bone, coal, ivory, limestone, or slate. Evidence of labret wear also appears in the site's wooden carvings and incised pebbles, which show people wearing labrets.

Historic accounts indicate that Alutiiq babies received a labret hole piercing as part of the process of entering society. Born in secluded huts, babies were washed twenty days after birth and their noses and chins pierced for jewelry before moving into the family home (Lisianski 1814:201). Over the course of one's life, it is likely that people increased the size of their labret to reflect age and achievement (Knecht 1995:641). In additional to tiny, thin labrets that may have been worn by children, Karluk labrets occur in distinct size groupings, with small, medium, large, and extra-large versions of each different shape. The site also produced hole stretchers, pieces of quickly carved alder branches designed to enlarge a person's piercing for a larger plug (fig. 7.13).

Figure 7.12. *Qukaciq*—labret. Labret preform carved from wood, 3 cm high, 2 cm wide, and 1.5 cm thick. Tool marks on the surface of this labret and its uneven top indicate an early stage of manufacture. The object has been roughly shaped, but not trimmed, sanded, or burnished. AM193.94:877.

Figure 7.13. *Qerllum neng'rsuutii*—labret-hole stretcher. Labret-hole stretchers made of alder branches with the bark attached. Like labrets, stretchers come in distinct small, medium, and large sizes, illustrating how people expanded their labret holes to accommodate the next size of lip plug. The *top* stretcher is 8.5 cm long and 2.5 cm in diameter. AM193.94:836, AM193.87:9259, AM193.87:9265.

A Piercing Question

Amy F. Steffian, Director of Research and Publication, Alutiiq Museum

When Western traders arrived in the Gulf of Alaska they found Native peoples with many unfamiliar customs. One of the most startling was the use of labrets—plugs of wood, bone, and stone fitted in holes below the lower lip. Native peoples pierced their faces to wear this form of jewelry. Some labrets were small, others large and elaborately decorated.

This practice horrified Westerners, who regarded facial piercing as grotesque and disfiguring (Dall 1884:82, 87; Davydov 1977:148; Emmons 1991:245–246; de Laguna 1956:205). Some even reported that when people removed their labrets to eat, food tumbled out of the holes in their faces (Holmberg 1985:38). Despite these dramatic descriptions, archaeological data from Karluk One indicate that Alutiiq people had a different view.

The practice of labretifry is ancient in the Alutiiq world. Labrets occur regularly in settlements up to three thousand years old (Clark 1984:139), appear in prehistoric petroglyphs (Clark 1970b; Haakanson et al. 2012), and are part of ancient drawings of Alutiiq people (Donta 1992). At Karluk One, archaeologists found hundreds of labrets, as well as evidence of labret manufacture and labret-hole stretchers. Narrow lengths of alder branches with a groove on each end helped people stretch the size of a piercing to accommodate a larger plug. Moreover, wooden dolls from Karluk One feature labrets. Many have a pair of large labrets carved at the sides of their mouths. These data illustrate that labrets were once a common part of Alutiiq daily life, but why did people to modify their faces in this way?

Anthropologists note that a person's possessions can carry messages about their identity (Wiessner 1983; Wobst 1977). Although members of a culture tend to make objects in similar ways, the style of some objects—their color, size, shape, and decoration—can vary between groups within a culture. People often use objects to show membership in a family or religious group, to signal their ties to a region, or to indicate their wealth, position, or achievements. Commonly used, easy-to-see objects—a parka, a kayak prow, a prominent piece of jewelry—can carry group-specific styles that help identify group members. Team uniforms are a good example of this concept in modern American society. Players on a sports team wear uniforms that identify them as members of that team. The uniforms help team members, opponents, and fans understand who belongs to the team and who does not. We think labrets acted similarly among Alutiiqs.

Instead of teams, patterns in the Karluk One labrets suggest labret styles identified families. Patrick Saltonstall and I found that the site's labrets occur in a set of distinct shapes (Steffian and Saltonstall 2001:14). Although there are a few unique labrets, almost all of the labrets are one of seven general shapes. Some look like top hats, others like a pulley or a pagoda. Each shape is distinct, and some shapes were worn in different parts of the face than others: below the lip or in the sides in the cheeks. Moreover, each shape has at least three sizes: small, medium, and large (fig. 7.14). Investigation of the labret shapes from

Figure 7.14. *Qukaciq*—labret. Ovoid labrets in three sizes. Labrets throughout the Karluk One collection appear in distinct size classes: small, medium, large, and sometimes extra large. AM193.94:821, AM193.94:893; Sheehan avocational collection AM38:2087.

other sites of the same age confirmed this pattern. There is a set of typical labret shapes from Kodiak, and each shape was made in a set of distinct sizes.

In addition to this pattern, some labrets were specially decorated, particularly large pieces. A large cleat-shaped labret from Karluk One features rows of inlaid salmon teeth. Another has a shallow carving of a bear's paw on its surface. These are one-of-a-kind decorations on a common labret shape.

What does this mean? We suspect that labrets helped to display a person's identity and that the shape of a labret and where it was worn likely represented a person's family. We envision that each of the seven styles found at Karluk One belonged to a particular extended family, so that groups of related men, women, and children wore the same shaped lip plug. In contrast, it appears that the size of a person's labret carried information about their age and achievements, with large sizes marking greater age and accomplishment. Finally, unique decorations probably recorded social position. A wealthy person or perhaps even a specialist in Alutiiq society—a healer or a religious leader—might have worn a specially decorated labret to show their position.

In short, labrets helped Alutiiq people navigate the social world. They were probably used in combination with clothing, jewelry, and tattoos to signal relatedness, to identify people who belonged to the same large family or perhaps a group of related families. Travel, trade, visiting, marriage, and warfare regularly brought people from different communities together, putting strangers face to face. Without even speaking, Alutiiq people could read key facts about each other by studying the style of their acquaintances' clothing and labrets.

In the historic era, both men and women wore labrets, although in different ways. Women wore a row of small labrets below their lower lips with as many as six plugs (Davydov 1977:148), or alternatively, hung strings of ornaments from these holes (Gideon 1989:58; Huggins 1981:5). In contrast, men wore a single large labret (Davydov 1977:150) or, based on carved human figures from Karluk, a pair of labrets (fig. 7.15). Drawings on incised pebbles from Karluk commonly show ancient people wearing a single large labret below the lower lip (Donta 1993:245). The placement of a person's labrets probably depended on style, as there are a variety of shapes in the collection. Labret style and placement also seem to have varied regionally. Incised pebbles from the Monashka Bay site on northern Kodiak Island commonly

Figure 7.15. *Samanam suarua'a*— shaman's doll, *agaa*—tool handle. Wooden figure wearing pairs of labrets. The base of this stake-like figure tapers to a stepped end so a tool bit can be attached. Knecht notes that the practice of wearing labrets shapes the mouth into a *V* shape, mimicking a bird's beak and perhaps symbolizing the close ties between people and birds (1995:623). Among the Alutiiq, birds are considered spiritually powerful creatures, as they can fly, swim, and walk on land (Korsun 2012:161). Birds were often the spiritual helpers of hunters. UA85.193:4063.

show people wearing multiple small labrets below the lower lip, decorated with hanging beaded strands (Clark 1964:127; Donta 1993:345). However, some also show people wearing a single large labret or a pair of labrets (Clark 1964:119).

In addition to size and placement, labret decoration varied. People of influence wore the most elaborate labrets, decorated pieces that advertised their wealth and power (Billings in Merck 1980:102). Karluk labrets suggest this practice. Some of the largest labrets in the collection are decorated. These one-of-a-kind pieces feature

Figure 7.16. *Qukaciq*—labret. Large wood and bone cleat-shaped labrets with unique decorations. The labret on top is 12.5 cm long, about 2.8 cm wide, and 2.8 cm deep. AM193.87:10774, UA85.193:3471, AM193.94:884, AM193.87:9262; Lind avocational collection, AM14:118.

insets of fish or sea otter teeth, surface carvings, and indentations to hold paint and ornaments (fig. 7.16–7.18). They are enormous, heavy labrets. Accentuated by unique decorations, each would have been a dramatic addition to a person's face. A person wearing such a labret would have been easily recognized as distinct.

Based on both historic and archaeological information, people's labrets shared information on their wearer's gender, age, passage through life events, and social position. We also believe they signaled a person's family, that different families wore different styles of labrets (Steffian and Saltonstall 2001; Steffian this chapter). Most of the wooden labrets from Karluk One fall into one of seven distinct shape classes (fig. 7.19–7.25), with each shape occurring in at least three different size classes. These seem to be labrets designed for wear by a group of people with members of different ages. The fact that Alutiiq people lived in large houses with members of their extended families, that broad distinctions separated families of different means, and that positions of leadership passed through families, all suggest that there may have been family-based clans within Alutiiq society (Jordan 1994:149). Variations in the size, shape, and decoration of labrets seem to mirror Alutiiq principles of social organization, suggesting that they helped people to understand and navigate interactions with others.

Figure 7.17. *Qukaciq*—labret. Detail of a large cleat-shaped labret with a nipple-like projection that held fur or baleen. AM193.87:9262.

Figure 7.18. *Qukaciq*—labret. Side view of a large, wooden, cleat-shaped labret with a teeth-like or pyramid-shaped decoration on the top. AM193.87:10774.

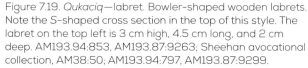

Figure 7.19. *Qukaciq*—labret. Bowler-shaped wooden labrets. Note the S-shaped cross section in the top of this style. The labret on the top left is 3 cm high, 4.5 cm long, and 2 cm deep. AM193.94:853, AM193.87:9263; Sheehan avocational collection, AM38:50; AM193.94:797, AM193.87:9299.

Figure 7.20. *Qukaciq*—labret. Top-hat-shaped labrets of wood. The labret on the top right is 3 cm high, 6 cm long, and 1.5 cm deep. AM193.94:849, UA85.193:6459, UA84.193:1155.

Figure 7.22. *Qukaciq*—labret. Pagoda-shaped labrets of wood and bark. The labret on the bottom is 2.5 cm high, 8.5 cm long, and 1.7 cm deep. AM193.94:790, AM193.94:893, AM193.M:577.

Figure 7.21. *Qukaciq*—labret. Ovoid and teardrop-shaped labrets of wood with a ridge down the center. The labret on the bottom is 3.2 cm high, 4.85 cm long, and 2.65 cm deep. UA84.193:898, AM193.94:821; Sheehan avocational collection, AM38:296.

Figure 7.23. *Qukaciq*—labret. Pulley-shaped labrets of wood. The bottom labret has an inset tooth and a hole. The labret on the right features an indentation, perhaps to hold paint or a small ornament. The labret on the bottom is 1.7 cm high, 7.25 cm long, and 3.7 cm wide. AM193.95:1217, AM193.M:575, UA85.193:4042.

Figure 7.25. *Qukaciq*—labret. Detail of a top-hat-shaped labret carved with two holes for attaching ornaments. Historically, Alutiiq people often hung strings of beads from their labrets. UA85.193:2475.

Figure 7.24. *Qukaciq*—labret. Antler labrets with holes and grooves for suspending strings of ornaments. UA85.193:4188, AM193.87:9284, UA85.193:2475.

Warfare

Evidence of a ranked social system dependent on the accumulation and redistribution of wealth also comes from artifacts related to war. The ties that linked people created divisions as well. Competition between families, communities, regions, and even different cultural groups was a part of the Alutiiq world (Davydov 1977:188). While many social interactions were positive—people from neighboring communities visited, traded, assisted each other, married, and shared in celebrations—people also clashed. Kodiak Islanders reportedly battled communities in the Aleutian Islands, the Kenai Peninsula, and Prince William Sound, and among their own communities (Black 1977:86, 2004b:140–142; Davydov 1977:159; Gideon 1989:13–14; Wrangell 1980:54). Some of these hostilities were ancient and enduring. For example, the Dena'ina of Cook Inlet are reported to have been "hereditary enemies" of the Kodiak Alutiiq (Osgood 1937:109), and conflict between Kodiak and Aleutian Island communities was frequent. Artifacts from Karluk One suggest that villagers participated in warfare, and historic sources indicate that communities of

southwestern Kodiak battled most commonly with people from the Aleutian Islands. In contrast, those on Afognak and Shuyak Islands at the northern entrance to the region fought most often with the Dena'ina Indians in Cook Inlet and the Prince William Sound Alutiiq (Black 2004b:141–142).

Descriptions of warfare are common in historic accounts from Kodiak. This reflects the conflict surrounding the conquest of the island. The strange European ships and people who arrived in island waters alarmed Alutiiq people, who defended their families, homes, stores, and harvesting areas as they would from any outsiders (Holmberg 1985:57). Similarly, Russian traders feared the size and strength of the Native population and its weaponry. They sought to subdue Alutiiq people and harvest Native labor to achieve their economic goals. Violent interaction was common and often recorded (Black 2004b; Davydov 1977:188–191; Lisianski 1814:179–180; Shelikhov 1981:39–40). As a result, there are detailed accounts of Alutiiq tactics and tools (Black 2004b).

Similar to punishment for a crime, warfare was often designed to revenge a wrong. Stealing and mockery were among the common reasons for an attack (Black 1977:84; Merck 1980:109). According to Blotov,

Figures 7.26a,b. *Alingnaillkutaq*—shield. Shield, front and back, with wooden braces lashed to the shield with spruce root. AM193.87:9361.

"Among themselves, one village may attack another, if they learn that a song of ridicule has been composed about them, or that so-and-so has been said not to be a warrior, or to be a poor hunter, but most of all if someone has been called a woman. The injured person declares the situation to his kinsmen, persuades them to aid him in vengeance, and finally they choose the time for a surprise attack." (Black 1977:86)

Warfare was typically a summer activity, the best time for traveling distances.

Alutiiq warriors were athletic, renowned fighters (Black 2004:142; Sauer 1802:176). They prepared for battle in the community house the evening before a raid. Here, the leader of the war party, a man of proven battle skills, provided drinking water, food, and gifts. Parkas, sea mammal skins, pieces of amber, dentalium shells, and beads were passed out in order of social standing

Figures 7.27a,b.
Alingnaillkutaq—shield.
Shield fragment front
and back. This piece features
a carved handle on the back. The
handle is part of the same piece of wood
used. The handle is 19 cm long, 6 cm wide, and
5 cm high. The entire shield is 66 cm long and 2 cm deep. Drilled holes
on the back of the piece indicate the former position of a shield brace,
a horizontal bar used to strengthen the shield and unite its pieces. The
front of this shield fragment features a carved zigzag design following the
object's upper and lower edges. Sheehan avocational collection, AM38:25.

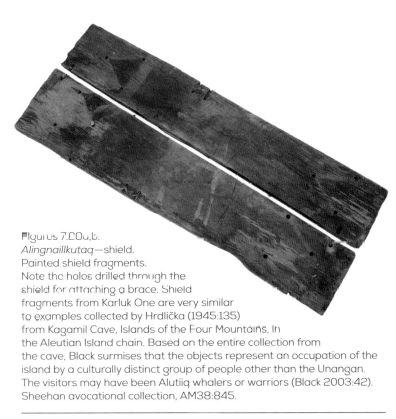

Figures 7.28a,b.
Alingnaillkutaq—shield.
Painted shield fragments.
Note the holes drilled through the
shield for attaching a brace. Shield
fragments from Karluk One are very similar
to examples collected by Hrdlička (1945:135)
from Kagamil Cave, Islands of the Four Mountains, in
the Aleutian Island chain. Based on the entire collection from
the cave, Black surmises that the objects represent an occupation of the
island by a culturally distinct group of people other than the Unangan.
The visitors may have been Alutiiq whalers or warriors (Black 2003:42).
Sheehan avocational collection, AM38:845.

following songs about heroic, ancestral acts of war. Men departed the following morning quickly and quietly, with only short farewells (Gideon 1989:42–43).

Raids were secretive, designed to surprise enemies and catch them unprepared or to lure unsuspecting victims into a trap (Black 2004:148; Sauer 1802:198). Many attacks occurred at night while people slept (Gideon 1989:44). Warriors were said to wait patiently for up to several days, watching their adversaries for the right moment to attack. Communities wary of an attack might post a sentry to watch for invaders. Often the first step in a raid was to dispatch the sentry (Black 2004:148).

There were also open battles. Historic accounts describe large groups of men advancing with a wooden shield wall, objects "of sufficient strength and thickness to withstand a musket ball, and large enough to shelter twenty or thirty men" (Sauer 1802:198). These portable walls were not only large but heavy. Accounts indicate they were made of three layers of cedar boards tied together with kelp and sinew (Black 2004:144; Coxe 1780:111).

Although shield wall parts have not been identified in the Karluk Collection, pieces of individual shields are present. These are made of heavy planks of wood, lashed together to form a roughly square shape (fig. 7.26a,b). Horizontal braces attached to the back of the shield united the pieces and were secured with spruce root or baleen lashing through pairs of holes drilled through the body of the shield. Some shield fragments feature carved wooden handles (fig. 7.27a,b), while others lack a handle and may have been carried by skin or fiber loops tied to the shield. Many of the Karluk shield fragments are decorated with carved designs or painting (fig. 7.28). Paint is most common on the outward facing surface of shields but also occurs on the inner surface.

Shirts of wooden armor were another form of protection. Made from narrow slats of wood or whalebone tied together with sinew, these garments functioned like a protective vest. They covered the torso, leaving the arms and legs free to move. Shoulder straps secured the front and the back panels together, and a tie on one side of the waist helped to fasten the garment to its wearer. These vests could be rolled up for storage and were flexible enough to be worn in boats, protecting warriors on the water (Sauer 1802:198–199). Over the front of the vest, warriors sometimes attached a breastplate, an extra layer of protection made by tightly lashing narrow rods of wood together (Black 1977:101). A collar of tightly woven sinew provided protection for the neck, and warriors wore hats of wood or thick animal skin (Black 2004:Figure 2; Gideon 1989:42).

The parts of wooden armor vests in the Karluk One collection are sturdy rectangles of wood with holes drilled at both ends for tying together (fig. 7.29). One example features the remains of a baleen tie. The collection includes both short slats and long slats, pieces most likely from different vest areas. The slats were tied together vertically, and appear in fig. 7.29 as they might have been assembled. Although there are very few examples of Alutiiq armor in ethnographic collections, a complete vest from Prince William Sound features short slats covering the chest and longer pieces below (Korsun 2012:350–351). Both types of Karluk armor slats are also similar in size and design to late prehistoric examples found at Palutat cave in Prince William Sound. Here, however, craftsmen used thin strips of leather to tie slats together (de Laguna 1956:228, 230).

Figure 7.29. *Qatgat*—armor. These armor slats are arranged in positions similar to their likely place in a complete vest. Slat armor pieces in the collection fall into two general shapes—short rectangular pieces (*top row*) and long bars with one slanted end (*bottom row*). The tapering ends of the long slats may be for a longer area on the front of the vest designed to cover the groin (cf. Korsun 2012:350). The extra holes drilled in the long slat (*third from the right*) may be for securing a cord to tie the vest closed. The short slats range from 9 to 14 cm long and 2 to 3.5 cm wide. The long slats range from 25 to 58 cm long and 2 to 4 cm wide. AM193.94:673; Panamaroff avocational collection, AM15:418; AM193.94:315, AM193.87:9511, AM193.87:9533, AM193.87:10242; Sheehan avocational collection, AM38:205; AM193.87:10595, AM193.94:4274; Panamaroff avocational collection, AM15:205; AM193.87:8246, AM193.95:510.

Warriors carried clubs, hatchets, spears, bows, and quivers filled with arrows (Black 2004:144–146, 148; Coxe 1780:110–111; Lisianski 1814:206; Shelikhov 1981:39–40). Shooting arrows at enemies was often the first stage of an attack, followed by the use of clubs, stone hatchets, and spears for close contact fighting. Other accounts suggest that warriors used ladders, bundles of grass, and pieces of birch bark to set fire to enemy property like houses and boats (Black 2004:146–148; Coxe 1780:111). Karluk One produced examples of a very distinctive style of club that appears to be a warrior's implement. Made from dense wood, these heavy implements are much bigger than the clubs used to stun fish and small game and appear more likely for use in battle. They feature a curved inner edge possibly effective for braining a person (fig. 7.30). Similarly, some of the site's spear, arrow, and adze parts, used for daily tasks, could have been employed as weaponry.

In open battle, men might advance as a group behind a shield wall, while archers moved singly along their sides. Boys sometimes accompanied the archers, carrying extra arrows (Black 2004:145–146). Raiding parties are reported to have surrounded those they were attacking, firing volleys of arrows from all sides (Shelikhov 1981:40).

Gathering loot was a central goal of raiding (Shelikhov 1981:39). War leaders distributed plunder to the members of their raiding parties, and clothing and food were especially prized. Raiding parties often traveled in *angyat* to carry not only participants but any hostages and plunder they might gain (Black 1977:86; Lisianski 1814:211). Warriors who captured prisoners were especially revered (Black 1977:92). Women, children, and teens were routinely taken hostage and men and the elderly killed (Black 1977:86; Merck 1980:97). Hostages were treated well and were often traded back to their communities in prisoner exchanges (Gideon 1989:44). Others served as laborers in their captors' homes (Black 2004:142; Davydov 1977:159; Sauer 1802:175). Whatever the fate of community members, it was customary to leave several people alive to tell the story of the raid (Black 2004:149).

While slavery was a widespread practice in the Gulf of Alaska (Townsend 1983), finding archaeological evidence of it is difficult. Slaves were not segregated but lived with their captors' families and worked alongside family members (Holmberg 1985:58). Thus, the activities of slaves mirrored those of other community members and are unlikely to have left distinct archaeological evidence. However, a small number of unique labrets could reflect their presence in Karluk (fig. 7.31). These labrets are like no other labrets in the collection. They are made of materials not available in the Kodiak region, and some are very similar to labrets found in the Aleutian Islands. While

Figure 7.30. *Piqrutaq* club. Carved from dense wood, this club is 54 cm long, about 6 cm wide, and 3.5 cm deep. The handle features a hole, perhaps for tying the implement to the warrior's boat or clothing. 193.94.306.

these labrets could have been obtained in trade or travel, left in Karluk by visitors, or made and worn as symbols of wealth, they might represent the labrets of people from distant communities captured in warfare (Jordan 1994:167).

Communities that suspected an attack would retreat to inaccessible camps on cliffs, small islets, or even the mountains, places where they had stockpiled water and food (Davydov 1977:173; Lisianski 1814:177, 180; Shelikhov 1981:39; Taylor 1965:20). Some of these places were fortress sites that could be defended with arrows or by dropping carefully positioned logs or rocks on attackers (Black 2004:148). An account from Kaguyak village describes how villagers piled greased boulders behind a wooden barrier on a hillside leading to their fortress. These boulders were then released as enemy warriors climbed the hill (Taylor 1965:20). Others places served as hiding spots for people to wait out a siege (Black 1977:86; Gideon 1989:44). Sentries, signal fires, and runners helped to warn communities of an impending attack or call for assistance from neighbors (Black 2004:146). Elders recall that despite competition between communities, when outsiders threatened a village, people from other communities united in its defense (Mulcahy 2003:81). At Karluk One, a mass grave holding the remains of four men and a male child, one man with an arrow in his pelvis, may represent the unfortunate victims of a raid (see Chapter 6).

Gaming

In contrast with the hostilities of warfare, friendly competitions took place through gaming. Traditional Alutiiq games ranged from outdoor community events like arrow-shooting contests to running, boating, wrestling, or swimming

Figure 7.31. *Qerllum mallarsuutii*—labret. Each one of these labrets is unlike any other found in the Karluk One collection, and all are made of materials not available in the Kodiak region. These labrets may have been worn by visitors to Karluk, people who married into the community, or captives taken from distant communities in warfare. UA84.193:1561, AM193.87:10630, AM193.87:9350.

competitions (Birket-Smith 1953:103–106; Golder 1903b:99; Reed 1962a). There were also a variety of indoor games typically played by men (Birket-Smith 1953:107–108; Davydov 1977:182–183; Lisianski 1814:210–211). Many of these games are still enjoyed in Alutiiq communities. Katya Chichenoff of Karluk remembered, "There was gambling, they'd come from different places on boats from Lazy B. They'd be anchored there and come on kayaks. And then the bay would be full" (Reed 1962a). According to Elders, such gatherings were raucous events that featured singing and gambling that might last all night. Evidence of gaming in the Karluk One collection appears in more than two thousand artifacts—objects likely used indoors, by men, for recreation, displays of skill, and gambling (Mishler 1997:191).

In addition to providing entertainment, gaming moved goods between the members of communities (Knecht 1995:575). Men bet everything from quantities of food and clothing to boats and houses on the outcome of matches (Davydov 1977:159; Knecht 1995:575; Lisianski 1814:210), wining and losing items to family members, friends, and neighbors. Those who were lucky at gambling were known to give away their personal possessions when they accumulated new items (Davydov 1977:182).

Like other activities in Alutiiq villages, there was a seasonal rhythm to gaming. Games were associated with the dark, stormy days of winter that kept people at home and more often inside. When they were not repairing tools, instructing youth, or preparing for festivals, men frequently competed and gambled. There were rules around gaming. In the distant past, some games were played in the community house, out of sight of women and children. In recent times, spiritually powerful games took place in an old sod house or someone's home (Mishler 1997:191). Sometimes, men waiting for the weather to change so they could travel would pass the time playing games (Davydov 1977:116). However, games were not played the evening before a hunt for fear of bad luck (Davydov 1977:183). Games

were also one of the activities enjoyed at winter festivals, gatherings that brought the members of neighboring communities together to socialize and celebrate the successes of the previous year (Holmberg 1985:46, 60).

Most of the Karluk artifacts associated with gaming are made from abundant, locally available materials—wood, bark, stone, and clay. Like other objects in the collection, they are carefully manufactured, carved to shape, and sanded to a fine finish. Nonetheless, many of the gaming pieces in the collection were discarded whole, suggesting that they were common, easily replaced objects (Knecht 1995:576). The large number of gaming pieces found on the floors of Karluk One houses supports this idea. Gaming pieces make up nearly 8 percent of the entire Karluk One collection, suggesting that gaming was not restricted to special events or private gatherings but a social and recreational activity very common in the daily life of families.

Gaming pieces in the Karluk One assemblage fall into five general groups—disks, darts, balls, dice, and possibly incised pebbles. Most of these pieces were probably parts of throwing games, where an item was tossed at a target or thrown to land in a specific position. As such, these subsistence-focused games required excellent hand-eye coordination and incorporated skills important to hunting (Mishler 1997:190).

Common to all of these games were tally sticks (fig. 7.32). Players kept score with small, cylindrical, wooden counters. More than six hundred tally sticks were recovered from Karluk One. Most are about 6 to 7 cm long, with a smooth finish and flat, carefully finished ends. Sticks were often piled beside players or in the middle of a gaming area where players could collect them (Lisianski 1814:211).

Figure 7.32. *Cit'suutet*—tally stick. Tally sticks from Karluk One fall into two general size classes. Most range from 6 to 7 cm long and 0.35 to 1 cm wide. However, there are a few very short tally sticks. These sticks are just 2 to 2.5 cm long and 0.5 to 0.7 cm wide. A few tally stick have been notched one or more times. One has a spiral cut around its length.

One game recorded by Russian traders and remembered by Alutiiq Elders is *Kakangaq* (Davydov 1977:136; Lisianski 1814:210; Merck 1980:109; Steffian and Counceller 2010:39–40). In this game, players throw wooden or bone disks at a target laid on a sealskin. According to one account, targets were typically round, made from bone, and the size of a coat button (Merck 1980:109). This account nicely matches the characteristics of a set of *kakangaq* disks collected on Woody Island in 1883 (Crowell and Lührmann 2001:38). Typically, two people compete, but teams of two can also play *kakangaq*. Each player gets five disks and takes turns tossing his disks at the target. The goal is to earn points by landing on or near the target and to dislodge the opponent's disks from scoring position. The first player to score twelve points wins (Steffian and Counceller 2010:39).

Kakangaq targets and disks were common finds at Karluk One. Targets from the site are generally small and carved of wood or bark (fig. 7.33). The disks are also made from wood and bark, although there are a few carved from whalebone. The disks vary widely in shape and size. Some are as large as a plate, others are tiny, perhaps even toys. A review of the collection shows there are four distinct size classes based on maximum width: large (>13 cm), medium (>7 and <13 cm), small (>4.5 and <7 cm), and miniature (<4.5 cm). Medium and small examples are the most common, accounting for 177 of the disks, or 72 percent. Most of the disks are trapezoidal, roughly square and gently domed in the center, but some are rectangular, round, or even oval (fig. 7.33). A small number of disks also have unique features. A few have pebbles set into their bases, to provide weight for throwing and knocking an opponent's disks off the target (fig. 7.34). Others

Figure 7.33. *Kakangaqutaq—kakangaq* disk, *kakangam napataa—kakangaq* target. The large wood target on top is 19 cm long, 16 cm wide, and 4 cm deep. The smallest wooden disk, which is painted black on the sides, is about 4 cm in diameter. The disk on the far right is bark. AM193.94:3594, AM193.87:10487, AM193.87:11377, AM193.87:11170, AM193.94:2878, AM193.87:10487.

Figure 7.34. *Kakangaqutaq—kakangaq* disk. On the left is half of a wooden disk designed to hold a stone weight. The two halves were pegged together. On the bottom is a *kakangaq* disk showing a slate pebble inserted into a carved-out section of a disk. UA85.193:2692, AM193.87:10916.

are decorated with carvings—geometric designs or a face. These decorations may have helped players to distinguish their pieces from those used by others or provided luck in the game. In short, the great variety of disks suggests that players

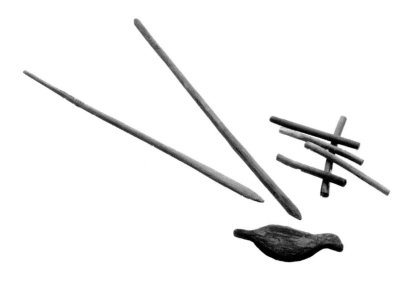

Figure 7.35. *Ruuwaq—augca'aq* dart. *Augca'aq* darts, bird target, and tally sticks. Today, artists typically carve targets in the shape of a porpoise or whale. *Whale darts* is another common name for this game. AM193.87:11304, UA85.193:2793, UA85.193:3352, UA85.193:4772g, UA85.193:3199c and e, UA85.193:4790a.

designed their own sets, individually tailoring the style of their *kakangaq* disks.

Like *kakangaq*, *augca'aq* is a throwing game still played in Kodiak Alutiiq communities. In this game, men toss darts at a whale or porpoise model suspended from a string about a couple centimeters off the floor. Each target is divided into areas with unique point values. Players kneel, as if in a kayak, and toss their darts at the hanging target, aiming for high scoring areas. Each player gets two darts and his own target. Players may work in teams of two or play singly. The first player to score twelve points wins the match, and the first player to win two matches wins the game. Players take their points from a pile of tally sticks in the middle of the playing area. When this pile is depleted, they take points earned from the tally sticks held by opponents (Steffian and Counceller 2010:38). Today, this game is typically played during the month of Lent, a period of quiet, modest living when the Russian Orthodox

faithful refrain from outdoor activities, including hunting (Mishler 1997).

Augca'aq darts in the Karluk collection are made of wood and have long narrow shafts with a flat, oval, pointed end (fig. 7.35). The Karluk darts are similar in shape to those made by modern craftsmen, though longer. The proximal ends of these darts, the part held in the throwers hand, typically taper to a narrow, squared-off end. Similarly, the ancient darts lack a sharp tip. Modern examples feature a pin set in the end (Crowell et al. 2001:12). One example from Karluk One has a copper tip, and another features a notch where a tip could be inserted, but most are self-pointed. It appears that the Karluk darts were designed to hit a target but not stick to it. The darts are largely undecorated, although one has remnants of paint on its surface.

There are just two possible *augca'aq* targets in the collection; both are lightweight, palm-size objects made of cottonwood bark. One is a bird-shaped piece, the other a badly worn carving with a hole for suspension.

Another known Alutiiq game represented in the Karluk One assemblage is *mangaq*, a dice game (Davydov 1977:183; Lisianski 1814:211). Today, people play this game with a small, five-sided piece of wood or bone. Each face of the die is a different size and carries a specific point value (Steffian and Counceller 2012:46). Players sit in a circle and toss the die. Each tries to make the die land on the smallest face to earn the most points. In the past, players used small figures carved of bone as die. One Russian observer noted that the die "is thrown up into the air, and if it falls on its bottom, two are counted; if on its back, three; and if on its belly, one only. This game consists in gaining twenty, which are also marked with short sticks" (Lisianski 1814:211).

Examples of die from Karluk are made of wood, bone, or ivory. This is one of the few artifact types where walrus ivory—a rare material in the collection—appears. Obtained from the western Alaska Peninsula, ivory was a valuable trade good. The use of this valuable material in making dice suggest that these artifacts were not discarded at the end of a game, but kept and reused. Most are roughly bullet shaped, narrower on one end than the other, with a flat bottom. This shape closely resembles a historic die drawing (Lisianski 1814:204). The Karluk specimens are interesting, however, as most appear to be representations of bears. One die is a sturdy, four-legged animal that may be a standing bear (fig. 7.36, top). Another is a detailed carving of a bear's head (fig. 7.37a,b). The shapes of other dice appear to be abstract representations of a bear's head.

Two other types of artifacts also appear to be game pieces. The first are small balls made of stone, clay, and even bark (fig. 7.38). There are 743 of these objects in the collection that range from about 2.5 to 5 cm in diameter. The great majority are naturally formed pebbles—water-worn and rounded spheres of granite, greywacke, and other stones, probably collected from the beaches of Karluk. However, spheres of andesite and basalt, materials not commonly available in the Kodiak region, were likely collected on the Alaska Peninsula or from deposits transported by mainland glaciers to the south end of Kodiak Island. Stone balls weigh from 3.7 to 292.7 grams (gm) with a median weight of 36 gm.

The twenty-two clay balls in the collection are molded from a dried but unfired, light grey glacial clay commonly found in the Karluk area (fig. 7.38, upper left). The clay is not tempered and has not been hardened by baking. They vary in size and weigh between 6.0 and 174.4 gm, with a median

Figure 7.36. *Maqat*—dice. Many dice recovered from the site are carved in the shape of a bear. All of the pieces shown, except for the ivory piece toward the upper left, likely represent a bear or bear's head. The wood die on top is 8 cm long, 4 cm wide, and 3.5 cm high. The walrus tooth die on the lower left is just 2.7 cm long, 1.3 cm wide, and 1 cm high. Panamaroff avocational collection, AM15:425; AM193.87:10824, UA85.193:3163, UA85.193:3413, AM193.87:9483, AM193.94:15, AM193.94:1563.

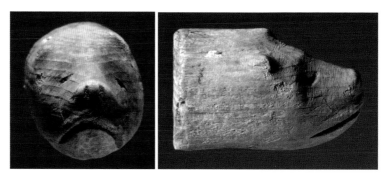

Figures 7.37a,b. *Maqat*—dice. Wooden die carved in the shape of a bear's head. This die is 3.35 cm long and about 2 cm in diameter. AM193.94:15.

Figure 7.38. *Mayaciingcuk*—gaming ball. Clay, wood, granite, and other stone gaming balls. These small, round spheres of stone may have been used in a tossing game. As reported by Chugach Alutiiq people, some may have been used in juggling (de Laguna 1956:223). The larger clay balls on the upper left are about 4 cm in diameter. UA85.193:2956, UA84.193:1069, UA84.193:1644a, UA84.193:2443, AM193.87:9704, UA85.193:4582, UA85.193:4270.

weight of 26.4 gm. Though lighter, ranging from just 7 to 23 gm, three wooden spheres are also similar in size to stone balls in the collection (fig. 7.38, lower left).

While it is possible that some of these stone balls were used in preparing food—heated in a fire and dropped in baskets to cook their contents, this appears unlikely. Rocks placed in a fire change color, develop a charred surface, and may crack. Only a few of the stone balls show evidence of heating. Moreover, these stones occur widely in houses, and in three cases, sets of stones were found together. These observations hint that the stones served a purpose other than cooking. A modern Alutiiq game provides a possible example of their use.

Today, Alutiiq children play a game called *yaamaq* (rock). Participants place two stakes in the ground, one at either end of the playing area. This game is typically played on the beach. Here, players select small, smooth rocks and line up behind one stake to toss a rock at the other. The goal is to hit the stake, but a point can be scored for being the closest rock to the stake (Steffian and Counceller 2012:128). This popular outdoor activity is both a common modern pastime and a game reported by Alutiiq Elders (Knecht 1995:577). The balls from Karluk One may have been collected for use in a similar tossing game. Based on their size and shape, lack of heating, common occurrence in houses, and discovery in groups, gaming seems a likely function for these objects.

This idea is also supported by variation in the spheres. Like the modifications seen in *kakangaq* disks (e.g., differences in size and shape, weighting, decoration), gaming balls range in size, weight, material, and color. One was smeared with red ochre. Another was polished. We know from Elders' accounts that gaming was very competitive and involved serious betting. It appears that people may have selected and crafted gaming balls in a variety of sizes and weights to enhance their success in competitions.

One final category of objects may also represent gaming pieces. These are incised pebbles, small piece of slate or greywacke with drawings of people scratched into their surfaces. Carved on both water-worn beach pebbles and tabular pieces of slate, these remarkable artifacts preserve drawings from the past (see fig. 7.3, 7.4 above). Some have geometric designs, while others depict faces, clothing, jewelry, and occasionally ceremonial gear (Clark 1974; Donta 1992, 1993, essay Chapter 7). Archaeologists note that incised pebbles occur at a very specific point in time. They are most common in deposits dating around 500 years old, appearing and disappearing in the archaeological record between about 650 and 400 years ago (Clark 1964, 1974; Donta 1993). While researchers remain uncertain about their function, Knecht suggests that they were gaming pieces—objects tossed at a target (1995:592–593). He notes that incised pebbles are common in the lower levels of Karluk One, a part of the site that contains many tally sticks but almost no *kakangaq* disks. Over time, incised pebbles disappear from Karluk houses, and *kakangaq* disk become common. *Kakangaq* disks or the *kakangaq* games may have replaced an older game that used incised pebbles instead of disks. Others believe that these small stones were part of spiritual life, depicting ancestors or even Alutiiq spirits (Donta 1993:263) or acting as amulets (Clark 1964:123). It is possible that they had multiple functions (fig. 7.39, 7.40).

Beliefs

The profound cultural changes that accompanied the conquest of Kodiak drove Alutiiq people to hide their beliefs and conceal ritual practices. The death of roughly 75 percent of the Kodiak Alutiiq population during the first fifty years of colonization (Clark 1974:7), enslavement, bigotry, and the introduction of new religious traditions suppressed older traditions. Accounts from the first decades of colonialism provide sparse information on Alutiiq beliefs and note that practices like shamanism, abhorred by Europeans, faded rapidly (Gideon 1989:60). Yet a close look at objects, legends, and cultural observations collected over the past two hundred years indicates that Alutiiq people continued to practice aspects of their ancestral religion and to share their worldview across generations (Crowell 1992:30; Drabek 2012; Pinart 1872). The principles of living in the Alutiiq world have been passed down through families—shared through stories and legends, demonstrated

Figure 7.39. *Yaamaruaq*—incised pebble. This incised slate pebble is 7 cm high and about 2.5 cm wide. The reverse side is rough and jagged, while the etched side has been polished. UA87.193:7108.

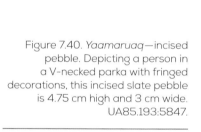

Figure 7.40. *Yaamaruaq*—incised pebble. Depicting a person in a V-necked parka with fringed decorations, this incised slate pebble is 4.75 cm high and 3 cm wide. UA85.193:5847.

in daily living, and embedded in technologies and artistic traditions.

A recent analysis of Alutiiq stories illustrates a set of commonly held, interrelated values. These include ties to home, stewardship of resources, sharing, listening, humor, and many more. All of these values are built on a foundation of respect for self, others, and the environment (Drabek 2012:144). Every object in the Karluk One collection broadly reflects this belief system. People raised with the community's values and who participated in its ritual life made each piece. While not every object reveals beliefs, the assemblage as a whole illustrates an enduring Alutiiq worldview. There is an Alutiiq ethos that pervades

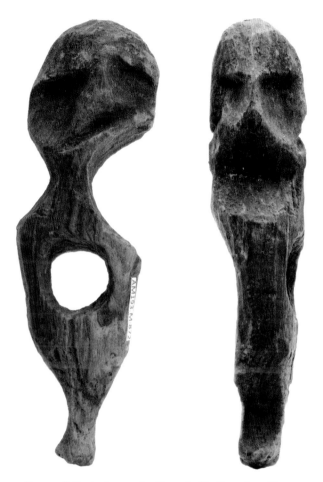

Figures 7.41a,b. *Agaa*—tool handle. Tool handle with crooked face on three sides and a hole through the center. The representation of three faces may represent the appearance of the tool's *sua*. AM193.M:872.

the collection and a number of items provide a glimpse of the ritual traditions that ordered life in Karluk.

The Alutiiq universe is not like the Western universe, where people control nature. In the Alutiiq world, people are part of a fluid living system where animals give themselves to people and everything is alive. People are never alone, as every plant, animal, and object is conscious, aware of its surroundings and the actions of others. Even the wind and the mountains have a human-like awareness (Birket-Smith 1953:120; Desson 1995:38). This consciousness is described as an

object's person, an internal being known in the Alutiiq language as a *suk* or *sua* (plural *sui*), or literally "its person." *Sui* monitor people's actions and must be pleased with their behavior to provide future prosperity. *Sui* who approve of human action will release the souls of plants and animals, so they may be reborn and reharvested (Crowell and Leer 2001:194). It is essential that people conform to universal values like thrift, cleanliness, and generosity to please the ever-present *sui* (Drabek 2012:125).

So important was appropriate behavior that a person's actions in life determined their place after death. Kodiak Alutiiq people traditionally believed that every person was reincarnated five times. Following a fifth and final death, the souls of good people went to the sky world and found prosperity. Those who had failed to behave respectfully in life became evil spirits in death. Some of these souls became part of the aurora borealis, while others rose from the grave in a ball of flames and flew west to the end of the universe. These souls suffered poverty and hunger after death (Black 1977:86; Desson 1995:49).

Representations of *sui* appear throughout the Karluk One collection. A variety of objects feature a small carving of a human-like face—the object's *sua* revealing itself (fig. 7.41a,b). Importantly, these faces appear on common household items, from tool handles to gaming pieces, ulu handles, a clasp, and a clam knife. The placement of these carvings underscores the spiritual awareness of their users and the interconnectedness of all things. Spiritual representations are not only associated with ritual items.

More broadly, the treatment of objects in the collection suggests an underlying respect for the *sua* of plants and animals. The majority of artifacts are carefully made and finished, including common, frequently discarded items such as tally sticks. Similarly, evidence of recycling occurs throughout the collection. Broken objects were fixed or reworked into new useful pieces, demonstrating care in the use of natural resources.

When interacting with the world, *sui* can take human shape. Transformation is a common theme in Alutiiq legends. There is a duality in Alutiiq cosmology, a blending of the tangible and spiritual worlds, a recognized reality that objects and animals are also human-like (Desson 1995:45; Knecht 1995:622). This duality also appears in the Alutiiq language that pervasively distinguishes between the real and nonreal (Drabek 2012:124). Alutiiq legends tell of people encountering animal *sua*. Sometimes, the *sua* is separate from the animal. In other stories, an animal has shed its skin to reveal its inner person or *sua*. It is not always possible to discern a *sua* in human form, but sometimes these beings shine or retain some of their animal characteristics (Desson 1995:40–41). Conversely, people themselves can transform into animals by putting on an animal skin (Crowell and Leer 2001:192). These tales remind people that the spiritual world is not distant, but pervasive. They also blur the distinctions between people and animals, illustrating that both are part of a broad, integrated cycle of life. The Karluk story of *How the Animals Came to Be Created* (Wallace, Chapter 5, originally collected by Alphonse Pinart) tells how a woman gave birth to all of the animals and in turn must eat animals to survive. This legend highlights the cyclical and intertwining relationship of all beings.

The spool shown on the cover of this book, and in fig. 6.89, illustrates the transformation process. It depicts a bird and a man, attached to each other, standing back-to-back, one and the same. The figures are the same size, and by turning the spool, one becomes the other. The bird sheds its skin to reveal its naked human form beneath, or perhaps the naked man dons a bird skin to become a bird. Similarly, a hand-size carving of cottonwood bark shows an array of human and bird faces (fig. 7.42a,b,c). Like the spool, it suggests duality and fluidity—the ability of one thing to be two and to move with ease between worlds or states of reality. The use of bird images on both carvings is not accidental. Birds are revered in the Alutiiq world for their ability to fly, swim, and shape-shift as they walk on land. They can traverse all layers of the universe (Korsun 2012:161). As such, birds were thought to deliver messages from spirits (Drabek 2012:11), "helping spirits" often appeared as birds (Crowell and Leer 2001:195), and people used birdcalls or whistles to converse with spirits (Demidoff 1962).

Within this vibrant, sentient world, there are many supernatural beings that both aid and obstruct people's activities. The Alutiiq universe is divided into layers, with five sky worlds and five worlds below Earth (Birket Smith 1953:10–121; Desson 1995:55). Each layer of these worlds is home to a set of powerful spirits. *Llam Sua*, the universe's person, lives in the fifth and most pure layer of the world. Recognized throughout the Alutiiq world (Crowell and Leer 2001:192), *Llam Sua* can be described as the *sua* of everything. He is invisible, all knowing/seeing (omniscient), immortal, and benevolent, the supreme spirit who assists human needs and is the weather god (Black 1977:86, 1981:1; Desson 1995:46; Drabek 2012:125). Elders today equated *Llam Sua* with the Christian God (Crowell and Leer 2001:192), although he is one of a series of Alutiiq deities. There is no known complete record of the Alutiiq pantheon, but historic accounts identify some of

Figures 7.42a,b,c. Bark carving showing bird and human faces. This transformative figure, like other maskettes in the collection, fits in the palm of the hand, at 13 cm high, 7 cm wide, and 2.5 cm deep. AM193.87:9352.

the other gods. *Kas'arpak*, the chief wise one and creator spirit, lived in the third sky world. This deity was the ancestor of all wise ones or *kas'at*, the revered spiritual leaders, storytellers, and religious teachers in Alutiiq society. After death, all *kas'at* joined *Kas'arpak* in the third layer of the universe (Desson 1995:138). In the first sky world lived the spirits of astrological bodies—the sun (*macaq*), moon (*iraluq*), stars (*agayat*), and aurora borealis (*quiqyat*). The moon was a spirit who wore a different mask each night (Black 1981:6), and the stars were one-eyed spirits who lay on the tundra and gazed down at Earth through holes in the ground (Golder 1903a:28–31). The aurora borealis held the spirits of dead warriors, meteors were men flying in a sphere of light, and comets were the excrement of stars (Birket-Smith 1953:120; Black 1981:7). This world was also the place where the souls of dead shaman and people

who had behaved well in life retired after their final death (Desson 1995:56).

Less is known about the worlds below Earth, sometimes interpreted as sea worlds. However, a story collected in Karluk in 1872 seems to describe a trip to this place and suggests that one way to access it was by descending a waterfall at the edge of the sea. In the lower worlds, a pair of brothers encountered evil beings and mask spirits (Desson 1995:61–62):

They say that at the extremity of the sea there was a large waterfall. Two brothers having ventured far away on the sea with their baidarka, reached this waterfall, and were thrown down without however suffering any harm. There they found fish who spoke a human language. They traveled in this new region and reached a land totally unknown to them. There lived evil feminine entities. They took several of them [with them?]. Then they left this place and went out to sea. They reached another land and found a settlement. There the same evil feminine entities lived and at night they killed one of the brothers. The one who survived ran away but reached a settlement where all the inhabitants wear the masks that the Aleuts [here Koniags are meant] use in their dances. Frightened he ran away and soon reached another settlement where lived men [and women] looking like those who live on earth, and there he married. . . . This man stayed in the settlement. It is located in the west.[1]

A set of three wooden box panels from Karluk One, found together on a house floor near a hearth, appear to show the layers of the Alutiiq universe with *Llam Sua* at its center (fig. 7.43a,b). Two of the panels, from opposite ends of the box, are painted with red and sparkly silver pigments; both have a series of concentric circles around a stylized face. One face rests in the center of three circles, another in the center of four. The later face has rays descending from its eyes, penetrating the rings and suggesting the type of supernatural vision attributed to *Llam Sua* and other deities or beings that journeyed between worlds. Concentric circles depicting the layers of the universe are also present on other artifacts in the collection. One incised pebble shows a series of three rings around a central depression (fig. 7.44). A leather mask cover has a painted, white spiral that gives the impression of concentric circles. Similarly, bases of many spruce root baskets feature three or four concentric rings of false embroidery, decorative work added to the surface of the weaving. Decorative work on basket bodies

Figures 7.43a,b. *Yaasiigem cania*—box panel. Painted box panels depicting the Alutiiq universe and its supernatural beings. When first excavated, some of the pigment that now appears black on these box panels was a sparkly silver color. While treating the panels with polyethylene glycol, this pigment faded to black. The use of reflective pigment supports the interpretation of these paintings as images of deities in their sky worlds. Alutiiq supernatural beings were thought to be filled with glowing light (Crowell and Leer 2001:192; Demidoff 1962). AM193.95:858, AM193.95:859.

Figure 7.44. *Yaamaruaq*—incised pebble. Incised piece of slate showing a concentric circle design. UA85.193:3645.

and rims features encircling bands, as do wooden masks and rattles surrounded by hoops.[2]

Other supernatural beings populated the earth. *Imam Sua*, who lives at the bottom of the sea, is the spirit of sea animals. *Nunam Sua*, who wears a parka covered in animals, is the spirit of forest. Both supernatural beings aided hunters and had holes in their hands that allowed animals to pass between the tangible and spiritual worlds (Birket-Smith 1953:121–122). Evil spirits were also encountered on Earth and believed to be the souls of dead people who behaved poorly in life. These beings—*iyat*, "one that is hidden" in the Kodiak Alutiiq language—were dangerous, flesh eating creatures recognized by their long pointed heads (Crowell and Leer 2001:195). On occasion, they were known to work with shamans and could become spirits.

In addition, Alutiiq people knew of giants, sea and lake monsters, enormous carnivorous worms, bigfoots, and little people (Desson 1995:52–53; Steffian and Counceller 2012:18, 53). Giants were believed to live in the mountains of the Alaska Peninsula, where their fighting caused volcanic activity. Little people—*sungcuk*—were tiny individuals, perhaps souls waiting to be reborn (Desson 1995:53). They were often known to help those in trouble, and an encounter with such a person could bring exceptional luck (Lantis 1938:149). However, other *sungcuk* play tricks on people. Tales of bigfoots and little people continue within Alutiiq culture and were shared by Karluk residents during the study of Karluk One.

Some of these supernatural beings may be shown in maskettes, small, stylized carvings of human faces (fig. 7.45–7.50). These masks are too small to cover the face. Most are hand-size, and some are tiny. Moreover, only some of them have hollowed backs. Others, like the maskette show in fig. 7.45, have a flat back as if the mask had been mounted on something. The function of these small carvings is not known, and they may represent several functionally different objects (Donta 1993:288). Ethnographic collections contain small mask-like carvings on the back of drum handles (Liapunova 1994:198–199; Varjola 1990:392). When people lifted their drums to play, the carving was visible to the audience. While some of the maskettes could have functioned this way (Donta 1993:284; Jordan 1994:157), others may have been used as talismans—carvings of spirit helpers carried by harvesters and travelers. Another possibility is that some miniature masks supported story-telling and religious education, helping to reinforce knowledge of the Alutiiq cosmos (Knecht 1995:676), or that they were part of plank masks. A nineteenth-century Kodiak mask collection features a number of plank-style masks to which small, though not miniature, face masks are attached (Haakanson and Steffian 2009:151, 152, 154, 155). Or perhaps dolls wore some of the

Figures 7.45a,b. *Giinaruangcuk*—maskette. This large maskette, carved of cottonwood bark, is 15 cm high, 9 cm wide, and 5 cm deep. It shows a stylized, smiling face. It features 8 holes around its edge, likely for fastening a small hoop. This face features the deeply carved nose and brow distinctive to Alutiiq mask carvings. AM193.87:11319.

tiniest masks. Human figurines are also relatively common in the collection, with a total of fifty-
four carvings. Some of the smallest maskettes
could have been used to dress these carvings.

Whatever their function, these maskettes are
relatively common in the Karluk collection. There
are seventy-four examples, all of which show
faces. These are not portraits of people, however.
The styles and designs of the carvings broadly
replicate full-size ceremonial masks found in historic collections, and thought to represent specific Alutiiq beings (Crowell 1992; Desson 1995;
Haakanson and Steffian 2009; Korsun 2012;
Liapunova 1994). Some maskettes show stylized
faces (fig. 7.46), others are miniature plank-style
masks (fig. 7.47, 7.48). At least ten have pointed
heads, matching the description of evil spirits
(fig. 7.49). Others feature a circular mouth, a
motif for whistling. Whistling is the way spirits
speak and a practice people reserved for ritual
performances (Desson 1995:186–187). Although
no two maskettes are identical, the carvings can
be grouped into sets of similar representations, a
number of which mirror historic Kodiak Alutiiq
masks. In short, these artifacts appear to be repli-
cas of ceremonial masks and miniature carvings
of supernatural beings. Interestingly, however,
their presence throughout Karluk One living
areas suggests that they did not carry the power
of full-size masks. As described below, masks
were potent religious objects used to call spirits
to winter festivals. They were often destroyed or
hidden in caves following ceremonies to protect
people from their power (Birket-Smith 1953:109;
Shelikhov 1981:81). Miniature masks, not treated this way, tell us what some of the ceremonial
masks from Karluk might have looked like (fig.
7.50), as just a few were preserved in the site.

Figure 7.46. *Giinaruangcuk*—
maskette. Bark maskette with an
incised design on the forehead.
AM193.94:1482.

Figure 7.47. *Giinaruangcuk*—maskette. Plank-style maskettes of bark.
The piece in the center is 10 cm high and 3.5 cm wide. UA84.193:1454,
UA85.193:2976, AM193.87:10559.

Figure 7.48. *Giinaruangcuk*—
maskette. Plank-style maskette
of bark with holes for hoop
attachment, 8 cm high and 5
cm wide. AM193.87:10559.

Figure 7.49. *Giinaruangcuk—*maskette. Bark maskette showing a being with a pointed head, a characteristic associated with evil spirits. AM193.95:915.

Figure 7.50. *Giinaruangcuk—*maskette. Selection of wood and bark maskettes. The largest bark maskette (left, with an uneven and pronounced brow line) is 11 cm high, 5 cm wide, and 2.5 cm deep. The smallest maskette (upper left, with a pointed head and *O*-shaped, whistling mouth) is 5 cm high, 2.85 cm wide, and 2.85 cm deep. Sheehan avocational collection, AM38:288; UA85.193:4778, UA85.193:4325, UA85.193:4026, AM193.94:2023, AM193.94:4139.

Sharing Knowledge Through the *Looking Both Ways* Exhibition

Aron L. Crowell, Alaska Director, Smithsonian Arctic Studies Center

Artifacts from Karluk One—extraordinary in their number, variety, and state of preservation—reveal innumerable details about Alutiiq/Sugpiaq life during the thirteenth through the fifteenth centuries AD. Perhaps more than any other archaeological site, Karluk One provides a tangible connection to the rich heritage of ancestral generations, and an anchor of cultural identity for the people of Kodiak Island.

Objects from Karluk One thus played a special role in the 2001 exhibition *Looking Both Ways: Heritage and Identity of the Alutiiq People*, produced by the Smithsonian Institution in collaboration with the Alutiiq

Museum (Crowell, Steffian, and Pullar 2001). Tools, containers, hunting equipment, armor, masks, labrets, toys, and figurative art from the Karluk archaeological site were displayed alongside hunting hats, clothing, and other ethnographic items purchased by the Smithsonian's William J. Fisher in villages of the Alutiiq/Sugpiaq region between 1879 and 1894. The two collections are complementary in many ways and reveal connections across time. For example, weaving patterns on a spruce root hat that Fisher purchased from a sea otter hunter at Karluk village in 1884 are similar to those seen on ancient spruce root basketry from the site (fig. 7.51).

Most significantly, organizers of the *Looking Both Ways* project turned to Elders and community members to interpret the meaning and cultural significance of the Karluk and Fisher collections. Knowledge shared by Elders was joined with a vast archive of historical and anthropological information, yielding a complex, many-stranded answer to the exhibition's central question: what does it mean to be Alutiiq?

During preparations for the exhibition in 1997, the recently created Alutiiq Museum and the Smithsonian Arctic Studies Center together hosted a five-day Elders' Planning Conference in Kodiak, attended by over forty representatives from seventeen villages on Kodiak Island, Prince William Sound, Cook Inlet, and the Alaska Peninsula (fig. 7.52). At this unprecedented gathering, Sven Haakanson Sr. said, "You've got to look back and find out the past, and then you look forward"—and suddenly the project had a name (Crowell 2004).

Elders discussed many items from the Karluk One collection during the conference, inspiring some of the exhibition's central themes. Martha Demientieff said, "If I see a basket that I think was used in the past for berry picking, that's not enough for me to know. What I do and what heals my spirit and makes my body healthy is to go out and pick berries in a basket, knowing that for maybe ten thousand years my ancestors have been doing this. That activity with that object does something for my body and for my spirit." A

Figure 7.51. *Awirnaq*—Spruce root hunting hat from Karluk. Painted and decorated with glass trade beads, dentalium shells, sea lion whiskers, and red cloth. Collected by William Fisher, 1884. E74720. Courtesy the Department of Anthropology, Smithsonian Institution.

Figure 7.52. Elders examine Karluk One artifacts at the Elders' Planning Conference for the *Looking Both Ways* exhibit, Kodiak, 1997. From left: Mary Peterson, Luba Eluska, Roy Madsen, Ivar Malutin, John Pestrikoff, Ignatious Kosbruk, and Jean Anderson. Courtesy Aron Crowell.

viewing of masks and human figurines from the site inspired a discussion about shamanism that examined both the beneficial and malevolent ways that the powers of the *kalla'alek* were employed. Several Elders remembered how shamans made wooden images of their enemies, similar to the Karluk One figurines, and cut these figurines or stuck them with pins to magically wound their victims. Others remembered how shamans used their abilities for good by foretelling the future and healing the sick and injured, aided by an extensive knowledge of medicinal plants.

Karluk One objects brought back memories of village childhoods, such as wooden dolls (different from shamans' figures) that girls waited all winter to bring out when the geese arrived—a ritual of rebirth and spring. A toy wooden bow reminded Elders of arrow-shooting contests held on the beach when they were boys. These and other types of objects found inside ancestral houses at Karluk One—a birch bark sewing bag, a whalebone mortar, fishing floats and sinkers, bentwood boxes—endured through time as elements of Alutiiq/Sugpiaq culture, surviving the cataclysm of Western contact to remain as familiar touchstones for late twentieth-century Elders.

It is this quality of connection across the centuries, and the attendant message of cultural survival and renewal, that makes the Karluk One collection such an irreplaceable resource for this and future generations.

Navigating the spirit world required the help of ritual specialists. Alutiiq communities had two very different types of religious practitioners—wise ones (*kas'at*) and shamans (*kalla'allet*). Both individuals interacted with the non-human world on behalf of their communities. *Kas'at* were revered for their knowledge of history and religious tradition. These specialists spoke directly to spirits, knew "how to do things," and had the power to change bad circumstances (Desson 1995:132, 157). *Kas'at* had two essential functions. First, they were responsible for sharing information about religious traditions. As experts in Alutiiq faith, they instructed others in human origins, the nature of the universe, and ritual practices (Desson 1995:136–138). This included teaching ritual dancing to youth. Second, *kas'at* oversaw the major winter hunting festivals, helping to organize and lead events (Lisianski 1814:208).

While the role of a *kas'aq* was public and based on sharing information, the role of a *kalla'alek*, shaman, was steeped in secrecy (Desson 1995:157). Shamans were both predictors of the future and spiritual intercessors (Campbell 1816:116). They knew the order of the universe and how to travel through the spirit world. Moreover, each shaman acquired as set of personal, helping spirits over their lifetimes. The word *kalla'alek* translates as "one who wields supernatural powers" and comes from the root word *kalliq*, meaning thunder (Alisha Drabek pers. comm. 2014). As such, they could ascertain the outcome of harvesting activities, travel, or warfare, change the weather, and provide spiritual healing for the sick (Desson 1995:138–139). When a person was ill due to misalignment with the spiritual world or the influence of an evil spirit, a shaman could intervene. This was a distinct type of healing, separate from that practiced by community healers trained in the use of medicinal herbs, massage, acupressure, bloodletting, and midwifery. These types of healers were typically women who managed people's physical health (Mulcahy 2001).

Both men and women could be shamans (Black 1981:2; Merck 1980:107), and there were a number of paths to the position. Shamanism was often passed through families, with the experienced shaman teaching the craft to an apprentice. Some children were selected for the position at birth. Other people became shamans because they displayed a talent for communicating with spirits or wished to learn the art (Davydov 1977:166; Gideon 1989:60; Holmberg 1985:59). In performing their services, shamans danced, sang, acted, and chanted, activities that resulted in a trance. They are often described as spinning or twisting and used special language (Desson 1995:134–135). In 1872, a shaman performing in Karluk spoke in a ritual language. Audience members did not understand his words, and they cannot be fully translated today, but those present knew the shaman was speaking with a spirit (Desson 1995:144–145). Sometimes, shamans performed naked, wearing only body paint and feathers in their hair (Black 1981:2). Other times, shamans might wear their clothes backward or don wigs, hats, or special gear. Shamanic paraphernalia collected from the Alaska Peninsula Alutiiq community of Ugashik in 1885–1886 include a rattle filled with charms, a whistle, a belt, bracelets, and a skin hat (Crowell and Leer 2001:209–210).

As shamans interacted with evil spirits and because they were themselves known to become evil, they were often distrusted. Alutiiq stories warn of the trickery of shamans, who could do things like call in the fog, create a giant wave, block travel, harness the assistance of animals, see in the dark, find people who were in hiding, transform a person into an animal, and kill (Golder 1903b:97, 1907:296). Today, Alutiiq Elders are

wary about discussing shamanic practices, although they persisted well into the twentieth century and included many good deeds (Crowell and Leer 2001:208; Drabek 2012:21). Due to the ambivalence surrounding the power of shamans, kas'at were more trusted and of higher social standing (Desson 1995:157). This distinction is apparent in the final resting places of these types of specialists. While the soul of a shaman ascended to the first sky world after death, that of a kas'at ascended to the purer second or third sky world. Shamans were also buried differently than other members of Alutiiq society. Their remains and gear were placed in a kayak and left in a high place, in a tree or on a cliff (Holmberg 1985:53). Perhaps like ceremonial masks, they were removed from the community to protect people from their power.

While there are no known records of the gear used by kas'at, historic sources indicate that shamans employed miniature boats, raven skins, animal carvings, and human figurines in their work. Some shamans even made models of the universe to use in seeing the future (Drabek 2012:126). A variety of human figurines recovered from Karluk may be related to shamanic practice. Shamans are reported to have led an annual doll festival at the conclusion of the winter ceremonial season. Here, they shared predictions for the coming year's harvest by hiding pieces of desired resources in a doll's clothing. A large piece of fish hidden on the doll signaled a productive fishing season, while a small piece predicted a poor season (Crowell 1992:27; Davydov 1977:170; Knecht 1995:688). Shaman also carved dolls in the likeness of people they wished to harm. Such a doll was damaged and left in a place where the unfortunate person would encounter it (fig. 7.53). Alutiiq Elders still recall this frightening practice and note that it

Figure 7.53. *Samanam suarua'a*—shaman's doll. Wooden female figure, back view. AM193.95:1013.

Figure 7.54. *Samanam suarua'a*—shaman's doll. Wearing labrets, this figure has a small protruding bump in the center of its stake-like body. It is 11 cm high, 3.5 cm wide, and 2 cm deep. AM193.95:1069.

Figure 7.55. *Samanam suarua'a*—shaman's doll. The protruding knob on the bottom of this doll may have been for inserting it into another object. The figure also displays a common feature seen in many human representations—a pronounced line from under the nose and cheeks to the raised mouth. It is 12 cm high, 3 cm wide, and 1.7 cm deep. AM193.94:4095.

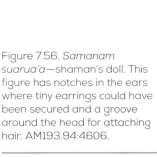

Figure 7.56. *Samanam suarua'a*—shaman's doll. This figure has notches in the ears where tiny earrings could have been secured and a groove around the head for attaching hair. AM193.94:4606.

could cause a person's death (Drabek 2012:132; Knecht 1995: 685–686).

A number of the human figures in the Karluk One collection are represented. Many of these figures feature detailed faces, on top of a stake-like body without arms or legs (fig. 7.54–7.56). Several are made on knots of wood (fig. 7.57a,b, 7.58). We interpret this type of figure as shamans' dolls as many have been damaged—cut, gouged, burned, or broken.

To aid their work, shaman carried charms, small talismans that provided spiritual assistance. These charms might be hidden in their gear, tied to a belt, or worn. Charms stored inside a historic rattle collected on the Alaska Peninsula in 1885–1886 include clippings of red and black hair, a piece of mica, a quartz crystal, and a sliver of wood (Crowell and Leer 2001:209). Hunters also carried talismans or stored them in their kayaks (Desson 1995: 1995:94–97). These highly personal items typically revealed themselves to a hunter, who then kept the objects private. Personal talismans were often stored out of view and not discussed (Black 1981:5; Drabek 2012:128).

Historic accounts suggest that small, rare objects functioned as hunting talismans. Chestnuts and beans washed up on the shore of Kodiak were considered good luck and might be worn around the neck (Davydov 1977:171; Holmberg 1985:50; Lisianski 1814:209). People also collected eagle feathers, bear hair, stones, and roots. Alutiiq Elders recall that both red and black stones functioned as talismans, or *nakernat*, and that men kept them in small boxes. Some of these stones were alive and required feeding (Drabek 2012:128). Other talismans glowed with spiritual power. An Alutiiq story tells of a hunter who found a luminous green stone that provided him with exceptional luck (Lantis 1938:149). Whalers,

powerful ritual specialists, used human flesh as a talisman, stealing the corpses of great hunters and leaders. From these bodies, they extracted fat and mixed it with a plant poison (Black 1981:5; Lisianski 1814:209). This made a chemically and spiritually potent potion that was smeared on whaling spear points.

Children also had charms. Alutiiq Elder Lucille Davis, who grew up in Karluk, noted that people saved the amniotic sack or a portion of the placenta when a child was born. This tissue was dried, folded, and placed in a small pouch for the child

Figure 7.58. *Samanam suarua'a*—shaman's doll. The function of this large, one-of-a-kind figure is unknown. Carved from knot of wood, it features a human face with one very large ear. The figure is large at 26 cm high, 18 cm wide, and 11 cm deep. This piece may represent the Man of Winter, a character from an Alutiiq legend told to noisy children. The tale warns that children who misbehave can cause bad weather and trouble many people. Lind avocational collection, AM20.

Figures 7.57a,b. *Samanam suarua'a*—shaman's doll. Made from a knot of wood, delicate carving marks are visible on the figure's head and neck. UA85.193:3733.

Figures 7.59a,b. *Nakernauteq*—amulet box. Hunters kept amulets in boxes, small containers they carried in the kayaks and kept hidden from view. Inside were personal talismans, or *nekernat*, that provided luck. This small 18 cm long, 6.5 cm wide, and 3.5 high wooden box carved in the shape of a fish, may be an amulet box. The opening of the compartment is 5 cm long and 2.5 cm wide. Lind avocational collection, AM14:5.

to wear around the neck as a protective charm. As the sack and placenta protected the child during pregnancy, they protected him or her in life (Hunt 2000:49–50). More broadly speaking, Alutiiq clothing was a form of talisman. The skins people wore retained the characteristics of the animals from which they were harvested, and these qualities could be passed to the person wearing the skin (Hunt 2000:45).

Karluk One also produced a variety of unique stones—quartz crystals, as well as green, black, and red stones. These items mirror descriptions of hunting talisman and may have functioned in this way (see fig. 4.21 and 7.38). A fish-shaped carving from Karluk One, perhaps representing a sculpin, may be a charm box. This small carving features a rectangular chamber in its base, the right size for holding small items. Alutiiq Elders who viewed the object suggested that it was a box for talismans and recalled family members who kept such boxes (fig. 7.59a,b).

Carvings of birds and sea mammals may also be talismans or representations of animal-spirit helpers. Some are carved into commonly used tools like ulu handles to acknowledge the connection with animals (fig. 7.60, 7.61). Others may

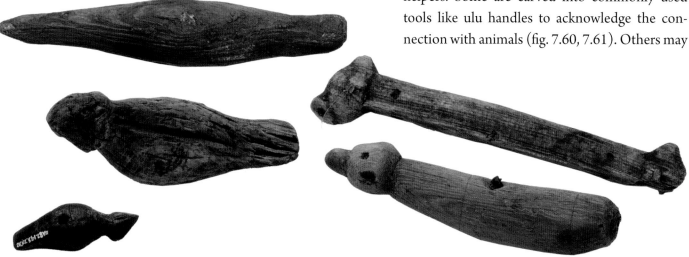

Figure 7.60. *Unguwallriangcuk*—zoomorphic figurine. Birds, including ptarmigans and puffins, are depicted in all these artifacts. The three pieces on the left have a tiny hole in the bottom center and their function is unknown. They could have been attached to another object. The two on the right are handles—a vessel handle and a tool handle. UA85.193:6476, AM193.94:4339, UA87.193:7532, AM193.87:10155, AM193.87:10675.

Figure 7.61. *Agaa*—vessel handle. Although faded, the sparkly black pigment is still visible on this finely carved handle. 16 cm long, 2 cm wide, and 2 cm deep, the bird on the left was broken and repaired with tiny pegs. UA85.193:4804.

be talismans. Birds are the most common animal carvings from the village. Puffins, with their angular heads are easily identified, but other species include ptarmigan and a long-necked bird (fig. 7.62, 7.63). Small bird carvings, covered with fine weaving, intricate embroidery, and strands of hair were collected on Kodiak in the nineteenth century and may represent talismans and/or decorations for hunting hats (Donta 1994:126; Holmberg 1985:46; Korsun 2012:259–261; Varjola 1990:238–239). In contrast, sea mammals, despite their economic importance, are less frequently represented (Knecht 1995:691, 694) (fig. 7.64). Alutiiq people note that young hunters went through a ritual process that helped each to discover the animals that would be their personal helpers throughout life. Each hunter had two such helpers, one for the land and one for the sea (Knecht 1995:623). Alutiiq Elder John Pestrikoff reported that as part of ritual preparations for hunting men selected and replaced animal carvings hung from the ceiling of the *qasgiq*. These carvings were suspended on a pole that was rocked back and forth during the ritual. The process of taking and replacing a carving brought animals to hunters and also ensured that fish and game would be reborn (Drabek 2012:127). It enacted the cycling of souls (cf. Crowell and Leer 2001:194).

Carvings of human figures may also have functioned as amulets. Alutiiq women without

Figure 7.62. *Unguwallriangcuk*—zoomorphic figurine. This small painted wooden puffin carving is just 3.6 cm long and 1.25 cm wide and high. UA87.193:7532.

Figures 7.63a,b. *Unguwallriangcuk*—zoomorphic figurine. This red and black painted wooden bird carving is 9 cm tall, 4 cm wide, and 5 cm deep. A knob on the bottom suggests that it was designed to adorn another object. UA85.193:4888.

Figure 7.64. *Unguwallriangcuk*—zoomorphic figurine. Seal carvings. The bottom piece is an ulu handle, with a slit for attaching a slate blade. After people and birds, sea mammals are the most commonly represented animals in the Karluk One collection. Interestingly, however, despite the widespread use of baleen and whalebone at Karluk One, whales are rarely shown in carvings. UA85.193:2556, UA85.193:2762.

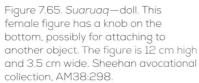

Figure 7.65. *Suaruaq*—doll. This female figure has a knob on the bottom, possibly for attaching to another object. The figure is 12 cm high and 3.5 cm wide. Sheehan avocational collection, AM38:298.

Figure 7.66. *Suaruaq*—doll. With traces of red pigment, this pregnant female figure is carved with ears. Sometimes, human figures were carved with ears, but often they were made without. The figure is 9 cm high, 2.8 cm wide, and 2.2 cm deep. AM193.87:19033.

children once kept dolls that represented "wished-for infant offspring, and amuse themselves with them, as if they were real infants" (Lisianski 1814:178). A number of wooden figurines from Karluk show female anatomy and pregnancy (fig. 7.65–7.67), including one dramatic example with a huge belly and hands supporting her lower back. These carvings may be fertility dolls or perhaps items used in fertility rituals (Knecht 1995:687). As a large family helped to ensure prosperity, both for its members and community leaders, the ability to produce many children was likely held in high esteem.

Rituals

Like the instruction provided by *kas'at*, shamanic practices, or the use of talismans, rituals helped Alutiiq people to maintain the proper balance between the natural and supernatural worlds (Drabek 2012:124). They emphasized the ties between people, animals, and the spirits, reminded participants of right behavior, and demonstrated cultural values. They also reinforced the social order (Donta 1992, 1993; Jordan 1994). Through displays of wealth, generosity, and social and spiritual connection, the wealthiest members demonstrated their power, fulfilled social obligations, and renewed social relationships. Rituals were both religious events and a major integrating feature of village life (Jordan 1994:153).

In classical Alutiiq society, people participated in both periodic rituals and annual festivals. Periodic rituals occurred throughout the year, as needed or desired (Crowell 1992:19). Some of these rituals celebrated achievements. For example, Alutiiq people held celebrations to mark the completion of a new house or a new *qasgiq*. In both instances, after community members joined forces to create the building, its owner provided

Figures 7.67a,b,c,d. *Suaruaq*—doll. Pregnant female figure is 16 cm high, 13 cm wide, and 6.5 cm deep. Although this figure was found with some human hair, conservators augmented its hair for display in the *Looking Both Ways* exhibit (Crowell et al. 2001). Interestingly, while her front side is very rounded, her backside is flat except for her arms. AM193.87:19090.

a celebratory meal in thanks (Gideon 1989:44; Matfay 1990).

Other rituals were preparatory, made in anticipation of new circumstances. The appointment of a new chief, hunting preparations, war preparations, and even planning for a large winter festival were preceded by rituals that involved different combinations of meals, steam bathing, gift giving, and interactions with the spirit world (Drabek 2012:127; Davydov 1977:183–184; Gideon 1989:41, 42–43). A child's first kill was a time of celebration. In the twentieth century, parents marked this achievement with a meal and by giving away the animal taken (Davis 2000, 1997a). Children were also initiated into the *qasgiq*. For this ritual, children wore special clothing, face paint, and feathers in their hair (Black 1981:5). The child danced and was introduced by his or her father, who presented the young person with a strip of his parka (Davydov 1977:184).

As clothing contained information on a person's social identity and could function as a talisman, these strips probably symbolized the universe of human and spiritual assistance available to a child as he or she entered the social and ceremonial life of an Alutiiq community. The initiation ended with a feast presented by the child's family.

There were also rituals associated with life passages—birth, puberty, marriage, and death. After the ritual seclusion associated with birth, mother and baby washed in a steam bath and then the child received piercings for a nose pin and labret. Following this process, the child was introduced to the family home (Lisianski 1814:201) and named by an Elder family member (Sauer 1802:195). Often, the newborn received the name of a deceased relative or famous person (Black 1981:3).

At the onset of menstruation, a young woman's family might host a feast for family and friends. Dressed in special clothing, the woman received tattoos, had her hair cut in a woman's style, and gave away her toys. Her parents might also give presents to those assembled. Then, she entered her first period of menstrual confinement. This process led to her reemergence as an adult member of society, ready for marriage and motherhood (Crowell 1992:22; Hunt 2000:62). A nineteenth-century account of this ritual indicates that the woman wore clothing of caribou calfskin from which all ornaments were removed. For boys, first-kill ceremonies may have been the equivalent of the menarche ritual held for girls. Among the Chugach Alutiiq, boys fasted for three days as part of this ritual and were dressed in clothes that resembled those of a baby (Birket-Smith 1953:87; Hunt 2000:63).

Marriage rituals varied, perhaps in part due to the social standing of the bride and groom. However, unions were marked with gift giving, steam bathing, feasting, and additional tattoos for the bride (Black 1981:3; Sauer 1802:177). A bride might also receive a set of new clothes from her father or her husband (Merck 1980:108). Sometimes, the groom publically received the title of dear son-in-law from his bride's father (Black 1981:3) and then spent time working for his father-in-law. Only when a husband demonstrated his ability to provide for his wife, or a child was born, did a couple move to their own home (Black 1977:85; Davydov 1977:182).

At death, a person was dressed in their best clothing for burial (Black 1977:96). In contrast, family members and close friends of the deceased painted their faces black, cut their hair, and in some case cut themselves (Lisianski 1814:189; Shelikhov 1981:54). When a person lost a husband or wife, the surviving spouse left the community for a time, moving to a neighboring village. If a woman lost a child, she went into seclusion (Lisianski 1814:200).

There are two common themes in these life-passage rituals, a period of waiting and alteration of a person's image. Passages were accompanied by an interval of transformation. People waited to acquire a new status, or in the case of death, they waited for the deceased to become part of the non-human world. They were also marked in lasting, physical ways visible to others. People wore or acquired new clothing. They adopted new hairstyles, and they visibly and permanently altered their physical appearances with tattoos and piercings. Based on the distinct size classes found in labrets from Karluk, enlarging one's labret hole may have been another modification associated with life passage rituals (Steffian essay Chapter 7). Whatever the case, these rituals helped to order the social world.

Archaeological evidence of periodic rituals is difficult to separate from evidence of daily life. While tools that could have been used for tattooing or face painting are present, these tools could also have been used for sewing and painting hunting gear. Thus, it is difficult to point to specific objects and suggest that they were used in celebrating first events or life-passage rituals. This is not the case for large annual festivals. One of the hallmarks of the Karluk One collection is the presence of festival gear (Donta 1994; Jordan 1994; Liapunova 1994). The collection contains 230 items used in recurring hunting ceremonies—feast bowls, drums, rattles, masks, and dance wands

These festivals were hunting rituals, designed to perpetuate the supply of game by appeasing the spirits who influenced life on Earth. Hunters interacted with the spirit world through masked dancing, recounting recent hunts and the great hunting achievements of ancestors. Their actions honored life-sustaining animals and enticed animal *sui* to release the souls of recently killed game. This helped to ensure an abundant supply of fish, birds, and sea mammals in the coming year. Winter festivals were also social events, gatherings where opulent clothing, speeches honoring ancestors, lavish meals, and generous gifts reinforced social relationships. Here, wealthy members of society demonstrated their position and created social obligations. Despite the relationships built between communities at such gatherings, they may have encouraged warfare. One way to obtain the large quantities of food and goods needed to host such gatherings was to loot another community (Jordan 1994:168).

While not every community hosted a festival every year, people were likely involved in yearly celebrations due to the reciprocal nature of these events (Crowell 1994:19; Desson 1995:269; Jordan 1994:151). One year a wealthy man in Karluk might hold a feast inviting neighbors from Uyak Bay, the next, a wealthy man from Uyak Bay might host the people of Karluk and Uganik, and so forth (Holmberg 1985:60). These events were typically held in early winter, beginning in December and lasting for weeks. Festivals were hosted by wealthy community leaders, organized by *kas'at*, and supported by community members. Preparations for a festival likely took several years, with the most intense work in the fall months preceding the event. People not only had to harvest, store, and prepare foods for their visitors, they had to make gifts, sew festival clothing, carve festival gear, compose festival songs and dances, and clean the community house (Jordan 1994:151). The planning process began in the community house:

> The one who wishes to give a feast calls all his neighbors to the kazhim.[3] When all have taken their appointed places along the benches, he brings in the tolkusha,[4] places it in the center, and takes up his place at the door. All then begin to sing in praise of his [the host's] kinsmen. At the end of the song,

he sits down on the floor and declares whom he intends to invite, what kind of present he shall give to each, and when he will send to summon the particular guest. Then he rises, gives gifts to the owner of the kazhim and to the old man whose duty it will be during the feast to entertain with conversation (tales) the guests, especially in the intervals between songs and dances, when one song or dance has ended and there is a lull before the next one. Finally, he himself offered the tolkusha to each man present, in order of seniority [rank]. They eat politely—in small quantities—so that there shall be enough for all. Having thanked their host for the food, all go home. (Gideon 1989:44–45)

In preparation for a festival, men from the host's community filled the *qasgiq* with fresh grass, patched its roof, and fumigated the structure with smoke. This work included appeals to animal *sui* for future hunting success (Davydov 1977:183–184). Decoration of the *qasgiq* followed with men hanging hunting weapons, decoys, stuffed animal skins, paddles, and boats from the ceiling. At least some of this gear was carved in miniature, like the items used by whalers to enact hunts (Davydov 1977:108; Desson 1995:174–175). The suspended gear served as both decoration and part of the staging for masked dancing. All of it was tied together allowing a person in the corner of the *qagiq* to pull a rope that made the objects sway. This mimicked the motion of the ocean and hunters in action, and it helped to transport guests into the world of the dance performances (Desson 1995:176). A large oil lamp in the center of the *qasgiq* was another common festival furnishing (Desson 1995:534–538).

Another potential prop was a story rock, a large painted stone with which dancers interacted. "In this spot there was also a stone with red spots

Figure 7.68. *Quliyanguaqutaq*—story rock. This large, heavy artifact has fourteen pecked depressions as well as a natural hole. Ten of the depressions are distinct. The other four are faint. Although its function is not known, the rock may have been a prop used in festival performances. An historic source reports people dancing around a rock painted with red circles. The pecked circles resemble elements of Alutiiq petroglyphs, designs pecked in stationary shoreline boulders. A rock formation near the mouth of the Afognak River feature similar circular depressions intermixed with cut lines (Clark 1979:286). Archaeologists recently uncovered a similar boulder in northern Alaska (Shirar et al. 2012). AM193.94:1984.

clothing, with painted faces, and wearing an array of headdresses, hats, and jewelry chosen for the occasion. Many of the incised pebbles from Karluk One show people in ornate headgear, perhaps made from feathers (Donta 1994:131). In the nineteenth century, when glass beads were abundant, people adorned themselves in beaded jewelry for celebrations (Davydov 1977:110). Similarly, ceremonial headgear collected on Kodiak in the nineteenth century features combinations of elaborate embroidery, tassels, tufting, quillwork, beading, lengths of human hair, and geometric designs. There are distinct styles for men and women, and each hat is unique (Korsun 2012:206–217, 228–229). These garments show the incredible work that went into preparing for festivals as well as the breathtaking displays of wealth, beauty, and artistry that finely dressed festival participants must have presented.

Guests were seated inside the *qasgiq* according to social status, with the most honored visitors nearest the door. There was also a special seat for the host (Desson 1995:159). Others filled benches along the walls or rested on the floor below. Men often sat on benches with their wives on the floor beside them (Gideon 1989:45).

The first activity was a meal. Boys from the host community offered guests fresh water and an abundance of food, oil, *akutaq* (a mixture of fat and berries), dried fish, and bird and animal meats (Desson 1995:159). The host always tasted each dish before passing it to his guests. Those assembled ate in order of social standing, passing bowls of food from one person to the next. Some of the food was served in decorated feast bowls (Korsun 2012:160 165). Examples of feast bowls were recovered at Karluk (fig. 7.69a,b, 7.70a,b). These long oval dishes have flat, flared ends. They are shaped like boats and were made in

painted on it, representing the burial place of one of their number considered to be famous, in whose honor the performance was taking place" (Davydov 1977:108). There are few details about the functions of such stones, but a large boulder from Karluk One, pecked with shallow indentations, may be an example (fig. 7.68).

Festivals began with the arrival of guests. Everyone attended the gathering, including women, children, and infants (Gideon 1989:45). Members of the host community waited on the shoreline, dancing and drumming in anticipation. When visitors' boats pulled on to the shore, community members waded into the ocean, picked up the guests, and carried them to the *qasgiq* (Shelikhov 1981:55). People arrived in their best

Figures 7.69a,b. *Qantaruaq*—feast bowl. The two parts of this large feast bowl were found in different parts of the site in different years and later fit back together. Even absent still-missing parts, the piece is quite large, measuring 51 cm long, 23 cm wide, and 19cm high. AM193.94:9, AM193.95:836.

many sizes. Some very large examples are suited for serving large groups (Black 1981:3; Gideon 1989:42–43). Others appear designed for family or even individual use. Some of the Karluk One examples have small, carved recesses along their rims or in their flared ends for inset decorations (fig. 7.71a,b). Most of these decorations have been lost, although a few retain circular pieces of shell. Food appeared throughout the festival, between dance performances and time for games and visiting.

Performances came next and were the heart of the festival. With music, dance, and acting, participants told hunting stories, gradually calling spirits to the *qasgiq*. Every performance was unique, designed to represent the people involved. For them, people created clothing and costumes, choreographed dances, carved masks, and authored songs. Moreover, performances often began by recounting recent family events before moving into well-known tales of ancestors and spirits. As a result, each festival was a dramatization made and enacted to reflect the festival host and a particular point in time. Despite the distinctive character of each performance, comparisons of historically observed festival dances suggest they followed a general framework (Desson 1995:Appendix 2).

Figures 7.70a,b. *Qantaruaq*—feast bowl. Karluk One produced no complete examples of feast bowls, except in miniature version. This piece cracked and was repaired, as evidenced by the two drilled holes on either side of the crack. Like many pieces in the collection, the bottom of this bowl shows cut marks. UA87.193:9253.

Figures 7.71a,b. *Qantaruaq*—feast bowl. Flared rim of a wooden feast bowl decorated with inset piece of shell. Baleen lashing was used to repair the vessel in the past, although the joining fragments were not recovered. Fragments of 41 full-size and miniature feast bowls were recovered at Karluk One. "Of dishes they have wooden platters and plates, carved from flat pieces of wood and decorated with bones, crystals, beads, and the teeth of various animals" (Billing in Merck 1980:207). AM193.M:898.

Figures 7.72a,b,c. *Cauyam puunga*—drum handle. Tiny inset teeth decorate the head of an animal on this drum handle. Teeth are also found on the shoulder of the handle at its end. This is the largest drum handle in the collection at 14.5 cm long and 3.5 cm in diameter. Lind avocational collection, AM14:4.

Participants in performances often included musicians—drummers, whistlers, and rattle shakers; a person who sat in the corner and rocked the gear that hung from the ceiling; both female and male dancers; and audience members (Desson 1995:Appendix 2). As the hunting gear and animals suspended from the ceiling began to sway, the audience might sway and one or more men beat drums. Drumming provided both accompaniment and atmosphere throughout the dances that followed. Men used a single, wooden drumstick to a beat circular, skin-covered drum

(Korsun 2012:389). Drums were made in different sizes and their tone changed by altering the tightness of the skin cover (Knecht 1995:681). Sometimes, men with rattles or whistles played with the drummers, playing both softly and with dramatic blasts at key moments. Whistling tended to occur near the end of a performance, as animal spirits drew near to the *qasgig* and were encouraged to enter.

Although no whistles were found at Karluk One, the site produced drum parts (fig. 7.72, 7.73) and fragments of a rattle (fig. 7.74). The drum parts include short, cylindrical wooden handles. One dramatic piece features a carving of a face at

Figure 7.73. *Cauyam awatiisqaa*—drum rim. There are no complete drum rims in the collection, so the diameter of these instruments is unknown. The fragment on top is 1.3 cm high and 8 mm deep, with the groove 2 mm wide. UA85193:5556, AM193.94:4298, UA85.193:3558.

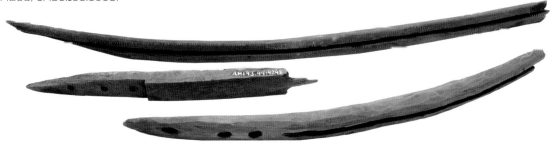

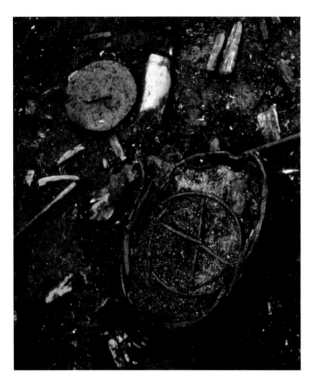

Figure 7.74. *Awirlursuutem awatiisqaa*—rattle hoop, *awirlursuutem tuknisuutii*—rattle cross brace. Photograph of the remains of a wooden rattle inside a bentwood vessel uncovered in the site. Alutiiq Museum archives, . "Their dances are proper tournaments, with a knife or lance in the right hand, and a rattle in the left; the rattle is made of a number of thin hoops, one in the other, covered with white feathers, and having the red bills of the seaparrot suspended on very short threads; which, being shaken, strike together, and make a very considerable noise" (Sauer 1802:176). AM628:482.S.

one end, inset with small teeth (fig. 7.72). Other examples are undecorated. All of the handles feature a deep notch, where the ends of the circular drum rim were united and attached. Rim parts from the collection are narrow, bent pieces of wood, with a groove along the outer edge where a string was fastened to hold a tight, flat, skin covering. Historically, these coverings were made of de-haired seal hide, a seal bladder, or even a halibut stomach. Drum rim ends, the parts fastened to handles, feature holes for lashing, as do the handles to which they were secured (fig. 7.73). The site also yielded a single drumstick, a narrow wooden baton with a rounded end.

The remains of a single rattle illustrate that prehistoric pieces closely mirror circular, puffin-beak rattles collected from Kodiak in the nineteenth century. The Karluk rattle features two concentric wooden hoops fitted with a two-piece wooden handle. The handle is made of narrow rectangular length of wood crossing in the center of the rattle (fig. 7.74) and extending across the edges of the hoops. Unfortunately, the pieces of this object have been spread through the large Karluk One collection and have yet to be relocated. As such, it is not possible to describe how the handles were attached to the rattle. However, nearly identical historic examples feature small, drilled holes in both ends to which the hoops were pegged. To these hoops, craftsmen tied many puffin beaks (Korsun 2012:xx, 294–303; Varjola 1990:242).

As the music played, dancers moved to the center of the *qasgiq*, naked or costumed (Merck 1980:101). Filled with people in heavy skin clothing, the *qasgiq* was hot and many performers danced without clothes. Dancers wore wooden masks and sometimes carried rattles, whistles, or hunting gear like knives and paddles (Korsun 2012:316). The performers crouched, swayed, jumped, and ran, mimicking the motions of hunters as they sang. Their songs recounted recent hunting trips and past hunting achievements.

Although not mentioned in ethnographic accounts or known from historic collections, two artifacts from Karluk One may be dance sticks carried by performers (fig. 7.75). Such sticks are used in certain Yup'ik festivals to commemorate extraordinary hunting feats or personal accomplishments, and each is decorated to tell a precise story (Fienup-Riordan 1996:137–139). One example from Karluk has a diamond carved on the center and an arched line on the end, much like Karluk One work boards that depict faces (see fig. 6.92). The other features small holes along the

Figure 7.75. *Lliil'rsuun*—dance stick. The dance stick on the right has what appears to be inset strands of baleen. These stands likely arched out of the stick like long hairs, creating movement as a dancer performed. This object is about 30 cm high, 4 cm wide, and 1 cm deep. AM193.94:1394, AM193.87:7284.

a song (Haakanson and Steffian 2009:Appendix). Between dances, the *qasgiq* might be fumigated with smoke (Desson 1995:161).

Women and audience members were part of performances. Groups of women danced in a line, moving very slowly as drummers sang about ancestors and the death of family members (Merck 1980:109). These dances recalled the skills and successes of ancestors and called on the spirits of the dead to assist in future hunts (Desson 1995:177–178). However, they were not entirely solemn. "During the women's dance, old men who are enjoying themselves make every possible effort to make some of them laugh, as according to their custom the father or husband of the woman who succumbs to teasing and laughs must pay a fine for the benefit of the old and the poor: it is enough for a wife or a daughter just to smile ever so slightly while dancing" (Gideon 1989:46). Similarly, throughout performances, audience members were directed to join in by singing, chanting, and making animals calls.

As the series of dances progressed, the atmosphere of the *qasgiq* became more mystical, even frightening, as spirits prepared to enter the room. The height of the event was the arrival of animal spirits, called in with shouting, whistling, and jangling of rattles. Other beings also entered the *qasgiq*, including both evil and helpful spirits, all of which masked dancers worked to appease (Desson 1995:265–266).

Alutiiq craftsmen carved masks in a variety of styles and sizes, but all depicted faces, and most were decorated with paint and encircling attachments. Face masks are the most common style in historic collections (Crowell 1992; Haakanson and Steffian 2009; Liapunova 1994). These masks feature a hollowed back, eyeholes, and sometimes a bite bar—a place for the dancer to hold the mask

edge with remnants of an inset material, perhaps baleen. These objects may be trade items, like the Yup'ik style caribou-tooth belt described above. Materials from a distance helped to illustrate the procurement skills of a leader, and their use in ceremonies would have provided a public display of such abilities.

Individual dances are recorded as lasting as much as forty-five minutes (Liapunova 1994), and performances included multiple dances. A festival held in Uyak Bay in 1872 featured a performance with thirteen dances, some of them specifically created for that event, others repeated like the chorus of a song (Desson 1995:166–169). Throughout these performances, male dancers wore masks representing supernatural beings—animal *sui*, deities, evil spirits, and ancestral spirits. Dancers were known to wear different masks for different parts of their performances, and craftsmen might carve a different mask for each verse of in his teeth. Some masks are roughly size of a human head. Others are much larger. Some nineteenth-century masks collected on Kodiak and Afognak islands are up to 60 cm long and weigh as much as 9 kg (20 lbs; Haakanson and Steffian 2009). These may have been suspended from the ceiling of the *qasgiq* during performances, so that dancers could perform behind them. The design of face masks varies from stylized faces that may represent specific supernatural beings, to more realistic carvings that may be portraits. Animals' faces are rarely represented in Alutiiq masks.

In addition to face masks, Alutiiq people carved two styles of plank masks. Some plank masks are largely two-dimensional. They are large, shaped and painted boards with slits cut for eyeholes and occasionally other minimally carved facial features (Haakanson and Steffian 2009:118–123, 144). Other plank masks feature a small three-dimensional face mask carving lashed to a large decorated plank (Haakanson and Steffian 2009:128, 151, 152, 154, 155).

Examples of both face masks and plank masks were found at Karluk One. While miniature face masks were relatively common, as described above, full-size face masks were rarer. There are just seventeen masks, including two complete carvings and fragments of fifteen others. The two complete examples do not resemble the miniature masks from the site. One is a bird mask (fig. 7.76a,b). Found in a storage box in a Karluk house, this unusual mask features a carving of a creature with large, circular eyes and a short beak, perhaps an owl. This mask is the only one from Karluk to picture an animal, and it closely resembles a historic Alutiiq mask preserved in the Pinart collection (Haakanson and Steffian 2009:115). Interestingly, the bird mask in the Pinart collection is also the only mask of seventy

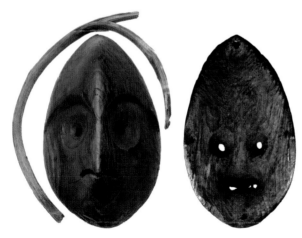

Figures 7.76a,b. *Giinaruaq*—mask. This mask and a piece of a hoop were found inside a storage box on house floor 2. The exterior of the mask is beautifully finished and smooth, while tool marks are still visible on its inside. In addition to the openings for the eyes and beak, there are four holes drilled in the edge of the mask for attaching a hoop. UA84.193:1044, AM193.87:11249.

Figure 7.77. *Giinaruaq*—mask. This full-size wooden mask is more portrait-like than the representations of faces shown in smaller masks. It measures 22 cm high, 16 cm wide, and 3.5 cm deep. On the backside are drill holes and significant charring, evidence from it also being used as a fire starter hearth. AM193.87:9260.

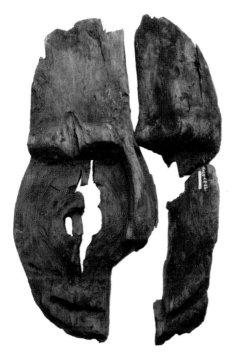

Figure 7.78. *Giinaruaq*—mask. There was such an abundance of material collected from the site, much of it fragmentary; pieces were often separated between collection, conservation treatments, and the collection's four relocations. These mask fragments were pieced together during the Alutiiq Museum's *Carlia'arluku*—To Care for Karluk One project in 2012. AM193.87:8406, AM193.87:10647, AM193.87:10648.

examples that shows an animal. Perhaps this owl-like being represents a specific character in Alutiiq cosmology.

The other complete full-size face mask is portrait-like (fig. 7.77). This cottonwood bark carving features a frowning face. It is ovoid, almost the size of an adult human head, and very symmetrical. It has a distinct brow and long, square nose, features found in stylized presentations. However, these features are not as abstract as seen in other masks, both in the Karluk One collection and historic Kodiak mask collections (Crowell 1992; Haakanson and Steffian 2009; Liapunova 1994). Six other fragmentary masks also show lower profile, portrait-like images (fig. 7.82). One poorly preserved mask, not shown here, is a fragmentary example from the burial of an adult male (Knecht 1995:668). Like a number of the figurines from the collection, this mask features an open mouth in a shape that suggests the person is wearing a pair of lateral labrets (Donta 1993:274). There is some evidence that masks were among the items offered at death (Donta 1993:272; Haakanson and Steffian 2009:Dedication). Perhaps the portrait-style masks from Karluk One were part of such a tradition. They might represent the deceased person or perhaps an ancestor.

Other mask fragments illustrate that villagers made stylized faces like those of the site's miniature masks and known from historic collections. This includes two fragmentary carvings with long, narrow, pointed heads, likely representing evil beings. One of these pointy-head beings is grinning and has a very long nose. Another piece, in many fragments, grins and has a curved nose (fig. 7.78). This curved nose also occurs in several maskettes. Two other mask fragments have long noses with prominent nostrils. Masks with prominent features like a curved nose, large nostrils, or a pointed head, may represent a specific spirit or type of spirit.

The assemblage also includes five plank masks: large, flat pieces of wood shaped but minimally carved to make masks. Several are circular. Others are rectangular on the bottom with a broadly curved top (fig. 7.79–7.81). All of these masks have eyeholes, openings gouged from the back of the mask through its front. Some also feature an opening for a nose and holes along the edges for attachments. One spectacular piece was found with a leather cover and a single hoop secured with two cross pieces (fig. 7.81a,b,c). Teeth marks indicate that the lower crosspiece functioned as a bite bar, a place where the dancer held the mask with his teeth. At the top of this mask, there is also a hole carved horizontally through the piece. This

Figures 7.79a,b. *Giinaruaq*—mask. This half of a large plank mask has a squared base and rounded top. The mask has a curved hoop associated with it. It might have once had another piece that attached to the front, or it might have been painted. The complete mask measures 45 cm high and 33 cm wide. AM193.87:8861.

Figures 7.80a,b. *Giinaruaq*—mask. Small oval plank masks carved of wood, front and back. The complete piece on the left is 16 cm high, 12 cm wide, and 1.3 cm deep. AM193.94:999, AM193.94:288.

Figures 7.81a,b,c. *Giinaruaq*—mask. Wooden plank mask with a painted leather cover and an encircling hoop. The wood mask has a painted design on it. Although faded, a white diagonal band and remnants of black pigment are still visible. The leather cover, found over the front of the mask, painted side down, features a concentric circular design painted in white. The rear of the mask features two horizontal support bars and a hole at the top—perhaps to attach an adornment or a strap that helped a dancer wear the mask. Sheehan avocational collection, AM38:2718, AM38:2719.

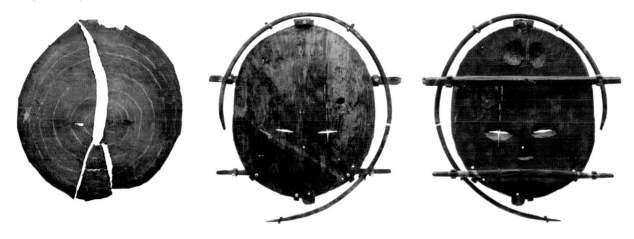

Figure 7.82. *Awatiisqaq*—mask hoop. The mask hoop on the left has holes for additional attachments, such as feathers or mask bangles. It also has knob ends for attaching to the mask. It may have been one of several pieces to form a hoop. Historically, mask hoops were made in a variety of styles, ranging from a full to a partial circle around the mask and from round to oval (Desson 1995:397). Sometimes, mask hoops were formed from one piece, and sometimes they were formed from several pieces of bentwood. UA84.193:1332, AM193.87:9000, AM193.87:11306.

Figure 7.83 *Awatiisqam ilakua'a*—mask bangle. Kayak paddle-shaped mask bangles. These bangles directly mirror kayak paddles, down to the angled tip design of some (see Figure 5.88). The use of paddle shapes for mask attachments supports the idea that masks were used in hunting rituals and mirror the journey that festival participants took from the *gasgiq* into the world of spirits. Paddles were also a common item carried by participants in festival dances. A number of the wooden mask bangles retain traces of red and black paint and white pigment. The longest mask bangle of this style is 24.5 cm long, while the smallest is 10 cm long. They average 10 to 20 cm long. UA84.193:1405, AM193.94:2410, AM193.87:9531, AM193.94:2730, UA85.193:3393

hole pierces the back of the mask horizontally. It may have been a place to secure an attachment that appeared above the mask or perhaps tie a strap to help a dancer wear the object.

We do not know why Alutiiq craftsmen carved plank masks or what they represent. The shape of the masks and the presence of eyes suggest faces, but their flat, plain, appearance also suggests that we cannot fully see the character represented. Leather coverings, like the one found at Karluk One suggests that additional details may have been shared in paintings attached to the front of these masks. This portrayal is notably distinct from the deeply carved features found on face masks.

Perhaps plank masks showed beings beginning to reveal themselves, those present but not fully unveiled. Whatever the case, the features of Karluk One plank masks are nearly identical in shape, design, and manufacture to nineteenth-century examples collected on Kodiak (Haakanson and Steffian 2009:118–123).

In addition to masks, the site produced fifteen fragments of bentwood mask hoops (fig. 7.82), forty-eight wooden fragments that could be either mask or rattle hoops, and 141 mask attachments, or bangles (fig. 7.83–7.87). Mask bangles are often painted and shaped like boat paddles, for both kayaks and *angyat* (fig. 7.83, 7.84). Others are

Figure 7.84. *Awatiisqam ilakua'a*—mask bangle. These mask bangles mirror the unique shape of *angyaq* paddles. UA84.193:1404, UA85.193:6318, AM193.94:1436, AM193.94:3750, AM193.94:3749.

Figure 7.85. *Awatiisqam ilakua'a*—mask bangle. Bangles are most often shaped like kayak and *angyaq* paddles, but Karluk One produced a variety of other shapes and variations. Some bangles have holes for adding attachments. The bangle on the right is painted with alternating red and black bands, a pattern seen in a number of objects from the site (see Figure 6.54 middle handle for an example). The dimensions of this bangle are 10.35 cm high, 5.6 cm wide, and 1 cm deep. The square part of the bangle is almost even at 5.8 cm high and 5.6 cm wide. UA87.193:7164; Sheehan avocational collection, AM231:31; AM193.87:9355.

shaped like crescents, squares, or whale tails (fig. 7.85, 7.86). The set of Karluk bangles closely resemble the attachments found on historic masks in size, shape, and even painted motifs (fig. 7.87, 7.88) (Haakanson and Steffian 2009:150–151; Liapunova 1994:190–194). All of the bangles have a narrow shaft below their decorative end, and most have a grooved or notched end for attachment to a mask hoop. Incised pebbles from Karluk One often show faces surrounded by long, narrow, U-shaped decorations angled away from the face. These pebbles may show people wearing masks surrounded by attachments (Donta 1994:130).

Festivals lasted days, even weeks, until the host's food stores were depleted (Lisianski 1814:209). The ceremonial season usually ended in late January. Guests left after the final activity, gift giving (Black 1977:85). Hosts provided their visitors with food for the trip home as well as generous gifts. Historically, these included parkas, pieces of amber, dentalium shells, and other items of wealth (Gideon 1989:46). The highest ranking

Figure 7.86. *Awatiisqam ilakua'a*—mask bangle. Mask bangle resembling the shape of a whale's tail. AM193.87:9354. While this mask bangle is an average size among those in the collection, there is another very similarly shaped whale-tail bangle that is much larger at 15.5 cm high, 7.5 cm wide, and about 1 cm wide, tapering in depth toward the tip of the whale's tail. The styling and workmanship involved in creating objects, such as mask bangles, reveals the skills and artistry of their crafters. AM193.87:9359.

Figure 7.87. *Awatiisqam ilakua'a*—mask bangle. Painted with red and black pigment, this bangle is delicate at just 8mm thick. It is 14 cm long and 1.2 cm wide. UA85.193:3393.

Figure 7.88. *Awatiisqam ilakua'a*—mask bangle. Boldly painted in black, which likely once sparkled with molybdenite-imbued pigment, the painted motif on this bangle is unique in the collection. AM193.87:9757.

visitors received the most lavish presents (Desson 1995:269). Hosts also gave away their personal possessions. Some cut up their best parkas and provided pieces of the garments to visitors as a parting gift (Davydov 1977:184). As clothing helped to signal a person's identity, parka pieces likely reminded guests of the social connections created by the host's generosity. More generally, gift giving was an essential piece of the ranking system. A wealthy leader was able to maintain his position and perpetuate the status of his family by giving. In essence, giving was insurance (Townsend 1980:136). A host was poor in belongings but rich in prestige following a successful festival (Desson 1995:269). Visitors left the festival with no ceremony, departing for home quietly (Gideon 1989:46).

The end of the festival season marked the beginning of the year and a new economic cycle. If the winter festivals were successful in pleasing the animal spirits, then the following year's harvest would be plentiful. If a wealthy man had hosted his friends and neighbors well, demonstrating his resourcefulness, he could begin to accumulate wealth again. As spring approached, people consulted shamans for predictions about the future, and the cycles of harvesting, storing, trading, raiding, manufacturing, and celebrating began again.

A Love of Old Things

Coral Chernoff, Alutiiq Artist

Coral Chernoff is an artist with deep family ties to the community of Kodiak. A student of Alutiiq arts for more than two decades, Coral is drawn to the beauty of natural materials. She harvests and processes the fish skins, bird pelt, seal gut, wood, and rye grass for her work, and her carvings, weavings, and skin sewing highlight their warm colors and rich qualities. For inspiration and information, she often looks to ancestral collections. Her journey to understand Alutiiq arts has taken her to repositories in France (Koniag, Inc. 2008) and Russia, as well as the Alutiiq Museum's collections room. Coral talked to Sven Haakanson Jr. in July 2012 about the importance of artifacts to her work, especially those in the Karluk One collection.

Everything in the collection has inspired me. Everything I lay my eyes on teaches me something—the shapes, the materials. Some of us just have a certain love for old or handmade things. When I look at the Karluk collection, the materials are beautiful to me. I love the look they have from being worn and used. They were touched in certain places over and over and over, and they have a worn, used look. I just love all that. I think it is so beautiful. There is something about all that old stuff that just grabs me. It makes me want to go out and explore. I like old, cultural, and handmade things, and I love great workmanship. That's what you see in all the old collections. Every single object shows topnotch workmanship.

As an artist, seeing well-made objects makes you want to be better. Every time I go into the collection room, I see something new. You can look at the same piece but see something new about it. If you turn an object in a certain light, all of a sudden you think, "Wow, I never saw that." Or you experience other things in your work, and you go back to an object you saw last year. All of a sudden it is something new. You've seen other parts, or you've gained another year of experience, so you see the object in a whole new way. You understand it better.

The artifacts I study show such amazing workmanship that sometimes they make me want to quit! But more often I'm excited by the knowledge people had to have to make these things. You have to understand the seasons you harvest the material, how to take care of it, and how to process it. And there isn't just one way to care for materials. There are multiple ways depending on the result you want. That's exciting for me. It's a steady challenge.

I've been basket weaving for twenty-two years, and I look at the baskets in these collections, and I wonder if I will ever get there. I'm thinking not, but I'll keep on trying! And then every time I look at them I'm that much more inspired. As you gain skill, you think, "Maybe I'll get to that level." When I'm in a slump, I come in here and look at the collection. When I leave, I'm full of ideas. I'm beside myself! I don't have enough time. Before I come, I'm bored and I don't know what to do. Then I go home and I just want to work, work, work, all through the night.

When you look at the size of the basket weaving, and how small and consistent it is. It's amazing. I know it's difficult. I'll go out and spend a whole summer collecting spruce root, and I won't be able to weave a decent-sized basket because I don't have enough root of one size. If you change up the size of your weaving material just a little bit, it jumps right out at you in the basket. You look at those old baskets, and they are incredible. They are so neat.

Making objects, learning and challenging myself, it fills something in me (fig. 7.89). This is why I keep doing it. It just feels important, so I do it. A lot of people say they want to learn how to make something, but they can't even show up for a full hour class. Unfortunately, this work is so time consuming that people don't make time for it. There is this whole outside world competing for our time and attention and telling us what's important. We get caught up in who has the latest iPhone, or who has more bling. It's hard. I know that when people fit this sort of study into their lives, they feel really good about it. I see that when I take people out to sit on the beach, feel the sun, and clean a puffin. This seems gross in everyday life, but when you are out there, on the beach, it's so different. It's neat to be able to share that experience with people. In that moment, they can experience our culture.

I encourage more people to come and look at the collections, I don't think you can look at them and not be affected. Especially if you are from Kodiak.

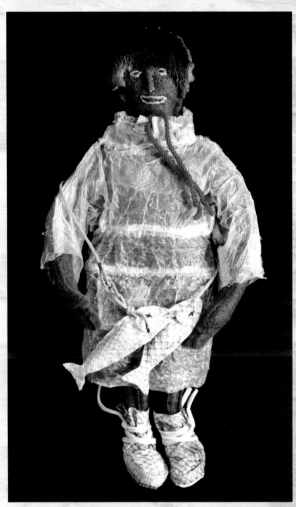

Figure 7.89. A young male figure wearing a seal gut parka and fish skin boots, by Coral Chernoff, AM701:1. Purchased with support from the Rasmuson Foundation.

Chapter Seven Notes

1. Story collected by Alphonse Pinart in Karluk, February 1872, and translated by Dominique Desson (1995:57–58). Bracketed comments are Desson's notes.

2. Concentric-circle motifs are also found on more ancient objects from southwestern Kodiak, including large coal labrets from Karluk Lagoon and Uyak Bay (Steffian 1992b:157). These pieces, which date to the Kachemak tradition, suggest that historically recorded concepts of the Alutiiq universe are at least 1,200 years old.

3. Community house or *qasgiq* in the Alutiiq language.

4. Black (1977:105) identifies *tolkusha* as a paste made from pulverized berries and dried root mixed with oil often eaten on special occasions. Alutiiq people call this food *akutaq*.

References

Alaska Department of Commerce, Community, and Economic Development
    2013 Community Database Online. Community Information Karluk, accessed November 2013. http://commerce.alaska.gov/cra/DCRAExternal/community/Details/2d985aa9-e05e-4dff-8e44-e14973dc3f9b.

Alaska Department of Fish and Game
    1985 *Southwest Region Vol. II: Human Use of Fish and Wildlife*. State of Alaska, Department of Fish and Game, Division of Habitat, Juneau.

Alpiak, Nick
    1983 Notes from Karluk. In *The Cama-i Book*, edited by Ann Vick, pp. 114–116. Anchor Books, Garden City, New York.

Alutiiq Museum and Archaeological Repository
    2011 Producing Petroglyphs. *Alutiiq Museum Bulletin* 15(3):1.
    2013 *The Wild Foods Cookbook*. Alutiiq Museum and Archaeological Repository, Kodiak.

Amorosi, Thomas
    1986 First Preliminary Report of an Archaeofauna from Uyak Bay and Karluk, Kodiak Island, AK. Report on file, Hunter Bioarchaeology Facility, Hunter College, Department of Anthropology, New York, New York.
    1987 The Karluk and Uyak Archaeofaunas: An Approach Towards the Paleoeconomy of Kodiak Island, Alaska. Paper presented at the 52nd Annual Meeting of the Society for American Archaeology, Toronto.

Anderson, Clara, and Amber Panamarioff
    2010 My Life as a Teenager. *Iluani* 23–25.

Anichtchenko, Evguenia
    2012 Open Skin Boats of the Aleutians, Kodiak Island, and Prince William Sound. *Études/Inuit/Studies* 36(1):157–181.

Arndt, Katherine
    2002 Russian Orthodox Church Histories of Southern Alaska Church Records Search. Compiled for the Alutiiq Museum and Archaeological Repository, Kodiak.

Balisle, Emily

2010 Sophie Kaltelnikoff Shepherd. *Iluani* 44–52.

Bancroft, Hubert Howe

1886 *History of Alaska, 1730–1885*. A. L. Brancroft and Company, San Francisco.

Barnaby, Joseph T.

1944 Fluctuations in Abundance of Red Salmon, *Oncorhynchus nerka* (Walbum), of the Karluk River, Alaska. *Fisheries Bulletin of the US Fish and Wildlife Service* 39(50):237–295.

Barnes, V. G., and R. B. Smith

1995 Brown Bear Density Estimation and Population Monitoring on Southwest Kodiak Island, Alaska. Manuscript on file, Alaska Department of Fish and Game, Kodiak.

Barsh, Russell

1985 Karluk River Study. Kodiak Area Native Association, Kodiak.

Bean, Tarleton H.

1890 *Report on the Salmon and Salmon Rivers of Alaska*. Government Printing Office, Washington, DC.

Birket-Smith, Kaj

1941 Early Collections from the Pacific Eskimo. *Nationalmuseets Skrifter Ethografisk Raekke* 1:121–163.
1953 The Chugach Eskimo. *Nationalmuseets Skrifter, Etnografisk Raekke, VI*. National Museum of Denmark, Copenhagen.

Black, Lydia T.

1991 *Glory Remembered: Wooden Headgear of Alaska Sea Hunters*. Alaska State Museum, Juneau.
1994 Deciphering Aleut/Koniag Iconography. In *Anthropology of the North Pacific Rim*, edited by W. W. Fitzhugh and V. Chaussonnet, pp. 133–146. Smithsonian Institution Press, Washington, DC.
2003 *Aleut Art*. Aleutian Pribilof Island Association, Anchorage.
2004a *Russians in Alaska: 1732–1867*. University of Alaska Press, Fairbanks.
2004b Warriors of Kodiak: Military Traditions of Kodiak Islanders. *Arctic Anthropology* 41(2):140-152.

Black, Lydia T., translator

1977 The Konyag (the inhabitants of the island of Kodiak) by Iosaf [Bolotov] (1794–1799) and by Gideon (1804–1807). *Arctic Anthropology* 14(2):79–108.
1981 Untitled Interveiw with Starik J. W. Chechenev. Manuscript on file, P-K 49, Box 1, Folder 12, Pinart Collection, Bancroft Library, University of California, Berkeley.
1990 Vasilii Ivanovich Kashevaroff manuscript from 1833, on file, Alutiiq Museum and Archaeological Repository Library, Kodiak.

Black, Lydia T., Donald W. Clark, and Katherine Arndt

ca. 2003 Karluk. In Crying in the Waves: A History of Kodiak Villages. Unpublished manuscript chapter on file, Alutiiq Museum and Archaeological Repository Library, Kodiak.

Campbell, Archibald

1816 *A Voyage Round the World from 1806 to 1812.* Archibald Constable Company, London.

Capps, Steven R.

1937 Kodiak and Vicinity Alaska. In *Mineral Resources of Alaska*, USGS Bulletin 868–B, pp. 93–134. US Printing Office, Washington, DC.

Carrlee, Ellen
2011 Karluk One Conservation Survey. Report on file AM193, Alutiiq Museum and Archaeological Repository, Kodiak.

Case, David
2012 *Alaska Natives and American Laws*. University of Alaska Press, Fairbanks.

Charliaga, Leonard
1980 Frieda Reft, A Very Interesting Lady. *Elwani* 9:86–88.

Christensen, Clyda
2010 Games. Alutiiq Museum and Archaeological Repository, Alutiiq Museum. Electronic document, http://alutiiqmuseum.org/language-studies/experience-alutiiq/alutiiq-recordings.html?pid=60andsid=107:Clyda-Christiansen-Games-mov, accessed October 2013.

Clark, Donald W.
1964 Incised Figurine Tablets from Kodiak, Alaska. *Arctic Anthropology* 2(1):118–134.
1966a Two Late Prehistoric Pottery-bearing Sites on Kodiak Island, Alaska. *Arctic Anthropology* 3(2):157–184.
1966b Perspectives in the Prehistory of Kodiak Island, Alaska. *American Antiquity* 31(3):358–371.
1970a The Late Kachemak Tradition at Three Saints and Crag Point, Kodiak Island, Alaska. *Arctic Anthropology* 6(2):73–111.
1970b Petroglyphs on Afognak Island, Kodiak Group, Alaska. *Anthropological Papers of the University of Alaska* 15(1):12–17.
1974 *Koniag Prehistory*. Tubinger Monographien zur Urgeschichte, Band 1. Verlag W. Kohlhammer, Stuttgart.
1979 *Ocean Bay: An Early North Pacific Maritime Culture*. Archaeological Survey of Canada, Mercury Series, Paper 86. National Museum of Man, Ottawa.
1982 An Example of Technological Change in Prehistory: The Origins of a Regional Ground Slate Industry in South-Central Coastal Alaska. *Arctic Anthropology* 19(1):103–125.
1984 Prehistory of the Pacific Eskimo Region. In *Arctic*, edited by David Damas, pp. 136–148. *Handbook of American Indians*, Vol. 5, W. C. Sturtevant, general editor, Smithsonian Institution, Washington, DC.
1986 Archaeological and Historic Evidence for an 18th-Century "Blip" in the Distribution of the Northern Fur Seal at Kodiak Island, Alaska. *Arctic* 39:39–42.
1997 *The Early Kachemak Phase on Kodiak Island at Old Kiavak*. Archaeological Survey of Canada, Mercury Series, Paper 155. Canadian Museum of Civilization, Hull.
1998 Kodiak Island the Later Cultures. *Arctic Anthropology* 35(1):172–186.
2008 Five Seasons with the Late Kachemak. *Alaska Journal of Anthropology* 6 (1and2):185–197.
2010 Ground Squirrels: The Mysterious Rodent of Kodiak. *Arctic Anthropology* 47(2):59–68.

Clark, Gerald H.
1977 *Archaeology on the Alaska Peninsula: The Coast of Shelikof Strait, 1963–1965*. University of Oregon Anthropological Papers, No. 13. Museum of Natural and Cultural History, Eugene.

Clifford, James
2004 Looking Several Ways: Anthropology and Native Heritage in Alaska. *Current Anthropology* 45(1):5–30.

Counceller, April G. L.
2010 *Niugneliyukut* (We Are Making New Words): A Community Philosophy of Language Revitalization. PhD dissertation, University of Alaska, Fairbanks.

Coxe, William

1780 *Account of the Russian Discoveries between Asia and America to Which Are Added the Conquest of Siberia and the History of the Transactions and Commerce Between Russia and China.* T. Caddel, London.

Coyle, Darla

1983 My Favorite Food is Alutiiq Ice Cream. *Elwani* 2:112–115.

Crowell, Aron L.

1986 An Archaeological Survey of Uyak Bay, Kodiak Island, Alaska. Manuscript on file, Alaska Office of History and Archaeology, Anchorage.

1992 Precontact Koniag Ceremonialism on Kodiak Island and the Alaska Peninsula: Evidence from the Fisher Collection. *Arctic Anthropology* 29(1):18–37.

1994 Koniag Eskimo Poisoned-Dart Whaling. In *Anthropology of the North Pacific Rim*, edited by W. W. Fitzhugh and V. Chaussonnet, pp. 217–242. Smithsonian Institution Press, Washington, DC.

1997 *Archaeology and the Capitalist World System: A Study from Russian America.* Plenum Press, New York.

2004 Terms of Engagement: The Collaborative Representation of Alutiiq Identity. *Études/Inuit/Studies* 28(1):9–35.

Crowell, Aron L., and April G. Laktonen

2001 *Súgucihpet*: Our Way of Living. In *Looking Both Ways: Heritage and Identity of the Alutiiq People*, edited by A. L. Crowell, A. F. Steffian, and G. L. Pullar, pp. 137–187. University of Alaska Press, Fairbanks.

Crowell, Aron L., and Jeff Leer

2001 *Ukgwepet:* "Our Beliefs": Alutiiq Spiritual Life and Traditions. In *Looking Both Ways: Heritage and Identity of the Alutiiq People*, edited by A. L. Crowell, A. F. Steffian, and G. L. Pullar, pp. 189–221. University of Alaska Press, Fairbanks.

Crowell, Aron L., and Sonja Lührmann

2001 Alutiiq Culture: Views from Archaeology, Anthropology, and History. In *Looking Both Ways: Heritage and Identity of the Alutiiq People*, edited by A. L. Crowell, A. F. Steffian, and G. L. Pullar, pp. 21–71. University of Alaska Press, Fairbanks.

Crowell, Aron L., Amy F. Steffian, and Gordon L. Pullar

2001 *Looking Both Ways: Heritage and Identity of the Alutiiq People.* University of Alaska Press, Fairbanks.

Dall, William W.

1884 On Masks, Labrets, and Certain Aboriginal Customs, with an Inquiry into the Bearing of their Geographical Distribution. *Third Annual Report of the Bureau of American Ethnology* (1881–1882), pp. 67–203. Smithsonian Institution, Washington, DC.

Davis, Lucille

1997a Notes on comments by Lucille Davis, originally from Karluk. Taken by Cindy Pennington, Maria Williams, Aron Crowell at the Arctic Studies Center, Anchorage, August 11, 1997. Alutiiq Museum Library, Kodiak.

1997b Looking Both Ways Elders conference video interview. Transcribed by Emma Brown for the Arctic Studies Center. Alutiiq Museum and Archaeological Repository Library, Kodiak.

2000 Lucille Davis, Alutiiq Elder. In *Gathering Native Alaskan Music and Words*, recorded by Kristi Olson, track 10. Surreal Studios/Nightwork Records, Anchorage, Alaska.

Davis, Nancy Yaw

1971 The Effects of the 1964 Alaska Earthquake, Tsunami, and Resettlement on Two Koniag Eskimo Villages. PhD dissertation, University of Washington, Seattle.

1979 Western Gulf of Alaska Petroleum Development Scenarios: Kodiak Native Sociocultural Impacts. Prepared for Mineral Management Service, Alaska Outer Continental Shelf Region Leasing and Environmental Office Social and Economic Studies Program. Technical Report 41. Cultural Dynamics Inc., Anchorage.

1986 A Sociocultural Description of Small Communities in the Kodiak-Shumigan Region. Prepared for Mineral Management Service, Alaska Outer Continental Shelf Region Leasing and Environmental Office Social and Economic Studies Program. Technical Report 121. Cultural Dynamics Inc., Anchorage.

Davydov, Gavriil Ivanovich

1977 *Two Voyages to Russian America, 1802–1807*. Translated by Colin Bearne and edited by Richard A. Pierce. Limestone Press, Kingston, Ontario.

Demidoff, Ralph

1962 *Ar'ursulek*—Whaler Story. Interview by Irene Reed. Transcribed in Alutiiq by Jeff Leer, Alaska Native Language Center, University of Alaska, Fairbanks.

Desson, Dominique

1995 Masked Rituals of the Kodiak Archipelago. PhD dissertation, University of Alaska, Fairbanks.

Dizney, Clarence

1952 Letter to Charles Lucier, September 7, 1952, Box 3, Folder 53. Charles V. Lucier Papers, 1903–2009, University of Alaska Anchorage, Consortium Library, Archives and Special Collections Department, Anchorage.

Dodge, Harry B., III

2004 *Kodiak Island and Its Bears*. Great Northwest Publishing, Anchorage.

Donta, Christopher L.

1988 Archaeological Indications of Evolving Social Complexity on Kodiak Island, Alaska. Masters thesis, Bryn Mawr College, Bryn Mawr, Pennsylvania.

1992 Incised Slate Images and the Development of Social and Political Complexity in South Alaska. In *Ancient Images, Ancient Thought: The Archaeology of Ideology*, edited by A. Sean Goldsmith, Sandra Garvie, David Selin, and Jeanette Smith, pp. 11–18. University of Calgary, Calgary.

1993 Koniag Ceremonialism. PhD dissertation, Department of Anthropology, Bryn Mawr College, Bryn Mawr, PA.

1994 Continuity and Function in the Ceremonial Material Culture of the Koniag Eskimo. In *Reckoning with the Dead: The Larsen Bay Repatriation and the Smithsonian Institution*, edited by Tamara L. Bray and Thomas W. Killion, pp. 122–136. Smithsonian Institution, Washington, DC.

Drabek, Alisha S.

2012 *Liitukut Sugpiat'stun* (We Are Learning to Be Real People): Exploring Kodiak Alutiiq Literature Through Core Values. PhD dissertation, University of Alaska, Fairbanks.

Dumond, Donald E.

1971 *A Summary of Archaeology in the Katmai Region*, Southwestern Alaska. University of Oregon Anthropological Papers, No. 2. Museum of Natural and Cultural History, Eugene.

1981 *Archaeology on the Alaska Peninsula: The Naknek Region, 1960–1975*. University of Oregon Anthropological Papers, No. 21. Museum of Natural and Cultural History, Eugene.

1988 The Alaska Peninsula as Super Highway: A Comment. In *The Late Prehistoric Development of Alaska's Native People*, edited by Robert D. Shaw, Roger K. Harritt, and Don E. Dumond, pp. 379–388. Alaska Anthropological Association, Anchorage.

2005 *A Naknek Chronicle. Ten Thousand Years in a Land of Lakes and Rivers and Mountains of Fire*. US Department of the Interior, National Park Service, Katmai National Park and Preserve, King Salmon, Alaska.

Egeland, G. M., R. Ponce, R. Knecht, N. S. Bloom, J. Fair, and J. P. Middaugh

1999 Trace Metals in Ancient Hair from the Karluk Archaeological Site, Kodiak, Alaska. *International Journal of Circumpolar Health*. January 58(1):52–6.

Emmons, George Thornton

1991 *The Tlingit Indians*. University of Washington Press, Seattle.

Etnier, Michael

2011 A Faunal Assemblage from Awa'uq (Refuge Rock): A Unique Record from the Kodiak Archipelago. *Alaska Journal of Anthropology* 9(2):55–64.

Fair, Susie

2006 *Alaska Native Art: Tradition, Innovation, Continuity*. University of Alaska Press, Fairbanks.

Farris, David W.

2009 Construction and Evolution of the Kodiak Talkeetna Arc Crustal Section, Southern Alaska. In *Crustal Cross Sections from the Western North American Cordillera and Elsewhere: Implications for Tectonic and Petrologic Processes*, edited by R. B. Miller and A. W. Snoke, pp. 69–96. Geological Society of America, Boulder.

Feuerstein, Brandt

1988 An Analysis of Kodiak Human Skeletal Remains and Burial Patterns from Bryn Mawr College Excavations 1985–1987. Senior Honors Thesis, Haverford College.

Fienup-Riordan, Ann

1996 *The Living Tradition of Yup'ik Masks*. University of Washington Press, Seattle.

2003 *Yuungnaqpiallerput The Way We Genuinely Live, Masterworks of Yup'ik Science and Survival*. University of Washington Press, Seattle.

Finney, Bruce I.

1998 Long-Term Variability of Alaskan Sockeye Salmon Abundance Determined by Analysis of Sediment Cores. *NPAFC Bulletin* 1:388–395.

Finney, B., I. Gregory-Eaves, M. S. V. Douglas, and J. P. Smol

2000 Impacts of Climatic Change and Fishing on Pacific Salmon Abundance over the Past 300 Years. *Science* 290:795–799.

Finney, B., I. Gregory-Eaves, J. Sweetman, M. S. V. Douglas, and J. P. Smol
  2002 Fisheries Productivity in the Northeastern Pacific Ocean over the Past 2,200 Years. *Nature* 416:729–733.

Fisher, W. J.
  1899 Notes accompanying collection of useful plants made by W. J. Fisher at Kodiak, in 1899. Vol. 1, Entries 1–48. SIA Acc. 12–038. Smithsonian Institution Archives, Washington, DC.

Fitzhugh, J. Benjamin
  1995 Clams and the Kachemak: Seasonal Dating and Implications of Seasonal Shellfish Use on Kodiak Island, Alaska. *Research in Economic Anthropology* 16:129–176.
  2003 *The Evolution of Complex Hunter-Gatherers: Archaeological Evidence from the North Pacific*. Kluwer Academic, New York.
  2004 Colonizing the Kodiak Archipelago: Trends in Raw Material Use and Lithic Technologies at the Tanginak Spring Site. *Arctic Anthropology* 41(1):14–40.

Fitzhugh, William W., and Aron Crowell, eds.
  1988 *Crossroads of Continents: Cultures of Siberia and Alaska*. Smithsonian Institution Press, Washington, DC.

Fitzhugh, William W., and Susan A. Kaplan
  1982 *Inua Spirit World of the Bering Sea Eskimo*. Smithsonian Institution Press, Washington, DC.

Foster, Catherine
  2009 Human Dietary Response to Resource Abundance and Climate Change. PhD dissertation, University of Washington, Seattle.

Gammon, Clive
  1984 Welcome to the Chocolate Factory. *Sports Illustrated*, September 17:34–40.

Gard, Richard and Richard Lee Bottorff
  2014 *A History of Sockeye Salmon Research, Karluk River, Alaska, 1880-2010*. US Department of Commerce, NOAA Technical Memorandom NMFS-F/SPO-125.

Gideon, Hiermonk
  1989 *The Round the World Voyage of Hiermonk Gideon*. Translated by Lydia Black and edited by Richard A. Pierce. Limestone Press, Kingston, Ontario.

Golder, F. A.
  1903a Tales from Kodiak Island. *The Journal of American Folklore* 16(60):16–31.
  1903b Tales from Kodiak Island II. *The Journal of American Folklore* 16(61):85–103.
  1907 A Kadiak Island Story: The White-Faced Bear. *The Journal of American Folklore* 20(79):296–299.
  1909 Eskimo and Aleut Stories from Alaska. *The Journal of American Folklore* 22(83):10–24.

Golovnin, Pavel Nicholaevich
  1979 *A Review of the Russian Colonies in North America*. Oregon Historical Society, Portland.

Goode, George Brown
  1887 *The Fisheries and Fishery Industries of the United States*. Section III, The Fishing Grounds of North America. United States Commission of Fish and Fisheries, Government Printing Office, Washington, DC.

Graburn, Nelson, H. H. Molly Lee, and Jean-loup Rousselot
  1996 *Catalog Raisonné of the Alaska Commercial Company Collection: Phoebe Hearst Museum of Anthropology*. University of California Publications in Anthropology, University of California Press, Berkeley.

Grantham, Anjuli
    2011 Fishing at Karluk: Nature, Technology and the Creation of the Karluk Reservation in Territorial Alaska. Masters thesis, University of South Carolina.

Griggs, Robert F.
    1921 The Valley of Ten Thousand Smokes: Our Greatest National Monument. *National Geographic* XL:219–292.

Haakanson, Sven D., and Amy F. Steffian
    2004 The Alutiiq Museum's Guidelines for the Spiritual Care of Artifacts. In *Stewards of the Sacred*, edited by Lawrence E. Sullivan and Alison Edwards, pp. 155–166. American Association of Museums, Washington, DC.

Haakanson, Sven D., and Amy F. Steffian, eds.
    2009 *Giinaquq—Like A Face, Sugpiaq Masks of the Kodiak Archipelago*. University of Alaska Press, Fairbanks.

Haakanson, Sven D., Amy F. Steffian, Jill H. H. Lipka, and Patrick G. Saltonstall
    2012 The Archaeology of Cape Alitak, Survey Investigations 2010. Technical Report Submitted to Akhiok-Kaguyak Inc. by the Alutiiq Museum, Kodiak.

Haakanson, Sven, Sr.
    1987 *Adaq'wy* Project Interview with Laurie Mulcahy, Kodiak Area Native Association, October 6. AM214:14. Alutiiq Museum and Archaeological Repository Archives, Kodiak.

Harvey, Lola
    1991 *Derevnia's Daughters: Saga of an Alaskan Village*. Sunflower University Press, Manhattan, Kansas.

Hausler, Philomena
    ca. 1990 Alutiiq terms for sod house parts. Illustration and notes on file, Alutiiq Museum and Archaeological Repository Library, Kodiak.

Heizer, Robert F.
    1943 Aconite Poison Whaling in Asia and America: An Aleutian Transfer to the New World. *Bureau of American Ethnology Bulletin* 133:415–468.
    1949 Pottery from the Southern Eskimo Region. *Proceedings of the American Philosophical Society* 93(1):48–56.
    1952 Notes on Koniag Material Culture. *Anthropological Papers of the University of Alaska* 1(1):11–24.
    1956 *Archaeology of the Uyak Site, Kodiak Island, Alaska*. University of California Press, Berkeley.

Henn, Winfield
    1978 *Archaeology on the Alaska Peninsula: The Ugashik Drainage, 1973–1975*. University of Oregon Anthropological Papers, No. 14. Museum of Natural and Cultural History, Eugene.

Heusser, Calvin J.
    1960 *Late-Pleistocene Environments of North Pacific North America*. American Geographical Society Special Publication No. 35. New York, American Geographical Society.

Hoffman, Brian W.
    2009 *2000 Years on the King Salmon River: An Archaeological Report for UGA-052*. Occasional Papers in Alaskan Field Archaeology, No. 2. US Bureau of Indian Affairs, Alaska Region, Branch of Regional Archeology, Anchorage.

Holmberg, Heinrich, J.

1985 *Holmberg's Ethnographic Sketches*. Translated by Marvin W. Falk and edited by Fritz Jaensch. University of Alaska Press, Fairbanks.

Hrdlička, Aleš

1944 *The Anthropology of Kodiak Island*. Wistar Institute, Philadelphia.

1945 *The Aleutian and Commander Islands and Their Inhabitants*. Wistar Institute, Philadelphia.

Huggins, Eli Lundy

1981 *Kodiak and Afognak Life 1868 1870*. Edited by Richard A. Pierce. Limestone Press, Kingston, Ontario.

Hunt, Dolores Cecelia

2000 The Ethnography of Alaska Clothing: Comparative Analysis of the Smithsonian's Fisher Collection. Masters thesis, San Francisco State University, San Francisco.

Jackson, Louise M.

1991 Nineteenth-Century British Ceramics: A Key to Cultural Dynamics in Southwestern Alaska. PhD dissertation, University of California, Los Angeles.

Jackson, Sheldon

1894 *Report on Introduction of Domesticated Reindeer into Alaska*. Reprint of Senate Executive Document 70, United States Department of Education, Washington, DC.

Johnson, Katherine

2002 *Buried Dreams: The Rise and Fall of the a Clam Cannery on the Katmai Coast*. National Park Service, Anchorage.

Jordan, Richard H.

1983 Karluk—Preliminary Report of the 1983 Bryn Mawr College Archaeological Investigations on Kodiak Island, Alaska. Bryn Mawr College, Department of Anthropology, Bryn Mawr, PA.

1986 Archaeological Investigations in Western Kodiak Island: A Progress Report. Bryn Mawr College, Department of Anthropology, Bryn Mawr, PA.

1987 The Kodiak Archaeological Project: 1987 Report of Activities. Bryn Mawr College, Department of Anthropology, Bryn Mawr, PA.

1992 A Maritime Paleoarctic Assemblage from Crag Point, Kodiak Island, Alaska. *Anthropological Papers of the University of Alaska* 24(1–2):127–140.

1994 *Qasqiluteng*: Feasting and Ceremonialism Among the Traditional Koniag of Kodiak Island. In *Anthropology of the North Pacific Rim*, edited by W. W. Fitzhugh and V. Chaussonnet, pp. 147–173. Smithsonian Institution Press, Washington, DC.

Jordan, Richard H., and Richard A. Knecht.

1988 Archaeological Research on Western Kodiak Island, Alaska: The Development of Koniag Culture. In *The Late Prehistoric Development of Alaska's Native People*, edited by Robert D. Shaw, Roger K. Harritt, and Don E. Dumond, pp. 356–453. Aurora Monograph Series, 4. Alaska Anthropological Association, Anchorage.

Kachadoorian, Reuben, and George Plafker

1967 Effects of the Earthquake of March 27, 1964, on the Communities of Kodiak and Nearby Islands. *Geological Survey Professional Paper* 542-F. United States Printing Office, Washington, DC.

Karlstrom, Thor N. V.

 1969 Regional Setting and Geology. In *The Kodiak Island Refugium: Its Geology, Flora, Fauna, and History*, edited by T. N. V. Karlstrom and G. E. Ball, pp. 20–55. Boreal Institute, University of Alberta, Calgary.

Kelly, Joe

 1998 Alutiiq terms given by Larry Matfay, March 12. Interview transcript on file, Alutiiq Museum and Archaeological Repository Library, Kodiak.

Kelly, Paul, and Kevin Carmody

 1991 *From Little Things Big Things Grow*. Warner/Chappell Music, Inc., Los Angeles.

Khlebnikov, K. T.

 1994 *Notes on Russian America. Parts II—V: Kadiak, Unalashka, Atkha, the Pribylovs*. Translated by Marina Ramsay and edited by Richard Pierce. Limestone Press, Kingston, Ontario.

Knagin, Julie

 2013 Video Interview. Alutiiq Wild Foods Project, AM723. Alutiiq Museum and Archaeological Repository, Kodiak.

Knecht, Richard A.

 1994 Archaeology and Alutiiq cultural identity on Kodiak Island. *Society for American Archaeology Bulletin* 12(5):8–10.

 1995 The Late Prehistory of the Alutiiq People: Culture Change on the Kodiak Archipelago from 1200–1750 AD. PhD dissertation, Bryn Mawr College, Bryn Mawr, PA.

 2000 Archaeology and Alutiiq Cultural Identity on Kodiak Island. In *Working Together: Native Americans and Archaeologists*, edited by K. E. Dongoske, M. Aldenderfer, and K. Doehner, pp. 147–154. Society for American Archaeology, Washington, DC.

Knecht, Richard A., and Richard H. Jordan

 1985 *Nunakakhnak*: A Historic Period Koniag Village in Karluk, Kodiak Island, Alaska. *Arctic Anthropology* 22(2):17–35.

Knecht, Richard A., S. Haakanson, and S. Dickson

 2002 *Awa'uq*: Discovery and Excavation of an Eighteenth-Century Alutiiq Refuge Rock in the Kodiak Archipelago. In *To the Aleutians and Beyond: The Anthropology of William S. Laughlin*, edited by Bruno Frohlich, Albert S. Harper, and Rolf Gilberg, pp. 177–191. Publications of the National Museum Ethnographical Series, Vol. 20. Department of Ethnography, National Museum of Denmark, Copenhagen.

Kodiak Alutiiq/Sugpiaq Repatriation Commission

 2008 Kodiak Alutiiq/Sugpiaq Repatriation Commission Manual. Alutiiq Museum, Kodiak.

Kodiak Island Borough

 1978 Kodiak Island Borough Resolution Number 78-64-R. Kodiak Island Borough, Kodiak.

Kopperl, Robert E.

 2003 Cultural Complexity and Resource Intensification on Kodiak Island, Alaska. PhD dissertation, University of Washington, Seattle.

Korsun, Sergei

 2012 *The Alutiit/Sugpiat: A Catalog of the Collections of the Kunstkamera*. University of Alaska Press, Fairbanks.

Krech, Shepard
      1989 *A Victorian Earl in the Arctic*. University of Washington Press, Seattle.

de Laguna, Frederica
      1939 A Pottery Vessel from Kodiak Island, Alaska. *American Antiquity* 4:334–343.
      1956 *Chugach Prehistory*. University of Washington Press, Seattle.

Langsdorff, Georg Heinrich
      1993 *Remarks and Observations on a Voyage Around the World from 1803–1807*. Translated and annotated by Victoria J. Moessner and edited by Richard A. Pierce. Limestone Press, Kingston, Ontario.

Lantis, Margaret
      1938 The Mythology of Kodiak Island, Alaska. *American Journal of Folk-lore* 51(200):123–172.

Lee, Molly
      1981 Pacific Eskimo Spruce Root Baskets. *American Indian Art Magazine* 6(2):66–73.
      2006 "If It's Not a Tlingit Basket, Then What is It?": Toward The Definition of an Alutiiq Twined Spruce Root Basket Type. *Arctic Anthropology* 43(2):164–171.

Lee, Richard B., and Irven DeVore
      1979 *Man the Hunter*. Aldine Publishing Company, New York.

Leer, Jeff
      1976 *A Conversational Dictionary of Kodiak Alutiiq*. Alaska Native Language Center, University of Alaska, Fairbanks.

Leer, Jeff, and Sven D. Haakanson
      2009 Appendix: Mask Songs. In *Giinaquq—Like A Face, Sugpiaq Masks of the Kodiak Archipelago*, edited by Sven D. Haakanson and Amy F. Steffian, pp. 177–179. University of Alaska Press, Fairbanks.

Lepola, Marcus
      2013 Alutiiq Bow. Northern Wilderness Skills and Traditions, electronic document, http://northernwildernessskills.blogspot.com/, accessed October 2013.

Liapunova, Roza G.
      1994 Eskimo Masks from Kodiak Island in the Collections of the Peter the Great Museum of Anthropology and Ethnography in St. Petersburg. In *Anthropology of the North Pacific Rim*, edited by W. W. Fitzhugh and V. Chaussonnet, pp. 175–203. Smithsonian Institution Press, Washington, DC.

Lisianski, Uri
      1814 *A Voyage Round the World, 1803–1806*. N. Isreal Amsterdam and Da Capo Press, New York.

Lobdell, John Edward
      1980 Prehistoric Human Populations and Resource Utilization in Kachemak Bay, Gulf of Alaska. PhD dissertation, University of Tennessee, Knoxville.
      1988 Harris Lines: Markers of Nutritional Stress in Late Prehistoric and Contact Period Eskimo Post Cranial Remains. In *The Late Prehistoric Development of Alaska's Native People*, edited by Robert D. Shaw, Roger K. Harritt, and Don E. Dumond. Aurora IV:47–55. Alaska Anthropological Association, Anchorage.

Luehrmann, Sonja
      2008 *Alutiiq Villages under Russian and U.S. Rule*. University of Alaska Press, Fairbanks.

Margaris, Amy V.

2009 The Mechanical Properties of Marine and Terrestrial Skeletal Materials with Implications for the Study of Forager Technologies. *Ethnoarchaeology: Journal of Archaeological, Ethnographic and Experimental Studies* 1(2):163–183.

Maschner, H., B. Finey, J. Jordan, N. Misarti, A. Tetwes, and G. Knudsen

2009 Did the North Pacific Ecosystem Collapse in AD 1250? In *The Northern World, AD 900–1400*, edited by H. D. G. Maschner, O. K. Mason, and R. McGhee, pp. 3–49. University of Utah Press, Salt Lake City.

Mason, Owen K., William J. Neal, and Orrin H. Pilkey

1997 *Living with the Coast of Alaska*. Duke University Press, Durham, NC.

Matfay, Larry

1990 Larry Matfay Interview about Barabaras. AM300. Alutiiq Museum and Archaeological Repository Archives, Kodiak.

1992 Interview with Joanne Mulcahy and Kodiak High School Alutiiq Studies Class, April 29, 1992. AM298. Alutiiq Museum and Archaeological Repository Archives, Kodiak.

Matfay, Larry, and Martha Matfay

1987 *Adaq'wy* Project Interview with Laurie Mulcahy, Kodiak Area Native Association, May 11. AM214-35. Alutiiq Museum and Archaeological Repository Archives, Kodiak.

McKeown, Martha Ferguson

1948 *The Trail Led North, Mont Hawthorne's Story*. MacMillan Company, New York.

Merck, Carl Heinrich

1980 *Siberia and Northwestern America 1788–1792*. Translated by Fritz Jaensch and edited by Richard A. Pierce. Limestone Press, Kingston, Ontario.

Milan, Frederick A.

1952 Letter to Charles Lucier, May 27. Box 9, Folder 9. Charles V. Lucier Papers, 1903–2009, University of Alaska Anchorage, Consortium Library, Archives and Special Collections Department, Anchorage.

1953 Archaeological Investigations at Karluk on Kodiak Island. Report on file, Alutiiq Museum, Kodiak.

1974 Archaeological Investigations at Karluk on Kodiak Island. In *Contributions to the Later Prehistory of Kodiak Island, Alaska*, edited by Donald W. Clark, pp. 81–85. Archaeological Survey of Canada, Mercury Series, Paper 20. National Museum of Man, Ottawa.

Minc, L.

1986 Scarcity and Survival: The Role of Oral Tradition in Mediating Subsistence Crises. *Journal of Anthropological Archaeology* 5:39–113.

Misarti, Nicole

2007 Six Thousand Years of Change in the Northeast Pacific: An Interdisciplinary View of Maritime Ecosystems. PhD dissertation, University of Alaska Fairbanks, Fairbanks.

Misarti, Nicole, B. Finney, J. Jordan, H. Maschner, J. Addison, M. Shapley, and J. Beget

2012 Early Deglaciation and Coastal Migration of First Americans along the North Pacific Rim. *Quaternary Science Review* 48(1–6).

Mishler, Craig

1997 *Aurcaq*: Interruption, Distraction, and Reversal in an Alutiiq Men's Dart Game. *American Journal of Folklore* 110(436):189–202.

2001 *Black Ducks and Salmon Bellies: An Ethnography of Old Harbor and Ouzinkie, Alaska.* Donning Company Publishers, Virginia Beach, VA.

Mishler, Craig, and Rachel Mason

1996 Alutiiq Vikings: Kinship and Fishing in Old Harbor, Alaska. *Human Organization* 55(3):263–269.

Morrison, Aubrey

2009 Analysis of Faunal Remains from KAR-035. In *Karluk Lake Archaeology: 2008 and 2009 Survey Results.* Interim Project Report prepared for the US Fish and Wildlife Service Alaska Office of Visitors Services and Communication, and the Kodiak National Wildlife Refuge, edited by Patrick Saltonstall and Amy Steffian, pp. 128–131. Alutiiq Museum, Kodiak.

Moser, Jefferson F.

1899 *The Salmon and Salmon Fisheries of Alaska, Report of the Operations of the United States Fish Commission Steamer Albatross for the Year Ending June 30, 1898.* Government Printing Office, Washington, DC.

1902 Salmon Investigations of the Steamer Albatross in the Summer of 1900. In *Bulletin of the United States Fish Commission*, Volume XXI for 1901. Government Printing Office, Washington, DC.

Moss, Madonna L., and Jon M. Erlandson

1992 Forts, Refuge Rocks, and Defensive Sites: The Antiquity of Warfare Along the North Pacific Coast of North America. *Arctic Anthropology* 29(2):73–90.

Mulcahy, Joanne B.

2001 *Birth and Rebirth on an Alaskan Island.* University of Georgia Press, Athens.

Mulcahy, Laurie

1986 *Adaq'wy*—The Time Has Come. Excerpts from Interviews with Elders of the Kodiak Island Area. Kodiak Area Native Association, Kodiak.

2003 The Native Village of Old Harbor and Its Traditional Government. In *Black Ducks and Salmon Bellies: An Ethnography of Old Harbor and Ouzinkie, Alaska*, edited by Craig Mishler, pp. 80–89. Donning Company Publishers, Virginia Beach, VA.

National Register of Historic Places

1980 Russian Orthodox Church Buildings and Sites in Alaska. Item 7, pp. 20–21. National Register of Historic Places Inventory—Nomination Form. US Department of the Interior, National Park Service, Washington, DC.

Naumoff, Alfred

1978 I'm Too Much of a Aleut. *Elwani* 6:61–63.

1979 95 And Still Going Strong. *Elwani* 7:90–92.

Nelson, Robert E.

1999 A Pollen Flora of Probable Late Early Miocene or Early Middle Miocene Age from Kodiak Island, Alaska. *Geological Society of America Abstracts with Programs* 31(7):A–463.

Nelson, Robert E., and Richard H. Jordan

1988 A Post Glacial Pollen Record from Western Kodiak Island, Alaska. *Arctic* 41(1):59–63.

Nobman, Elizabeth
  1993 *Nutrient Value of Alaska Native Foods*. US Department of Health and Human Services, Indian Health Service, Alaska Area Native Health Service, Anchorage.

Nunn, Patricia
  2007 *Climate, Environment, and Society in the Pacific during the Last Millennium*. Elsevier Science, Philadelphia.

Oleksa, M.
  1992 *Orthodox Alaska: A Theology of Mission*. St. Vladimir's Seminary Press, Crestwood, NJ.

Orth, Donald J.
  1971 *Dictionary of Alaska Place Names*. Geological Survey Professional Paper 567. Government Printing Office, Washington, DC.

Osgood, C.
  1937 *Ethnography of the Tanaina*. Yale University Publications in Anthropology, 16. Yale University, New Haven, CT.

Partlow, Megan
  2000 Salmon Intensification and Changing Household Organization in the Kodiak Archipelago. PhD dissertation, University of Wisconsin, Madison.

Partnow, Patricia
  2001 *Making History*. University of Alaska Press, Fairbanks.

Peteet, D., and D. Mann
  1994 Late-Glacial Vegetational, Tephra, and Climatic History of Southwestern Kodiak Island, Alaska. *Ecoscience* 1:255–267.

Petrof, Ivan
  1884 *Report on the Population, Industries, and Resources of Alaska*. Department of Interior, Census Office, Government Printing Office, Washington, DC.

Pierce, Richard, translator
  1981 *Mikhail Dmitrievich Teben'kov: Atlas of the Northwest Coasts of America from Bering Strait to Cape Corrientes and the Aleutian Islands with Several Sheets on the Northwest Coast of Asia*. Limestone Press, Kingston, Ontario.
  1990 *Russian America, 1741–1867: A Biographical Dictionary*. Limestone Press, Kingston, Ontario.

Pinart, Alphonse L.
  1872 *Catalogue des Collections Raportées de L'Amerique Russe*. Imprimerie de I. Claye, Paris.
  1873 Eskimaux et Koloche, Idees religieuses et traditions des Kaniagmioutes. *Revue d'Anthropologie* 2:673–680.

Porter, Robert
  1895 Population and Resources of Alaska at the Eleventh Census: 1890. In *The Miscellaneous Documents of the House of Representatives for the First Session of the Fifty-Second Congress 1891–92*, Vol. 50, Part 9. Government Printing Office, Washington, DC.

Pratt, Kenneth
  1990 Economic and Social Aspects of Nunivak Eskimo "Cliff-Hanging." *Arctic Anthropology* 27(1):75–86

Pullar, Gordon L.

    1992 Ethnic Identity, Cultural Pride, and Generations of Baggage: A Personal Experience. *Arctic Anthropology* 29(2):182–191.

    2009 Historical Ethnography of Nineteenth-Century Kodiak Villages. In *Giinaquq Like a Face*, edited by S. D. Haakanson and A. F. Steffian, pp. 41–60. University of Alaska Press, Fairbanks.

Pullar, Gordon L., Richard A. Knecht, and Sven D. Haakanson Jr.

    2013 Archaeology and the Sugpiaq Renaissance on Kodiak Island: Three Stories from Alaska. In Inuit Memories and Archaeological Reconstructions: Contemporary Reifications of the Inuit Past, special issue, *Études/Inuit/Studies* 37(1):79–94.

Rasic, Jeff

    2011 University of Alaska Museum of the North Laboratory Report 2011-11. On file AM193, Alutiiq Museum and Archaeological Repository, Kodiak.

Rausch, R. L.

    1969 Origins of the Terrestrial Mammalian Fauna of the Kodiak Archipelago. In *The Kodiak Island Refugium: Its Geology, Flora, Fauna, and History*, edited by T. N. V. Karlstrom and G .E. Ball, pp. 216–234. The Boreal Institute, University of Alberta, Calgary.

Reed, Irene

    1962a Interview with Katya Chichenoff, Karluk. SU961R1962c . Alaska Native Language Archives, Fairbanks.

    1962b Interview with Katya E., Karluk. SU961R1962c . Alaska Native Language Archives, Fairbanks.

Righter, Elizabeth, and Richard H. Jordan

    1980 Report of Comprehensive Archaeological Reconnaissance and National Register Eligibility Tests at the Terror Lake Hydroelectrical Project Site, Kodiak Island, Alaska. WAPORA, Berwyn, Pennsylvania. Report Submitted to International Engineering Company, San Francisco.

Rogers, Ronnie

    1989 Determination of Recent Shoreline Changes at Karluk Lagoon Kodiaks Island, Alaska (1952–1988) Using an Analytical Photogrammetric Approach. Masters thesis, University of Georgia, Athens.

Roppel, Patricia

    1985 *Salmon from Kodiak: A History of the Salmon Fishery of Kodiak Island, Alaska*. Alaska Historical Commission Studies in History No. 216. Alaska Historical Commission, Anchorage.

Roscoe, Fred

    1992 *From Humboldt to Kodiak 1886–1895*. Edited by Stanley N. Roscoe. Limestone Press, Kingston, Ontario.

Rostad, Michael

    1980 Mary's Never Contrary and Her Garden Grows Just Fine. *Kadiak Times.* Friday, October 10, p. 8.

    1988 *Time to Dance: Life of an Alaska Native*. A. T. Publishing, Anchorage.

Rousselot, J. L., and V. Grahammer

    2002 *Catalogue Raisonné de la Collection du Château-Musée de Boulogne-sur-Mer, France*. In *Kodiak, Alaska*, edited by E. Desveaux. pp. 206–243. Adam Biro, Paris.

Russell, Priscilla

    1991 Kodiak Alutiiq Plantlore. AM4. Alutiiq Museum Kodiak.

Saltonstall, Patrick G.

    1997 Archaeology of the Settlement Point Site. Report prepared for the Afognak Native Corporation, Kodiak.

Saltonstall, P. G., and A. F. Steffian

    2006 *The Archaeology of Horseshoe Cove: Excavations at KOD-415, Uganik Island Kodiak Archipelago, Alaska.* Occasional Papers in Alaskan Field Archaeology, Vol. 1. United States Department of the Interior, Bureau of Indian Affairs, Office of Regional Archeology, Anchorage.

    2007 Archaeology of the South Olga Lakes, Kodiak Archipelago, Alaska. Report prepared for the US Fish and Wildlife Service by the Alutiiq Museum, Kodiak.

    2010 Karluk Lake Archaeology: 2008 and 2009 Survey Results. Report prepared for the US Fish and Wildlife Service by the Alutiiq Museum and Archaeological Repository, Kodiak.

Saltonstall, Patrick G., Amy F. Steffian, and Mark A. Rusk

    2012 *The Penguq Site in Alaska Peninsula Prehistory.* Occasional Papers in Alaskan Field Archaeology, Vol. 4. United States Department of the Interior, Bureau of Indian Affairs, Office of Regional Archeology, Anchorage.

Sarychev, G.

    1806 *An Account of a Voyage of Discovery to the North-east of Siberia, the Frozen Ocean, and the North-east Sea.* Richard Phillips, London.

Sauer, Martin

    1802 *An Account of a Geographical and Astronomical Expedition to the Northern Parts of Russia.* A. Strahan, London.

Service, Elman

    1962 *Primitive Social Organization: An Evolutionary Perspective.* Random House, New York.

Shaw, Jennie D.

    2008 Driftwood as a Resource: Modeling Fuelwood Acquisition Strategies in the Mid-to-Late Holocene Gulf of Alaska. PhD dissertation, University of Washington, Seattle.

Sheehan, Glenn

    1983 Archaeological Field Notes from Karluk Lake. AM193. Alutiiq Museum and Archaeological Repository, Kodiak.

Shelikhov, Gregorii I.

    1981 *A Voyage to Russian America, 1783–1786.* Translated by Marina Ramsey and edited by Richard A. Pierce. Limestone Press, Kingston, Ontario.

Shepherd, Sophie Katelnikoff

    2010 "Fishing at Karluk." Alutiiq Museum and Archaeological Repository, Kodiak. Electronic document, http://alutiiqmuseum.org/language-studies/experience-alutiiq/alutiiq-recordings. html?pid=60andsid=100:Sophie-Katelnikoff-Shepherd-Fishing-at-Karluk-mov, accessed October 2013.

Shirar, Scott, Jeff Raisic, Eric Carlson, and Mareca Gutherie

    2012 Rock Art in the Far North: A Local Style of Petroglyphs from the Central-Western Brooks Range. Poster Presented at the Annual Meeting of the Alaska Anthropological Association, Seattle.

Shugak, Marie
>1978a I'm Marie Shugak. *Axtakuqing* 1(1):26.
>1978b Old Story. *Axtakuqing* 1(1):26.

Simon, James J. K., and Amy F. Steffian
>1994 Cannibalism or Complex Mortuary Behavior? An Analysis of Patterned Variability in the Treatment of Human Remains from the Kachemak Tradition of Kodiak Island. In *Reckoning with the Dead: The Larsen Bay Repatriation and the Smithsonian Institution*, edited by Tamara L. Bray and Thomas W. Killion, pp. 75–100. Smithsonian Institution Press, Washington, DC.

Smith, Kevin P.
>1983 Archaeological Field Notes from Karluk Lake. AM193. Alutiiq Museum and Archaeological Repository, Kodiak.

Smith, Tim
>2005 *Island Journey with the Evangel*. The Evangel at Karluk: A Photo Album. Electronic document, http://www.tanignak.com/island%20journey%20with%twentiethe%20evangel%205.htm, accessed December 2013.

Smithsonian Institution Arctic Studies Center
>1997 Looking Both Ways Elders Conference tapes. Alutiiq Museum and Archaeological Repository Library, Kodiak.

Solovjova, Katerina, and Aleksandra A. Vovnyanko
>2009 The Fur Rush: A Chronicle of Colonial Life. In *The Alaska Native Reader History, Culture, Politics*, edited by Maria Shaa Tláa Williams, pp. 28–41. Duke University Press, Durham, NC.

Sowls, A. L., S. A. Hatch, and C. J. Lensink
>1978 *Catalog of Alaskan Seabird Colonies*. United Sates Department of the Interior, Fish and Wildlife Service, Biological Services Program, Washington DC.

Stamp, Bobby
>1987 *Adaq'wy* Project Interview with Laurie Mulcahy, Kodiak Area Native Association. AM214-34A. Alutiiq Museum and Archaeological Repository Archives, Kodiak.

Steffian, Amy F.
>1992a Archaeological Coal in the Gulf of Alaska: A View from Kodiak Island. *Arctic Anthropology* 29(2):111–129.
>1992b Fifty Years After Hrdlička: Further Investigations at the Uyak Site, Kodiak Island, Alaska. *Anthropological Papers of the University of Alaska* 24(1and2):141–164.
>1996 Archaeological Salvage Excavations at Karluk One: Report form the 1995 Field Season. Prepared for Koniag, Inc., Anchorage. Alutiiq Museum and Archaeological Repository, Kodiak.
>2000 Letter to Peter Corey, Sheldon Jackson Museum, March 26. On file, Sheldon Jackson Museum, Sitka.

Steffian, Amy F., and April Laktonen Counceller
>2010 *Alutiiq Traditions. An Introduction to the Native Culture of the Kodiak Archipelago*. Alutiiq Museum and Archaeological Repository, Kodiak.
>2012 *Alutiiq Word of the Week: Fifteen Year Compilation*. Alutiiq Museum and Archaeological Repository, Kodiak.

Steffian, Amy F., and Richard A. Knecht
    1998 *Karluk One*. Pictures of Record, Weston, CT.

Steffian, Amy F., and Patrick G. Saltonstall
    2001 Markers of Identity: Labrets and Social Organization in the Kodiak Archipelago. *Alaska Journal of Anthropology* 1(1and2):1–27.
    2004 Settlements of the Ayakuli: Red River Drainage, Kodiak Archipelago, Alaska: Comprehensive Project Report. Report Prepared for the US Fish and Wildlife Service. Alutiiq Museum and Archaeological Repository, Kodiak.
    2005 Tools but Not Tool Kits: Traces of the Arctic Small Tool Tradition in the Kodiak Archipelago. *Alaska Journal of Anthropology* 3(2):3–35.
    2014 Prehistoric Settlements of the Midway Bay Peninsula, Old Harbor, Alaska. Report prepared for the Old Harbor Native Corporation. Alutiiq Museum and Archaeological Repository, Kodiak.

Steffian, Amy F., and James J. K. Simon
    1994 Metabolic Stress among Prehistoric Foragers of the Central Alaskan Gulf. *Arctic Anthropology* 31(2):78–94.

Steffian, Amy F., Jim Begét, and Patrick Saltonstall
    1996 Prehistoric Alutiiq Artifact Provides Oldest Documentary Record of Ancient Volcanic Eruptions in Alaska. *Alaska Volcano Observatory Bi-Monthly Report*, March/April 8(2):12–13.

Steffian, Amy F., Elizabeth B. Pontti, and Patrick G. Saltonstall
    1998 Archaeology of the Blisky Site: A Prehistoric Camp on Near Island, Kodiak Archipelago, Alaska. Report prepared for the Kodiak Island Borough. Alutiiq Museum and Archaeological Repository, Kodiak.

Steffian, Amy F., Patrick G. Saltonstall, and Robert E. Kopperl
    2006 Expanding the Kachemak: Surplus Production and the Development of Multi-Season Storage in Alaska's Kodiak Archipelago. *Arctic Anthropology* 43(2):93–129.

Steffian, Amy F., Patrick G. Saltonstall, and Linda F. Yarborough
    In press Maritime Economies of the Central Gulf of Alaska after 4,000 BP. In *Oxford Handbook of Arctic Archaeology*, edited by T. Max Friesen and Owen K. Mason. Oxford, Oxford University Press.

Stewart, Hilary
    1982 *Indian Fishing Early Methods on the Northwest Coast*. University of Washington Press, Seattle.
    1984 *Cedar: Tree of Life for the Northwest Coast Indians*. University of Washington Press, Seattle.
    1996 *Stone, Bone, Antler and Shell: Artifacts of the Northwest Coast*. University of Washington Press, Seattle.

Stuart, Gene S.
    1988 *America's Ancient Cities*. The National Geographic Society, Special Publications Division, Washington, DC.

Taylor, Kenneth I.
    1965 The Political Structure of a Koniag Eskimo Village of the 1960s. Karluk, Kodiak Island, Alaska. Manuscript on file, Alutiiq Museum and Archaeological Repository Library, Kodiak.
    1966 A Demographic Study of Karluk, Kodiak Island, Alaska, 1962–1964. *Arctic Anthropology* 3(2):211–240.

Tennessen, Travis
    2010 Trouble in Paradise: Conflict over Introduced Wildlife on Alaska's Kodiak Archipelago. PhD dissertation, University of Wisconsin, Madison.

Territory of Alaska Department of Education
    1952 Letter to Charles Lucier, May 8, 1952. Box 3, Folder 53. Charles V. Lucier Papers, 1903–2009, University of Alaska Anchorage, Consortium Library, Archives and Special Collections Department, Anchorage.

Tiffany, Warren I.
    1995 Letter to Jerry Sheehan, November 30. AM237. Alutiiq Museum and Archaeological Repository Archives, Kodiak.

Tikhmenev, P. A.
    1978 *A History of the Russian-American Company*. Translated by Richard A. Pierce and Alton S. Donnelly. University of Washington Press, Seattle.

Townsend, Joan B.
    1980 Ranked Societies of the Alaska Pacific Rim. *Senri Ethnological Studies* 4:123–152.
    1983 Precontact Political Organizations and Slavery in Aleut Society. In *The Development of Political Organization in Native North America*, 1979 Proceedings of the American Ethnological Society, edited by E. Tooker, pp. 120–132. American Ethnological Society, Washington, DC.

Troyer, Willard A.
    1962 Size, Distribution, Structure, and Harvest of A Kodiak Bear Population. Masters thesis, Montana State University.

Tunohun, Mike
    1987 Interview with Laurie Mulcahy for the Kodiak Area Native Association. AM214:38:A. Alutiiq Museum and Archaeological Repository, Kodiak.

United States Army Corps of Engineers
    2007 Erosion Information Paper: Karluk, Alaska. Alaska Baseline Erosion Assessment. United States Army Corps of Engineers, Alaska District, Anchorage.

United States Department of the Interior
    1987 Kodiak National Wildlife Refuge: Comprehensive Conservation Plan, Environmental Impact Statement, and Wilderness Review, Final. United States Department of the Interior, Fish and Wildlife Service, Anchorage.

Utermohle, Charles
    1988 Koniag Burial Patterns: Examples from Karluk (KAR-001). Paper presented at the 15th Annual Meeting of the Alaska Anthropological Association, Fairbanks.

Van Daele, Larry
    1990 Denning Characteristics of Brown Bears on Kodiak Island, Alaska. *International Conference on Bear Research and Management* 8:257–267.

Varjola, Pirjo
    1990 *The Etholén Collection. The Ethnographic Alaskan Collection of Adolf Etholén and His Contemporaries in the National Museum of Finland*. National Board of Antiquities of Finland, Helsinki.

Vlasoff, Bonnie

2007 *Our Kotel'nikov Journey from Okhotsk, to Fort Ross, to Ouzinkie*. Publication Consultants, Anchorage.

West, Catherine F.

2011 A Revised Radiocarbon Sequence for Karluk-1 and the Implications for Kodiak Island Prehistory. *Arctic Anthropology* 48(1):80–92.

West, Catherine F., Stephen Wischniowski, and Christopher Johnston

2011 Little Ice Age Climate: *Gadus macrocephalus* Otoliths as a Measure of Local Variability. In *The Archaeology of North Pacific Fisheries*, edited by Madonna Moss and Aubrey Cannon, pp. 31–44. University of Alaska Press, Fairbanks.

Wiessner, Polly

1983 Style and Information in Kalahari San Projectile Points. *American Antiquity* 48(2):253–276.

Wilson, Judith G., and James E. Overland

1986 Meteorology. In *The Gulf of Alaska Physical Environment and Biological Resources*, edited by Donald W. Hood and Steven T. Zimmerman, pp. 31–54. US Printing Office, Washington, DC.

Wiswell, Ella L.

1979 *Around the World on the Kamchatka 1817–1819*. Hawaiian Historical Society, Honolulu.

Wobst, H. M.

1977 Stylistic Behavior and Information Exchange. In *For the Director: Essays in Honor of James B. Griffin*, edited by C. Cleeland, pp. 317–342. University of Michigan Anthropological Papers, No. 61, Ann Arbor.

Workman, William B.

1966 Archaeological Reconnaissance on Chirikov Island, Kodiak Group: A Preliminary Report. *Arctic Anthropology* 3(2):185–192.

Wrangell, Ferdinand P.

1980 *Russian America Statistical and Ethnographic Information*. Translated by Mary Sadouski and edited by Richard A. Pierce. Limestone Press, Kingston, Ontario.

Yarborough, Linda F.

1976 Archaeological Reconnaissance at South Karluk Lake. Preliminary Field Report. University of Alaska, Fairbanks. Report on file, Alaska Office of History and Archaeology, Anchorage.

Yarborough, M. R., and L. F. Yarborough

1998 Prehistoric Maritime Adaptations of Prince William Sound and the Pacific Coast of the Kenai Peninsula. *Arctic Anthropology* 35(1):132–145.

Zimmerly, David W.

2000 *Qayaq Kayaks of Alaska and Siberia*. University of Alaska Press, Fairbanks.

Glossary

New Words for Old Things: Creating Alutiiq Terms for Karluk One Artifacts

April Laktonen Counceller, Assistant Professor, University of Alaska, Kodiak College

As part of the *Kal'unek—From Karluk* project, fluent Kodiak Alutiiq speakers are breathing additional life into a museum collection by giving modern Alutiiq names to prehistoric artifacts (Glossary fig. 1). Doing so lays intellectual claim to this collection, emphasizing cultural continuity, and reinforcing pride in Alutiiq heritage. Bringing these material items into the modern lexicon asserts how they are critical for our contemporary understandings of Alutiiq culture and history and demonstrates their value not only to archaeologists and scholars but to community members as well.

Glossary Figure 1. New Words Council members with ties to Karluk examine artifacts to determine Alutiiq names. Front row from left: Sophie Shepherd, Kathryn Chichenoff, and Clyda Christensen. Back row from left: Theresa Carlson, Helen Malutin, and Barbara Hochmuth, 2012. Photo by Patrick Saltonstall.

The Kodiak Alutiiq New Words Council (NWC), also known as the *Nuta'at Niugnelistet* (New Word Makers), works to create words where holes exist in the modern Alutiiq language after surviving two centuries of linguistic oppression. As a founding organizer for the NWC, I have worked with fluent Elders and second-language speakers in the group for over five years. Initiated under a National Science Foundation Documenting Endangered Languages Program grant in 2007, the group is loosely modeled after the Hawaiian Lexicon Committee, a body that has developed new Hawaiian terms for more than two decades (Kimura and Counceller 2009). Terminology committees like the Alutiiq NWC and the Hawaiian Lexicon Committee craft terms for threatened languages in order to help them maintain a place in the modern world, keeping them viable for current generations (Counceller 2010).

As part of the Kal'unek project, however, Kodiak Alutiiq speakers have turned their attention from producing terms for modern items, such as computers and ATM machines, to a category of ancient items. The NWC has been working to document, reawaken, or create terms for Karluk One objects, so that Alutiiq words—rather than just English—can be used to discuss and describe treasured cultural artifacts. From this point forward, exhibits, publications, and presentations about the artifacts excavated in Karluk can be accompanied by Alutiiq language terms, reinforcing the living language and culture even in items seemingly frozen in the past.

When the project was first proposed to the New Words Council, members agreed to participate, despite the very different focus of the Kal'unek project. They agreed with the Alutiiq Museum staff that the Karluk One collection is special and deserves to be showcased in the same way as other Alutiiq archaeological and ethnographic collections in museums around the world. The idea of connecting the archaeological items to Alutiiq terms reinforced the connection felt by today's Alutiiq communities with ancestors who wielded the tools and ceremonial items found in the collection.

Museum staff members provided a list of needed artifact terms broken into broad categories reflecting their usage, function, and the overarching structure of the Kal'unek publication. These categories do not reflect Alutiiq perspective on organizing the material but rather categories the museum choose, and those often found in ethnographies, to subdivide the large assemblage. They include economic, household, and spiritual life, each with numerous subcategories (Glossary table 1). The NWC's task was to translate each category and recall, locate, or develop terms for each artifact type listed within each group.

Late in 2011, fluent Elders and semi-fluent learners began reviewing the list of English artifact terms from Karluk One that would need Alutiiq names. We organized the list into categories reflecting the type of artifact name:

1. modern (m): names currently part of the modern Alutiiq lexicon
2. historical (h): obsolete names documented by explorers and traders during the historical period
3. created (c): names given by the NWC to objects lacking known modern or historical names.

Each of these classes went through a process of identification or creation and approval by the NWC.

Working in small group sessions at first, fluent speakers identified the terms that occur in the modern lexicon. These words would not need to be created, only compiled. Existing terms primarily include items for which there is a contemporary use, a modern equivalent, or that were used in Alutiiq communities within the last one hundred years. For example, the word *ulukaq*, "ulu" is an item still in use in the modern day, although today's functional examples are made with metal rather than slate blades. Another example is *ruuwaq*, "arrow." Many Elders remember practicing and playing with bows and arrows in their youth, although these traditional hunting weapons are not regularly made or used in Alutiiq communities. Another common category of existing terms are those for games and game pieces, which were actively played in Alutiiq communities until the mid-to late-twentieth century and are still occasionally used today.

Some items not in modern usage or memory have modern equivalents and names, even though the modern and ancient tools may look very different. This group is primarily composed of tools like whetstones, adzes, and hammerstones. Rather than develop new words for these items, speakers chose to extend the definitions of certain items to include their prehistoric counterparts. For example, a splitting adze was termed a *tupuuʀuq*, which is an Alutiicized Russian term for an axe. Clearly this term would not have been used before contact, but the NWC decided that modern speakers could use this term for both a modern axe and a precontact adze.

Expanding definitions rather than creating new words serves a number of functions. It simplifies the job of the committee, whose time and effort need to be conserved for more complex terminology development. It signals to today's speakers and learners what the function of that item is, without having to translate to English or understand archaeological jargon. Most importantly, this choice makes a statement about cultural continuity. Just as assigning modern language terms to an archaeological collection makes a statement about cultural affiliation by the NWC, the use of common words for ancient and modern items makes an overt statement about community perceptions of cultural continuity.

After compiling the words in current and expanded use, I worked with Elders to develop a preliminary short list of needed words that could be predicted or intuited according to Alutiiq etymological patterns. These words do not currently exist in the lexicon, but fluent speakers considered the creation of Alutiiq terms for these items "obvious." One of these words was *iqum patua* or "point sheath" (literally "point's cover" in Alutiiq). This preliminary list of created words went before the full NWC for review and approval, and most were passed with little or no modification. Some of the "obvious" words were crafted by adding an Alutiiq suffix to existing words of Alutiiq or Russian origin. An example of this type is the word for "maul," *muʀut'uuruasinaq*, which consists of the Aluticized Russian word *molotó* ("hammer") and the Alutiiq postbases *-ruaq* ("kind of like") and *-sinaq* ("big ___").

The next category of words needing development were somewhat less predictable, so I reviewed Alutiiq root words from my own Alutiiq language studies, using documents such as Jeff Leer's Kodiak Alutiiq Dictionary (Leer 1978) and his forthcoming multidialect Alutiiq dictionary (Leer n.d.). In these documents, I discovered words that had been recorded during the Russian period, as well as archaic and modern-root words, which could be combined with postbases and suffixes to create new words based on existing or historical morphemes. The old words and some of my suggested creations were put before the NWC for review.

Although certain words that existed during the Russian period had been found in written documents by Leer, the NWC still needed to review them. The existence of a word historically or in a related dialect is not a guarantee of modern community acceptance. Remembered or previously documented words regularly come before the council for discussion, and the NWC then chooses whether to adopt these terms. One of the historically documented terms that is no longer in use or living memory is *qatgat* ("armor"). Elders recognized the term as being related to the remembered word *gaateq* ("chest") and approved the option to use the historically documented word. Similarly, the word *kakangaqutaq* (a disc used in playing *kakangaq*) was seen to have the same roots as the contemporary word for the game (*kakangaq*); although not in current use, the word was readily confirmed by the NWC. A historically documented term for twined cordage, however, sounded obscure to the NWC members, who declined to use that term.

The final group of items needing names were less familiar to NWC members, as the objects had fallen from use long before modern memory. Some of the more obscure items—harpoon components and fishing rigs—initially proved difficult for the NWC because, although there may have been a name for the larger item, the parts making up that item seemed outwardly indistinguishable to the lay community member. Preliminary ideas for these items translated as "thing" or "spear part," showing the lack of information about each item's specific function. To enable more specific terminology development, Alutiiq Museum staff members Patrick Saltonstall and Marnie Leist were invited to bring some examples of these items to a NWC meeting and demonstrate their function to the group (Glossary fig. 2, 3). Saltonstall and Leist displayed the items alongside other parts of the larger tool. They showed how the toggling piece of a harpoon worked, what materials each component was traditionally made of, and for what reason. Based on this information, the NWC developed terms like *ayaqum pegsuutii* ("spear foreshaft"), which translated literally as "the spear's thing for letting go." The term *ayaqum arunart'staa* ("socket piece" or, literally, "the spear's thing for heaviness") was directly linked to information provided on the heavy material used for that component of a harpoon assembly.

Ultimately, the list of words developed for this project by the Kodiak Alutiiq New Words Council was an exercise in community education and an act of recoupling traditional material and linguistic culture. Community members were

Glossary Figure 2. Alutiiq Museum curator Patrick Saltonstall shares harpoon assemblies with Elder Florence Pestrikoff at a meeting of the Kodiak Alutiiq New Words Council, 2012. Photo by Marnie Leist.

Glossary Figure 3. New Words Council members Susan Malutin, Florence Pestrikoff, Mary Haakanson, Nina Gronn, and Julie Knagin study a fishing rig with assistance from Alutiiq Museum curator Marnie Leist, 2012. Photo by Patrick Saltonstall.

given an opportunity to collaborate with museum professionals to co-create terms that shed light on the use of materials and tools in classical society. In developing names for items otherwise held in stasis in the Alutiiq Museum's collections, fluent Kodiak Elders reached back through history to reclaim items touched by their ancestors in an effort to awaken the tools and demonstrate their value for future generations.

Glossary Table Alutiiq words for Karluk One artifacts

ECONOMIC LIFE	SUUMACILLPET *[M] ("OUR PAST WAY OF LIVING")[C]
Collecting	*Pingtaallriit[m]*
digging stick	*laakarsuuteq[c], laakalisuun[c], mamaayarsuun[m]* ("clam stick")
clam knife	*mamaayam nuusaa[c]*
Fishing	*Iqallugsurtaallriit[m]*
fish harpoon	*ayaqum iqua[c] (cirunemek canamauq:* "it is made from antler")
leister side prong	*akeq canisqaq[c]*
leister center prong	*akeq qukasqaq[c]*
leister socket	*iqum tuumiaqsuutii[c], kakiswik[h]*
fishhook shank	*iqsam ilakua'a[c] (raatnek canamauq:* "it is made from a rib")
fishhook barb	*iqsam iqua[c]*
line weight	*kicauteq[m], kitsuuteq[c]*
spacer bar sinker	*kitsuut'ruaq[c]*
rig spreader	*canamasqaq[c], iqsaguarsuuteq[c]*
snood	*Iʀafkum kupuraa[c]*
plummet	*kitsuuteq[c]*
lure	*narya'aq [m]*
stunning club	*piqrutaq[m]*
net sinker	*kitsuuteq[c]*
net float	*pugtaq[m]*
anchor	*kicaq[m]*
line leader	*Iʀafkum tuumiaqsuutii[c]*
Hunting	*Pisurtaallriit[m]*
ground lance (bayonet)	*takesqat iquit[c]*
point sheath	*iqum patua[c]*
chipped point	*iquq[m], kukeglugaq[h]* ("arrowhead")
chipped knife	*nuusiq[m]*
ground knife	*nuusiq[m]*
knife handle	*nuusim puunga[c]*
ground point	*ipegca'imasqaq iquq[c]*
end blade	*iquq[m]*
gorge	*saqullkam naryarua'a[c], qatuqmaq[h]* (literally means "choking thing")
toggling harpoon point	*iquq[m], paiktuq[h]*
non-toggling harpoon point/dart	*iquq[m], qalugyaq[h]*
arrow point	*ruuwaq[m]* (term for the whole arrow)
socket piece	*ayaqum arunart'staa[c]* ("the spear's thing for heaviness")
foreshaft	*ayaqum pegsuutii[c]* ("the spear's thing for letting go")

Hunting, continued	*Pisurtaallriit*[m], *continued*
shaft	*ayaqum puunga*[c] ("the spear's handle/grip")
dart butt	*ayaqum nullua*[c]
finger rest	*suawik; lliiwiat*[c]
throwing board	*nuqaq*[m]
throwing board pin	*nuqam kuuliangcua*[c]
bow	*qitguyaq*[m]
arrow shaft	*ruuwaq*[m]
sinew twister	*qikarllum qipsuun*[c]
gutskin jacket-cuff clip	*kanagllum tayarnaa*[c]
drag handle	*agaq*[m]
wound plug	*mallarsuuteq*[c]
net	*kugyasiq*[m]
knife	*nausisinaq*[c] (N), *nuusisinaq*[c] (S)

Trapping	*Kapkaanartaallriit*[m]
snare pin	*negam ilakua'a*[c]

Boating	*Aiwitaallriit*[m]
kayak part	*qayam ilakua'a*[c]
angyaq part	*angyam ilakua'a*[c]
paddle	*anguat*[m]

HOUSEHOLD LIFE	**ENGLUMPTHNI**[M] **("IN OUR HOUSE")**

Building & Woodworking	*Englulitaallriit*[m] (N) / *Unglulitaallriit*[m] (S) ("house building")
splitting adze	*tupuuʀuq*[m]
planing adze	*stʀuusaq*[m]
adze handle	*tupuuʀum puunga*[c]
wedge	*kliitaq*[m]
maul	*muʀut'uuruasinaq*[c]; *mulut'uuruasinaq*[c], *muʀut'uurpak*[c]
plank	*qupuraq*[m], *alasarnaq*[h]

Cooking & Storing	*Kenirtaallriit*[m] ("they used to cook"); *Ang'ataallriit*[m] ("they used to keep things")
vessels (bentwood & other)	*yaasiiguaq*[c]
basket	*inartaq*[m]
mat	*pal'awik*[m]
vessel lid	*patuq*[m]
vessel handle (and others)	*agaa*[m]
gravel tempered pottery sherds	*qikumek canamasqat*[c]
box panel	*yaasiigem cania*[c]/*yaasim cania*[c]
mortar	*ciiwik*[c]

pestle	*ciisuun*^c
spoon	*laus'kaaq*^m (N); *luus'kaaq*^m (S)
fire-starter hearth	*ken'liwik*^c
fire-starter drill	*ken'lisuutem ukit'suutii*^c, *nucuutaq*^h (whole tool)
fire-starter drill handle	*ken'lisuutem agaa*^c
fire-drill bow	*ken'lisuutem qitguyaa*^c
fire starter	*ken'lisuuteq*^c
oil lamp	*laam'paaq*^m, *naniq*^m
ulu (including ulus w/handles)	*ulukaq*^m
ulu handle	*ulukam agaa*^c
plug	*mallarsuuteq*^c
tube	*cupllukaruaq*^c

Sweat Bathing	*Maqitaallriit*^m
rock paddle	*yaamat tuumiaqsuutait*^c
rock tong	*yaamat tuusuutait*^c, *tuullek*^m
water scoop	*qalutaq*^m

Playing	*Wamtaallriit*^m/*Wamqutat*^m ("toys")
children's doll	*suaruaq*^m
miniature/toy	*mikt'sqaq*^m ("small thing")
kayak carving	*qayangcuk*^c
kayak figurine	*suaruangcuk*^c ("mini doll")
angyaq carving	*angyangcuk*^c
model kayak part	*qayangcum ilakua'a*^c
model angyaq part	*angyancum ilakua'a*^c

Manufacturing	*Pilitaallriit*^m, *Canataallriit*^m
awl	*siilaq*^m
needle	*mingquteq*^m
spool	*qikarllum elgwia*^c, *qikarllum egwia*^c
work board	*amit neng'rsuutait*^c
gut scraper	*k'ligsuun*^c
rodent-incisor carving tool	*k'ligsuun*^c
tool handle	*agaa*^m (literally "its handle")
drill	*ukit'suuteq*^m, *napaaliaq*^m
drill handle	*ukit'suutem puunga*^c
chisel/tool bit	*kliitaq*^m ("wedge"), *canasuutem iqua*^c
net gauge	*kugyasim uspersuutaa*^c
peg	*kuuliangcuk*^c
stake	*kuuliaq*^h
cordage/lashing	*iʀafkuq*^m
biface	*iquruaq*^c

Manufacturing, continued	*Pilitaallriit*[m]*, Canataallriit*[m]*, continued*
flake tool	*yaamam ipgaa*[c]
cobble scraper	*k'ligsuuteq*[c]
chipped scraper	*k'ligsuun*[c]
U-shaped abrader	*k'liguasuuteq*[c]
hammerstone	*mulut'uuk*[m]*; muʀut'uuk*[m]
hone	*ipegcaisuuteq*[c]*; ip'gcaisuun*[c]
abrader	*rasqaq*[m]
burnishing stone	*rirsuuteq*[c]
whetstone	*minguutaq*[m]*, ipegucaq*[m]
flaker	*qupkualisuun*[c]
worked piece/debitage	*yaamam ilakuall'raq*[c]

SOCIAL & SPIRITUAL LIFE	*PITAALLRIAKUT*[M] **("HOW WE USED TO LIVE")**

Warring	*Anguyagtaallriit*[m]
armor	*qatgat*[h]
club	*piqrutaq*[m]
shield	*alingnaillkutaq*[h]

Gaming	*Wamenguartaallriit*[m]
kakangaq disc	*kakangaqutaq*[h]
kakangaq target	*kakangam napataa*[c]
augca'aq dart	*ruuwaq*[m]
gaming ball	*mayaciingcuk*[c]
dice/game piece	*maqat*[m]
tally stick	*cit'suutet*[c]*, ciqsuutet*[c] *(N)*
incised pebble	*yaamaruaq*[c]

Personal Adornment	*Cucunarkua'itaallriit*[m]
labret	*qerllum mallarsuutii*[c]*, qukaciq*[h]
labret-hole stretcher	*qerllum neng'rsuutii*[c]
bead	*pinguaq*[m]
pendant	*uyamillkuaq*[m]
fastener/button	*puukicaaq*[m]
caribou tooth belt	*tuntum guutai*[c] (caribou teeth); *qilau'un*[c]*, piil'taaq*[c] ("belt")
nose pin/ring	*paciiruam kulut'rua'a*[c]*, maitaq*[h]

Festivals	*Katurtaallriit*[m]*, Kac'imatallriit*[h]
feast bowl	*qantaruaq*[c] *(N); alutaruaq*[c] *(S)*
mask	*giinaruaq*[m]*; maas'kaaq*[m]*; giinaquq*[h]
maskette	*giinaruangcuk*[c]*, maas'kaaruangcuk*[c]

mask hoop	*awatiisqaq*[c]
mask bangle	*awatiisqam ilakua'a*[c]
drum handle	*cauyam puunga*[c]
drum rim	*cauyam awatiisqaa*[c]
drumstick	*kaugtuutaq, kaugsuun*[m]
amulet box	*nakernauteq*[c] ("container for talismans/good luck charms")
rattle hoop[m]	*awirlursuutem awatiisqaa*[c]
rattle cross brace[m]	*awirlursuutem tuknisuutii*[c]
dance wand	*lliil'rsuun*[c]
rattle part	*awirlursuutem ilakua'a*[c]
shaman's doll	*samanam suarua'a*[c]; *kalla'alam suarua'a*[c]
story rock	*quliyanguaqutaq*[c]
zoomorphic figurine	*unguwallriangcuk*[c]

ADDITIONAL WORDS DISCOVERED/CREATED:

ilakuaq[h]: piece of something (removed)

canamasqaq[c]: thing that was made (a thing)

canasuuteq[c]: thing for making (tool)

puunga[c]: handle (such as a stick handle for an outboard, not a round handle)

naugneq[h]: knot in a cord/rope

qilleq'artuq[h]: knotted

qillerngauq[m]: braided

(N) Northern Kodiak Alutiiq
(S) Southern Kodiak Alutiiq
[m] modern (word currently in use)
[h] historical (word appearing in historic documentation)
[c] created (word created or derived by the Kodiak Alutiiq New Words Council)

Glossary References

Counceller, April
> 2010 *Niugneliyukut* (We are Making New Words): A Community Philosophy of Language Revitalization. PhD dissertation, University of Alaska, Fairbanks.

Kimura, L., and April Counceller
> 2009 Indigenous New Words Creation: Perspectives from Alaska and Hawai'i. In *Indigenous Language Revitalization: Encouragement, Guidance and Lessons Learned*, edited by J. Reyhner and L. Lockard, pp. 121–139. Northern Arizona University, Flagstaff.

Leer, Jeff
> 1978 *A Conversational Dictionary of Kodiak Alutiiq*. Alaska Native Language Center, University of Alaska, Fairbanks.
> n.d. *Multi-dialect Alutiiq/Sugpiaq Dictionary*. On file, Alaska Native Language Center, University of Alaska, Fairbanks.

Appendix I

Sources of Eighteenth- and Nineteenth-Century Ethnographic Information on the Kodiak Alutiiq People

The eighteenth- and nineteenth-century historic and ethnographic information shared in this book comes from accounts by the people list below. These brief summaries are intended to help readers understand how each person was connected to the Kodiak region. For a more detailed account of many of these people, we recommend *Russian America, 1741–1867: A Biographical Dictionary*, by Richard A. Pierce, 1990, Limestone Press, Kingston, Ontario.

Arkhimandritov, Illarion (1820–ca.1872)
    A mariner and cartographer of Aleut and Russian ancestry, Arkhimandritov was hired by Russian American Company as a skipper. In 1846, Teben'kov ordered him to map large areas of the central Gulf of Alaska coast, including the shores of the Kodiak Archipelago. One of his maps preserves the name of the Karluk resettlement village Nunakakhnak.

Bean, Tarleton Hoffman (1846–1916)
    Bean was an American fisheries biologist from Pennsylvania who studied Alaskan fisheries in the late 1800s. He visited Kodiak in 1880 and 1889 to report on the salmon industry for the US government. He spent August of 1889 in Karluk, where he photographed the village. He also visited Karluk Lake and slept in a sod house on Camp Island.

Billings, Joseph (1761–1806)
    A British mariner who served as an officer in the Russian navy, Billings led an expedition to Alaska in 1790 and visited Kodiak from June 28 to July 6.

A short excerpt of his diary, with ethnographic observations from Kodiak, is printed in the account of the expedition's naturalist C. H. Merck (see below).

Bocharov, Dmitrii Ivanovich (unknown)
    Bocharov was a Russian mariner who sailed to Kodiak in 1783 with entrepreneur Grigorii Shelikhov and helped to build the Three Saints Bay colony. In subsequent years, Bocharov worked with Gerasim Izmailov on coastal surveys, exploring the Aleutian Islands and the central Gulf of Alaska and making maps. They charted the southwest coast of Kodiak Island and created a map that shows the village of Karluk.

Bolotov-Archmandrite Ioasaf (1761–1799)
    An educated Russian cleric who led the first Russian Orthodox mission to America, Archmandrite Ioasaf arrived on Kodiak in 1794 and stayed until 1798. His account, translated and published by Lydia Black (1977), provides details of Alutiiq life from the early years of Russian colonialism.

Campbell, Archibald (1787–after 1816)

Campbell was a Scottish seafarer who worked on a Russian American Company cargo vessel. Campbell came to Kodiak in 1807, after the ship on which he was working wrecked on Sanak Island in the Aleutians. Attempting to return to Sanak, he was shipwrecked again, in Zachar Bay on Kodiak's western coast. Campbell froze his feet trying to walk to Karluk with his shipmates and was eventually taken to the village in an Alutiiq kayak. His brief account of the incident includes some details of village life. Campbell spent a year on Kodiak, departing in December 1808.

Coxe, William (1747–1828)

An English clergyman and historian, Coxe tutored the children of English aristocrats living in Russia. Here, he collected and published manuscripts on the Russian explorations of the Pacific. This included an account of Russian seafarer Stephan Glotov (d. 1769), who wintered on the coast of southern Kodiak Island in 1763.

Davydov, Gavriil Ivanovich (1784–1809)

Davydov was a young, educated, Russian naval officer who visited Kodiak twice between 1802 and 1803 in service to the Russian American Company. He traveled around the archipelago by kayak and spent a winter in the region. His extensive journals provide some of the most detailed information on Alutiiq traditions from the turn of the nineteenth century.

Delarov, Evstratti Ivanovich (ca. 1740–1806)

Delarov was a Greek explorer, mariner, and entrepreneur who led multiple explorations to Alaska in Russian service. He became the chief manager of the Shelikhov-Golikov Company, the predecessor of the Russian American Company. Delarov and a company of men under his command wintered in Karluk and built its Russian artel in 1787. He left Kodiak in 1792.

Fisher, William J. (1830–1903)

Fisher was a US tidal observer stationed in Kodiak in 1879. He collected cultural objects and natural history specimens for the Smithsonian Institution until the late 1800s. He married an Alutiiq woman and lived on Kodiak till his death in 1903. His notes include observation on local plants and their uses.

Gideon (1770–1843)

An educated member of the Russian Orthodox clergy, Hiermonk Gideon served as a missionary on Kodiak Island from 1804–1807. He was sent to Alaska to investigate conditions of the Russian Orthodox Church and traveled to Kodiak on the *Neva*, a ship commanded by Russian Naval officer Uri Lisianski. His journal provides a detailed account of Alutiiq life in the early days of Russian rule.

Golovnin, Vasilii Mikhailovich (1776–1831)

Golovnin was a Russian naval officer and a highly respected ship captain. He sailed to Kodiak in 1818, visiting the island July 7–8. His account provides many details on the maritime environment and a few observations on Alutiiq culture.

Holmberg, Heinrich J. (1818–1864)

A Finish naturalist and amateur ethnographer, Holmberg visited Kodiak from April to October 1851. His detailed account of Alutiiq culture includes summaries of earlier Russian explorers' observations as well as his own observations.

Huggins, Eli Lundy (1842–1929)

Huggins was a US Army soldier stationed in Kodiak from 1868 to 1870, immediately following the purchase of Alaska from Russia. Huggins's journal entries discuss Alutiiq culture and communities in the first years of American rule, particularly on northern Kodiak and Afognak islands.

Izmailov, Gerasim Grigor'evich (1745–ca.1796)

A formally trained Russian navigator, Izmailov sailed to Kodiak in 1783 with entrepreneur Grigorii Shelikhov and helped to establish the colony at Three Saints Bay. In subsequent years, Izmailov worked with Dmitrii Bocharov on coastal surveys, exploring the Aleutian Islands and the central Gulf of Alaska and making maps. They charted the southwest coast of Kodiak Island and created a map that shows the location of Karluk.

Kashevarof, Vasilii Ivanovich (unknown)
The son of a Russian merchant, Kashevaroff was an employee of the Russian American Company who visited Kodiak in 1830. An unpublished translation of his notes, dated 1833 and given to the Alutiiq Museum by Lydia Black, provides details on company facilities in Karluk.

Khlebnikov, Kirill Timofeevich (1784–1838)
A Russian American Company official, scholar, and author, Khlebnikov traveled widely in Alaska and California in the first decades of the nineteenth century. He became the chief clerk of the Russian American Company in Alaska in 1816 and acted as the company's leading administrator, diplomat, and trader for nearly two decades. From his post in Sitka, he kept exceptionally detailed notes on life in Russian America. His records include reports on life in the Kodiak Archipelago with information on Russian enterprises in Karluk.

Langsdorf, Georg Heinrich von (1774–1852)
A German naturalist and physician with an interest in anthropology, Langsdorf accompanied

Nikolai Rezanov to Kodiak in 1805. He visited Kodiak briefly in 1805 and again in 1806, taking notes that provide some ethnographic detail on Alutiiq traditions.

Lisianski, Uri (1773–1837)
Lisianski was an officer in the Russian navy. He commanded the ship *Neva*, one of two vessels under the command of Kruzenshtern that traveled in the Pacific. Lisianski visited Kodiak in 1804 and again in 1805 in support of the Russian American Company's commercial pursuits and is known for making important charts of the coast. Lisianski traveled widely in the archipelago, and his account provides many details on Alutiiq culture at the turn of the nineteenth century.

Merck, Carl Heinrich (1761–1811)
Merck was a German naturalist and physician who visited Kodiak for a week in the summer of 1790 as a member of the Billings Expedition. His account of Kodiak provides detailed summaries of both the natural environment and Alutiiq culture, particularly the social aspects of Alutiiq society.

Petrof, Ivan (1842–unknown)
Petrof was a Russian-born US Army soldier, language expert, and writer who studied Alaskan history. He visited Kodiak in October of 1880 while working for the US Census and in 1881 was posted in Kodiak as a customs collector. He lived on the island for four years. His summary of Native culture, published with the 1881 census, mixes the observations of Russian explorers with his own.

Pinart, Alphonse Louis (1852–1911)
A French linguist and anthropologist, Alphonse Pinart traveled to Alaska at age nineteen to study Native languages. He visited Kodiak in the winter of 1871–1872, collecting legends, linguistic information, and ethnographic information and objects. His collection includes the largest known assemblage of historic Alutiiq masks. Pinart visited Karluk in the winter of 1872 during a kayak trip around the archipelago.

Appendix I Figure 1. Interior of the *Ascension of Our Lord*, 1983. Bryn Mawr College Archaeological project, Alutiiq Museum archives, AM278:66.S.

Sarychev, Gavrill Andreevich (1763–1831)
Sarychev was a Russian naval officer and hydrographer who visited Kodiak for a week in the summer of 1790 as a member of the Billings Expedition. His brief account of Kodiak provides a few observations on Alutiiq culture.

Sauer, Martin (unknown)
Sauer was an Englishman who served the Russian navy under the command of Joseph Billings. He visited Kodiak for a week in the summer of 1790 as a member of the Billings Expedition. He was Joseph Billings's personal secretary. His account of Kodiak contains a broad overview of Alutiiq culture.

Shalamov, Tikhon (unknown–1933)
Shalamov was the Russian Orthodox priest for the Kodiak parish for twelve years around the turn of the twentieth century. The parish included the community of Karluk, where Father Shalamov visited periodically. He wrote about the economic and social effects of salmon canneries on the Karluk community in 1896.

Shelikhov, Grigorii Ivanovich (1747–1795)
A Russian merchant, Shelikhov led the conquest of Kodiak Island in 1784 and established the first Russian settlement in Alaska at Three Saints Bay. He traveled around the archipelago for almost two years, between 1784 and 1787. Shelikhov is known to have exaggerated some information, particularly his very large estimate of the size of the Alutiiq population.

Teben'kov, Mikhail (1802–1872)
Teben'kov was a Russian naval officer and cartographer who worked as the chief manager of the Russian American Company from 1845 to 1850. He published an atlas of maps in 1852 that includes a map of Karluk.

Tikhanov, Mikhail (1789–1852)
A Russian artist trained at the Academy of Arts in St. Petersburg, Tikhanov accompanied Golovnin to Alaska, leaving Russia in 1817. He visited Kodiak and painted some of the first images of Alutiiq people. His portraits show both men and women and record important details of clothing, personal adornment, and tools.

Tikhmenev, Petr Aleksandrovich (ca.1820–1888)
A Russian naval officer and a scholar, Tikhmenev served the Russian America Company as a historian. He chronicled company history from Shelikhov's conquest of Kodiak to the final days of Russian rule in the 1860s.

Wrangell, Ferdinand Petrovich (1797–1870)
A German mariner and officer in the Russian navy, Wrangell became the chief manager of the Russian American Company and governed its Alaskan operations between 1829 and 1835. He visited Kodiak in July of 1818 for about two weeks and again at some point during his tenure as company director.

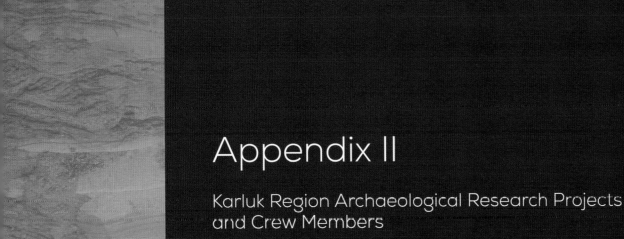

Appendix II

Karluk Region Archaeological Research Projects and Crew Members

1982 Bryn Mawr College Reconnaissance

Glen Sheehan—Principal Investigator
Kevin Smith

1983 Bryn Mawr College Survey and Excavations

Richard Jordan—Principal Investigator
Claudia Chang
Alexander Dolitsky

Appendix II Figure 1. Crew members, August 1984, in Karluk School. Back row from left: Miriam Kahn and Dick Taylor; second row standing from left: Kevin Smith, Mary Loemker, Amy Steffian, Nurit Goldman, Philomena Hausler, Rick Knecht; front row kneeling from left: Barbara Cellarius, Catherine Reft, and Marie Shugak. Photograph by Richard Knecht Sr.

John Hanrahan
Rick Knecht
Andy Millstein
Joanne Mulcahy
Glenn Sheehan
Kevin Smith
Marianne Smith

1984 Bryn Mawr College Survey and Excavations

Richard Jordan—Principal Investigator
Barbara Cellarius
Eddie Charliaga
Nurit Goldman
Philomena Hausler
Lucas Jordan
Richard Jordan III
Miriam Kahn
Richard Knecht Sr.
Rick Knecht
Colleen Lazenby
Mary Loemker
Darrin Malutin
Alicia Reft
Joyce Reft
Katherine Reft
Marie Shugak
Kevin Smith
Darryl Squartsoff
Robin Squartsoff
Amy Steffian
Dick Taylor

1985 Bryn Mawr College Survey and Excavations

Richard Jordan—Principal Investigator
Daniel Albrecht
Guy Balutta
Lanita Collette
Aron Crowell
David Lee Crowell
Dee Crowell
Philomena Hausler
Kirsten Hoffman
Lucas Jordan
Richard Jordan III
Rick Knecht
Jennifer Krier
Frederica de Laguna
Colleen Lazenby
Philip McCormick
Joshua Meikrantz
Andy Millstein
Phillip Mitchell
Bob Nelson
Patrick Saltonstall
Jerry Sheehan
Marie Shugak
Teri Silvio
Darryl Squartsoff
Robin Squartsoff
Amy Steffian
Charles Utermohle
Beth Ann Workmaster

1987 Bryn Mawr College Survey and Excavations

Richard Jordan—Principal Investigator
Tom Amorosi
Cecil Charliaga
Eddie Charliaga
Chris Donta
Ben Fitzhugh
Brandt Feuerstein
Nurit Goldman
Pam Innes
Natalie Harrison

Appendix II Figure 2. Crew members, 1985. Left to right, from top of stairs down: Rick Knecht, Colleen Lazenby with ulu, Frederica de Laguna, Beth Ann Workmaster, Lucan Jordan, Richard Jordan, Marie Shugak, Richard H. Jordan III, Kirsten Hoffman, Josh Meinkrantz; standing from left: Aron Crowell, David Lee Crowell, Dee Hunt, Jennifer Krier, Philip McCormick, Amy Steffian, Patrick Saltonstall, Teri Silvio, Philomena Hausler, Jerry Sheehan, and Daniel Albrecht. Alutiiq Museum archives, AM628:474.

Appendix II Figure 3. Crew members, 1987. Courtesy Colleen Lazenby. From the top row, left to right, going down the stairs: Gordon Pullar, Colleen Lazenby, Richard Jordan holding Celeste Jordan, Chris Donta, Phillip Kugzruk, Ben Fitzhugh, Maura Moulton, Mike Moulton, Philip McCormick, Amy Steffian, Eddie Charliaga, Susan Wenzel, Beth Workmaster, Brandt Feuerstein, Alicia Reft, Nurit Goldman, Nancy Lind, Cecil Charliaga.

Appendix II Figure 4. Survey Crew, May 2009, East Arm of Karluk Lake. From left: Aubrey Morrison, Patrick Saltonstall, Rose Kinsley, and Mark Rusk. Alutiiq Museum archives, AM620.

Kirsten Hoffman
Celeste Jordan
Richard Jordan III
Philomena Hausler Knecht
Rick Knecht
Phillip Kugzruk
Colleen Lazenby
Nancy Lind
Philip McCormick
Wendy McLaughlin
Maura Moulton
Michael Moulton
Alicia Reft
Ronny Rogers
Patrick Saltonstall
Jerry Sheehan
Amy Steffian
Laura Scolnick
Lauren Surachi
Katie Wenzel
Susan Wenzel
Katharine Woodhouse-Beyer
Beth Ann Workmaster

1994 KANA Culture Center Salvage Excavations

Rick Knecht—Principal Investigator
Jim Beget
Carrie Browden
Tori Chya
Pete Cummiskey
Brian Davis
Chris Donta
Kitty Earl
M. Gillespie
Sven Haakanson Jr.
Andy Hall
Steven Hall
Philomena Hausler Knecht
Cheryl Heitman Meunier
Tom Kizzia
Naomi Klauda
Joan Knecht
Rachel Miller
Jeff Peterson
Mark Rusk
Patrick Saltonstall
Teacon Simeonoff
Amy Steffian
Hans Tschersich
Phillip Tschersich
Katharine Woodhouse-Beyer
Anne Zope

1995 Alutiiq Museum Salvage Excavations

Rick Knecht—Principal Investigator
Elizabeth Pontti Eufemio
Patrick Saltonstall
Amy Steffian

2008 Alutiiq Museum Survey

Patrick Saltonstall—Principal Investigator
Rose Kinsley
Mark Rusk
Chase Tingle

2009 Alutiiq Museum Survey

Patrick Saltonstall—Principal Investigator
Rose Kinsley
Aubrey Morrison
Mark Rusk

2011 Alutiiq Museum Survey

Patrick Saltonstall—Principal Investigator
Molly Odell
Mary Pearce
Mark Rusk

2012 Alutiiq Museum Survey

Patrick Saltonstall—Principal Investigator
Jill Lipka
Matt Van Daele

Appendix II Figure 5. Survey Crew, May 2011, Camp Island, Karluk Lake. From left: Patrick Saltonstall, Mary Pearce, Molly Odell, and Mark Rusk. Alutiiq Museum archives, AM620.

Quyanaa—Thank You

For more than thirty years, beautifully preserved artifacts excavated from the Karluk One village site have fueled the Kodiak Alutiiq heritage movement. No other collection has figured as centrally in returning Alutiiq history to community awareness or promoting an accurate view of the richness of Kodiak's Native past. Archaeological investigations can have a profound impact on the present when conducted in partnership with indigenous communities. The Karluk archaeological project is such an example, thanks to the foresight of Alutiiq leaders and the collaborative spirit of researchers.

It is not possible to identify everyone who assisted with the Karluk project or the subsequent care of collections. Hundreds of people participated, and the process continues. However, the organizations, communities, and individuals who stewarded this effort deserve acknowledgment for their contributions.

The Kodiak Area Native Association (KANA), under the direction of Dr. Gordon Pullar, recognized the value of heritage education to health. In their efforts to serve Alutiiq people, KANA formed a culture committee to promote the exploration of Alutiiq history, language, and culture. For their vision, willingness to work with a team of archaeologists from distant Philadelphia, and steadfast support, we dedicate this volume to Dr. Pullar and the KANA Culture Committee. In succeeding years, KANA continued to care for the Karluk collection. Rick Knecht, working for the KANA Culture and Heritage department, brought the collections back to Kodiak and then helped KANA leaders Kelly Simeonoff and Rita Stevens build it a permanent home—the Alutiiq Museum.

In the United States, archaeological sites and their contents belong to landowners, who must provide permission for research. Koniag, Inc. and its leaders, Uwe Gross, John Merrick, and Frank Pagano graciously allowed archaeological investigations on corporation land and studies of resulting collections. Moreover, when the Karluk River changed its course in 1995 and began to rapidly erode Karluk One, Koniag, Inc., under the leadership of Dennis Metrokin, provided funding for salvage excavations and object conservation. More recently, Koniag supported archaeological surveys of its lands along Karluk Lake and River, providing the Alutiiq Museum with a broader context in which to understand the excavated finds from Karluk Lagoon. Additionally, Koniag assisted collections care by collaborating with the Alutiiq Museum on two grants from the Institute for Museum and Library Services. Koniag leaders Will Anderson, Charlie Powers, and Chuck Reft made these activities possible and provided the valuable assistance of staff members Matt Van Daele and Alex Panamaroff III.

The community of Karluk was home to about ninety-one people when the Bryn Mawr College crews arrived to study Alutiiq prehistory. The influx of dozens of scientists and students over six summers had a sizable impact on the small village. Like the archaeological sites, scientific studies became a part of Karluk's history. Karluk residents extended the visitors assistance, expertise, and friendship, and allowed their children to participate in the research, including the Balutta, Charliaga, Chya, Lind, Malutin, McCormick, Panamaroff, Pavlov, Reft, Sheehan, Sikes, Shugak, Squartsoff, and Waselie families. And when the meandering mouth of the Karluk River washed the site away, many community members also salvaged artifacts from Karluk's beaches and sent them to the Alutiiq Museum. The size and breadth of the Karluk One assemblage directly reflects their generosity.

Funding for the fieldwork came from grants and support provided by the National Science Foundation, KANA, Koniag, Inc., and the US Fish and Wildlife Service, as well as support from Bryn Mawr College, the Smithsonian Institution's Arctic Studies Program, the Kodiak Island Housing Authority, Chuck Dieters, Pete Cummiskey, and numerous other people and organizations. Most of the students who participated in the project paid their own way to Karluk.

Each raised the money for airfare, rain gear, and a contribution to the cost of groceries for the privilege of participating.

Bryn Mawr College, the University of Alaska Fairbanks, and the Kodiak Area Native Association all provided temporary housing for the Karluk One collection, as researchers preserved and studied the artifacts, and the Kodiak community worked to develop the Alutiiq Museum. Since 1995, the collection has been the centerpiece of the Alutiiq Museum's holdings, and its care supported by the Alutiiq Heritage Foundation. This consortium of Alutiiq organizations governs and funds the repository, and includes the Kodiak Area Native Association, Koniag, Inc., Afognak Native Corporation, Akhiok-Kaguyak, Inc., Leisnoi, Inc., Natives of Kodiak, Inc., the Old Harbor Native Corporation, and the Ouzinkie Native Corporation.

The idea for this publication evolved from the Alutiiq Museum's investigations of ethnographic collections. For the past decade, staff members have been locating and studying ancestral Alutiiq objects in the world's museums. This work is providing Alutiiq people with powerful connections to traditions and enhancing understandings of cultural identity. Yet the collection that sparked the Alutiiq heritage movement and that rests in the Alutiiq Museum at the heart of the Alutiiq world, had not been shared in an accessible publication. The Kal'unek project addresses this need. It represents an effort at cultural connection through the Karluk One artifacts. This book extends the reach of the collection, creates a tool for understanding its place in Alutiiq history, and invites continued cultural learning.

This book also documents community knowledge. It preserves the experiences and observations of the people who participated in the

Karluk Archaeological project, records the far-reaching impacts of archaeology in the Alutiiq world, and reunites the Karluk One objects with Alutiiq names with help from first-language Alutiiq speakers. Members of the New Words Council who contributed their knowledge to the creation of the glossary included Elders Nick Alokli, Sally Carlough, Kathryn Chichenoff, Clyda Christensen, Fred Coyle, Irene Coyle, Mary Haakanson, Barbara Hochmuth, Julie Knagin, Helen Malutin, Susan Malutin, Florence Pestrikoff, and Sophie Shepherd, and community members Christian Carlson, Teresa Carlson, Leilani Dias, Alisha Drabek, Nina Gronn, Sean Hales, Marya Halvorsen, Lynda Lorenson, Agnes McCormick, Julia Naughton, Gayla Pedersen, and Kari Sherod.

Finally, Kal'unek reflects the ongoing efforts of the Alutiiq Museum to maintain the highest standards of collections care. In 2010, Koniag, Inc. received grant funds from the Institute for Museum and Library Services (IMLS) to complete and computerize an inventory of the excavated collection. Developed between 1983 and 1995, the collection is the result of six distinct excavations, cleaned, cataloged, conserved, and stored through multiple laboratory projects. With federal funding, the Alutiiq Museum was able to combine and standardize the collection's catalogs, while organizing and reclassifying Karluk One's holdings. The grant project also addressed the condition of the collection. Ellen Carrlee of the Alaska State Museum reviewed the conservation of objects and provided suggestions for additional stabilization to assist in preserving the objects for future generations. This collections care work, led by Marnie Leist with assistance from Carrie Barker and Patrick Saltonstall, provided the foundation for Kal'unek.

A second grant from IMLS supported the development of this publication by the staff of the Alutiiq Museum. Amy Steffian acted as the project manager, working with contributors to develop the manuscript, write and edit the text, create maps, and complete funding proposals. Marnie Leist oversaw caption writing, aided contributors, and assisted with the photography, creation of the glossary, text development, and manuscript assembly. One of her greatest contributions was editing the many photographs in this volume. She located and organized images, and prepared photographs for publication. Sven Haakanson Jr. helped to initiate and direct the project, led efforts to photograph the Karluk One collection, and interviewed contributors for short essays. April Laktonen Counceller worked with the Kodiak New Words Council to develop a glossary of Alutiiq terms for Karluk One's major artifact classes and documented this process. Marya Halvorsen and Alisha Drabek assisted her. Patrick Saltonstall researched historic images of Karluk, located excavation information and photographs in the museum's archives, contributed to the text, and participated in editing. Alisha Drabek spearheaded fundraising work, developed illustrations, assisted with editing, and made the project a museum focus to ensure its completion. Jill Lipka prepared illustrations. Natalie Wadle located reference material, scanned slides, and helped to organize the book's many illustrations. Danielle Ringer interviewed an essay contributor, and Katie St. John and Frank Peterson Jr. administered the project, managing funding, reporting, and many other essential details.

Additional assistance for the publication came from reviewers Donald Clark, Alisha Drabek, and an anonymous colleague, who provided helpful evaluation, fact checking, and essential editing.

Daniel Albrecht, Katherine Arndt, Donald Clark, Alisha Drabek, Mike Etnier, Nurit Goldman Finn, Bruce Finney, Anjuli Grantham, Richard Knecht, Colleen Lazenby, Nicole Misarti, Scott Shirar, Kevin Smith, Matt Van Daele, and Katharine Woodhouse-Beyer provided helpful information. We also recognize the expert assistance of the University of Alaska Press. This small non-profit organization provides an essential service in Alaska, transforming scholarly works on the state's environments, cultures, and history into accessible publications. Joan Braddock, James Engelhardt, Amy Simpson, Sue Mitchell, and Krista West were critical partners in this project, and we thank them for their professional stewardship of Kal'unek.

Koniag, Inc., the Kodiak Area Native Association, the CIRI Foundation, the Alaska State Museum Grant-in-Aid program, and the Alaska Humanities Forum all provided major grants to support publication costs. We thank them most sincerely. Publication was also made possible by generous gifts from Gordon Pullar, Catherine Foster West, Emily Lewis, Patrick and Zoya Saltonstall, Polly Saltonstall, Donald Clark, Steve Hall and Amy Steffian, Amy V. Margaris, Jill and Joseph Lipka, Beth Ann Workmaster, Barbara Cellarius, Erica Guyer, Sven and Balika Haakanson, Aron Crowell, Ben Fitzhugh, Pat Kozak, Colleen Lazenby, Mark Rusk, Jeremy and April Counceller, Marnie Leist, Elmer Lotter, and Karen Carson, and the support of the Alutiiq Heritage Foundation and the University of Alaska Press.

These many contributors illustrate the team effort that underlies Kal'unek. It reflects the spirit of collaborative research that began on Kodiak with the Karluk archaeological project and continues to infuse heritage studies and programming at the Alutiiq Museum.

About the Authors

Amy Steffian serves as Director of Research and Publication at Kodiak's Alutiiq Museum and Archaeological Repository. In addition to serving on the museum's administrative team, Steffian leads research, develops educational programs, and creates exhibits and publications. A focus of her work has been community-based archaeological projects that advance historical preservation and public understanding of Kodiak's past.

Sven Haakanson Jr. is the curator of Native American anthropology at the University of Washington's Burke Museum and a member of the Old Harbor Alutiiq Tribe. Since 2000, Haakanson has worked to share Native American perspectives with museums and museum practices with Native people. In 2007, his work was honored with a MacArthur Foundation Fellowship.

Marnie Leist manages the Alutiiq Museum's large, diverse collections, leads special collections projects, and serves as the coordinator of the Island-wide Alutiiq/Sugpiaq repatriation commission. Leist's work with the Karluk One collection includes rehousing the collection, standardizing definitions and terminology, and photographing objects.

Patrick Saltonstall is the Curator of Archaeology at the Alutiiq Museum, a Native governed cultural center and repository in Kodiak, Alaska, where he cares for collections, leads field and laboratory research, oversees historic preservation projects, and shares archaeology with the public. His research projects focus on understanding the evolution of Alutiiq societies, the development of village life, and the evolution of fishing practices.

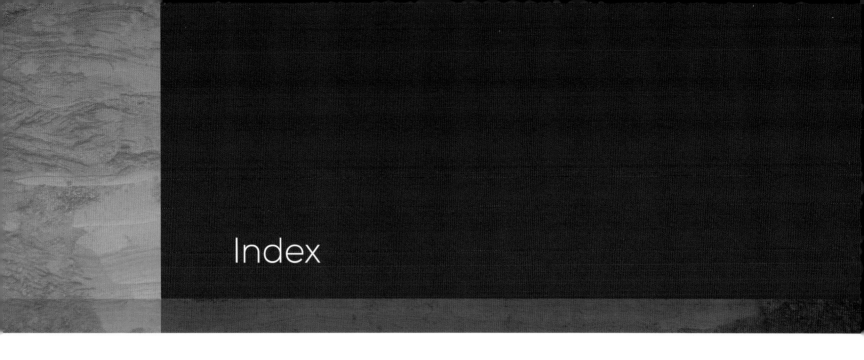

Index